P9-DEZ-570

The Affective and Cognitive Domains:

Integration for Instruction and Research

The
Affective and
Cognitive Domains:

Integration for
Instruction
and Research

Barbara L. Martin, Kent State University
and
Leslie J. Briggs, Florida State University

Educational Technology Publications
Englewood Cliffs, New Jersey 07632

LB 1570.M3669 1986

Library of Congress Cataloging-in-Publication Data

Martin, Barbara L.
   The affective and cognitive domains: integration for
instruction and research.

   Bibliography: p.
   Includes index.
   1. Lesson planning. 2. Curriculum planning.
3. Instructional systems. I. Briggs, Leslie J.
II. Title.
LB1570.M3669   1986   371.3   85-16143
ISBN 0-87778-193-1

Copyright © 1986 Educational Technology
Publications, Inc., Englewood Cliffs, New Jersey 07632.

All rights reserved. No part of this book may be
reproduced or transmitted, in any form or by
any means, electronic or mechanical, including
photocopying, recording, or by information
storage and retrieval system, without permission in writing from the Publisher.

Printed in the United States of America.

Library of Congress Catalog Card Number:
85-16143.

International Standard Book Number:
0-87778-193-1.

First Printing: January, 1986.

Foreword

Leslie J. Briggs was an educational psychologist who represented a tradition of dedication to high ideals and standards in research. I was privileged to have a close professional association and friendship with Les beginning in the early fifties, when we were engaged in training research in an Air Force laboratory, continuing over our years of collaboration in the writing of textbooks, and throughout an extended period as faculty colleagues in a graduate program in instructional systems design at Florida State University.

His research typically began with a painstaking analysis and definition of a problem, usually a problem of how students could be helped in their learning. He took the time to observe students in learning situations, and to reflect upon these observations in order to formulate carefully the question to be answered by research. Naturally the form taken by the research questions he decided upon were influenced by prevailing theory; but they were strongly constrained by the observable conditions of the learning situation that he wished to understand. As for the research itself, it was always done with great care, and with enormous respect for the evidentiary value of empirical data. The most immediate rewards of research came from the examination of the quantitative results of an investigation.

Another feature of Briggs' research arose from his strong interest in gadgets of the variety sometimes called training devices, or teaching machines. Perhaps this interest was initially stimulated by his mentor, Sidney Pressey, the inventor of an early teaching machine. During his period of involvement with Air Force training research, Les devised a number of training devices intended to improve and make more efficient the learning of technical skills by airmen. These devices included those directed at skills of maintaining specific electronic equipment, and also those intended to teach more generally a great variety of procedural and declarative knowledge. He welcomed the opportunity to describe these devices, and the evidence of their effectiveness, in several articles prepared during the period of peak interest in programmed instruction and teaching machines. His view, as expressed in these articles, is that there are many ways in which properly designed equipment can be used to aid the processes of learning and memory.

Obviously a psychologist who approached research on human learning with this kind of orientation and experience was a natural leader for the newly defined field of instructional design and development. This was the field of graduate study being developed at Florida State University, and one to which Les Briggs made many contributions. In the beginning, his wise counsel on the design of courses and dissertation topics had substantial effects on the formulation of the curriculum and program procedures. Over a period of years, he directed the work of a good many students who have become successful practitioners and teachers of instructional design. His colleagues have always recognized a Briggs' student as one who has a special source of intellectual strength derived from disciplined thought and hard work.

Les also devoted much effort to the preparation of materials for instruction of graduate students. His course on design of instructional materials became and has remained a keystone in the curriculum for the instructional systems program. The content came from his books and articles, and also from carefully prepared exercises that provided students with practice in the procedures of instructional design. As one would expect from his writings, Briggs strongly believed in the efficacy of practice exercises, simulated problems, and student constructions; and he devoted much time to the preparation of these items for his course in instructional design. An equal amount of time, surely, was spent in their revision, reflecting a similarly strong commitment to the process of formative evaluation.

The contributions Les Briggs has made to the field of

instructional design will last for many years—through his writings, through his students, and through the memories his colleagues have of his dedication to high scientific and professional ideals. The present work, undertaken enthusiastically in collaboration with a younger colleague, reflects the breadth and originality of his thought, and will surely take its rightful place in the body of work that is his legacy to us.

Robert M. Gagné
August, 1985

Preface

The design, development, and implementation of curricular and instructional programs to promote human learning has become big business in the United States. Traditionally learning was the arena of schools, school systems, and colleges and universities. Now, a vast array of other people and institutions has joined these forces and they, too, are going about the business of designing and implementing instruction. Professionals in non-traditional education settings, such as in the factories and boardrooms of business and industry, in the laboratories and classrooms of hospitals and medical schools, and in all varieties of military training facilities, spend billions of dollars annually to educate and train people to perform all types of tasks and occupations. In addition, a host of industries, employing many thousands, has sprung up all over the country to design and develop materials that enhance and facilitate learning. Perhaps the most notable of these industries are those related to the computer. New software packages and hardware systems hit the markets daily, all promising to increase learning, to make learning more efficient and effective, and/or to motivate learners. Few people, it seems, go untouched; everyone is either an educational producer, consumer, or critic.

Some trends seem clear. First, education and schooling are no longer the exclusive domain of schools. Life-long learning is a necessary, desirable, and valued part of the educational process. Second, new technological innovations, such as videodiscs and microcomputers, are continuing to have an impact on education and learning. Third, the composition of the learning audience has changed. Corporate executives, physicians, government officials, and women who work at home are continuing their education.

These adult learners are participating in all types of experiences, from on-the-job training to self-help weekends and workshops. Fourth, educational settings have changed. Classes and workshops are held in schools, employment places, community centers, field settings, and churches. Fifth, the individuals who teach are no longer confined to those who have had four years of college and a degree in teacher education. Technicians move up through company ranks to become trainers; subject matter experts working with instructional designers become the new educational specialists; and doctors and military personnel who are content experts but have never had a course in designing or implementing instruction now conduct workshops, design courses, and implement curricula. Sixth, new and/or expanded educational theories have been developed that describe learning processes or prescribe instructional goals, strategies, and methods. The stronghold of behaviorism has lessened, and cognitive inquiry, cognitive-information processing, and humanistic and developmental ideologies and theories have been revised, modified, or developed to meet new needs. Seventh, research and statistical methods have changed. Quantitative and experimental methodologies are increasingly sharing space in journals with qualitative research and ethnographic methodologies. Smaller sample sizes and the on-going development of hypotheses based partly on studying the context of an educational setting are featured. Finally, the focus of curricular and instructional content has broadened. Affective aspects of the curriculum are now being incorporated into lessons and units. Attention to attitudes, values, ethics, morals, and the self-esteem of learners is demanding time, energy, and effort alongside the important cognitive dimensions of curricula.

Instructional technologists and instructional designers have become increasingly aware of these trends, and they have directly or indirectly assisted in developing and testing new theories, offering practical suggestions, and demonstrating how alterations, modifications, and extensions of theories and practices can be designed and implemented. Notable strides have been made with new learner populations in non-traditional settings using technological innovations. New theories have been developed and tested, and new research designs and methodologies have been explored.

What has received relatively little attention by instructional technologists and designers is *the development of instruction that incorporates affective goals, objectives, and strategies into educational programs and practices. Likewise, the relationships between cognitive and affective behaviors have not been investigated.*

It is the purpose of this book to demonstrate how affective and cognitive components of learning can be integrated for instruction and research purposes. Since the major portion of educational effort has been directed toward development of cognitive knowledge, a first step in integrating the domains is to get some clearer understanding of what affective behaviors are and how they develop. Once this is done, goals, objectives, instructional sequences, and evaluation measures that integrate affect and cognition can be developed and described.

In Part I of this book, we set the broader context within which our contribution toward the integration of affective and cognitive components of instruction will be made. In Part II, we review related research and its implications for practice. In Part III, we offer a procedure called *audit trails* for determining how to sequence affective and cognitive objectives for instruction in a variety of learning settings so as to achieve life-long needs and goals. In Part IV, we deal with education and training for affective and cognitive objectives for specialized situations for adult learning. In Part V, we deal with designing lessons directed toward both affective and cognitive outcomes. In Part VI, we review our progress and look to the future.

This book is intended for teachers, curriculum specialists, instructional designers, and other educational professionals, and for persons responsible for training in a variety of settings. It is also intended to suggest new areas of effort for researchers.

In essence, this book suggests a way to sequence lesson objectives and to design lessons intended to result in both affective and cognitive outcomes, and to connect life-long goals more directly with curriculum and instruction. We believe that actual application of the recommended techniques could result in major gains in the effectiveness of instruction. We have striven to acknowledge the tremendous complexity of the problem on one hand, but also to offer concrete guidelines for practice.

We have tried to build upon the prior work in taxonomies of outcomes, development theory, and instructional theory and practice. We owe a special debt to Robert M. Gagné, who first demonstrated the important relationships among categories of desired educational outcomes, sequencing of instruction, instructional events, and conditions of learning. We have adopted his work especially in the domain of intellectual skills, and we have expanded his work in the affective domain. We have then addressed the problem of integrating instruction in the affective and cognitive domains.

If readers are curious as to how the two authors of this book happened to discover their mutual interest in the problem of how to integrate instruction in the affective and cognitive domains, see the sub-heading *Our Work*, near the end of Chapter 14. There we explain how we discovered our mutual interest, which led us to write this book.

B.L.M.
L.J.B.

Table of Contents*

*Since each chapter opens with a detailed outline of contents, we list here
only the titles of book parts and book chapters.

Acknowledgments

I would first like to thank Susan Maxwell for spending many long hours typing this manuscript. She went well beyond the call of duty time after time. I would also like to thank the staff at the Center for Studies in Vocational Education, Marcy P. Driscoll, and Cynthia Wallat for their enthusiasm about this book from the beginning. Special appreciation is also due Arvella Briggs for her encouragement and support. She was instrumental in many ways, even after Les died, and I thank her for her friendship. Finally, I would like to thank my mother for encouraging me to spend a year at Florida State and for her continued support.

B.L.M.
September, 1985

The Affective and Cognitive Domains:

Integration for Instruction and Research

Introduction to Part I:
The Problem and a Proposed Solution

In the *Preface* to this book, we noted that the management of instruction is no longer the exclusive province of schools, home, and church, as was the case in the past. Almost all private and public organizations and institutions now conduct instruction, especially for adults. There is now a widespread demand for instruction in basic and specialized skills, and for increased attention to the development of attitudes, values, ethics, and self-actualization.

Unfortunately, the old theories of learning and instruction and traditional models of teaching do not point clearly to techniques by which both cognitive and affective behaviors may be developed by instruction which brings a planned integration of cognitive and affective objectives. Separate groups of people, among both researchers and practitioners, have dealt separately with instruction for cognitive and affective outcomes. This is the problem we address in this book. Our goal is to help overcome this separation of the two domains by offering techniques for integrating instruction in cognition and affect, and to more directly tie curriculum and instruction to life-long needs and goals.

In the two chapters which comprise Part I, we expand upon both the problem and the proposed approach to a solution for it. In Chapter 1, we state our eclectic theoretical posture while announcing that we adapt a system design strategy for searching for a solution. In that chapter we give our first overview of our approach to a solution. There we also acknowledge the need to first clarify the affective domain so that we can make maximum use of theory, research, and models of teaching in building our approach to designing instruction to solve the problem of the separation of the two domains. We accept the complexity encountered in our view of the affective domain as consisting of all types of instructional objectives which cannot be classified as cognitive or psychomotor.

In opening Chapter 2, we pause to acknowledge the many influences upon learning which arise from sources outside the classroom as well as from those within the classroom. We then present an overview of the questions to be answered in design of curriculum and instruction. Finally, we identify and briefly discuss some dozen component processes in our recommended approach to the integrating of instruction in the cognitive and affective domains. This early introduction of those components, we hope, will give the reader a first framework for the more detailed description of our model for instruction, which fills Parts III, IV, and V of this book.

Part II of this book presents our review of research in all components of the affective domain. It may be of special interest to theorists and researchers. Some practitioners may wish to go directly from Part I to Part III. However, we have placed Part II where it is because it is the data background from which we derived many of the practical applications presented in Parts III, IV, and V.

In Part I, many of the important instructional and curricular design components for our model of instruction are first mentioned. Later on, there is intentional redundancy in the sense that we "return again," or "spiral" our discussion and elaboration of the building blocks in our design approach. We hope by doing this to enable the reader to gradually accumulate understanding of our intended meaning of each concept or building block.

We have undertaken an important task of enormous complexity. In Parts I and II, we attempt to acknowledge that complexity while giving some order to it. We also attempt to point out aspects of the total problem which we do not address directly in the more applied technique portions of the book. We hope that other researchers and practitioners will find this book to be of assistance in their criticism, adaptation, or adoption of some of the techniques we recommend.

Chapter 1

The Problem of Domain Separation and an Approach for Integration

INSTRUCTIONAL THEORY

THE NEED TO STUDY DOMAIN INTERACTIONS

THE AFFECTIVE DOMAIN

Domain Taxonomies

Means vs. End

Curricular and Instructional Spirals

Summary of the Affective Domain

APPROACHES TO INTEGRATING THE AFFECTIVE AND COGNITIVE DOMAINS

Sequencing of Instruction

Lesson Design

SUMMARY

Chapter 1

The Problem of Domain Separation
and an Approach for Integration

Educational researchers, theorists, and practitioners have to date conceptually separated affective and cognitive behaviors into two distinct domains. The original purpose of this separation was to clarify the behaviors in each domain and to facilitate research and study of the behaviors. Evidence of the effect of this conceptual separation can be seen in the instructional theories, models of teaching, and instructional design models that have been developed. While most agree that the two domains interact in actual learning, each domain has been studied and taught with little attention to its counterpart. We believe that this oversight can be corrected, and that the two domains can and should be integrated in the design of instruction.

In this first chapter, we begin to explore the problem of domain separation and to search for a solution (domain integration). The purposes of this chapter are to:

1. Explain how the development of a more comprehensive instructional theory can assist in organizing a solution to the problem.
2. Describe the nature of the problem.
3. Give an overview of our approach to a solution to the problem.

INSTRUCTIONAL THEORY

Instructional theories are developed to organize ideas, data,

7

hunches, and educated guesses into frameworks that provide a comprehensive but parsimonious description of how to influence learner achievements. There are two primary ways to construct a theory: a deductive approach and an inductive approach. A theory developed deductively provides a reasonable, legitimate, and conceptually consistent set of rules and constructs that can be defined logically but that has not been subjected to empirical verification. These theories often begin with a researcher's synthesis of literature reviews, logical thought, knowledge of practice, and application of sheer brain power. On the other hand, an inductively developed theory begins with empirical data that describe and explain some phenomena and then builds on those data to derive generalizations with greater explanatory power. Verified findings form the core of an inductively derived theory.

Neither of these theory building types is pure, and there are problems with both approaches. Top-down or deductive theories are only as good and useful as the original propositions. If the logic used in deriving the propositions is incorrect, the propositions will be incorrect. In addition, considerable time will have been spent attempting to verify the propositions and conducting unnecessary, though not necessarily wasted, research. Bottom-up or inductive theories, though steeped in research findings, are often limited in scope and, therefore, in explanatory power. The miniature models that are built come almost directly from the data, are usually somewhat restricted, and often address low-level questions. Likewise, they are rarely integrated with other theories dealing with similar issues and findings.

According to Snelbecker (1974), theory building is an important activity because theories enable us to (a) systematize findings and reduce complex phenomena by organizing and tying together seemingly unrelated events or results; (b) generate hypotheses and, therefore, guide research efforts; (c) make predictions about expected findings; and (d) provide explanations that essentially help answer the question *why*. While no theory is all-inclusive nor a panacea that explains or solves all problems, theories do provide a starting point for a search for solutions. They help us ask specific questions, focus our research efforts, and enable us to begin to discover some answers.

What we have set out to do in this book is to develop a framework for an instructional theory that will help us synthesize what we know about the development of attitudes, values, and feelings with what we know about the development of intellectual abilities. We have used a deductive theory building approach, and our focus has been on instructional theories rather than learning theories. Instructional and learning theories differ in that the former is primarily concerned with applications and practical principles about how to influence learner changes, whereas the latter deals with descriptions and predictions about how and why learning occurs.

The strategy we used for developing a theoretical framework was deductive. We have recognized a problem, that is, that there has been little integration of cognitive and affective behaviors in instruction and research. We have seen examples of the problem in practice; we have searched the literature for clues about the origin and solution to the problem; and we have expended both time and effort thinking about a way to approach the problem. The result is the beginning of a theory that enables us to systematize findings, generate hypotheses, make some predictions, and provide guidance to practice. We have made major strides in some areas, less in others.

In this first chapter, we begin by providing some background into the problem and our theoretical orientation for discussing it. We then give an overview of how integration of cognitive and affective behaviors might proceed. In later chapters we will delve further into specific aspects of the problem and the solution.

THE NEED TO STUDY DOMAIN INTERACTIONS

Educational psychologists and researchers have found it convenient, for theory construction and research purposes, to divide the varieties of human learning and learning outcomes into three conceptually distinct categories or domains: the *cognitive* domain, the *affective* domain, and the *psychomotor* domain. This division was, for the most part, arbitrary since psychologists and educators agreed that in actuality, that is, in teaching and real-life learning situations, no true separation of cognitive, affective, and psychomotor states was possible (Bloom, 1976; English & English, 1958; Fishbein, 1967, Gagné, 1970; Gordon, 1970; Gephart & Ingle, 1976; Payne, 1976; Rokeach, 1960; Transgaard, 1973; Wyer, 1974).

While it is generally accepted that no true separation of the domains can occur in any practical learning situation or in any comprehensive theory of learning or instruction, educators have studied the domains as though they are separate, distinct entities. For example, a cursory examination of learning and instruction theories, models of teaching, and domain taxonomies demonstrates that researchers have, for the most part, addressed one domain or the other (Ausubel, 1963; Bruner, Goodnow & Austin, 1967; Gagné, 1977; Gephart & Ingle, 1976; Krathwohl, Bloom & Masia, 1964; Rogers, 1951, 1969).

In addition to the conceptual separation of the domains in the professional literature, we also recognized three "in practice" types of evidence of failure to address domain interactions. The first was discovered when studying the educational change literature on the adoption of innovations. The adoption process, described in the literature as an example of how any kind of learning occurs, is only successful when both cognitive and affective behaviors are developed in the audience responsible for implementing the change. That is, implementers must develop both the cognitive skills and behaviors necessary for implementing an innovation and positive attitudes toward the innovation. Research into the adoption process has stated fairly strongly that the failure of many adoption efforts can be attributed to the potential implementer's lack of positive attitudes toward the innovation. Usually, the cognitive skills were developed, i.e., most adopters understood and could use a particular innovation, but most did not have favorable attitudes toward it. Change agents had spent their time developing the client's cognitive abilities, but had failed to develop appropriate affective behaviors. Partly as a result of this oversight, many adoption efforts failed.

The second type of evidence of the neglect of attention to integration of affective and cognitive outcomes in the design of instruction is found in the models of teaching developed by educators and others. Joyce and Weil (1980) have summarized a number of such models of teaching. When each model is examined, it is found to be a contribution to teaching in either the affective or cognitive domain, but not to both. Thus the integration sought in this book was lacking in our review of models of teaching.

The third kind of instance of lack of attention to domain interaction was seen in the literature and practical applications of instructional design procedures. Actually, it was not that domain interactions were not acknowledged, but that techniques for influencing motivation and other affective behaviors were rarely addressed (Briggs, 1984). The powerful influences of a motivated learner and motivational materials coupled with any given learner's attitude toward a subject, school, or learning are well documented in educational and psychology literature. Yet, instructional designers have spent very little time developing theories or models that address affective behaviors and even less time integrating them with cognitive behaviors. This fact is also noted by Reigeluth (1983a, p. 79).

The neglect of the domain integration problem is also evident in other respects. For example, the events surrounding the "Sputnik era" prompted an almost total dedication to the cognitive aspects of the curriculum. Many of the "new curricula projects" were developed to teach learners cognitive skills, strategies, and knowledge. Little attention was paid to the affective aspects of the curricula. Although a hidden affective goal was sometimes claimed, it was obscured and not directly taught.

In spite of the above instances of the neglect of domain integration in current practices and delivery systems, there is a growing demand for attention to the affective domain. Public schools, medical schools, and business and industrial settings are now paying direct attention to the development of learners' attitudes, values, morals, ethics, human relationships, and self-esteem. The public seems ready to demand both competence in cognitive skills and attention to affective needs.

It was primarily recognition of the above instances of separation of the domains and the renewed interest in affective behaviors that led us to undertake the theory building work that is the topic of this book. Division of behavior into three domains has resulted in at least two major unfortunate consequences: (a) the *interactions* of learning in each domain with learning in the other domains has remained obscure, and (b) few guidelines have been developed to show how objectives should be sequenced and taught to achieve the goals in all three domains. Our intent is to remove the artificial barriers that have arisen among the domains, with special reference to showing how to *integrate* the affective and the cognitive domains, in both instruction and research. We thus exclude the psychomotor domain from our work, while acknowledging its role as an important domain in education and in training.

THE AFFECTIVE DOMAIN

One reason why integration of the affective and cognitive domains has rarely been attempted is that affective behaviors are difficult to conceptualize and to evaluate. Because of this, the most effort and time have gone into thinking about, studying, evaluating, and teaching the cognitive aspects of behavior. Cognitive behaviors are easier to specify, operationalize, and measure than are affective behaviors. Evidence of this can be seen in the extensive taxonomic work done in the cognitive domain by researchers such as Bloom (1956), Gagné (1962, 1965, 1977), Guilford (1967), and Gerlach and Sullivan (1967).

The affective domain poses a unique set of problems for educators. First, the definition of the domain and the concepts that comprise it are so broad and often unfocused that all aspects of behavior not clearly cognitive or psychomotor are lumped together in a category called the affective domain. For example, all of the following terms can be found associated with affect: self-concept, motivation, interests, attitudes, beliefs, values, self-esteem, morality, ego development, feelings, need achievement, locus of control, curiosity, creativity, independence, mental health, personal growth, group dynamics, mental imagery, and personality. As educators we are directly or indirectly concerned with each of these, and since they appear not to be cognitive or psychomotor, the catch-all phrase has *become* "the affective domain."

The definitional problem is further compounded when one

looks within and between disciplines for clarification. Some psychologists define affect as a physiological or biological state; educators and other psychologists interested in behavior changes define affect as a cognitive type process (Bills, 1976).

These definitional problems are at least partly responsible for another set of problems related to affective behaviors. The lack of definition and focus has made measurement of and research related to the domain difficult; and it has made translation of affective behaviors into classroom practices inadequate. Bills (1976) states:

> ... 1) We are not close to an agreement about what affect is or what to call it. 2) What we are trying to measure is so unclear to us that we cannot develop instruments with acceptable psychometric qualities, and ... I have concluded that unless we can achieve a better concept of affect, we will never be able to deal with it in our classrooms or in our research (p. 10).

In addition to these definitional and measurement problems, there are other problems associated with the affective domain. These include:

1. The belief by some educators that affective goals are so long range and intangible that regular classroom time restrictions (e.g., periods, semesters, years) prohibit development and measurement of affective outcomes (Bloom, Hastings, and Madaus, 1971).
2. Fear that discussions of values, attitudes, morals, and other aspects of the domain may be viewed as indoctrination or "brainwashing" (Bloom *et al.*, 1971).
3. Recognition that in the affective domain the *absence* of behaviors is often as important, if not more so, than the presence of behaviors.
4. The inability to identify and specify affective behaviors because our language does not always lend itself to clarity.
5. Uneasiness about some of the methods associated with attitude change, e.g., classical conditioning, operant conditioning, and persuasive communications.
6. Disagreement and confusion about whether affective behavior are *ends* (outcomes) or *means* to ends.

While acquisition of affective goals and learning outcomes is a priority in many educational settings, the problems associated with the domain often make success difficult to achieve. Not only is the domain hard to define, operationalize, and measure, but educators are concerned about how to go about influencing affective behaviors without indoctrinating learners or compromising their own professional ethics. Yet, the task of integrating the cognitive and affective domains is only possible when we have (a) some clearer notions of the scope and boundaries of the affective domain, and (b) some way to differentiate between abstract and poorly defined concepts. We address some of these problems in greater depth later in the book, but briefly consider several of these here.

Domain Taxonomies

The classification of behaviors into taxonomies is one way researchers in many fields have set boundaries to delineate an area and have organized ideas and concepts within those boundaries. In education, there are a number of cognitive taxonomies (Bloom, 1956; Gagné, 1977; Gerlach & Sullivan, 1967; Guilford, 1967) and several affective taxonomies (Brandhorst, 1978; Gephart & Ingle, 1976; Krathwohl *et al.*, 1964). In the cognitive domain, the taxonomies of Bloom (1956) and Gagné (1977) are perhaps the best known; in the affective domain, the taxonomy proposed by Krathwohl *et al.*, (1964) is best known.

The three best-known taxonomies provide a classification of learning outcomes and a way to generate and classify test items, but only the taxonomy by Gagné (1977) is sufficiently embellished to assist a teacher or instructional designer in planning and developing optimal methods of instruction. Other taxonomies, such as the one by Gephart and Ingle (1976) of the affective domain, provide lists of categories, terms, or types of responses, but do not delineate specific ways to generate test items and lesson designs for each type of outcome desired.

Taxonomies of different types serve different purposes. We have labelled them as *prescriptive* or *descriptive* in much the same way that Reigeluth (1983b) has differentiated between prescriptive and descriptive theories. A prescriptive taxonomy includes not only learning outcomes, but also is specific enough that test items and optimal methods of instruction can be derived from it. Only the taxonomy by Gagné (1977) can be said to be truly prescriptive. The affective taxonomy by Gephart and Ingle is on the other end of the spectrum; it provides only a categorization of types of responses, e.g., visceral, emotional, but does not give clear, operational outcomes, nor does it include sufficient information to develop evaluation items and to design techniques, or methods and strategies. It is, however, a more inclusive taxonomy (it includes more elements of the affective domain) than the one developed by Krathwohl *et al.*, and hence is useful in a *different* way, e.g., to check the scope of instructional planning (but not the design of lessons).

We believe this difference between prescriptive and descriptive taxonomies is important for two reasons. First, when beginning to develop a theory of instruction, the more prescriptive the taxonomy the more useful the theory will be to others who wish to use it to design instruction. Second, prescriptive taxonomies classify educational outcomes or behaviors rather than instructional means or methods. In the affective domain, this difference between ends and means is often unclear. For example, is motivation an outcome to be planned for and evaluated (and, therefore, included in a taxonomy) or is motivation a strategy, a means to an end? If it is a means, does it belong in a taxonomy? The next two sections will shed some light on this issue.

Means vs. Ends

In planning instruction it is important to attend to the ends (goals) first, then to the means (teaching strategies). In practice, the distinction between means and ends is a sticky one and often not very clear. It is, however, an important distinction, especially when developing a taxonomy, theory, or lesson plan. When dealing with instruction for the affective domain, there is often a general hesitancy to state affective goals or outcomes. In part, this may be due to the educator's fear that she/he is indoctrinating learners, or that goal setting in the realm of values and attitudes is unethical, or that stating affective goals is out of the jurisdiction of the instructor's role or the instructional setting. Therefore, strategies or means are stated, leaving a specific outcome undefined. We believe it is important to distinguish between affective outcomes and affective means, leaving the choice of whether or not to state affective outcomes to each designer of instruction.

The distinction we make is conceptually simple. *Means* refer to learning environments and educational activities and strategies that *facilitate* acquisition of an affective behavior. Some examples include discussion groups, value clarification exercises, role playing situations, and a variety of types of media. The emphasis in a learning activity is on what is occurring *during the activity* rather than what outcome it leads to. While objectives are often stated for learning activities, they generally explain what will take place *during* the activity; e.g., the learner will share his or her feelings; the learner will participate in a discussion about his or her values.

Affective *ends* or outcomes refer to behavior changes expected to occur as a *result* of engaging in activities. Therefore, an instructor may state an outcome, such as, "The student will demonstrate a commitment to maintaining good health." The instructor would then arrange for relevant activities (to occur over a period of time) as well as establish a pleasant environment that would influence that outcome. The purpose of the *outcome* is to focus on what result is expected, such as a commitment to good health, demonstrated by decisions made. The *means* used to help learners achieve the outcome might include a trip to the health museum, watching films, or participating in group discussions.

This distinction is not always easy to make, but it is important to keep in mind for two reasons. First, it is ends or outcomes, not means, that are most often categorized in domain taxonomies. These categories of learner behaviors can be influenced and are intended to be influenced by educational activities and strategies. The categories we give in some later chapters are outcomes; in other chapters, on sequencing and lesson design, we will deal also with means.

Second, an outcome implies evaluation. If an outcome is specified, presumably there is some way to evaluate whether the learner did or did not achieve that outcome. For affective behaviors, evaluation can take the form of questionnaires, interviews, self-reporting strategies, and behavior observations. Usually, evaluation is conducted at a time after the activities have been employed that were intended to facilitate the behavior change. However, the same measurement techniques can be used to evaluate both ends and means. An instructor can, on one hand, evaluate the success of a particular learning activity (a means) to determine whether or not the learners participated, if they were motivated, or whether or not they enjoyed the activity; on the other hand, and often at a later date, the instructor can use similar measurement techniques to determine whether the activity led to some prespecified goal or end.

Curricular and Instructional Spirals

Affective outcomes often take a long time to establish, and regular classroom time allocations often restrict their development. The development of a value or a value system is an example of this. Values, defined as a group of inclusive attitudes, do take considerable time to develop. A two day workshop or even a semester course may not be sufficient to establish a value. If that is the case, what recourse do educators have if they wish to influence important affective outcomes?

We have relied on the use of *curricular and instructional spirals* to aid in solving this problem. What we mean by this is that a designer can (a) use the affective goal of one lesson or unit as the necessary prerequisite and building block for the achievement of an affective or cognitive goal of another lesson or unit; or (b) the result of a strategy used in one lesson or unit can become the outcome of a future lesson or unit. For example, if the goal of a unit is development of a commitment to excellent personal health (a value), the outcomes of particular lessons or units may involve commitment to developing good eating habits (an attitude), commitment to developing a personal physical fitness program (an attitude), and commitment to avoid taking drugs (an attitude). In our example, the three attitudes plus several cognitive objectives can be developed prior to attempting to develop the value, since these attitudes are contained within the value structure. As another example, a lesson that was particularly successful in motivating learners to action may be the precipitating influence for stating a new outcome, and may also become the input for further developing motivated learners in another lesson or unit.

This idea of spirals is not new; it is basically the same strategy used with cognitive behaviors. It is a backward chaining approach where the outcome or behavior of one lesson becomes the necessary input or antecedent for the achievement of a higher level, more inclusive, outcome. These outcomes can be planned or unplanned; they build on one another, and, over time, they have some significant impact on affective behaviors that are long range and at first glance seemingly difficult, if not impossible, to influence. This spiralling can occur at the stages of either lesson-design, unit-design, curriculum-design, or even at the stage of design of life-long learning. We will have more to say about this in Part III of this book, where we illustrate how to develop an "audit trail" consisting of many objectives that operate over time in a cumulative fashion to permit achievement of life-long goals and objectives.

Summary of the Affective Domain

This section has been devoted almost exclusively to a discussion of the affective domain and some of the problems associated with it. This may seem odd since the topic of this book is *integration* of the affective and cognitive domains. However, the task of integration is impossible without some clearer and firmer notion of what the affective domain is and how to influence affective behaviors. In this section, we have, therefore, begun to delineate its parameters and its problems to give the reader some insights into the task we have attempted. As the affective domain becomes clearer, as we hope it will in this book, our task of integrating the domains will be possible.

APPROACHES TO INTEGRATING THE AFFECTIVE AND COGNITIVE DOMAINS

There is a wide variety of ways that could be used to study and integrate the affective and cognitive domains. Not only could one approach integration from any one of several broad frameworks, like philosophy, psychology, biology, and religion, but also from perspectives that cross a number of these frameworks. As an example, one might integrate a mystical and a rational/scientific orientation, using ideas from philosophy, psychology, biology, and religion. Still another way might be to approach integration from a physiological/psychological orientation by studying brain dominance patterns; i.e., the affective right hemisphere and the cognitive left hemisphere. Other orientations might be to study particular content areas, such as art or music, that have strong affective and cognitive components.

Within a discipline such as psychology, educators with varying perspectives could, and probably would, approach the task of integrating the domains differently. Psychologists or educators could address the different orientations of a "whole person" versus a "school outcomes" versus a "learning environment" approach. These could be further differentiated along "developmental," "behavioral," and "cognitive" theory orientations. Although the list of possible approaches is not infinite, it is certainly large.

The theory approach we have used is eclectic. We have not limited ourselves to any particular philosophical or psychological theory or orientation. We have used the ideas, instructional and learning theories, and models of teaching that come from all of the following psychology and education research traditions: social, behavioral, cognitive, developmental, and humanist.

Our technique for designing instruction, however, comes from the framework of instructional systems theory. As such, we describe and discuss various ways of setting goals and objectives in the two domains and how to integrate them. We also demonstrate how to sequence instruction for the objectives that have been identified, and we show how lessons can be designed that simultaneously influence the achievement of both affective and cognitive behaviors. We, therefore, support the notion of systematically designed instruction. Following the lead of Gagné (1977) and Gagné and Briggs (1979), we utilize the major concepts of (a) a taxonomy of outcomes, (b) a sequencing strategy, and (c) a lesson design model for working toward the integration of instruction in the affective and cognitive domains. We have already discussed taxonomies; we now give an overview of the other two components, sequencing and lesson design.

Sequencing of Instruction

An important aspect of designing instruction is the determination of how to sequence instruction for the objectives that have been identified. When the objectives consist of *intellectual skills* (a part of the cognitive domain), the analysis of the subskills into the form of a learning *hierarchy* (Gagné, 1977) is an important aid for sequencing those objectives. However, it still remains to be decided how the intellectual skill objectives are to be sequenced in relation to *information* objectives (another part of the cognitive domain), and in relation to objectives in the affective domain. To assist in this larger aspect of sequencing, Briggs and Wager (1981) demonstrated the use of instructional curriculum maps (ICMs). While Briggs and Wager presented general suggestions on how objectives may be sequenced to enhance domain interactions in terms of how learning in one domain facilitates learning in another, our purpose is to make this step in instructional design more explicit and concrete. Our notion of an audit trail of curricular and instructional spirals will also be made more explicit in Part III of this book. We therefore later present illustrations of sequences designed to maximize the contributions of each domain (affective and cognitive) to learning in the other domain. At the same time, our illustrative audit trails show how to close the present gap between broad statements of life-long needs and goals and the sequence of instruction within the curriculum.

Lesson Design

According to the approach outlined in this book, after the sequencing of objectives in the cognitive and affective domains has been determined, individual lessons are designed to achieve the objectives. Here, again, we build upon the pioneering work of Gagné (1977), who demonstrated how lessons, particularly in the cognitive domain, may be organized around the accomplishment of nine *instructional events*. Examples of how these nine events for the cognitive domain are used in lesson design are found in Gagné and Briggs (1979), Briggs (1977), Briggs (1970), and Briggs and Wager (1981). One purpose of this book is to re-examine the applicability of those nine instructional events to affective outcomes, and to the integration of affective and cognitive outcomes.

Important guidelines for how to accomplish the nine instructional events for each of various subcategories of the cognitive domain, and for the subcategory of attitudes (in the affective domain) have also been presented by Gagné (1977) in the form of *conditions of learning*. These *conditions*, unlike the nine instructional events, are *different* for each type of learning outcome. Throughout this book we search out further conditions of learning for the affective domain, since Gagné restricted his affective conditions to the learning of attitudes and to the single method of human modeling as a way to establish attitudes.

There are few examples of designing lessons for the affective domain, either in textbooks or in curriculum development, and there are still fewer examples of designs for integrating the two domains; we later provide some examples.

In later chapters, we will identify the specific subcategories of outcomes for which Gagné has identified relevant conditions of learning. In this book, we extend the conditions of learning to subcategories of the affective domain beyond the subdomain of attitudes.

SUMMARY

Prior work has contributed to our understanding of the cognitive and affective domains, *when viewed separately*. In this book, we undertake the neglected task of how the two domains interact, or may be made to interact, by how we sequence objectives and how we design lessons. In short, our task has been to develop a framework for an instructional theory that shows how to *integrate* the two domains, both conceptually and practically.

Drawing upon the work of others, especially Gagné in the cognitive domain, and Krathwohl *et al.*, in the affective domain, we offer guidelines for both practice and further research. We thus contribute to planning how to integrate instruction in the two domains, and we identify some new *conditions of learning*, especially for the affective domain. In doing so, by the use of audit trails, we also close a gap in present practice—a gap between life-long goals and the curriculum.

Chapter 2

The Broader Context of the Problem and Our Contribution Toward a Solution

THE BROADER CONTEXT OF THE PROBLEM

Determiners of Learning in Elementary and Secondary Schools

Home Environment
Intelligence
Motivation
Public Policy
Self-Esteem and Attribution
Time on Task
Teacher-Pupil Relationships
Teaching Methods and Quality of Instruction
Learner Strategies
Attitudes and Values
Peer Influence
Instructional Media

Determiners of Learning for Adults

Personal Goals
Organizational Policies
Expectations of the Future
Life Styles
Feelings and Emotions

Summary of Influences Upon Learning

OUR CONTRIBUTION TOWARD A SOLUTION

An Overview of Curriculum and Instruction

Who
What
Why
When
Where
How

The Major Components in Our Approach

Needs Assessment (Audit Trails)
Taxonomies of Outcomes
    Checking audit trails for completeness
    Checking lesson designs
    Interpreting learning research literature
    Planning instructional events
Sequencing of Instruction
Lesson Design
    Objectives
    Selecting instructional events
    The external conditions of learning
    Designing materials and activities
    Evaluation

SUMMARY

Chapter 2

The Broader Context of the Problem and Our Contribution Toward a Solution

In Chapter 1 we stated the problem that our knowledge of the affective and cognitive domains has been dealt with separately, by separate groups of people. The result has been that there is a lack of integration of the two domains in both research and instructional practice.

Also, in Chapter 1, we indicated that our contribution toward a solution of this problem will focus upon two primary curriculum and instructional practices: (1) the sequencing of instruction, and (2) lesson design. In the latter part of this chapter we elaborate on those two major practices, and we show their relationship to the affective domain and the cognitive domain. Before doing so, however, we pause to review broadly many influences upon learning which are beyond the scope of this book. We make this digression for several reasons: (a) to acknowledge the limitations of this book, (b) to admit that our contribution toward a solution of the problem is a modest one, (c) to emphasize the enormous complexity of the problem, and (d) to encourage others either to add to and correct our limited area of effort, or to pick up work on other areas we have only acknowledged but not worked upon.

THE BROADER CONTEXT OF THE PROBLEM

It is self-evident that many persons and influences determine what and how people learn. We have chosen only to sketch broadly here the wide range of influences upon learning which go beyond the solution strategies treated in detail in this book. We include influences upon learning accomplished by both children and adults. As we shall see, many of these influences are exerted by people other than educators. While this book is addressed to teachers, curriculum developers, instructional designers, trainers, and materials and media developers, many influences are exerted by people other than those who have professional responsibility for instruction.

Since this book is intended for those who teach adults as well as for those who teach children, we list separately these determiners of learning for elementary and secondary school learners and for adults. There are, of course, some long-term effects which begin early in life and persist into adulthood, but for convenience we list the influences separately. We pause only for the briefest discussion of each influence, and we make no pretense of being able to defend our rank order of them in importance.

Determiners of Learning in Elementary and Secondary Schools

We have no quantitative way to appraise the relative strength of the various determiners of learning that we list here. However, our subjective estimate is that we take them up roughly in their *rank order of strength of influence upon learning*. We have no way to show the interactions among the influences, nor are we prepared to defend our subjective rank ordering. Our main purpose, as stated earlier, is to acknowledge the many influences or determiners of learning which are not included in our major concentration upon sequencing of instruction and lesson design. However, we do suggest that simply being aware of all these influences should benefit both educators and others who also influence schooling and adult education. We even hope that listing these influences will help us, the authors, to present our central contribution in a more insightful manner.

Home Environment
There can be little doubt that a home environment which encourages learning and places a high value upon it is a major factor in both the achievement of children and upon their

attitudes toward education. It is well known, for example, that children read more if their parents read more. There is a positive correlation between the amount of parental education and children's school achievement. Occupation of fathers is related to achievement of their children. Presumably, similar findings about occupations of mothers will be forthcoming.

A broad perusal of the fifth edition of the *Encyclopedia of Educational Research* (Mitzel, 1982) turns up much evidence of the influence of home environment upon children's school achievement. In fact, it is the strength of this influence which may account for the modest results of many school improvement programs. It is not that parents must be highly educated for their children to become highly educated. Rather, the need is for parents to support and encourage learning, and to be role models of life-long learning. The old custom of parents' reading books to children in the evenings may have been supplanted all too much by television watching. It may be hoped that if we are changing from an industrial society to an information society, as some claim, home influences will again be exerted to place a higher value upon learning.

Intelligence

While there have been many criticisms of standard measures of intelligence, the fact remains that the scores on such measures are positively correlated with achievement. The nature-nurture battle continues to be waged. In earlier years the controversy centered upon the relative strength of genes versus training as the determiners of intelligence. In recent years racial bias in intelligence tests and in schooling has been the focus. There are calls for tests which tap originality and creativity rather than acquired knowledge and skills. However these issues may be resolved in the future, and allowing for changes in both tests and the curriculum, we would expect intelligence, however defined and measured, to remain high among influences upon learning.

Motivation

We begin by noting that motivation can be both a cause and an effect of learning. The conventional wisdom is that motivation causes achievement. So teachers for years have attempted to "motivate" the learner first. Recently there has been more recognition that a teacher can arrange for learning to be successful, and this success fosters further learning. This idea is operationalized in many forms of competency based instruction, in individualized instruction, and in precision teaching. In a later chapter, we will see that Keller (1983) has broken down the concept of motivation into four major aspects: interest, relevance, expectancy, and satisfaction, and he has recommended teaching strategies for each. Motivated learners and motivational materials do have a positive influence upon learning.

Public Policy

In a later chapter, we mention some of the shifts in influence of federal, state, and local government upon the curriculum of elementary and secondary schools. But public policy and legislation also extend (some would say intrude) beyond curriculum matters.

Mitchell and Encornation (1984) have pointed out that policy goals have shifted over the years. Beginning in 1920, the goal was for efficiency in the schools, but equity emerged as the primary issue from the 1950s through the 1970s. Now, in the 1980s the goal has shifted to quality. The authors go on to summarize the mechanisms that state legislatures have employed to implement policy. These mechanisms are: structural reorganization, revenue generation, resource allocation, program definition, personnel training and certification, student testing and assessment, and curriculum materials development. Thus, public policy determines access to school, the nature of the curriculum, and how teachers are certified. Public policy thus relates to who may be educated, and where, as well as to classroom grouping, curriculum, and indirectly to methods and quality of instruction.

Self-Esteem and Attribution

While self-esteem and attribution are distinct conceptually, operationally they are related. Bar-Tal (1978) defines an attribution as "the inference that an observer makes about the causes of behavior—either his own or another person's" (p. 259). One aspect of attribution theory is "locus of control." A person who perceives outside influences as the determiners of his or her success or failure is called an "external." A person who perceives his or her own ability and effort as the determiners of success or failure is called an "internal." An internal reacts to success with increased pride, and over a period of many successes, is likely to develop positive self-esteem, other factors being equal.

Later chapters will deal in more detail with motivation and self-esteem. The point, of course, in the context of this book, is to attempt to design sequences and lessons so as to harness the power of intelligence, motivation, and self-esteem into long-term constructive learning and personality development.

Time on Task

Of all the specific variable that have been studied relating to teaching arrangements and procedures, time on task may be the most powerful. This variable, we say with some chagrin, is probably more powerful than teaching methods or quality of instructional materials. Some legislators have assumed that lengthening the school day and school year will increase achievement, presumably because time on task would be increased. However, several studies have indicated that only a small portion of each school day is spent with on-task activities. Our suggestion is to increase the interest and challenge of activities and materials, thereby increasing the amount of time learners will spend on task, and at the same time to enhance motivation and self-esteem. Present instructional design practices appear to result in relatively effective learning, but we believe this level could be improved by the use of recommendations made later in this book about sequencing and lesson design to better integrate progress in the affective and cognitive domains.

Teacher-Pupil Relationships

Earlier research has studied the effects of classroom climates named democratic, autocratic, and laissez-faire. The democratic climate has often been found to enhance pupil comfort, and sometimes achievement. If these data were re-analyzed to separate results for "internals" and "externals," this would perhaps make the data more meaningful. Such an analysis, however, falling into the general category of research into trait-treatment interaction, or learning styles, would perhaps be hard to apply. Any research confirming different learning styles has the penalty of low efficiency when put into practice, because of the need for multiple teaching approaches for the objective. Perhaps creative programming of computers and microcomputers can help overcome this difficulty. If computers can be interactive with varying entry skills, as in present programs, perhaps they could be made to be interactive with varying personal traits such as locus of control.

The general topic of the contributions of teachers to the achievement of affective and cognitive objectives is addressed in a later chapter.

Teaching Methods and Quality of Instruction

Research in teaching methods has led several writers to conclude that any method can be effective if the teacher is comfortable with the method and pursues it with enthusiasm. This is one justification for the traditional practice of allowing great latitude to teachers in regard to method.

We are somewhat uncomfortable with the above, rather generally accepted, conclusion. First of all, some research studies or methods do not verify and document how accurately and consistently the intended method is applied. Second, many of the methods studied are not replicable; there is no guarantee that other teachers could apply it the same way, nor that a given teacher could do it the same way twice. It is difficult, therefore, to generalize about particular methods to many teachers. Third, there may be undetected trait-treatment interactions which are obscured by the data analysis method used. We therefore believe that improvements are needed in methods research, including how to relate the method to the type of outcome represented in the objectives. But as matters now stand, it may be that teaching method accounts for only five percent of achievement variance, as some have concluded.

"Quality of instruction" is also a difficult influence to address, partly because of a philosophical circular dilemma. We could define quality as adherence to specified rules in designing and delivering the instruction, or we could define it empirically as the extent to which pupils achieve the objectives. Thus if we follow the "systematic approach" to designing the instruction, we specify and sequence objectives, and we design lessons using the appropriate instructional events and conditions of learning, such as those stated by Gagné and Briggs (1979). According to theory, if we are skilled practitioners, our instruction should be empirically effective (pupils would earn high scores in tests over the objectives). If the students do in fact score well on the tests, we have no problem. But if they don't score well, was the theory defective or was our *application* of the theory defective? Or were the students not trying to learn, or did they lack the assumed entering skills? Tough questions. It is difficult to validate a teaching theory, even if scientifically derived, when our method of instruction and the theory testing depend in part on our artistic competency. This mixture of art and science complicates the entire matter of teaching and learning, but we must try to live with it.

Aside from these problems, and by any definition of quality of instruction *presently within our state of the art*, we estimate, with chagrin, that quality of instruction must be ranked relatively low as we have it here, among other more powerful influences upon learning. *However*, if we do make progress in achieving instruction which better integrates the affective and cognitive domains, we believe we can eventually move the state of the art to a degree of quality which would push this topic higher on our list of influences upon learning. Our own part in this desired result would rest upon our handling of sequencing of objectives in the two domains, and upon our skill in identifying conditions of learning to be incorporated into lessons containing affective and cognitive objectives. If our overall approach proves to have merit, others could join in this approach to the further improvement of quality of instruction. Of course, other approaches may prove more fruitful.

Learner Strategies

We had difficulty deciding where to place learner strategies in our rank order of influences upon learning. In a broad sense, no academic learning takes place without some cooperative activity on the part of the learner. But in a more narrow sense, we have no good basis for knowing the relative influence of learning strategies that are directly taught to the learner by the teacher and strategies developed by the learner's own efforts.

A complicating factor is that our use of "learner strategy" refers to two distinct kinds of activities, which Gagné (1977) terms, respectively, "internal conditions of learning" and "cognitive strategies." We also embrace information processing in our use of learner strategies.

Internal conditions of learning include the prior learning which the learner brings as prerequisites to a new learning task or objective. The term also includes the learner's study habits and way of attending to instruction. When we add the term "cognitive strategies," we are referring both to a process of learning and an outcome. The learner develops major sets of cognitive strategies over a lengthy period of time. Some of these strategies may be used only in a single subject, like mathematics, while others may be used for all new learning. Gagné uses this term as an outcome domain in the sense that strategies are an outcome of learning, but he also treats them as learning processes.

To further complicate matters, the term "information processing" has been adopted to identify one kind of learning theory. This theory tends to imply that all people learn by the same processing mechanisms and that all types of learning outcomes (domains) are achieved by the same process. While we agree that there are some universal characteristics of brain functioning, in the physiological sense, we regard information processing as a theory of memory rather than a theory of learning. So we regard how memory is used in practical learning situations as only one aspect of the individual learner's strategies for new learning.

However, the main reason for listing learner strategies here is to raise the question of the extent to which strategies are to be included in instruction and the extent to which the learner is left to devise his or her own strategies.

Derry (1984) has proposed to directly teach some learning strategies before the lesson content is presented, and then program the computer to help the learner recall the strategies when learning problems are encountered.

Again, working to enhance motivation and self-confidence, coupled with learner strategy instruction, could represent an improvement in the state of the art in instructional practice.

Attitudes and Values

We would tend to place this topic higher in our rank order of influences in the broad sense that little school learning would take place in the event of completely negative attitudes and values concerning learning and schooling. Yet, because little is done explicitly to influence attitudes and values in instructional situations, we have placed it here.

Also, as for other topics in this list, we consider attitudes and values as both inputs to learning and outcomes of learning. Just as motivation is a pre-determiner and a result of successful learning, so are attitudes and values. As we delve into the role of attitudes in later chapters, we will recognize increasingly the interactions among many of these influences upon learning in our present list.

Peer Influences

As children mature, the relative influence of various "significant others" in their lives changes. The parents are all-important in infancy and early childhood, and then peers begin an influence which increases with time.

Beyond this simple observation, we might just remind readers to think to recall from their experiences the appearance of influence from other persons, such as teachers, spouses, supervisors, public figures, and others.

Instructional Media

We have deliberately used the term *instructional* media because we have nothing to offer concerning the debate over the good or evil of commercial television. We do not deny the power of commercial television—we just wish it were used more for instructional purposes for goals toward which our personal biases predispose us. That said, we refer now to media used in schools and training institutions.

There have been several "models of media selection," for use in education and training. These have been reviewed by Reiser and

Gagné (1983), who have also offered their own model, which attends to consideration of characteristics of the learners, the nature of the objectives, and principles of learning.

Short of outright inappropriate selection of media, such as audio recordings for the deaf or conventional print for the blind or the non-reader, there are few generalizations to be drawn from research that compares the effectiveness of one medium with that of another. Our conclusion is that *the message is more important than the medium*. That is to say, we believe that careful design of the software is the key to instructional effectiveness. If, for example, one adopts the model of lesson design proposed by Gagné and Briggs (1979), one would select media or combinations of media which permit the presentation of each of the nine "instructional events" called for in that model of lesson design. These nine events are discussed later in this book. In that model, the teacher is considered a medium, so any of the nine instructional events may be provided for by either the teacher or by other media. It has been shown that this model can be applied either by teachers (Briggs, 1977, Chapter 8) or by teams of instructional developers (Carey & Briggs, 1977).

However, to accomplish the instructional events in such a way as to adjust to learner differences, an *adaptive* medium may often be preferred. A later chapter will deal with media in the context of the purpose of this book.

In conclusion, while we rank media selection low in relative influence in the present state of the art, we foresee more creative uses of media not only to adapt to varying entry skills but also to affective characteristics of the learner. Eventually, more creative design of software should move this topic much higher in our list of influences upon learning.

Determiners of Learning for Adults

In the previous section of this chapter, we have listed determiners of learning in elementary and secondary schools. Many of these determiners or influences pertain also to adult learning, and perhaps the relative strength of influences shifts somewhat over the years.

We now list *additional influences* pertaining to *adult learning*.

Personal Goals

While many determiners of learning in childhood, such as intelligence, motivation, and self-esteem, may continue as powerful determiners of adult learning, the personal goals of the adult begin to become clarified and to exert greater influence. These goals are manifested in decisions, such as whether to enter college or the world of work. Of course, some may attend college primarily for social reasons, but others enter with serious interests which prove to be permanent. Needless to say, the school or work decision reflects the prior attitudes, values, and achievement of the person. For college students, the choice of a major may be directly linked to a life-long occupational or professional goal. Also in early adulthood, the goals relating to work, marriage, and long-term material security may conflict, and only gradually be resolved into a life pattern. The decisions made in this process, in turn, will partly determine the persons who are to become significant others—spouses, colleagues, bosses, employing organizations, etc. Separate chapters in this book deal further with adult learning in undergraduate school, professional schools, and military and industrial organizations.

Organizational Policies

For adults not entering professions through professional schools, policies of employing organizations may be closely related to continued learning and career progression. Company policy may determine whether any career progression is possible, and if so, the mechanism for progression, e.g., experience, training, or a combination of both. Further formal training or education thus may be closely linked to career plans. Training in some organizations may be of short duration and narrow in scope, while other organizations may provide a life-long sequence of job progression interspersed with increasingly broad or specialized training. Some organizations operate their own schools, and others sponsor advanced university education.

While most employing organizations are involved in training and education now, the scope of this may expand because of shifts in demand for various occupations. There have been several forecasts by many publication sources of the nature of these shifts in job demands. While forecasting the future is an uncertain enterprise, young people would do well to study the forecasts. The majority of futurists believe that we can at least devise alternate scenarios of the future showing what results could be expected from alternate national policy decisions yet to be made. Notice could be taken by adults of the occupational implications of some of the forecast material.

Expectations of the Future

Many young people are understandably doubtful whether it is worthwhile to plan for the future. The complexity and seriousness of world and national problems can indeed lead to pessimism. Some futurists are pessimistic and some are optimistic, but both camps agree that if the right decisions are made, the problems can be solved. Hawkin, Ogilvy, and Schwartz (1982) point out that a prospect of doom can paralyze action just as certainly as naive hopes render action unnecessary. They outline seven plausible scenarios, based on a program of research at Stanford Research Institute. While the major problems they cite—depletion of energy resources, hunger, erratic weather, and threat of nuclear war—are not strictly educational or occupational matters, the education of all citizens is a needed step toward increasing the probability that the necessary decisions will be made. The implication: a more broadly educated citizenry is needed to select political leaders.

Life Styles

We use the term "life styles" in a broad sense. We do not refer to sexual preferences or living arrangements, but to overall adult goals. Mitchell (1983) conducted a major mail survey of over 800 specific questions to a sample of over 1,600 American adults aged 18 and over, living in the 48 contiguous states. The data were analyzed into a typology which "comprises four comprehensive groups that are subdivided into nine life styles, each intended to describe a unique way of life defined by its distinctive array of values, drives, beliefs, needs, dreams, and special points of view:

> Need-Driven Groups
> > Survivor Life style
> > Sustainer Life style

> Outer-Directed Groups
>> Belonger Life style
>> Emulator Life style
>> Achiever Life style
> Inner-Directed Groups
>> I-Am-Me Life style
>> Experiential Life style
>> Societally Conscious Life style
> Combined Outer and Inner-Directed Groups
>> Integrated Life style (pp. 3-4).

Mitchell goes on to say that some adults stay fixed in one lifestyle while others move from one style to another over a period of their adult years. The causes of such progression are very complex. Mitchell lists these influences as determiners of status and degree and nature of change: events and circumstances, age, history, unresolved childhood and other experiences, changing paradigms, natural development, and evolution. It is clear that learning of either an incidental sort or a planned learning course must play a large role in the directions in which a person moves over the years. As some persons gain everyday experiences, they review goals and aspirations and deliberately plan changes in their lives, some of which may require formal education or training for realization of the planned change. Other persons appear to just drift along on the same level. Also, some individuals seem almost to "inherit" their place in the scheme from parent status, while others actively seek change of status. We must suppose that such planned changes often create a market for further education and training services. Other changes may relate to occupational shifts not requiring further training or retraining.

Feelings and Emotions

This influence could have been listed under either childhood or adult influences upon learning. We often think of feelings and emotions as *reactions* to experiences, including educational experiences, but recent literature suggests that feelings and emotions are *determiners* of what the person seeks to learn. Like motivation and attitudes, feelings and emotions can be both determiners and consequences of learning. We will look briefly into this literature in a later chapter.

Summary of Influences Upon Learning

We have named and briefly discussed a great variety of influences upon learning by both children and adults. We have done this partly to present a condensed overview of many influences which are not addressed in detail in this book. This helps to set the broader context within which rest the curricular and instructional techniques which are the main focus of this book. We also hope this will indicate to the reader that we, the authors, are not narrow specialists in our total view, even though we concentrate the major portion of this book upon a few aspects of curriculum and instruction, and even though we are professionally identified as instructional designers applying a systems approach to instruction.

Having reviewed this broader context of many influences upon learning, we next turn to an overview of the research and techniques which will be emphasized most in the remainder of this book.

OUR CONTRIBUTION TOWARD A SOLUTION

In the opening portion of this chapter we gave an overview of the broad context of total influences upon learning within which our contribution toward a solution to the problem of domain interactions will be developed in this book. We now take a similar broad view of the total scope of planning a curriculum or course of study before outlining the components of our approach to instruction to integrate the domains.

An Overview of Curriculum and Instruction

Whether one is planning an entire school curriculum or designing a single course or special training program, a useful check on the total plan is to see if the following questions are answered in the plan: Who? What? Why? When? Where? How? We now address each question in turn.

Who

The people who are to be taught and the people who are to do the teaching must receive deliberate attention. The characteristics of the intended learners should be noted systematically so that the instruction is planned to meet their needs through application of teaching means which are appropriate for them. This information about the learners may come from school records, test data, or personal contact with the learners. The instruction is then designed so as to match the characteristics of the learners both as to the ends to be sought (goals, outcomes) and the means to be employed (methods and materials for learning).

The characteristics of the teachers or trainers also must be considered to be sure that *their* characteristics are compatible with the ends and means that are adopted. The skills and attitudes of the instructors, as well as their knowledge of subject matter, need to be matched to the ends and means to be selected. The instructors' knowledge of student characteristics is also widely recognized as crucial.

What

What is to be taught is expressed in the form of the goals and objectives of the instruction. Objectives may be specified at several levels: lesson objectives, unit objectives, course objectives, or curriculum objectives. Sometimes the objectives are expressed in the form of "instructional curriculum maps" (ICMs) which list objectives in the cognitive and affective domains (Briggs and Wager, 1981). For the sub-domain of intellectual skills, the development of learning hierarchies (Gagné, 1977) is useful. Or, objectives may simply be listed in a descending order of complexity, as in our example of audit trails in Part III of this book.

The practice of listing intended objectives does not prohibit the emergence of unanticipated outcomes, as many have claimed. We see no reason why a teacher cannot work with preplanned objectives as well as respond flexibly to unexpected outcomes.

Why

The detailed objectives adapted for a curriculum or a course must be justifiable by reference to some long-term outcomes, such as life-long goals. This matter is dealt with for both education and training in Part III of this book. Thus objectives for each lesson, unit, and course must contribute to the attainment of some longer-term goal. A mechanism for plotting such linkages between groups of detailed objectives and broader goals is presented in our illustrative audit trails in Part III.

When

For public education at the elementary and secondary level, laws determine when children enter school and how long they must remain. But the matter of just when specific objectives should be taught is left largely up to the schools and the curriculum planners. The question of "when" is not a trivial one. The development of the child as well as sequencing considerations enter into good planning for when each cognitive or affective objective may be undertaken.

For adults, there is more flexibility as to when education is continued or special training begun. This is taken up in Part III.

Where

Again, for children in public schools, where they attend is determined by law and local rules. The major determiner is place of residence. Race may no longer place some children in inferior schools, nor may all exceptional children be segregated from other children.

For adults, choosing the locus of further education or training is often related to career plans, as discussed in Part III.

How

This refers to the methods, media, and techniques of teaching, or the means. Much of this book is devoted to background and techniques relating to the planning of sequences of lessons for objectives in the affective and cognitive domains.

The Major Components in Our Approach

We have gone to some length, in the opening section of this chapter, to discuss the broader context within which our contribution to the solution of the identified problem is embedded. As said before, we hoped that doing so would help us, the authors, to retain a broad perspective when presenting the details of our work. We also hoped that this broader context would help the reader evaluate our contribution, and to decide whether to employ it in practice or research.

We have chosen in this book to classify the details of our work in accordance with the following outline of components in our approach to building a theory for the integration of instruction for affective and cognitive goals:

1. Needs Assessment (Audit Trails)
2. Taxonomies of Outcomes
3. Sequencing of Instruction
4. Lesson Design
    a. Objectives
    b. Instructional events
    c. Internal conditions of learning
    d. External conditions of learning
    e. Learning materials, activities, and media
    f. Evaluation

The following sections of this chapter represents an overview and introduction to the components in the above outline. All these components will be encountered in more detail later in this book.

Needs Assessment (Audit Trail)

Robert Mager has said "if you don't know where you are going, no telling where you will end up." This was a way of saying that we should be sure of our intended goals (ends) before we decide how to reach them (means). Another way of expressing the same idea is "don't bother about solutions before you have a problem."

These ideas have been expressed more formally and in considerable detail by Kaufman and English (1979) in their treatment of methods of needs assessment and needs analysis.

In Part III of this book, we present the technique of "audit trails" as our way of approaching needs assessment. An audit trail represents an attempt to not only identify life-long goals, but also to design curricula and courses by listing a continuous sequence of objectives from elementary school to adult life. In Part III we discuss what we believe is a major problem in present practices in curriculum and instruction—the separation of responsibility for (a) long-term goals (needs), (b) intermediate goals (curriculum), and (c) short-term goals (instruction day by day). This separation, in combination with the separation of the cognitive and affective domains as discussed in Chapter 1, becomes the "problem" that we address.

An audit trail not only seeks to bring continuity among lesson objectives, course objectives, curriculum goals, and life-long goals, but it also seeks to bring integration of affective and cognitive objectives. The example audit trails in Part III encourage us to believe that a more thorough effort in this direction would improve both curriculum and instruction. More broadly yet, we see the audit trail as a potential mechanism for coordinating the work entailed in needs assessment, curriculum development, and the sequencing of instruction.

Taxonomies of Outcomes

This topic is treated in detail in Chapter 3. Here we will merely list and briefly discuss several uses of taxonomies, as they relate to the design of instruction.

Checking audit trails for completeness. When a first draft audit trail has been developed, the individual objectives in it can be classified, using a taxonomy for the cognitive domain and a taxonomy for the affective domain. Doing this will reveal gaps or empty taxonomy categories. We can then review the audit trail to determine whether some of the gaps should be filled, by adding new objectives. This process is a systematic way to check our objectives for balance, breadth, and completeness. It will remind us to review the sequencing of objectives to enhance domain interactions—the contribution of affective learning to cognitive learning, and the reverse.

Checking lesson design. As discussed elsewhere in this book, the classification of each objective into a taxonomy category can remind us to review lesson plans to see if they incorporate appropriate conditions of learning. As shown in Chapter 1, we must consider two kinds of conditions of learning when designing lessons: (a) internal conditions, reflecting presence or absence of essential prerequisites for the lesson, and (b) external conditions to be provided by the teacher or by the lesson materials. Since the external conditions are different for each category in a taxonomy, classifying the objective reminds us to recall or look up the appropriate external conditions of learning.

In a later chapter, we list these external conditions; many of them, especially for the cognitive domain, were originated by Gagné (1977). Most of the conditions for the affective domain were identified by the authors. Referring to these lists of conditions frequently when designing lessons is recommended.

A large amount of our effort in preparing to write this book was to make inferences from the research literature concerning the affective domain in order to originate new conditions of learning.

Interpreting learning research literature. For the designer who attempts to apply the learning research literature, a taxonomy is useful to classify the category of learning outcomes represented in each research report. From the researcher's point of view, a taxonomy helps to identify the boundaries of outcomes within which the research can be generalized. One of the confusing problems about the learning research literature is that there is no clear general agreement on what the category labels in taxonomies mean. Thus the reader of the reports may have to search the article for objectives and test items in order to infer the category of outcomes represented by the research study.

Planning evaluation instruments. The classification of objectives into a taxonomy is a helpful guide to the development of tests measuring achievement. Briggs and Wager (1981) have offered concrete guides to developing such tests, using the standard verbs for each taxonomy category listed by Gagné and Briggs (1979). Some additional standard verbs are implied by the taxonomy of the affective domain by Krathwohl *et al.* (1964). These listings have aided the authors in developing both conditions of learning and standard verbs for the affective domain.

As shown in Chapter 1, achievement tests have two distinct values for the teacher and other designers of instruction. First, they can be used to evaluate and improve the lessons and the materials (formative evaluation), and second, they can be used to evaluate revised lessons and to assess the achievement of the students (summative evaluation).

Sequencing of Instruction

The above discussion of needs assessment and audit trails has conveyed much of what we wish to say here about the sequencing of instruction.

The major remaining point is that a re-examination of our audit trails and lesson plans can alert us to a continuous consideration of how to interface cognitive and affective objectives. So there is the question of how to sequence objectives *within* each domain and *between* the two domains. Learning hierarchies can help decide sequencing within the intellectual skills sub-domain of the cognitive domain. Instructional curriculum maps represent a visual display to help us make and review decisions about sequencing between the domains, and within domains other than the intellectual skills subdomain.

The reader may wish to inspect the audit trails in Part III and decide whether some improvement upon the sequencing could be made.

Lesson Design

We adopt a basic approach to lesson design first developed by Gagné (1977), and elaborated upon and further illustrated by Gagné and Briggs (1979), Briggs (1977), and Briggs and Wager (1981).

These references contain some format aids useful in designing lessons. Here we will briefly discuss the following components of this approach to lesson design:

1. Objectives.
2. Instructional events.
3. External conditions of learning.
4. Materials, activities, and media.
5. Evaluation.

Objectives. Using the audit trail as a guide, the designer identifies lessons and series of lessons to implement the portion of the audit trail for which he or she is responsible. Each lesson may have one or more objectives in either the affective or cognitive domain, or both. The objective(s) is noted by the designer to guide the lesson design work, and in our model, the objective is also communicated to the learner unless there is a reason for not doing so, as is often the case with affective objectives.

Selecting instructional events. Gagné (1977) has identified nine instructional events which are the building blocks in this model of instructional design. These nine events are listed, discussed, and illustrated in the several texts referred to in the opening portion of this chapter section on *lesson design.* Those same texts also present examples of lesson designs. Most of the sample lesson designs in those texts and most of the known applications in design projects are for objectives in the cognitive domain. One task we face later in this book is to examine the relevance of those nine events for affective objectives.

One purpose of lesson design is to decide which of the nine events are necessary, considering the sophistication of the learner in providing his own events. For some learners and some lessons, only a few of the events may be provided by the teacher or by the instructional materials, media, and activities. For other learners and other lessons, all the events may be presented one or more times during a lesson.

The nine events, as listed by Gagné and Briggs (1979, p. 157) are:

1. Gaining attention.
2. Informing the learner of the objective.
3. Stimulating recall of prerequisite learning.
4. Presenting the stimulus material.
5. Providing "learning guidance."
6. Eliciting the performance.
7. Providing feedback about performance correctness.
8. Assessing the performance.
9. Enhancing retention and transfer.

Each of these events is intended to activate internal information-processing activities, one of the components of the *internal events of instruction.*

After the designer decides which of the nine events are needed for a lesson, the next step is to decide how to implement the events chosen. This implementation involves (a) a plan to incorporate the relevant external conditions of learning into the events of the lesson, and (b) the design and development of the physical materials or communications and learner activities needed to accomplish the events. These two aspects of implementation are addressed next.

The external conditions of learning. Whereas the nine events of instruction listed above are presumed to be applicable for all learners and all types of desired outcomes, the conditions of learning are different for each category of outcome in taxonomies. That is to say, the matter of what is communicated to the learner and how it is communicated during instruction vary according to the type of outcome represented by the lesson objective. This variation among lessons representing different outcome categories tends to occur for two of the nine events: presenting the stimulus and providing guidance to learning.

In regard to presenting the stimulus, *what* is presented and *how* it is presented varies with the category of intended outcome. For example, in the memorization type of objectives, the instructor presents the exact words to be remembered and recited by the learner, as in memorizing a poem or a set of words and their associated symbols, as in mathematics. On the other hand, in teaching a rule, such as how to find the area of a circle, the teacher states the rule and demonstrates examples of applying the rule, but the learners are not asked to reproduce solutions to the same examples, rather the solution to *different* examples.

In regard to guiding learning, in the case of memorizing a poem, the teacher directly prompts the learner by giving the next line of the poem when the student is blocked in reciting at a particular point. But when learners are trying to find the area of a particular circle, the teacher would give indirect hints when needed, such as "what is the value of pi?" or "what is the relationship between diameter and radius?"

Stated differently, two external conditions of learning for memorized material are to present the exact stimulus material to be learned, and to provide direct prompts. The external conditions for learning to apply rules are to provide a variety of sample solutions and give indirect hints when a learner falters when trying to work a new example.

A summary of the external conditions of learning to be incorporated into the events of instruction for different types of outcomes is presented in Part IV of this book.

So the nine events or building blocks are the same for all lessons, but the conditions of learning incorporated into the events vary among lessons, depending upon the type of outcome reflected in the lesson objective.

Designing materials and activities. In some lessons, all the events of instruction are accomplished by the teacher and by learners' responses to the teacher. In other lessons, several media may be employed to accomplish the nine events. Selection of a medium for each instructional event can bring a precision to teaching which may be lacking in a less analytic method of lesson planning. When it has been decided which medium will be used for each event, then the actual lectures, discussions, activities, and materials and media can be planned in a word-by-word, picture-by-picture, and action-by-action level of detail, as in writing a script. Often the first brief outline of how each event will be accomplished is called a "prescription," and the full-scale verbatim presentation for the event is called a "script." See Briggs and Wager (1981) for examples of prescriptions and scripts.

Evaluation. The lessons first designed can be empirically evaluated by the process called formative evaluation, which includes giving a test after the lesson and making an item analysis of the results. Formative evaluation can also involve other procedures, as outlined by Dick (1977a). The total purpose is to improve the instruction before the next use of the lesson designs, and to have a preliminary estimate of how well the instruction is succeeding in enabling the learners to reach the objectives.

After instruction has been revised by the above procedure, a summative evaluation can be undertaken (Dick, 1977b) to (a) assess the effectiveness of instruction in achieving the objectives, (b) to detect unplanned outcomes, and (c) to make decisions as to whether to keep the program or to adopt a different one.

The two evaluation stages just discussed have been widely used for cognitive objectives. The evaluation of progress for affective objectives will receive attention later in this book.

SUMMARY

In this chapter we have presented a broad outline of the many pre-determiners or influences upon learning in order to set the total context of this book.

We then presented a brief overview of questions to be answered by design of curricula and courses in education and training.

Within these two general contexts, we sketched out the major components in our approach to the problem of how to integrate instruction in the affective and cognitive domains. In so doing, we identified some well-established practices in designing instruction for the cognitive domain, and we alluded to new elements we have added for the affective domain and for integration of the two domains.

We expressed the hope that preparing this chapter would help the authors keep aware of the broader context within which we are seeking solutions to the problem we have addressed. We also expressed the hope that these overviews would help prepare readers for the remaining chapters, and would lead them to realize that we are aware of many facets of the problem which we could not address in this book.

We are sobered by the complexity of the task we have undertaken, and we acknowledge that we have made only a modest beginning to the solution of the problem we have addressed.

We have identified our professional affiliation with that not completely popular group called "instructional system designers" or "educational technologists." Whatever the previous views of the readers concerning that group may be, we hope this chapter has convinced you that we are not just narrow technicians. After you have finished reading the book, we would not be displeased if you would regard us as "humanistic instructional technologists."

In any event, we hope this book adds a new dimension to instructional technology. We are confident that we have identified an important problem. How well we have dealt with it we leave to your judgment.

Introduction to Part II:
The Research Background
and Instructional Implications

In Part II of this book we present the research background that we used for deriving instructional implications for integrating the affective and cognitive domains. We also present internal and external conditions of learning for each component of the affective domain that we discuss. Before proceeding to describe the contents of Part II, we first want to offer a working definition of the affective domain.

In Chapter 1, we provided a general overview of the affective domain, and we listed some problems that we and other researchers have encountered when trying to define and make use of the affective domain. We did not, however, provide a clear, concise definition of the domain. Rather, we reported terms and constructs that have been used in descriptions of the affective domain, or terms and constructs that are included in taxonomies of the affective domain. Granted, this is not a satisfactory definition. We attempt to rectify that here.

In general, the affective domain is comprised of all behaviors concerned with emotions and feelings. Ringness (1975) defines the affective domain in the following way: "Strictly speaking, any behavior that has an emotional tone lies within the affective domain, which is why emotions themselves belong to it. Some behaviors have a more highly cognitive component than emotions, per se, yet also have a definite emotional tone. Thus, interests, tastes, preferences, attitudes, values, morals, character, and personality adjustment are important parts of the affective domain" (pp. 19-20).

Gephart and Ingle (1976) spent considerable space in their paper trying to define the affective domain; they never do present *one* definition, but instead give several. They also offer a number of ways *not* to define the domain. They say, "The affective domain is an abstract categorical term which references a class of concepts. As such, it has no synonyms" (p. 186). They go on to say that the affective domain is at a higher level of abstraction than either a term like emotion, or one like affect. "The affective domain is the term for the whole class and as such is the most abstract concept in the taxonomy" (p. 187). In addition, they point out that the three domains, cognitive, affective, and psychomotor, are "three useful explanatory fictions" because we never "see 'pure' affective behavior or 'pure' cognitive behaviors, etc." (p. 186). Their "definition" is, in part, the terminology they include in their taxonomy. We present their taxonomy in Chapter 3.

We used the definition of Ringness (1975) and those given by Gephart and Ingle (1976) to help us formulate our own definition of the affective domain. Since there are no pure behaviors, and because of our interest in integrating the affective and cognitive domains for instructional purposes, we have used a working definition that combines the affective and cognitive aspects of any behavior. We were interested in behaviors that had a strong emotional tone coupled with a cognitive capability.

The definition that guided our work is: The affective domain is a category term which catalogs a class of *behaviors that have both an emotional tone and a cognitive component; both components are required for expression of the behavior.* Like Gephart and Ingle, we (a) use the term affective domain as a superordinate category, and (b) use the components we included in the domain to assist us in understanding and defining the domain.

In Part II of this book we provide examples of how other people have defined the affective domain, and we provide a number of constructs that can be included in the domain. We do not believe we have exhausted all the possible components that could be included, nor are we convinced that all the constructs we have included should be included, e.g., social development and attributions. So, by our working definition and our inclusion of the constructs found in Part II, we present a first stab at forming some boundaries for the affective domain.

We begin Part II with a chapter on domain taxonomies. In Chapter 3, we present an overview of several taxonomies of the cognitive domain and several taxonomies of the affective domain. These taxonomies "define" or set boundaries for each respective domain. We attempt to compare the taxonomies within a domain, and we offer a critique of the major ones. We end the chapter with a brief summary of research that has attempted to integrate the affective and cognitive domains.

In the remaining chapters of Part II, Chapters 4 through 7, we examine individual components of the affective domain. We close each chapter with the internal and external conditions of learning that we derived for each component. Following the convention from the cognitive domain established by Gagné (1977) and Gagné and Briggs (1979) we adopt the notion of "conditions of learning." We have included both *internal* and *external conditions of learning.* The internal conditions refer broadly to the conditions that must be present in the learner before learning can occur, e.g., recall of prerequisite information. The external conditions refer to conditions outside the learner that facilitate learning, e.g., presentation of examples of concepts by an instructor or by the instructional materials. Unless otherwise noted, the internal and external conditions that we present are useful for instructional situations in which there are children, adolescents, or adult learners.

In Chapter 4, we present research on the development of attitudes and values, and attitude change. We first provide an overview of attitude change theories, and then we present five theories to discuss in more detail. They are: (a) The Yale Approach, (b) Dissonance Theory, (c) Cognitive Balancing, (d) Social Judgment Theory, and (e) Social Learning Theory. In Chapter 5, we present a discussion of the development of moral and ethical behavior from several philosophical perspectives. We then discuss in some detail Lawrence Kohlberg's theory of moral development. In Chapter 6, we focus our attention on self-development. We first present an overview of personality theories, and then we present several selected theories or constructs that we describe in more detail. These include: (a) the work of Alfred Adler, (b) the position of Carl Rogers, (c) three concepts from social learning theory—self-efficacy, self-regulatory behavior, and locus of control, and (d) the learned helplessness construct from attribution theory. At the end of each chapter, we discuss the internal conditions required for each component, and we list external conditions for each component.

In Chapter 7, we present four additional components of the affective domain: (a) emotional development and feelings, (b) interest and motivation, (c) social development and group dynamics, and (d) attributions. A section of Chapter 7 is devoted to each component. We have made a slight format change in this chapter. Rather than discussing the internal conditions, as we did in Chapters 4 through 6, we have listed them. We felt that the internal conditions were straightforward and often similar to those presented in the previous three chapters, and therefore did not require discussion. The external conditions for each component are also listed as they were in Chapters 4, 5, and 6.

Our review of research in Part II is by no means exhaustive. We did not attempt to do a complete literature review of each category. We have, however, selected what we believe to be representative theories or aspects of theories that would assist us in our task of integrating the affective and cognitive domains. Although we have only briefly addressed representative theories, or parts of theories, we hope we have done them justice.

Ringness (1975) stated in the Preface of his book, "The fact that attitudes and values are learned presents us with our greatest hope for the future." We concur. We hope the conditions of learning we have derived from our literature review will enable teachers, instructional developers, and curriculum specialist to do a better job planning for instruction that involves behaviors in the affective domain.

Chapter 3

Domain Taxonomies:
Descriptions and Research

CHARACTERISTICS OF TAXONOMIES
OF EDUCATIONAL OUTCOMES

A Taxonomy as a Classification System

The Complexity of the Taxonomy

Descriptive and Prescriptive Taxonomies

TAXONOMIES OF THE COGNITIVE DOMAIN

Gagné's Taxonomy

Major Categories of Learning Outcomes
Intellectual skills
Learning Hierarchies

Summary

Bloom's Taxonomy

Condensed Outline of the Taxonomy
Validation Studies
Criticisms of Bloom's Taxonomy

Summary

53

OTHER COGNITIVE TAXONOMIES

Summary

TAXONOMIES OF THE AFFECTIVE DOMAIN

Krathwohl, Bloom, and Masia's Taxonomy

Condensed Outline of the Taxonomy
Validation Studies
Criticisms of the Affective Taxonomy
Summary

The Gephart and Ingle Taxonomy

The Brandhorst Taxonomies

Other Affective Taxonomies

Summary

RESEARCH INTEGRATING THE COGNITIVE AND AFFECTIVE DOMAINS

SUMMARY

Chapter 3

Domain Taxonomies:
Descriptions and Research

In this chapter, we review the various taxonomies of the cognitive and affective domains and the research related to them. Most of the research has been conducted on the domains separately; however, several studies have been conducted, or are being conducted, that have attempted integration. In addition to these studies that directly address domain integration, another group of studies has been conducted that demonstrates causal or correlational interactions among subcategories of the domains or constructs related to a domain. Studies showing that positive attitudes toward a content area or subject yield higher achievement scores than do negative attitudes are one example. While these studies do not directly relate to domain taxonomies, they do demonstrate the interaction of cognitive and affective behaviors.

We begin this chapter by explaining what taxonomies are and how they can be used. Then we review the major taxonomies of both domains and the research related to them. Last, we review research done on the interactions of the domains, including a brief review of interaction studies not directly related to domain taxonomies.

CHARACTERISTICS OF TAXONOMIES
OF EDUCATIONAL OUTCOMES

A taxonomy provides for the orderly classification of objects, substances, plants, animals, or processes. A taxonomy in physics allows us to classify substances as liquids, solids, or gases. A taxonomy in botany allows us to classify plants by their characteristics. A taxonomy in zoology allows us to classify animals by their characteristics. What do educational taxonomies enable us to do? This is the central question addressed in this chapter.

Various educational researchers have offered taxonomies in the broad domains of (a) cognitive outcomes, (b) affective outcomes, and (c) psychomotor outcomes. In this book we are concerned with how to integrate instruction for the simultaneous achievement of cognitive and affective objectives. This task of achieving such integration becomes necessary because, generally speaking, different researchers have tended to concentrate their efforts in only one of these domains. This has resulted in the creation of three separate bodies of knowledge, without sufficient attempts to show how all three may be drawn upon for the purpose of designing instruction.

While three different sets of researchers have labored to produce the three types of taxonomies and their three corresponding areas of knowledge, taxonomies have not been sufficiently *used*, in teaching, research, or instructional design. Thus, one often reads a journal article reporting a learning experiment without being certain as to the type of outcome being dealt with, because the author of the article has not clearly classified the objectives, tests, and learning materials. The same can be said for many lesson plans and for many instructional materials produced by designers.

Most areas of research or practice would benefit by greater and more precise use of taxonomies. We hope to illustrate this in this book. But first we must examine the present status of educational taxonomies and the research relating to them. We do this first by examining the general characteristics of taxonomies, and second by discussing separately taxonomies in the cognitive domain and in the affective domain.

A Taxonomy as a Classification System

Just as a taxonomy of animals allows us to classify thousands of individual specimens by assigning them to appropriate categories in the taxonomy, a domain taxonomy in education allows us to classify terms, concepts, goals or outcomes, assessment instruments, and/or lesson plans that are directed toward a particular outcome. A taxonomy of terms or concepts usually shows the breadth of the domain. A *taxonomy of educational outcomes* allows us to classify thousands of instructional goals or objectives into appropriate categories. The basic requirement of such a taxonomy is a set of clearly defined categories for whichever domain or domains of outcomes it addresses. Taxonomies of educational outcomes allow us to classify (a) goals, objectives, and observed outcomes, (b) test items attempting to measure the stated objectives, and (c) lesson plans directed to the teaching of the stated objectives. These three uses of a taxonomy help us bring *congruence* among objectives, instruction, and measurement of the attainment of the objectives by the learners. By designing lessons to achieve this congruence, we have used a systematic procedure to enhance the effectiveness of the instruction, and by communicating this congruence to the learners we hope to gain their trust in the honesty of our intentions. This can promote an atmosphere of "working together" in the educational effort.

The Complexity of the Taxonomy

The more complex the taxonomy, the more precision we may attain in both the classification of objectives and in the design of instruction. For example, a zoology taxonomy listing only phyla as categories would not be as precise as a taxonomy also providing subordinate categories called genus, species, etc.

As will be seen later in this chapter, the taxonomies we review, in both the cognitive and affective domains, vary somewhat in their degree of complexity. A difficulty we will encounter is that it is not possible to translate directly from one taxonomy to another, because the individual categories and sets of categories do not appear to describe exactly the same types of objectives or outcomes. For this reason, in designing either a lesson or a research study, we will be forced to select one taxonomy for use. We are tempted to conclude that communication would be simplified if researchers and designers agreed to use *one* taxonomy for each domain. That would appear ideal at least in the short run. But of course we may not reach such an agreement. In the long run, it may be best that we don't, but at present our task is complicated by the lack of equal "coverage" by the taxonomies in a single domain.

Descriptive and Prescriptive Taxonomies

We have used the terms descriptive and prescriptive to refer to taxonomies of different types. Actually it is not the taxonomy itself that is descriptive or prescriptive, but rather the taxonomy plus the materials and explanations that accompany it. If the taxonomy authors provide sufficient materials to allow objectives, test items, and/or lesson plans to be derived from the taxonomy, we have labelled it prescriptive. So, a prescriptive taxonomy may be accompanied by an entire model or theory for the design of instruction, all organized around the categories in the taxonomy. In that case, the author of the taxonomy has not only provided the taxonomy itself; he or she has also shown us how to use it in designing lessons and instructional materials.

A descriptive taxonomy, on the other hand, is one that permits reliable classifications of terms, labels, and sometimes even objectives and test items, but generally does not include the supporting materials to allow a user to design lessons. It generally describes a range of concepts or terms, but does not allow for prescriptions.

Descriptive and prescriptive taxonomies, however, are not discrete categories; rather, they form a continuum. One taxonomy of the affective domain, the one proposed by Gephart and Ingle (1976), is described by the authors as a list of terminology, but it is actually a categorization of affective behaviors or responses. They say the classification is only a "suggested direction" and that they felt quite unsure about the placement of some of the terms. No operational definitions are given, no objectives or test items provided, and no directions, hints, or ideas about how to go about designing instruction are given. Of all the affective taxonomies we review, it is the most inclusive, but also the least prescriptive.

The cognitive taxonomy developed by Gagné (1977) is the most prescriptive one we will review. He has provided not only a classification system, but also the major components of a theory of instructional design. His theory, further expanded by Gagné and Briggs (1979), and by Briggs and Wager (1981), offers the following *prescriptive* concepts and procedures:

1. A list of nine instructional events which form the building blocks for designing lessons and instructional materials and activities, for all categories in the taxonomy.
2. A set of conditions of learning, differing for each category of outcomes in the taxonomy.
3. The technique of deriving learning hierarchies which displays the relationships and assumed directions of transfer of learning among the categories. This technique has been expanded upon, in the form of instructional curriculum maps, by Briggs and Wager (1981).

This brief list of some of the features of the taxonomy by Gagné has been presented here to explicate the meaning of the word "prescriptive." More details about Gagné's taxonomy are provided in the next section of this chapter.

TAXONOMIES OF THE COGNITIVE DOMAIN

Gagné's Taxonomy

While the taxonomy by Gagné (1977) includes a single category of motor skills and a single category of attitudes, his major contribution has been in the cognitive domain. We have chosen, for convenience, to classify his taxonomy as one for the cognitive domain. However, in our account of his work, we will include his limited coverage of motor skills and attitudes.

Gagné identified five categories of learning outcomes that can result from instruction. They are: (a) intellectual skills, (b) cognitive strategies, (c) verbal information, (d) motor skills, and (e) attitudes. For each category he described internal and external conditions of learning specifically related to that category, and he described nine events of instruction that are instrumental for designing instruction across all categories. Internal conditions of learning refer to those abilities or capabilities within the learners that are necessary for learning to occur, hence, the term internal. They are usually in the form of prerequisites—skills, knowledge, attitudes, and motor skills—that were previously developed or learned and stored in memory. External conditions are those that can be arranged for in instruction and are, therefore, external to the learner. Gagné gives specific and different internal and external conditions for each type of learning outcome and for each subcategory of intellectual skills. For example, internal conditions for verbal information learning are (a) a pre-existing set of organized knowledge, and (b) the appropriate encoding strategies. For attitudes, internal conditions include (a) prerequisite concepts directly related to the attitude to be learned, (b) ability to identify important characteristics of a human model, and (c) concepts related to the personal action that the attitude prompts. External conditions for verbal information learning include (a) providing a meaningful context, (b) increasing the distinctiveness of cues, and (c) providing opportunities for repetition; for attitudes they include (a) providing opportunities to observe the human model, and (b) reinforcing the choice of personal action. These different conditions of learning for each type of learning outcome enable a designer to organize and plan instruction for each category of outcomes. We will provide a more in-depth coverage of conditions of learning in a later chapter.

In addition to the conditions of learning, Gagné also gives nine events of instruction that correspond to and facilitate the internal structures and processes of learning, e.g., expectancy, coding, memory, etc. These nine events occur during a learning situation, and their function is to provide the external conditions of learning for the class of outcomes under consideration. Unlike the conditions of learning, these events are the same for each type of outcome. The nine events are:

1. Gaining attention.
2. Informing the learner of the objective.
3. Stimulating recall of prerequisite learnings.
4. Presenting the stimulus materials.
5. Providing learning guidance.
6. Eliciting the performance.

7. Providing feedback about correctness of the performance.
8. Assessing the performance.
9. Enhancing retention and transfer.

These will also be made more explicit and clear in a later chapter.

Gagné's inclusion of conditions of learning and events of instruction with his taxonomy is extremely useful for designers, instructors, and teachers. The breadth of coverage—categories of outcomes including attitudes, motor skills, and three components of the cognitive domain—plus the conditions of learning and events of instruction, make this taxonomy useful for planning instruction, and applicable across many learning situations. It is a more prescriptive taxonomy than most.

Major Categories of Learning Outcomes

In this book, we refer to three broad "domains"—cognitive, affective, and psychomotor. However, Gagné refers to *five* domains. Three of his "domains"—intellectual skills, cognitive strategies, and information learning—are what we call the "cognitive domain." His "motor" skills are a component of the psychomotor domain, and his "attitudes" are a component of the affective domain.

Gagné has classified human learning into five domains categorized by learned capabilities. He defines learning as "a change in human disposition or capability, which persists over a period of time, and which is not simply ascribable to processes of growth" (Gagné, 1977, p. 3). These capabilities, which are unobservable as such, can be observed in a learner's behavior; that is, we infer from an observed behavior that a learner has acquired a particular capability. These capabilities result in the different outcomes and when they are planned for, they are stated as instructional objectives (Aronson & Briggs, 1983).

Gagné's five varieties of learning outcomes (domains) are:

1. *Intellectual skills*—The capabilities that enable the learner to use *symbols* to organize, interact with, and make sense of the world. The two basic forms of symbols, language and numbers, can be used in a variety of ways (e.g., reading, writing, distinguishing, combining, classifying, quantifying, etc.) toward this end. The use of symbols to

discriminate, form concepts and rules, and solve problems makes up the category of outcomes called intellectual skills. We classify such skills as part of the cognitive domain.

2. *Cognitive strategies*—The capabilities that govern the learner's own thinking, learning, and remembering behaviors. These are personal systems for guiding thinking, remembering, and problem solving, and they enable the learner to manage his own internal processes. We consider this one component of the cognitive domain.

3. *Verbal information*—Factual information that is either stored in the memory or can be looked up. It consists of labels or names, single facts, memorized sequences, and organized information. We consider this one component of the cognitive domain.

4. *Motor skills*—The capabilities of executing movement in any number of organized motor acts; they include the proper execution of movement and skills in a routine or sequence. We consider this one component of the psychomotor domain.

5. *Attitudes*—When a learner has acquired a mental state or tendency that influences his choice of a personal action, he has acquired an attitude. These states or tendencies are observed as *choices* rather than as actual performances. We consider this one component of the affective domain. See Chapters 4, 5, 6, and 7 for a discussion of other components of the affective domain.

Gagné (1962, 1970, 1977) has focused his attention on the cognitive domain (intellectual skills, cognitive strategies, and verbal information); and, within that domain, he pays particular attention to intellectual skills. While each of the human capabilities is important, Gagné (1977) and Gagné and Briggs (1974, 1979) suggest that intellectual skills are the most pervasive in school learning because they interact with all other kinds of learning. They are hierarchically ordered, and they are of central importance to school learning. We therefore next turn to the specific categories within the intellectual skills components of the cognitive domain.

Intellectual skills. Intellectual skills have been divided into seven types of learning, which form categories of mental processing ranging from least complex to most complex. They are: (a) making stimulus-response connections, (b) chaining, (c) making verbal associations, (d) making discriminations, (e) learning concepts, (f) learning principles and rules, and (g) solving problems. The first three categories are very basic and are learned in early childhood, so they usually are not significant components of school learning (Gagné & Briggs, 1974, 1979). Therefore, only the last four categories of intellectual skills will be emphasized. Examples of objectives representing the four categories are found in Chapter 14. The four categories are:

1. *Discrimination.* A capability of making different responses to stimuli that differ from each other along one or more physical dimension" (Gagné & Briggs, 1979, p. 63).

2. *Concepts.* Gagné and Briggs (1979) describe two types of concepts: (a) concrete concepts—"a capability that makes it possible for an individual to identify a stimulus as a member of a class having some characteristics in common, even though such stimuli may otherwise differ from each other markedly" (Gagné & Briggs, 1979, p. 64); (b) defined concepts—a capability that makes it possible to "demonstrate the 'meaning' of some particular class of objects, events, or relations" (Gagné & Briggs, 1979, p. 66).

3. *Rules.* The ability of the learner to respond with some "regularity over a variety of specific situations. In other words, the learner shows that he is able to respond with a *class* of relationships among *classes* of objects and events" (Gagné & Briggs, 1979, p. 67).

4. *Problem solving* (higher order rule using). The ability to solve problems or classes of problems by combining simpler rules to form more complex ones and then using these rules to solve real or intellectual problems (Gagné & Briggs, 1979).

Gagné (1962, 1970, 1977) hypothesized that these intellectual skills form a continuum of skills from simple to complex, and that they are hierarchically related. That is, the learning of a complex skills requires mastery of the subordinate skills, or conversely, each subordinate skill is prerequisite to higher level skills. The levels of skills are cumulative in nature; the lower level skills form the basis for learning the higher level skills. Gagné (1977) refers to this as positive vertical transfer, because the learning of lower skills contributes to or supports the learning of higher skills.

Learning hierarchies. Since the intellectual skills are hypothesized to be both hierarchically ordered and cumulative, "the central issue is how . . . prerequisites of learning are to be identified" (Phillips & Kelly, 1975, p. 360). Gagné (1970, 1977) suggests that they can be identified by making a detailed analysis of the intellectual skills required to perform the given task. The result is a *learning hierarchy* which "is an arrangement of intellectual skill objectives into a pattern which shows the prerequisite relationships among them" (Gagné & Briggs, 1979, p. 147-148).

An objective is an operational definition that states what an individual will be able to do after instruction. It describes a test performance. It is a nonambiguous statement which, according to Gagné and Briggs (1979), defines: (a) the "operations" (action verb) one must perform to achieve the objective; (b) the special circumstance, i.e., the test stimulus, the tools, constraints, time allotments, etc., under which the "operations" will be demonstrated; and (c) the inferred capability indicated by the test performance. In methods of writing objectives presented by other authors, the statement also includes the criterion for a required acceptable performance (e.g., *how well* the learner must perform).

In order to formulate a learning hierarchy, one begins with a statement of a terminal objective and then performs an instructional analysis by asking the question, "What prerequisite skills must the learner possess to perform this task given only verbal instructions?" This question is repeated until an ordered set of prerequisite skill objectives is generated. The result is a learning hierarchy which "identifies a set of intellectual skills that are ordered in a manner initiating substantial amounts of positive transfer from skills of lower position to connected ones of higher position" (Gagné, 1970, p. 239).

In order to verify this proposition that intellectual skills are hierarchically ordered and cumulative, considerable research has been conducted. A preliminary study was conducted by Gagné (1962) in which he attempted to teach seven ninth grade boys how to find "formulas for the sum of *n* terms in a number series" (p. 358). Nine prerequisite skills were identified in the learning hierarchy; each one was taught to the seven students by means of a simple teaching machine. The students received a pretest to determine their level of competence prior to instruction, and they received a posttest after instruction. Six of seven students achieved success on the final task, and Gagné observed that none of the students acquired a higher level skill without first mastering those skills which were predicted to be prerequisite. In summary, he states, "These results provide additional evidence compatible with the idea of the learning hierarchy" (Gagné, 1962, p. 362).

Other studies (Gagné & Paradise, 1961; Gagné, Mayor, Garstens, & Paradise, 1962) also supported the hypothesis of the hierarchical arrangement of intellectual skills; however, White (1973) noted some specific methodological problems with the early studies and questioned the "proportion of positive transfer" index that was used. Subsequently, more recent studies (Gagné & Bassler, 1963; Kolb, 1967-68, Merrill, Barton, & Wood, 1970; Resnick, 1967; Resnick & Wang, 1969) have been conducted that provide varying degrees of support for the hierarchical model of intellectual skills. As the methodological problems associated with some of the earlier studies were overcome, primarily as a result of suggestions by White (1973, 1974a, 1974b), the support for the hierarchical model increased. "It now appears well established that hierarchies do represent patterns or maps of prerequisite intellectual skills leading to the terminal skill or skills in a piece of subject matter" (White & Gagné, 1974, p. 20). White (personal communication, 1984) further stated that he conducted his last "hierarchy study" in 1979 and, at that time, was tempted to state in an article that no further validation work was necessary on the hierarchical order of intellectual skills. The validity of the ordering of the intellectual skills was sufficiently established, he said, that the hierarchy postulate no longer required extensive study.

The term "learning hierarchy" has normally referred only to the learning of intellectual skills, and the method of research has been the conduct of learning experiments. However, Hurst (1980b), employing a different research method, demonstrated hierarchical relationships between cognitive and affective objectives. This study, described later in this chapter, was one of the stimuli leading to the writing of this book.

Summary

Gagné's taxonomy of learning outcomes can be characterized by its breadth, that is, the inclusion of attitudes, motor skills, verbal information, cognitive strategies, and intellectual skills, and also by its prescriptive nature, i.e., the internal and external conditions of learning and the nine events of instruction. Gagné's taxonomy has been both applauded and criticized. For example, Snelbecker (1974) says, "One concern . . . is that the taxonomy . . . may be overly biased toward those learning aspects which have been studied by psychologists. . . . the taxonomy, therefore, may not adequately deal with the kinds of learning changes which are of greatest concern to educators" (p. 475). Hilgard and Bower (1966), however, regard the taxonomy developed by Gagné as "the beginning of a unified theory" of learning (p. 569). We believe it is a significant and extremely useful taxonomy. The taxonomy, coupled with the design model (Gagné, 1977; Gagné & Briggs, 1979) has been judged by Reigeluth (1983a) to represent the oldest and most comprehensive model of instructional design among those summarized in the book he edited.

Bloom's Taxonomy

The *Taxonomy of Educational Objectives, Handbook 1: Cognitive Domain* was developed by a group of college educators and researchers, headed by Benjamin Bloom, and published in 1956. The purpose of the *Taxonomy* was to develop a classification system that would enable educators and others to communicate more clearly about test items, educational objectives, and testing procedures.

Work on the *Taxonomy* was begun in 1948, guided by several principles and priorities intended to facilitate the purpose stated above. First, the classification of objectives was to reflect the distinctions teachers make about student behaviors. Second, the taxonomy was to be logically developed and internally consistent. Third, the classification system was to be consistent with present understanding of psychological phenomena. And, fourth, the taxonomy was to be completely descriptive and neutral with regard to educational philosophies. Although these priorities were important guidelines set by the researchers, they agreed that the key ingredient of the *Taxonomy* was educational meaningfulness, and that other priorities might have to be sacrificed slightly to meet this criterion.

In developing the *Taxonomy*, a choice had to be made about what phenomena should be classified. The developers decided to use the student behavior which an objective and test item is *intended to elicit*. "Therefore, the taxonomy is designed to be a classification of the student behaviors which represent the intended outcomes of the educational process" (Bloom, 1956, p. 12). In making this choice, other phenomena were rejected: subject matter, educational processes, and the student behavior which an item actually evokes. Regarding the last phenomena, Kropp and Stoker (1966) state, "they [Taxonomy developers] acknowledged that the behaviors which an item is intended to evoke and those which it actually evokes might be different due to the prior experience of the examinees" (p. 2).

With this in mind, the student behaviors were categorized into six major categories and within each category into specific subgroups. All categories were arranged hierarchically, from most simple to most complex. "Our attempt to arrange educational behaviors from simple to complex was based on the idea that a particular simple behavior may become integrated with other equally simple behaviors to form a more complex behavior. Thus our classification may be said to be in the form where behaviors of type A form one class, behaviors of type AB form another class, while behaviors of type ABC form still another class" (Bloom, 1956, p. 18).

A condensed version of the taxonomy appears on the following page. We have defined only the six major categories and have listed the accompanying subcategories. The complete *Taxonomy* with illustrative test items has been published numerous times and can be easily located. Readers are urged to check Bloom (1956) and Bloom, Hastings, and Madaus (1971) for complete descriptions of the categories and subcategories.

This taxonomy is not accompanied by a model of instructional design, as was the taxonomy by Gagné. Thus, we classify this taxonomy as descriptive, and Gagné's as prescriptive.

Condensed Outline of the Taxonomy

Taxonomy of Educational Objectives: Cognitive Domain

KNOWLEDGE

1.00 *KNOWLEDGE*: ". . . . the recall of specifics and universals, the recall of methods and processes, or the recall of a pattern, structure, or setting . . . The knowledge objectives emphasize most of the psychological processes of remembering. . . ." (Bloom, 1956, p. 201).
　　　1.10 *Knowledge of Specifics*
　　　　　1.11 Knowledge of Terminology
　　　　　1.12 Knowledge of Specific Facts
　　　1.20 *Knowledge of Ways and Means of Dealing with Specifics*
　　　　　1.21 Knowledge of Conventions
　　　　　1.22 Knowledge of Trends and Sequences
　　　　　1.23 Knowledge of Classifications and Categories
　　　　　1.24 Knowledge of Criteria
　　　　　1.25 Knowledge of Methodology
　　　1.30 *Knowledge of the Universals and Abstractions in a Field*
　　　　　1.31 Knowledge of Principles and Generalizations
　　　　　1.32 Knowledge of Theories and Structures

INTELLECTUAL SKILLS AND ABILITIES

"Abilities and skills refer to organized models of operation and generalized techniques for dealing with materials and problems. . . . The abilities and skills objectives emphasize the mental processes of organizing and reorganizing materials to achieve a particular purpose. The materials may be given or remembered" (Bloom, 1956, p. 204).

2.00 *COMPREHENSION*: "This represents the lowest level of understanding. It refers to a type of understanding or apprehension such that the individual knows what is being communicated and can make use of the material or idea being communicated without necessarily relating it to other material or seeing its fullest implications" (Bloom, 1956, p. 204).

2.10 *Translation*
2.20 *Interpretation*
2.30 *Extrapolation*

3.00 *APPLICATION*: "The use of abstractions in particular and concrete situations. The abstractions may be in the form of general ideas, rules of procedures, or generalized methods. The abstractions may also be technical principles, ideas, and theories which must be remembered and applied" (Bloom, 1956, p. 205).

4.00 *ANALYSIS*: "The breakdown of a communication into its constituent elements or parts . . . Such analyses are intended to clarify the communication, to indicate how the communication is organized, and the way in which it manages to convey its effects, as well as its basis and arrangement" (Bloom, 1956, p. 205).

4.10 *Analysis of Elements*
4.20 *Analysis of Relationships*
4.30 *Analysis of Organizational Principles*

5.00 *SYNTHESIS*: "The putting together of elements and parts so as to form a whole. This involves the process of working with pieces, parts, elements, etc., and arranging and combining them in such a way as to constitute a pattern or structure not clearly there before" (Bloom, 1956, p. 206).

5.10 *Production of a Unique Communication*
5.20 *Production of a Plan, or Proposed Set of Operations*
5.30 *Derivation of a Set of Abstract Relations*

6.00 *EVALUATION*: "Judgments about the value of material and methods for given purposes. Quantitative and qualitative judgments about the extent to which material and methods satisfy criteria. Use of a standard of appraisal. The criteria may be those determined by the student or those which are given to him" (Bloom, 1956, p. 207).

6.10 *Judgments in Terms of Internal Evidence*
6.20 *Judgments in Terms of External Criteria*

Validation Studies

One of the most extensive attempts to examine the structure and content validity of the *Taxonomy* was done by Kropp and Stoker (1966). Students in ten secondary schools, grades nine through twelve, were tested on one of four forms of tests developed to measure levels of social studies and science content. Each test had two parts: (a) multiple choice items for Knowledge Comprehension, Application, and Analysis, and (b) free-response items for Synthesis and Evaluation.

Kropp and Stoker stated at the outset of the discussion of their study that "we have serious reservations about the propriety of our effort to validate the taxonomy" (p. 17). Their reservations revolved around the difference between "intended" student behaviors and "actual" student behaviors. Since the taxonomy developers classified the behaviors that an objective "intended to elicit," not those behaviors actually portrayed by students, Kropp and Stoker stated that if one held rigorously to that stipulation, inter-rater reliability would be the only true way to assess the validity of the taxonomy structure. While Kropp and Stoker acknowledged the intended versus actual behavior distinction, they proceeded "on the assumption that the usefulness of the taxonomy in educational planning and research depends upon the empirical demonstration that the structure of the taxonomy portrays actual student behaviors" (p. 17).

The results of their extensive study neither completely supported nor failed to support the taxonomy structure. They did conclude that the tendency in the data was to support the hierarchical structure; however, for the natural science form of the test, they reported a systematic reversal in the order of Synthesis and Evaluation.

In other studies reported by Kropp and Stoker, varying degrees of support for the hierarchical order of the taxonomy were found. When the studies used trained raters, the results generally conformed to the hypothesized structure. Kropp and Stoker suggested that raters could in fact classify the behaviors that an item is *intended to evoke*. When the studies used "taxonomy-type data," the results were mixed. For example, McQuire (cited in Kropp & Stoker, 1966) used an abridgment of the taxonomy and found a reversal of Synthesis and Evaluation. A study conducted by Smith (cited in Kropp & Stoker, 1966) used sublevels of the taxonomy. His results did not support the taxonomic ordering (Kropp & Stoker, 1966).

The data provided by Kropp and Stoker have been used in

many other studies; two are reported here that do not support the hypothesized ordering. In a continuation of the Kropp and Stoker study, Madaus, Woods, and Nuttall (1973) found a branching pattern occurring after Application, with Analysis on one stem and Evaluation and Synthesis on the other. Miller, Snowman, and O'Hara (1979) also found a Y-shaped structure that was similar to that found by Madaus, Woods, and Nuttall.

Hill and McGaw (1981) reported still other studies and one of their own. In their review they quote Seddon (1978), "Evidence regarding the validity of the psychological assumptions underlying the taxonomy is both meager and inconclusive." Although the results of the studies are mixed, there does seem to be fairly strong and consistent support for the lower levels of the taxonomy (Hill and McGaw, however, demonstrated support of the structure only when the knowledge category was deleted). Less support has been found for the three upper categories.

Criticism of Bloom's Taxonomy

De Landsheere (1977) lists four criticisms of the Bloom taxonomy. First, she states that the taxonomy has *real, but limited validity*. The criteria for classification are not the same across subcategories, e.g., a scale of products is used in Knowledge, Analysis, and Synthesis, but specifications of operations, not products, are used in Comprehension. In addition, the categories are not mutually exclusive.

Second, there is lack of reliability across the categories due primarily to the vagueness of the category descriptors. The labels refer to mental operations and not to observable events (Bormouth, 1970, reported in De Landsheere, 1977).

Third, De Landsheere states that the taxonomy is of limited usefulness for curriculum development. While useful for formulating objectives and structuring learning sequences and assessment procedures, it artificially separates content and thinking, and it separates substantive behavior and thinking.

Finally, the taxonomy is weighted toward Knowledge (with nine subcategories) rather than the higher mental processes. In addition, it is impossible to use the taxonomy without reference to the specific background of the individual. "The taxonomic level at which an individual behaves in a given situation, at a given moment, depends on his former experience. There is an obvious difference between the individual who solves a specific problem for the first time . . .; and the individual who has met the same problem before and can produce the solution from memory. In both cases, however, the answers can be the same" (De Landsheere, 1977, p. 107).

One additional criticism from a psychological vantage point has also been made. Bloom and his associates have focused their efforts on school-related work and examination questions. This is viewed by many as psychologically weak and arbitrary. De Landsheere (1977) points out, "Between Bloom and Gagné, we find the traditional opposition between educational pragmatism, usually brought about by the need for immediate action, and the analytical rigour of the psychologist who might like to explain or, at least, to describe the behavioral process, before acting" (p. 104).

Many of the criticisms of Bloom's Taxonomy that De Landsheere (1977) makes are also made by Furst (1981). The Furst critique is more easily accessible than is the one by De Landsheere; interested readers are referred to Furst (1981) for an excellent review of Bloom's Taxonomy.

Summary

The taxonomy developed by Bloom (1956) is probably the most widely used and best known of the cognitive taxonomic schemes in education. It has some definite weaknesses: the distinctions between the category classifications are neither clear nor sharp, they are not mutually exclusive, and the taxonomy structure is only minimally supported. However, the taxonomy has had an enormous influence on education and has prompted educators to clarify, classify, and develop objectives and test items at varying levels. De Landsheere (1977) states that even if the taxonomy does nothing more than make teachers more aware of the enormous place factual knowledge takes in school learning and of the relatively low regard of higher cognitive processes, the time and effort devoted to its development and use are still exceedingly worthwhile, and the criticisms of it are of negligible importance.

Other Cognitive Taxonomies

A number of other cognitive taxonomies have been developed that either describe different ways of addressing the cognitive dimension or that describe different means of analyzing objectives. Because each is described elsewhere and because they are not directly suited to our purposes, we refer the reader to the original sources for a more detailed account of each. In this section, we either list and give a short description of other taxonomies or describe a type of taxonomy, e.g., taxonomies that analyze constituent parts of objectives.

Guilford's Model (1967) was designed to describe the structure of intellect. This non-hierarchical model allows any intellectual factor to be described by three unique properties: operation, content, and product. The model is presented by a three-way matrix in which there are five *operational* categories (evaluation, memory, convergent production, divergent production, cognition), four *content* categories (figural, symbolic, semantic, behavioral), and six *product* categories (units, classes, relations, systems, transformations, implications). Each cell of the matrix represents an intellectual factor that is a unique combination of operation, content, and product.

While this model was not designed to be used for the analysis or production of educational objectives, it appears that it could be used for that purpose. Guilford states, the model "clearly indicates the kinds of exercises that must be applied to develop intellectual abilities" (De Landsheere, 1977, p. 114). Schools, Guilford said, focus too much time on cognition and memorization of semantic units. The model could be used to facilitate development of objectives that emphasize other products (classes and relations) and other operations (evaluation). Hence, an objective might be: to evaluate symbolic relations.

De Landsheere (1977) reports *Merrill's* work with Gagné's and describes the Gagné-Merrill Taxonomy. Merrill's contribution, she said, was to add two categories to Gagné's original ones: complex skill in the psychomotor domain, and naming in the cognitive domain. He includes conditions of learning for each.

However, Merrill (1983) has also developed *Component Display*

Theory (CDT). It is a narrower, but more detailed theory than the one developed by Gagné (1977) and Gagné and Briggs (1979). CDT applies only to the cognitive domain and within that domain it deals only with aspects of instruction related to a single idea, for example, a single concept or rule. CDT classifies objectives on two dimensions: level of performance (Find, Use, and Remember) and type of content (Fact, Concept, Procedure, and Principle). Objectives can, therefore, be written that require remembering a concept, using a rule, or some other combination. This prescriptive model, while narrow, is compatible with Gagné's system and is already proving to be useful for defining objectives and prescribing instruction (Reigeluth, 1983a).

Gerlach and Sullivan developed a category system for cognitive behaviors that listed observable learner behaviors. They did this because they felt Bloom's Taxonomy describing mental processes was of limited usefulness. The six categories they devised are ordered from simple to complex, but cannot be said to be a true hierarchy or "considered as a real taxonomy" (De Landsheere, 1977, p. 124). The categories are: Identify, Name, Describe, Construct, Order, and Demonstrate. This taxonomy is actually a checklist for insuring that a range of behaviors is included in the curriculum. It is useful for describing and formulating testable hypotheses. The taxonomy is slanted toward school learning and mastery-type objectives; no mention is made of creative productions, generalization, or transfer of skills (De Landsheere, 1977, p. 125).

Gropper (1983) stated that there are two types of taxonomies: those that classify objectives as intact wholes, and those that analyze and dissect objectives into their component parts. All of the taxonomies we have presented are of the first type—those that classify complete, intact objectives. The second type is defined as, "those behavioral models that analyze objectives for the discriminations, generalizations, and associations that make up a total chain. Each objective is analyzed for its specific *mix* of these constituent skills" (Gropper, 1983, p. 49). While we recognize the potential benefits of such a classification, e.g., to determine the unique as well as common requirements of a given objective, we do not believe this approach is most useful for our task of integrating and synthesizing the cognitive and affective domains. Interested readers should check Gropper (1983) for examples and clarification of taxonomies of this type.

Summary

In this section we have presented several taxonomies of the cognitive domain. The two best known were developed by Gagné (1977) and by Bloom (1956). Gagné's taxonomy includes cognitive, affective, and psychomotor outcomes, but his focus has been on the cognitive domain and within that domain on intellectual skills. Gagné has defined internal and external conditions of learning and nine events of instruction that are useful for designing and implementing instruction. Different internal and external conditions are required for each category and subcategory of outcomes; however, the same nine events of instruction can be used across categories. Learning hierarchies are useful for planning learning sequences and identifying prerequisites. Briggs and Wager (1981) expanded on this technique by developing instructional curriculum maps. The taxonomy developed by Gagné is a prescriptive one.

Bloom (1956) developed a cognitive taxonomy with six major categories and accompanying subcategories. Unlike Gagné's taxonomy that defined psychological criteria for learned capabilities, Bloom categorized objectives by the mental processes that learners were expected to perform, e.g., analysis, synthesis. The most frequent and justifiable criticism of the Taxonomy is that the categories are neither sharp nor clear, and are not mutually exclusive.

The other taxonomies we presented provide additional ways of analyzing and categorizing objectives, but none are as complete or as well-documented as the two by Gagné (1977) and Bloom (1956). They do, however, give us some insight into the numerous ways of describing the cognitive domain and of developing a useful taxonomy.

TAXONOMIES OF THE AFFECTIVE DOMAIN

Krathwohl, Bloom, and Masia's Taxonomy

When Bloom and his colleagues began their work on classifying objectives, they intended to develop "a complete taxonomy in three major parts—the cognitive, the affective, and the psycho-motor domains" (p. 7). The cognitive taxonomy was the first to be published, in 1956, the affective was second, and the third was never completed by them because the authors stated that they "find so little done about it [psychomotor behaviors] in second-ary schools or colleges, that we do not believe the development of a classification of these objectives would be very useful at present" (pp. 7-8).

The authors stated that development of the Affective Taxono-my was considerably more difficult than was the development of the Cognitive Taxonomy. Several problems plagued their work from the start: lack of clarity in the objectives, inability to find an adequate organizing principle, and concern about whether or not such a taxonomy would be useful to and used by educators. Because of this, the idea of developing the affective taxonomy was almost dropped, but insistence from educators and measurement specialists prompted Krathwohl and Bloom to complete the task. They were aided by Masia, who wrote the sections on testing, and a host of other critiquers and critics. The Affective Taxonomy was published in 1964.

A major difficulty in constructing this taxonomy was lack of a basis for structuring the domain. The "simple to complex" and "concrete to abstract" principles used in the cognitive domain did not seem adequate for the affective taxonomy. After much consternation and search, the authors discovered an ordering principle that allowed them to construct a meaningful continuum. The principle was *internalization*, ". . . the process by which the phenomenon or value successively and pervasively becomes part of the individual" (Krathwohl *et al.*, 1964, p. 28). Although the original hope was to organize the taxonomy by definitions, the authors reported that the various terms and meanings of affective constructs, e.g., attitudes, values, etc., were nearly impossible to define, so the idea of ordering the taxonomy according to definitions was abandoned and internalization was selected.

In discussing internalization as the major organizing principle, the authors stated, "This ordering of the components seemed to describe a process by which a given phenomenon or value passed from a level of bare awareness to a position of some power to guide or control the behavior of a person" (p. 27). It seemed to be a viable ordering principle for "objectives which emphasize a feeling tone, an emotion, or a degree of acceptance or rejection . . . [for example] interests, attitudes, appreciations, values, and emotional sets or biases" (p. 7).

There are five major categories of the Affective Taxonomy with subcategories for each. The Taxonomy was intended to be hierarchical. The authors acknowledged the arbitrariness of the category divisions and stated that they felt more secure about the major divisions than they did about the subcategories. A condensed version of the Taxonomy is presented below. We have defined the major divisions and have briefly described the subcategories. Illustrative objectives and test items are included in the original work and readers are referred to it for a more in-depth discussion of the Taxonomy.

Condensed Outline of the Taxonomy

Taxonomy of Educational Objectives:
Affective Domain

1.0 RECEIVING (ATTENDING): "At this level we are concerned that the learner be sensitized to the existence of certain phenomena and stimuli; that is, that he be willing to receive or to attend to them" (Krathwohl, *et al.*, p. 176).

    1.1 *Awareness*: "the learner will merely be conscious of something—that he take into account a situation, phenomenon, object, or state of affairs" (p. 176-177).

    1.2 *Willingness to Receive*: "at worst, . . . , the learner is not actively seeking to avoid it [stimuli]. At best, he is willing to take notice of the phenomenon and give it his attention" (p. 177).

    1.3 *Controlled or Selected Attention*: "There is an element of the learner's controlling the attention here, so that the favored stimulus is selected and attended to despite competing and distracting stimuli" (p. 178).

2.0 RESPONDING: "... perhaps it is correct to say that he [learner] is actively attending. ... we use the term to indicate the desire that a child has become sufficiently involved in or committed to a subject, phenomenon, or activity that he will seek it out and gain satisfaction from working with it or engaging in it" (p. 178).

    2.1 *Acquiescence in responding*: "We might use the word 'obedience' or 'compliance' to describe this behavior. The student makes the response, but he has not fully accepted the necessity for doing so" (p. 179).

    2.2 *Willingness to respond*: "The key to this level is in the term 'willingness,' with its implication of capacity for voluntary activity" (p. 179).

    2.3 *Satisfaction in response*: "The additional element ..., is that the behavior is accompanied by a feeling of satisfaction, an emotional response, generally of pleasure, zest, or enjoyment" (p. 179).

3.0 VALUING: "Behavior categorized at this level is sufficiently consistent and stable to have taken on the characteristic of a belief or an attitude. The learner displays this behavior with sufficient consistency in appropriate situations that he comes to be perceived as holding a value" (p. 180).

    3.1 *Acceptance of a value*: "At this level we are concerned with the ascribing of worth to a phenomenon, behavior, object, etc. ... Beliefs have varying degrees of certitude. At this lowest level of valuing we are concerned with the lowest levels of certainty; ..." (p. 181).

    3.2 *Preference for a value*: "Behavior at this level implies not just the acceptance of a value ..., but the individual is sufficiently committed to the value to pursue it, to seek it out, to want it" (p. 181).

    3.3 *Commitment*: "Belief at this level involves a high degree of certainty ... [The person] acts to further the thing valued in some way, to extend the possibility of his developing it, to deepen his involvement with it and the things representing it. He tries to convince others and seeks converts to the cause" (p. 182).

4.0 ORGANIZATION: "As the learner successively internalizes values, he encounters situations for which more than one value is relevant. Thus the necessity arises for (a) the organization of the values into a system, (b) the determination of the interrelationships among them, and (c) the establishment of dominant and pervasive ones" (p. 182).

    4.1 *Conceptualization of a value*: "At this level the quality of abstraction or conceptualization is added. This permits the individual to see how the value relates to those he already holds or to new ones that he is coming to hold" (p. 183).

    4.2 *Organization of a value system*: "Objectives properly classified here are those which require the learner to bring together a complex of values, possibly disparate values, and to bring these into an ordered relationship with one another" (p. 183).

5.0 CHARACTERIZATION BY A VALUE OR VALUE COMPLEX: "At this level of internalization the values already have a place in the individual's value hierarchy, are organized into some kind of internally consistent system, have controlled the behavior of the individual for a sufficient time that he has adapted to behaving this way; and an evocation of the behavior no longer arouses emotion or affect except when the individual is threatened or challenged" (p. 184).

> 5.1 *Generalized set*: "A generalized set is a basic orientation which enables the individual to reduce and order the complex world about him and to act consistently and effectively in it" (p. 184).
>
> 5.2 *Characterization*: "..., the peak of the internalization process, ... Thus, here are found those objectives which concern one's view of the universe, one's philosophy of life, ... As the title of the category implies, these objectives are so encompassing that they tend to characterize the individual almost completely" (p. 185).

The figure produced on the following page (Krathwohl *et al.*, 1964, p. 37) is a useful summary of the Taxonomy. It shows some common terms associated with the affective domain and how they relate to the Taxonomy levels. See Figure 3.1.

Validation Studies

Central to the Taxonomy is the assumption that the lower level behaviors are prerequisite to higher level behaviors, that is, the behaviors are cumulative and hierarchical. However, evidence for the hierarchical validity of the Taxonomy is sparce and unconvincing; very few studies have been conducted. A fairly extensive study was conducted by Lewy (1968) that provided both descriptive and empirical support for the Taxonomy, however, the study did not include the fifth level of the Taxonomy, Characterization, and the fourth level, Organization, did not order exactly as expected. Lewy concluded that there was validity for the lower levels of the Taxonomy, Receiving, Responding, and Valuing, but that his study should be considered a pilot analysis. More work was necessary, he said, especially on the upper levels of the Taxonomy.

Connelly (1972) used Guttman Scalogram Analysis to determine the extent to which objectives designed for an education

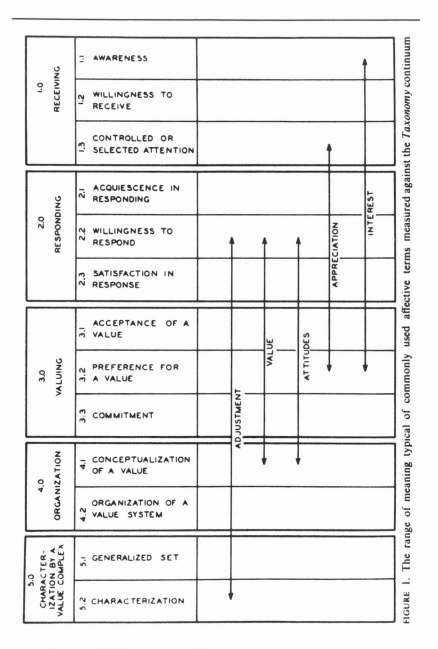

FIGURE 1. The range of meaning typical of commonly used affective terms measured against the *Taxonomy* continuum

Figure 3.1. From Krathwohl, Bloom, and Masia. 1964, p. 37.

course were hierarchical. One objective was formulated for each major category of the Affective Taxonomy. The results (coefficients of reproducibility ranging from .89 to .94) "reflected highly the hierarchical ordering imposed by the Affective Taxonomy. These results would seem to support the assumption that the categories of the Affective Taxonomy form a hierarchy" (p. 82).

Purcell (1968) utilized the Taxonomy rationale and continuum to develop and order items on attitude scales. Once completed, he asked 25 judges to order the items from most unfavorable to most favorable. The results indicated that the scale order of the items as determined by the judges and the order of the Taxonomy were significantly related (correlations ranged from .75 to .86). Purcell concluded that the levels of the Taxonomy are correctly ordered.

In an attempt to further validate the Taxonomy, Purcell used Guttman Scalogram Analysis to analyze the results obtained from administering the attitude scales to 150 students. While the coefficients of reproducibility were high, Purcell felt that other factors (e.g., coefficients which suggested a homogeneous group with respect to attitude) may have biased the data and he, therefore, reserved judgments about a hierarchical order of the Taxonomy based on this analysis.

Two additional studies also lend some support to the hierarchical order of the Taxonomy. Both studies were part of larger studies of domain interaction (these studies will be reported later in this chapter) and both used ordering theory (Airasian & Bart, 1975; Bart & Airasian, 1974; Bart & Krus, 1973), a deterministic model capable of generating linear and non-linear sequences, to analyze the data. In the first study (Hurst, 1978, 1980b), twenty-nine volunteer elementary teachers in varying stages of implementing a new curriculum called Individually Guided Education (IGE) were assessed at each level of the Taxonomy. With the exception of the Valuing level that did not order prerequisite to the Organization level, the data supported the hypothesized structure of the Taxonomy.

In the second study (Dinero & Martin, 1983), seventy-five preservice teachers enrolled in a one semester education course on models of teaching were assessed on the three lower levels of the Taxonomy. Four ordering theory analyses were run using 2.5

percent, 4 percent, 5 percent, and 10 percent tolerance levels. Only at the 10 percent tolerance level did the categories scale as hypothesized, i.e., Receiving → Responding → Valuing.

Martin (1984a) concluded, "Both studies provide some support for the taxonomic schema although methodological problems—a small sample and some missing data in Study I, scoring concerns in Study II—and use of a deterministic model prompt cautious interpretation of the results. In general, it appears that Receiving, Responding, Valuing, and Characterization scale as predicted. However, the branching patterns that appear at various levels, most notably at Valuing and Organization (and that also appear in some analyses of the Cognitive Taxonomy), suggest that perhaps a cumulative hierarchy structure may not be consistently found" (p. 12).

All the studies do provide some degree of support for the Taxonomy categories; they seem to be correctly ordered. Support, however, appears to be strongest for the lower levels: Receiving, Responding, and Valuing. The most tenuous connection occurs between the Valuing and Organization levels where either a branching pattern emerges or where the link is not established.

Criticisms of the Affective Taxonomy

There have been a number of criticisms of the Affective Taxonomy; several of the most striking and important ones are listed here.

First, the Taxonomy is too general and abstract. De Landsheere (1977) states that both the concept of internalization and the objects of internalization (values, attitudes, etc.) have not been carefully operationalized and, hence, are not always helpful. The Taxonomy authors are aware of the problem and suggest that the Taxonomy be used at the curriculum construction rather than at the instructional planning level. (In Chapters 8, 9, and 10 of this book, we have nevertheless attempted to reflect both levels in our illustrative audit trails. The practice may be useful even in spite of lack of complete research support, and the criticisms.) De Landsheere (1977) comments on the vagueness of the schema, comparing the utility of the cognitive and affective taxonomies. She says, "After studying the latter, the classroom teacher feels rather frustrated: he is convinced that important principles, concepts, categories have been discussed and documented, but he does not really feel better off to educate and evaluate in the affective domain" (p. 137).

Martin (1984a) also comments on this problem. "The difficulty in developing objectives and items that accurately reveal the intent of the various categories of the Taxonomy is no small feat. The authors make no secret and no excuses about the problems they incurred when developing the Taxonomy and making distinctions between and among categories. Using the sample objectives and items as a guide is helpful, but does not totally alleviate the problem. ... Since virtually no revisions or clarifications of the Taxonomy have been made in the last twenty years and it is doubtful that they are forthcoming, researchers and educators will have to interpret the categories as best they can, making distinctions between categories on both a conceptual and logical level" (p. 13).

Another criticism of the Taxonomy is that it is limited in its coverage of affective constructs. De Landsheere (1977) states that the Taxonomy reduces the affective dimension to "liking or disliking" and that this is only one aspect of the domain. For example, self-development and motivation have not been included. De Landsheere states, "The criterion 'internalization' (...) is society or culture centered; it indicates a movement from exterior to interior. The other aspect to be considered is self-development. And for it, we need another taxonomy" (p. 146).

Summary

The Affective Domain Taxonomy, developed by Krathwohl *et al.*, is the best known and most prescriptive of the affective taxonomies we will discuss. Although it has been criticized as being too general, overly dependent on cognition, and limited in scope, it is widely used, and it is a landmark in the development of a schema that addresses the domain. Research does show some support for the hierarchical order of the six major categories; support for the three lowest levels is more compelling than for the upper levels.

The Gephart and Ingle Taxonomy

The taxonomy proposed by Gephart and Ingle (1976) is a descriptive taxonomy and of a completely different nature than the one proposed by Krathwohl *et al.* First, it is a tentative affective taxonomy which the authors define as a "suggested direction" for organizing the domain. Second, it is a taxonomy of terminology; it organizes the wide array of affective terminology into different levels of abstraction. In this respect, it is very different from the taxonomy by Krathwohl *et al.* The latter classifies levels of operations, e.g., receiving, responding, and valuing, whereas the former classifies terms and concepts that have not been defined or operationalized.

Although Gephart and Ingle have "serious reservations about the validity of the placement of the terms" (p. 189), we feel that their tentative taxonomy gives an excellent overview of the scope and breadth of the affective domain. The taxonomy includes two major branches: Physiological Responses or Behaviors and Psycho-Social Responses or Behaviors. Each branch has subcategories. (See Figure 3.2). The authors included dotted lines to show that the taxonomy is not necessarily inclusive and that other categories may exist.

The authors suggest that the psycho-social responses are those most closely related to the fields of education and psychology; the physiological behaviors are more closely related to the medical fields. For example, somatic responses (e.g., internal changes in blood pressure, temperature, etc.) and visceral responses (e.g., "sensors for external stimuli and muscle contractions and expansions") are associated with the nervous system and may not be of major concern to educators.

Although this taxonomy is tentative, descriptive, and intended to show different levels of abstraction or specificity of terms, it is a most useful classification. It provides a wide range of possible behaviors, many not included in the Krathwohl *et al.* Taxonomy, and shows the expansiveness of the affective domain.

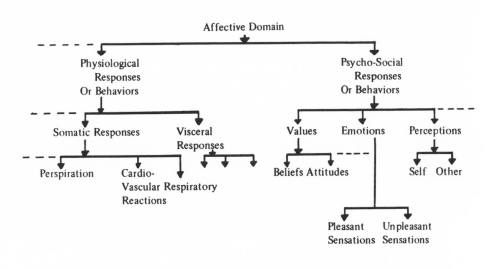

Figure 3.2. Taxonomy from Gephart and Ingle, 1976, p. 188.

The Brandhorst Taxonomies

Brandhorst (1978) has developed two and proposed a third taxonomy that identifies still other important dimensions of the affective domain. Brandhorst argues that self-development is an educational end in itself; a goal currently being shortchanged by the public school system. He states that most affective taxonomies, and specifically the paradigm by Krathwohl *et al.* (1964), are associated with Maslow's D-cognition construct "which is purposive, a means to an end" (p. 7). He suggests that affective taxonomies need to be developed which are associated with the construct of B-cognition, conceptualized by Maslow as an end in itself.

It is the end intended that differentiates B cognition from D cognition. B cognition seeks no end outside itself, it is concerned with intrinsic satisfaction and appreciation. D cognition, on the other hand, is functional and instrumental. Using Maslow's B-cognition as a basis, Brandhorst defined four goal constructs which are ends in themselves. They are: effectance, efficacy, competence, and analytic-coping ability. He then developed two taxonomies and proposed a third that defined goals which are ends in themselves: a taxonomy with an ego-involvement orientation, a taxonomy with a motivational orientation, and a taxonomy with a moral development orientation.

The categories of the ego-involvement taxonomy are based on "the order of qualities of personality style as observed in behavior" (p. 9), and include the categories of: objectivity, empathy, response delay, impulse suppression, and transformation. The motivation orientation taxonomy is based on the assumption that active aesthetic appreciation is necessary for optimal psychological and physical health and that an aesthetic end product (e.g., a dance, painting, etc.) is less important than the process of aesthetic creation. The categories of this taxonomy are: perceptual awareness, perceptual synthesis, risk taking, concentration, and playfulness. Brandhorst also suggests the need for a third taxonomy with a conceptual-relational orientation associated with moral reasoning, but does not define a category system for it.

Brandhorst's taxonomies are based on "behavior in learning experiences" (p. 9) and, therefore, are themselves means rather than ends, but he argues that specifying these behaviors as outcomes forces them back to the D-cognition construct. Since he is referring, at least in part, to "means" or what he calls the "experience outcome unity" (p. 9), his taxonomy is not directly comparable to the Krathwohl, *et al.* (1964) and Gephart and Ingle (1976) taxonomies. His taxonomies are useful, however, in identifying other important dimensions of the domain.

Other Affective Taxonomies

A few other taxonomies will be briefly mentioned. These taxonomies are included only to show the variety of ways the domain has been classified.

Nunnally (1976) and Hoepfner *et al.* (1972) developed the two taxonomies below:

Nunnally (1976)	Center for Study of Evaluation (Hoepfner *et al.*, 1972)
Sentiments	Personal Temperament
Interests	Social Temperament
Values	Attitudes, Opinions, Beliefs
Attitudes	Needs
	Interests
	Values

Payne (1976) reviewing and comparing the taxonomies of Krathwohl *et al.* (1964), Hoepfner *et al.* (1972), and Nunnally (1967) pointed out that commonalities existed among them in (a) the terms used, i.e., "interests," "attitudes," and "values," and (b) the characteristics associated with various facets of affect (e.g., affective variables are learned, have specific referents, and vary in degree of interrelatedness).

Foshay (1978) described six different domains of learning. Four of the six domains appear to have affective elements or behaviors included within them:

- The Intellectual: Similar to Bloom's Cognitive.
- The Emotional: Development of feelings and emotions.
- The Social: Development of social organization; moral development.
- The Physical: Psychomotor skills; development of physical self-concept.
- The Aesthetic: Formal, technical, sensuous, and expressive response to an object of contemplation.
- The Spiritual: Relating to the search for ultimate meaning (Foshay, 1978, p. 24).

Foshay has also given an example of an objective related to each of the six domains.

Finally, Raven (reported in De Landsheere, 1977) conducted a series of studies in England to determine the importance of affective or non-academic objectives in the educational enterprise. He amassed a great deal of data but two findings are of interest:

1. Students and teachers ranked the same two objectives as

first and second in importance: (a) to take responsibility and (b) to develop one's personality.

2. Neither students nor teachers felt that schools did an adequate job in developing these objectives.

Although Raven does not develop a taxonomy, his list of affective objectives is extensive and his research showed the discrepancy between what is desired by students and teachers and what actually occurred in schools. The objectives provided and the data he has collected could be used to develop or add to a taxonomy.

Summary

In this section we have presented several taxonomies of the affective domain. Krathwohl, Bloom, and Masia (1964) developed the best known and most often used taxonomy. It has six major categories and is organized around the concept of internalization. Although most useful at the curriculum construction level, it has also been used extensively to develop and/or categorize objectives for instruction and research purposes. It has been criticized as being too general, too vague, and too limited, but it is the only taxonomy we know of that is useful for classifying objectives of the affective domain. De Landsheere (1971) states that it actually has more limitations than weaknesses.

The taxonomy by Gephart and Ingle (1976) is descriptive and identifies the scope of the domain. It includes two major divisions, physiological responses and psycho-social responses, and subcategories for each. The psycho-social behaviors are the ones of most interest to educators.

Brandhorst (1978) developed two and proposed a third taxonomy emphasizing self-development as an educational goal. He used Maslow's B-cognition construct as a basis and proposed an ego-development taxonomy and a motivation orientation taxonomy; he suggested the need for a moral reasoning taxonomy.

Three other taxonomies, Nunnally (1976), Hoepfner *et al.* (1972), and Foshay (1978), were presented that show other conceptions of the affective domain. A study by Raven was also reported. The "development of personality" was identified by students and teachers as a top priority objective.

The inclusion of these taxonomies with their multitudes of categories and subcategories shows the range of behaviors educators and researchers have used to describe and organize the affective domain. If one thing seems clear, it is that not only must categories like attitudes, values, and morals be included in the affective domain, but a category of behaviors related to self-development must also be included. Any taxonomy or classification scheme without it will certainly be incomplete.

RESEARCH INTEGRATING THE COGNITIVE AND AFFECTIVE DOMAIN

There have been very few studies that demonstrate the relationships between behaviors in taxonomies of the affective and cognitive domains, even though researchers such as Bloom (1956), Gagné (1977), Gagné and Briggs (1979), and Krathwohl *et al.* (1964) state that the two dimension are inseparable. Krathwohl *et al.*, addressing the arbitrary nature of classification schemes, states that "When one looks for the relations between the subcategories of the two domains, one finds that they clearly overlap" (p. 49). This overlap, they say, is most apparent between (a) Receiving (1.0) in the affective domain and Knowledge (1.0) in the cognitive domain; and (b) at the upper levels of the taxonomies where values are being developed. The ability to organize and integrate values into a value system requires, at the very least, Comprehension (2.0), and certainly Analysis (4.0) and Synthesis (5.0). It may also require Evaluation (6.0).

Gagné and Briggs (1974, 1979) also recognized the interrelationships between cognitive and affective behaviors. They stated: "The desired attitude may involve choice of some action which in turn requires intellectual skills . . ., the implication is that such skills must have been previously learned; and if they are not, they should be acquired before the learning of the attitude is undertaken" (1974, p. 107).

One of the first studies that focused on empirical validation of the simultaneous ordering of the two domains assessed the relationships of 24 cognitive and affective behaviors (Hurst, 1978, 1980b). Ordering theory, a deterministic measurement model which allows for branching networks, was used. The affective behaviors were ordered according to the Affective Taxonomy (Krathwohl *et al.*, 1964), and the cognitive behaviors were ordered according to the cognitive subdomain of intellectual skills (consisting of concepts, rules, and higher-order rules) and the subdomain of verbal information both developed by Gagné.

The results indicated an integrated hierarchical pattern with four levels. The lowest level behaviors were affective: awareness, willingness to receive, and satisfaction in response. Then a second tier of lower level cognitive behaviors appeared: general knowledge, simple rules and concepts, and operating procedures. These cognitive skills led to more refined attitudes: valuing and organization. Finally, these attitudes resulted in higher level cognitive understanding coupled with a willingness to use the content. The author concluded, "The results indicated that the cognitive skills and attitudes necessary to achieve a given goal are integrally related. Had the two domains been separate entities or only minimally related, the empirical hierarchy would have shown two separate and independent branches—one cognitive and one affective" (Hurst, 1980b, p. 300).

To illustrate the relationships between the two domains, we have included two sequences of objectives taken from the Hurst (1980b) study. The first sequence was empirically validated; the second was not.

In the sequence below, objective number 1 is cognitive. The learner (who is a teacher) must demonstrate his or her (cognitive) ability to develop an instructional plan using the components of Individually Guided Education (IGE). In objective number 2, the learner must voluntarily choose to develop a plan. This affective objective is purely a behavior of choice; however, in order to exhibit the behavior the learner must have the necessary cognitive prerequisites. Objective number 3 is actually the terminal performance in the sequence, and as such has other supporting prerequisites in addition to the ones shown. Voluntarily implementing IGE requires the prerequisite cognitive capabilities to do so, and prerequisite affective behaviors, such as belief in the worth of IGE. In this case, the learner not only has the ability to generate an instructional plan, but has also chosen to do so. These two objectives, plus others, lead to the goal of voluntarily implementing IGE. The learner must therefore not only have the necessary cognitive skills to implement IGE, but must also be sufficiently committed to IGE to choose to implement it.

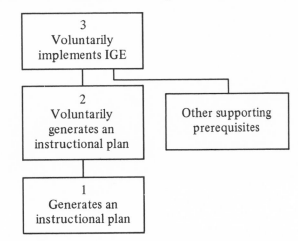

In the next sequence, the hypothesized relationships were not established. It was hypothesized that a general awareness of IGE (affective-receiving) would be prerequisite to a general knowledge of IGE (cognitive-information) and both would be prerequisite to choosing to seek further knowledge about IGE (affective-responding). The hypothesized sequence was:

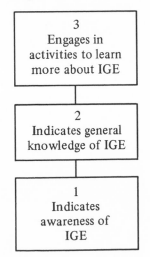

The validated sequence showed awareness (1) directly prerequisite to responding (3) and both of these prerequisites to the cognitive knowledge objective (2). In addition, other objectives intervened between those hypothesized. The validated sequence was:

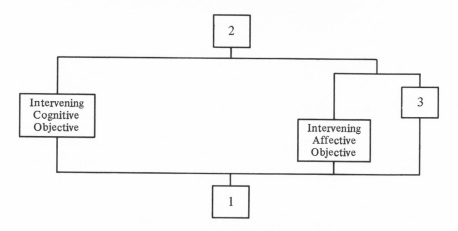

Although this validated sequence demonstrates the relationships between the two domains, the specific hypothesized relationships were not supported.

Another study demonstrating the relationships between the lower levels of Bloom's Cognitive Taxonomy and Krathwohl's Affective Taxonomy lends further support to the simultaneous ordering of the two domains (Dinero & Martin, 1983). Ordering theory and Rasch scaling were used to analyze data collected from 75 students enrolled in a one semester course on models of teaching. The results did demonstrate the relationships between the two domains, but the authors stated that specific findings were tenuous. The following relationships between the two domains were supported: Receiving/Awareness was directly prerequisite to Knowledge; Receiving/Awareness was directly prerequisite to Responding (it was hypothesized to be mediated by Knowledge); both Knowledge and Responding were directly prerequisite to Valuing (Knowledge was hypothesized indirectly prerequisite to Valuing). One hypothesized relationship between the two domains was unsupported: Application was hypothesized prerequisite to Valuing, but it did not scale as hypothesized. Because of methodological and other concerns, the authors concluded that only minimal support for the relationships between specific categories of the two domains could be established; however, more generally, the two domains do build upon each other.

Young (1984) is currently conducting an experimental classroom learning study to determine the effects of various sequences of cognitive and affective objectives. One group will receive instruction emphasizing information and intellectual skills objectives first and attitude objectives second; a second group will receive instruction in the reverse order; a third group will receive an integrated sequence using Gagné's intellectual skills, attitude, and verbal information outcomes. Young hypothesized that the group receiving attitude instruction first will score higher on measures of cognitive achievement, attitudinal revision, and changes in behavioral intentions than the other two groups. Her results should be forthcoming in the near future.

These are the only studies we found that demonstrated the relationships between behaviors described in the various cognitive and affective taxonomies. Considerable research, however, has been conducted on other relationships between cognition and affect. For example, Allender (1983) provided an excellent overview of the research that has been done linking the two domains. He cited examples of research or review articles on all the following: mutually attainable cognitive and affective objectives in the open classroom; psychological education in which objectives are intended to promote intellectual and emotional development; affective activities that promoted significantly improved cognitive skills in areas such as reading; use of small groups and other forms of social interactions or cooperative learning that facilitate cognitive learning; the use of mental imagery to aid cognitive learning; promoting experiences that use both the cognitive left brain and the affective right brain; imagination training; and emphasis on student directed learning to achieve both cognitive and affective gains.

Krathwohl *et al.* (1964) also cited research in which cognitive objectives have been used as a means to affective goals, and vise versa. They made reference to motivation, inquiry training, discovery learning, and positive learning environments as ways the affective and cognitive domains are or can be linked. They said: "Thus a cognitive skill is built and then used in rewarding situations so that affective interest in the task is built up to permit the next cognitive task to be achieved, and so on" (p. 60). They used the analogy of two ladders side by side—one cognitive and one affective; by alternating between the two ladders (domains), the simultaneous achievement of behaviors in both domains can be accomplished.

Bloom (1976) also linked the two domains. He made a case for the direct relationship between school achievement and affect, but he did not provide research findings. He described three categories of achievement related to affect: (a) subject related affect, (b) school related affect, and (c) academic self-concept.

Subject related affect refers to positive attitudes toward a given subject or task and can be operationally defined as whether an individual would voluntarily engage in additional learning tasks given the opportunity. Since the student and/or the teacher make some judgments about the adequacy of a student's performance regarding any given subject, this type of affect is highly influenced by the student's perceptions of his or her competence. Therefore, Bloom suggested that the teacher strive to promote student success, thereby increasing subject related affect.

School related affect is a composite of subject related affect. The more successful the student is in all subjects, the more positive is his or her view of school and learning. Bloom stated that school related affect is relatively stable after the primary grades.

Both subject and school related affect directly influence a third category of affective consequences, *academic self-concept*. As the student continues in school and is relatively successful or unsuccessful, he or she begins to form judgments about himself as a learner and perhaps as a person. The judgments he makes, therefore, move from external evaluations of subjects and school to internal evaluations of self. These evaluations of self related to school generalize to other aspects of self. Bloom stated that "low academic self-concept increases the probability that an individual will have a negative general self-concept" (p. 156). He then took these ideas a step further by linking school and subject related affect, academic self-concept, and general self-concept to the individual's mental health by suggesting that success or failure in school may affect ego development, general anxiety levels, and the ability to handle stress and frustration. Thus, he certainly sees a strong link between cognitive and affective outcomes.

In summary, it is practically impossible to deny the existence of the interrelatedness of the cognitive and affective domains. The first studies we reported dealt directly with the relationships between domain taxonomies. Even though there are few of these studies and the results are either tentative or forthcoming, the other research we reported that demonstrates interrelationships suggests that linking the domain taxonomies is a promising line of inquiry. The study being conducted by Young will certainly be a valuable contribution.

Much of the other research we reported explored the causal relationships between affective and cognitive teaching strategies or means (e.g., inquiry and discovery learning, environmental influences, etc.) on cognitive and/or affective outcomes (e.g., achievement and self-esteem). The evidence for the relationships is both strong and compelling.

We have little doubt that the two domains interact significantly in instruction and learning. We concur with Smith (1966), who pointed out: "To teach any concept, principle, or theory is to teach not only for its comprehension, but also for an attitude toward it—the acceptance or rejection of it as useful, dependable, and so forth. . . . Suffice it to say it is possible for a learner to understand and be quite proficient in a subject matter area and still have a deep aversion and other negative affect toward the discipline (Bloom, 1971, p. 225).

SUMMARY

In this chapter, we have focused our attention on educational taxonomies. We gave an overview of taxonomies and their purposes, differentiating between prescriptive and descriptive taxonomies, and we reviewed specific taxonomies of the cognitive and affective domains. The taxonomies proposed by Bloom (1956) and Gagné (1977) in the cognitive domain and those of

Krathwohl *et al.* (1964) and Gephart and Ingle (1976) in the affective domain are the ones we found most useful for our task of integrating the two domains.

In addition to reviewing taxonomies, we also provided an overview of other research and conceptualizations of the interactions between the cognitive and affective domains. There is little doubt that the two domains interact in significant ways.

Although the affective domain and the taxonomies that describe it are still unclear in many ways, we are beginning to get a sense of a few critical issues that must be considered before proceeding. First, in addition to attitudes, values, feelings, and motivation, self-development must be included in any comprehensive taxonomy of the affective domain. How and where are important questions. Second, before integration can proceed, a choice will have to be made about the nature of the organizing principle of a taxonomy. Should we use categories of constructs, like attitudes, or should we use learner strategies, e.g., valuing, analysis? Next, how prescriptive must a useful taxonomy be? Also, does it need to be cumulative and hierarchical to be most useful?

In the chapters that follow, we proceed by exploring several major affective constructs—attitudes, values, morals, ethics—and defining the internal and external conditions of learning for each. Using the idea of conditions of learning, we believe we have the tools to use affective constructs in our conception of the affective domain. These conditions of learning can be major components of a theoretical framework linking the two domains.

Chapter 4

Attitudes, Values, and Attitude Change

ATTITUDES AND VALUES

Definitions

The Relationship Between Attitudes and Values

Attitude Dimensions

Components of Attitudes
The affective component
The cognitive component
The behavior component

Types of Attitudes
Affective associations
Intellectualized attitudes
Action-oriented attitudes
Balanced attitudes
Ego-defensive attitudes

Summary

ATTITUDE CHANGE THEORIES

Overview of Attitude Change Theories

97

Critique of Attitude Change Theories

Selected Theories Having Instructional Implications

The Yale Communication and Attitude Change Program
Dissonance Theory
Cognitive Balancing
Social Judgment Theory
Social Learning Theory

EDUCATIONAL IMPLICATIONS

Internal Conditions

External Conditions

Persuasive Communications
  Sources
  The message
  The audience

Dissonance Theory
  Establishing dissonance
  Dissonance reducing techniques
Modeling
Other Techniques

External Conditions for Values Development

OVERVIEW OF THE EDUCATIONAL TASK

Chapter 4

Attitudes, Values, and Attitude Change

In every description or taxonomy of the affective domain, the concept or category *attitude(s)* is included. Usually, *values* are also included since they are defined as clusters of attitudes. The pervasiveness of attitudes and values as the predominant category of the affective domain prompted us to include them in this first section of the book, and to devote more time and space describing and reporting attitude literature than we will spend on other dimensions of the affective domain.

Attitude change and attitude measurement research have played a major role in the development of social psychology. Allport states: "The concept of attitudes is probably the most distinctive and indispensable concept in contemporary social psychology" (Zimbardo, Ebbesen, & Maslach, 1977, p. 19). Yet, the bodies of research associated with various aspects of attitudes, e.g., formation, change, and measurement, are vast and diffuse, and the concept of attitude is confusing due to variations in both terminology and definitions.

Even if confusion about attitude terminology did not exist, a comprehensive review of the relevant literature would be virtually impossible. Since our interest in discussing attitudes and values is ultimately to provide instructional implications in the form of conditions of learning, we have made selective decisions to meet our needs and have organized this chapter into three major subsections. The first gives a brief overview of attitudes and values, their definitions, and two important dimensions of attitudes, i.e., attitude components and attitude typologies. The second section reviews some major attitude change theories. There is no attempt in this section to review research related to these theories. We will at times make very general statements about the adequacy and scope of the research as reported by other authors, but we have done no examination of the research ourselves. The final section of this chapter outlines instructional implications based primarily on the attitude change theories discussed in section two.

ATTITUDES AND VALUES

Definitions

Like descriptions of the affective domain, definitions of the attitude concept vary widely. Fisher (1977, cited in Adams, 1983) states that there are more definitions of attitude than of any other concept in social psychology. Kiesler, Collins, and Miller (1969), reporting McGuire (1968), state that the disagreements or variations in meaning revolve around five varying conceptions of attitude dimensions:

(1) the psychological locus of attitudes, i.e., as a mental, emotional, perceptual, or cognitive state;
(2) attitudes as a response versus a readiness or set to respond;
(3) how attitudes are organized;
(4) the extent to which previous experience affects attitude development and learning; and
(5) the function of attitudes as directive-knowledge or dynamic-motivational.

Some of these dimensions can be seen in the five definitions of attitude that follow:

> An attitude is a mental and neutral state of readiness, organized through experience, exerting a directive or dynamic influence upon the individual's response to all objects and situations with which it is related (Allport, 1935, p. 810).

> . . . an enduring organization of motivational, emotional, perceptual, and cognitive processes with respect to some aspect of the individual's world (Krech & Crutchfield, 1948, p. 152).

> ...the intensity of positive or negative affect for or against a psychological object. A psychological object is any symbol, person, phrase, slogan, or idea toward which people can differ as regards positive or negative affect (Thurstone, 1946, p. 39).

> Attitude is primarily a way of being "set" toward or against certain things (Murphy, Murphy & Newcomb, 1937, p. 889).

> ...an enduring, learned predisposition to behave in a consistent way toward a given class of objects; a persistent mental state of readiness to react to a class of objects as they are conceived to be. This readiness state has a directive influence upon the feelings and action related to the object ... All attitudes are social in the sense they are influenced by social factors (English & English, 1958, cited in Silber, 1961, p. 11).

In general, definitions of attitude can be made from either a cognitive perspective, i.e., the evaluation of an individual's cognitions or beliefs, or from a motivational perspective, i.e., the readiness of the individual to respond or act to motives that have been aroused (Newcomb, Turner, & Converse, 1965). Attitudes, say Newcomb *et al.* (1965), are comprised of a number of psychological processes. In order to understand them we must know something about what motivates behavior, how they are organized, and how the relationships of past and present experience influence behavior. "The attitude concept seems to reflect quite faithfully the primary form in which past experience is summed, stored, and organized in the individual as he approaches new situations. Such experience is best described as a residue (but nonetheless highly organized) of cognized objects to which experience has lent affective color or valence" (p. 41-42).

Although we have not adopted any particular definition of attitude, we believe that attitudes are internal states that influence behavior. We can infer these states from actions and words. The link between attitudes and behavior is a tenuous one, although most theorists agree that the more highly organized and more strongly valenced an attitude or attitude cluster, the more likely we are to find congruence between the attitude and behavior. We will have more to say about this in a later part of this section.

The Relationship Between Attitudes and Values

Values are viewed by most psychologists as a collection of attitudes or attitude clusters that become more and more inclusive. English and English (1958, cited in Silber, 1961) define values as "of much the same character as attitudes, but with a more explicit judgment factor. A value is the degree of worth ascribed to an object or activity . . ." (p. 12).

Katz and Stotland (1959) state that values are groups of attitudes organized around some central idea such as a political or religious system. A value system is highly personalized and is generally organized into a hierarchical or networking pattern. Therefore, it implies some "logical subordination and superordination of attitudes" (p. 432). It is also both possible and likely that attitudes may be part of more than one value system.

In addition to describing the structure of a value system, Katz and Stotland (1959) also relate value systems to an individual's self-concept. An individual's value system is an important part of his/her view of self. When values are jeopardized, the individual may feel that his ego is being threatened. This may, in turn, produce an emotional response. They suggest that this relationship between value systems and self-concept may have important implications for modifying and changing attitudes.

Newcomb *et al.* (1965) describe values as attitudes integrated into several broad patterns. They state that "values are readily seen as special cases of the attitude concept . . . values can be considered as the ultimate development of those many processes of selection and generalization that produce long-range consistency and organization in individual behavior" (p. 45). Figure 4.1 shows their conception of the relationship between attitudes, values, motives, and drives.

While the conception of attitudes and values shown in Figure 4.1 appears to come from a motivational point of view, Newcomb *et al.* (1965) state that they conceive attitudes to be "at a crucial intersection between cognitive processes (such as thought and memory) and motivational processes (involving emotion and striving)" (p. 40). They envision a variety of motives, some based primarily on cognitive adaptation to the environment (that is, a

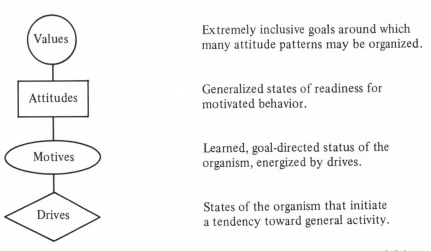

Figure 4.1. The relationship between values, attitudes, motives, and drives.

Note: The above figure was taken from *Social Psychology: The Study of Human Interaction* (p. 45) by T.M. Newcomb, R.H. Turner, and P.E. Coverse, Copyright © 1965; New York: Holt, Rinehart, & Winston. Used with permission.

person's need to know and understand his/her world) and some based on internal states that lead to the development of attitudes and that influence motivated behavior. These attitudes develop over time into broader, generalized structures called values.

There is no body of literature on values development and change that compares to the attitude change literature. Some attitude change theories address attitude organization and attitude clusters, but it is not always clear whether the descriptions refer to several independent attitudes (grouped together in some way), attitude sets, or values. Presumably, attitude sets or attitude groups are not the same as values, since attitude sets may vary in the number of attitudes, their intensity, stability, inclusiveness, valence, etc. We will not try to sort out these confusions and differences, but where possible, will make recommendations for developing values based on our view that values are highly integrated sets of attitudes.

Attitude Dimensions

We turn our attention now to the structure of attitudes and to various types of attitudes. These dimensions may serve to explain, if not clarify, some of the discrepancies in the previous definitions. A brief discussion of types of attitudes follows naturally from the components of attitude structure.

Components of Attitudes

An attitude is conceptualized as having three components: affect, cognition, and behavior. The affective or evaluation component and the cognitive component most directly influence the formation of an attitude and its subsequent change or stability. The behavior component is usually conceived as a *tendency* to act or respond to the attitude object.

The affective component. This component refers to an evaluation or emotional response to the attitude object and is generally thought to be the central core of attitudes. The affective component cannot exist entirely without the cognitive element, since an object must be at least recognized to be evaluated; however, the cognitive component can play a minimal role. The difference between intellectual evaluation and attitudinal evaluation lies in the affective component of attitudes. The latter refers to a liking or feeling toward an object.

The affective component is often measured in terms of both logical position and intensity. Degrees of logical position refer to where, on a continuum, an individual's attitude statements can be placed toward, for example, integration-segregation or some other positional dimension. Intensity refers to the strength of an attitude and is the most common measure of an attitude. Position and intensity are, of course, closely linked.

The cognitive component. The cognitive component refers to an individual's belief or knowledge about the attitude object. Katz and Stotland (1959) give three characteristics of the cognitive component: (a) the degree of differentiation, that is, the number of beliefs or cognitive elements, (b) the degree of integration of the cognitive elements, i.e., how they are organized into patterns or structures, and (c) the generality or specificity of the beliefs.

These three characteristics can vastly influence the nature of the cognitive component.

The behavior component. The behavioral component usually refers to a tendency to act, although Zimbardo *et al.* (1977) state that this component involves an individual's overt behavior toward the attitude object. In discussing the relationship between the cognitive and behavioral component, Katz and Stotland (1959) shed some light on the confusion surrounding attitude as a *tendency* or an *action.* ". . . if the person has a detailed knowledge of appropriate channels of social action, we would say that his attitude has a behavioral component. Accordingly, we would predict that the person favorably disposed toward a political party will be more likely to vote if he knows where the polling place is and when it is open, and if he believes his vote is important for the outcome, than the person who lacks such beliefs related to the action orientation" (p. 432). Since the cognitive component provides the knowledge of appropriate and inappropriate action patterns, the two components are closely linked. Still, the key to the behavioral component appears to be an action *orientation.* Correct prediction of overt actions is probably enhanced by knowing the individual's tendency to act.

Types of Attitudes

Katz and Stotland (1959) have organized attitudes into five types, each reflecting varying degrees of the three components described above and taking into account various human needs. Katz and Stotland hypothesize that attitudes reflecting different components and motives will require different change strategies. Although the attitude change theories do not generally specify a particular type of attitude, Katz and Stotland's typology is similar to one group of attitude change theories.

Affective associations. This type of attitude is almost exclusively affective in nature with little or no cognitive and behavioral orientation. These attitudes are developed through past associations with an attitude object because they meet some immediate need; the need, however, is not instrumental, it is contiguious. Because of the relatively little cognitive content associated with these attitudes, they are isolated and are not an integral part of a value system(s). They are also difficult to change unless new associations are made.

Intellectualized attitudes. Attitudes of this type have major cognitive components, some affectivity, and very little behavioral orientation. Hence, it is difficult to predict an individual's behavior from them. These attitudes tend to be strongly connected to cognitive structures and, therefore, beliefs form the basis of complex value systems. The motivation for these attitudes is a need to understand the world and make sense of it as well as a need for self-consistency. These attitudes can be changed primarily through changes in the cognitive structure.

Action-oriented attitudes. When a need can be met simply and directly, action-oriented attitudes are often invoked. These attitudes have very limited cognitive structure, in fact, cognitive structures often serve to block such attitudes through over-intellectualization. When the path to a goal can be met through social action, these attitudes are used to meet the need. Action-oriented attitudes are often difficult to change unless the need satisfaction can be altered, new paths to the goal become available, or a change in the need satisfaction aspect of the object occurs.

Balanced attitudes. These attitudes develop from ego and biological needs and include affective, cognitive, and behavioral components. The cognitive dimension is fairly well differentiated, which leads to the identification of clear pathways to a goal. This, along with specific beliefs that justify a course of action, activates the behavioral component, which is later rewarded. Such attitudes are learned through trial-and-error and can be altered by changing the contingencies, changing the cognitive aspects of the attitude, and redirecting or identifying new pathways toward a goal.

Ego-defensive attitudes. Ego-defensive attitudes are also balanced, that is, they contain all three components. The difference lies in their source of motivation. While balanced attitudes are more closely associated with acceptable goals and needs, ego-defensive attitudes arise from inner conflict, and behavior is often directed toward objects that are not a viable means for resolving the conflict. These attitudes can be changed to some extent through cognitive reorganization, but the primary means is through personality change, e.g., better self-understanding.

Summary

Summarizing this section on defining attitudes and values is somewhat like trying to simultaneously hold ten corks under water. Attitudes can be defined from either a cognitive or motivational point of view, or at some juncture between the two. Values are highly integrated clusters of attitudes, yet attitudes can cluster into groups that are not values. That is, attitude sets can influence a variety of behaviors, but not be directed toward an inclusive goal. Attitudes are composed of three components, affective, cognitive, and behavioral, that influence to a greater or lesser degree particular types of attitudes and therefore, the change strategies that are best used with each. There is a group of attitude change theories, the Functional or Type Theories, that reflect this appealing categorization of attitudes; however, the criticism of such theories is that the categories are arbitrary and that determining a particular type of attitude is difficult, if not impossible. Likewise, some theories direct their attention toward different attitude components (although this is not always explicit in the discussion of the theories), while other theories make no reference, implicitly or explicitly, to the components.

We included this section to show the diversity of attitude definitions and conceptions and to help the reader understand the problems and confusion educators face when trying to derive instructional implications for this dimension of the affective domain. In the next section we review major attitude change theories; again we encounter considerable diversity.

ATTITUDE CHANGE THEORIES

Theorizing and research on attitude change is a fairly recent endeavor. Although some work was done during World War II, the Yale Attitude Change Program by Hovland, Janis, and Kelley done in 1953 represented the first major thrust in the field (Kiesler *et al.*, 1969). This work set the stage for many subsequent theories.

Like many theories in learning and instructional psychology, attitude theories can be grouped into two broad categories: behavioral and cognitive. The behavioral theories address attitude change from "outside" the individual, that is, from the perspective of environmental or social influences. Much of Hovland's work on the communicator, source credibility, and persuasive communications comes from this orientation. Also included in this category are theories that deal directly with reinforcement, modeling, and other external stimuli, such as peer pressure.

The cognitive theories look "inside" the individual to study attitude development and change. Some factors addressed by these theorists are personality traits and structures, the brain, hormones and the nervous system, cognitive structures, mental states, types of attributions, undeveloped or underdeveloped moral systems or codes, and poor intellectual functioning. The theorists in this group are interested in how one's internal psychological and/or physiological functioning influence attitudes and behaviors.

We assume, as do most social and educational psychologists, that both internal and external factors affect attitude change. Strict adherence to one set of theories or another provides a biased view. Kiesler *et al.* (1969) review a 1963 work by Campbell on the nature of attitudes in which Campbell attempts to synthesize or at least reconcile the behavioral and cognitive approaches. Campbell says that the major difference between the theories is in the connotation of theoretical terms, that is, either objective or subjective connotations. "Campbell argues that, whether the connotation is subjective or objective, the language of most theories is *functionally* equivalent. He would argue, for instance, that the statement 'I perceive that the current administration is dishonest and incompetent' is functionally equivalent to the statement, 'I voted against the administration. " (Kiesler *et al.*, 1969, p. 82). He goes on to say that use of particular data gathering techniques, e.g., self-report versus behavioral observation, have fueled the fire of differences between the two groups.

There is a large body of attitude measurement research and literature that we will not discuss. The way different theorists have collected data and measured the attitude concept has considerable bearing on the findings and later development of the theories. The techniques include a variety of self-report measures, observational measures, and physiological reactions. In a later chapter, on designing instruction, we will briefly describe some of these attitude measurement techniques.

Overview of Attitude Change Theories

We have relied heavily on three books while writing this section. *Influencing Attitudes and Changing Behavior* (Zimbardo, Ebbesen, & Maslach, 1977) is an introductory text in social psychology. *Theories of Attitude Change* (Insko, 1967) is a comprehensive review of attitude change theories and is often cited as a source for in-depth coverage of the various theories. Insko (1967) suggests that the book be used as a handbook or reference. *Attitude Change* (Kiesler, Collins, & Miller, 1969) is also a comprehensive review. It was selected primarily because it organized the major theories into groups, for example, Consistency Theories, and because it reviews some theories not included in the book by Insko (1967). The labels used to define or identify theories or theory groups vary among authors, e.g., Consistency and Balance Theories are used to refer to some of the same theories, and specific reasons for inclusion and exclusion of particular theories are not clear. In addition, the text by Zimbardo *et al.* (1977) lists theories not included in either of the other two, e.g., Social Learning Theory, and gives a more cursory examination of the theories. Table 4.1 lists the names of the theories included in the three books.

Only two theories are discussed in all three books: the Yale Attitude Change Program by Hovland, Janis, and Kelley (1953), and Dissonance Theory by Leon Festinger (1957). These two theories, plus (a) Social Judgment Theory, also called Assimilation-Contrast Theory, by Sherif and Hovland, (b) Cognitive Balancing, or Affective-Cognitive Consistency, by Abelson and Rosenberg, and (c) Social Learning Theory, by Bandura, will be the theories we focus on in this section. We have selected these because they are either well-known, well-developed, appealing because of the instructional implications that can be derived from them, or because they have been previously used by instructional developers or educational psychologists in addressing attitudes (e.g., see the discussion of Social Learning Theory in reference to Attitudes in Gagné, 1977, and Gagné & Briggs, 1979).

Before beginning this discussion, we have included an overview of all the major theories. Table 4.2 lists the major premises of the

Table 4.1

Attitude Change Theories Listed by Reference Author Used

Zimbardo, Ebbeson, Maslach	Insko	Kiesler, Collins & Miller

1. Yale Attitude Change Approach
2. Group Dynamics Approach
3. Cognitive Dissonance
4. Attribution Theory
5. Social Learning Theory
	1. Reinforcement Theory (Yale)
	2. Assimilation-Contrast Theory
	   Sherif & Howland
	3. Adaptation-Level Theory
	   Helson
	4. Logical-Affective Consistency
	   McGuire
	5. Congruity Theory
	   Osgood & Tannenbaum
	6. Belief Congruence
	   Rokeach
	7. Balance Theories
	   Heider & Newcomb
	8. Affective-Cognitive Consistency
	   Rosenberg & Abelson
	9. Dissonance Theory
	   Festinger
	10. Psychoanalytic Theory
	   Sarnoff
	11. Inoculation Theory
	   McGuire
	12. Type Theories
	   a. Smith, Bruner, & White
	   b. Katz
	   c. Kelman
		S-R and Behavioral Theories
		1. Attitude as Implicit Response-Doob
		2. Yale Communication and Attitude Change
		3. Persuasion and Acquisition of Attitudes
		4. Skinnerian "Radical Behaviorism"
		5. Inoculation Theory
		Consistency Theories
		1. Heider's Balance Theory
		2. Structural Balance Cartwright & Harary
		3. Cognitive Balancing Rosenberg & Abelson
		4. Osgood Congruity Model
		5. Newcomb's Strain Toward Consistency
		Dissonance Theory
		1. Festinger (original conception of dissonance theory)
		2. Brehm & Cohen
		3. Aronson
		Social Judgment Theory
		Functional Theories
		1. Smith, Bruner & White
		2. Katz
		3. Kelman

attitude change theories cited in the three books we have consulted, excluding the five just mentioned. We are indebted to the authors of these books since we have borrowed from their extensive work, using their categories, labels, and descriptors. Table 4.2 gives the reader a broad, although somewhat superficial, overview of the current state-of-the-art literature on attitude change theories.

Critique of Attitude Change Theories

We have organized the attitude change theories into four groups. The theories in the first group, the *S-R or Behavioral Theories*, use learning theory and an understanding of learning processes to address attitude change. Because there are so many learning theories on which to draw, these theories represent individual efforts rather than a unified theoretical approach. In general, these theories focus on stimuli in the environment, i.e., communication characteristics and "objective" feedback, usually in the form of rewards and punishments, to study attitudes. Of primary interest to these theorists is (a) identifying communication characteristics, and (b) finding a suitable way to quantify the stimulus condition.

Kiesler *et al.* (1969) list several shortcomings of the behavioral theories. First, they question the extent to which the experiments used test the actual theory or some analogy or translation of it. Second, they state that there are considerable data to suggest that certain rewards designed to produce overt statements of attitude do not actually change the attitude. Third, they fear that these theories have oversimplified the attitude change process. Fourth, they note that the jump from the animal lab to use of human subjects is a big, perhaps a problematic, one. And, finally, they note that there is little theoretical interaction among the researchers in this group. This has resulted in many single theories with few, if any, coordinated findings.

The *balance or consistency* theories look inside the individual to study attitude change rather than at outside influences, as do the behavioral theorists. The primary assumption is that individuals strive for consistency and that inconsistency produces stress or tension. Consistency is viewed from a number of perspectives, e.g.,

Table 4.2

Overview of Major Attitude Change Theories

Attitude Theory Groups	Name or Identifying Label	Theorists	Basic Premise(s)
Stimulus Response and Behavioral Theories	Attitude as an Implicit Response	Doob	Attitudes are seen as a mediating process. Attitudes are formed in much the same way that classical and instrumental conditioning occur. $S^r \rightarrow$ attitude and attitude $\rightarrow$ behavior bonds are learned. Attitudes are conditioned to singular or multiple stimuli to produce a response.
	Yale Communication and Attitude Change Program	Hovland, Janis & Kelley	See Table 4.4
	Persuasion Based on Analogies with Conditioning and Selective Learning	Weiss	An application of Hull-Spence behavior theory where opinion statements are similar to a stimulus and arguments are similar to a reinforcer. Uses variables such as drive, argument strength, source credibility, etc. A very narrow theory.
	Skinnerian "Radical Behaviorism"	Bem	Attitudes are largely determined by the context or external environment where attitude statement is made. Clues in the environment tell us how we feel internally.
	Inoculation Theory	McGuire	This theory focuses on making attitudes resistant to change and uses a biological analogy to do so, i.e., creating resistance. Persuasive attacks against "truisms" that are seldom attacked are effective because appropriate defenses have not been raised. This is because of: (a) lack of practice and (b) lack of motivation. The theory suggests inducing resistance by altering the communication, e.g., adding a motivating element.

Table 4.2 (Continued)

Attitude Theory Groups	Name or Identifying Label	Theorists	Basic Premise(s)
Consistency or Balance Theories	Balance Theory	Heider	This is the basic consistency model. It is a phenomenological approach. The contention is that balanced states are stable and resist change; unbalanced states are unstable and move toward balance. Two types of relations, *sentiment* (attitudinal) and *unit* (person, event) form the basis of the theory. The usual relationship involves triads, e.g., a person, an event, and a relation.
	Strain Toward Symmetry	Newcomb	An application revolving around interpersonal relationships where "communication acts" are highlighted; attention is focused on specific interpersonal attraction and influence. Strain refers to out of balance systems; communication is the means for strain reduction.
	Structural Balance	Cartwright and Harary	They revised and extended the basic model by quantifying balance, making it objective.
	A Structural Balance Model	Feather	This model is oriented toward relationships between communication elements: the source, the communication, the issue and the receiver as they influence attitude change. It is considered an improvement over the basic balance model.
	Congruity Model	Osgood and Tannenbaum	Congruity or balance is dependent on the magnitude of the affective relationship, e.g., *how much* P likes O and S. When two objects of differing evaluation are linked by an assertion, the evaluation of each will move toward equilibrim.

Table 4.2 (Continued)

Attitude Theory Groups	Name or Identifying Label	Theorists	Basic Premise(s)
Consistency Theories (cont'd)	Belief Congruence	Rokeach	Drawing on Congruity Theory, stimuli are linked by an assertion referred to as a characterized subject (CS). The CS forms the basis of several evaluations an individual makes about the subject(S) and the characterization of the subject(C), e.g., their mutual relevance and their relative importance. An important concept in this theory is overassimilation, i.e., an evaluation of CS that is more polarized than either C or S. The importance of the theory is most closely related to work done on prejudical behavior.
	Logical-Affective Consistency Theory	McGuire	Two postulates form the basis of this theory: (a) an individual's belief are arranged *logically* and (b) beliefs tend to be congruent with one's wishes and desires. Wishful thinking distorts logical consistency. When inconsistency is recognized, beliefs will change toward greater consistency. The theory is regarded as incomplete, but a promising line of inquiry because it views beliefs as logically arranged.
	Dissonance Theory	Festinger	See Table 4.4.
Functional or Type Theories	Functional Theory	Katz, et al.	A phenomonological approach to attitude development and change relying heavily on motivational bases. Katz list four functions attitudes can perform for the personality: (a) instrumental, adjustive, and utilitarian, (b) ego defensive, (c) knowledge, and (d) value-expressive.

Table 4.2 (Continued)

Attitude Theory Groups	Name or Identifying Label	Theorists	Basic Premise(s)
Functional or Type Theories (cont'd)	Functional Theory	Smith, Bruner & White	Basically similar to Katz's theory except for the categorization of functions. The authors give four different categories: (a) social adjustment, (b) externalization, (c) object appraisal, and (d) quality of expressiveness. Attitude change strategies are dependent on the attitude's function, e.g., an object appraisal function is most responsive to new information.
	Compliance, Identification, and Internalization	Kelman	The theory implies that one must know how an attitude was acquired in order to change it effectively. Three processes of attitude change are identified: (a) *compliance*—acceptance is based on a system of rewards; (b) *identification*—acceptance is based on the individual's relationship to another individual or a group; (c) *internalization*—acceptance is based on how intrinsically rewarding or congruent the idea is to an individual's value system. For each process, Kelman gives antecedent (e.g., motives and social influence) and consequent conditions (e.g., the conditions where the attitude can be expressed).
Miscellaneous Theories	Psychoanalytic Theory	Sarnoff	Based on a Freudian model, this theory relies heavily on understanding the motives that produce internal tension. A positive attitude is developed toward objects that reduce tension, an unfavorable attitude toward objects that interfere with this process. Likewise, attitudes are formed when they facilitate ego-defensive reactions such as denial and projection.

Table 4.2 (Continued)

Attitude Theory Groups	Name or Identifying Label	Theorists	Basic Premise(s)
Miscellaneous Theories (cont'd)	Attribution Theory (This is actually a term given to various theories concerned with investigating causal perception.)	Jones Kelley Weiner	This theory attempts to describe how people formulate reasons for their own and other's actions. The two types of attributions are: (1) *situational* or external and (2) *dispositional* or internal. Attitudinal influence strategies must take into account a person's subjective view of reality, i.e., their perception of the attributional bases of behavior. Knowledge of attributional bases helps identify an individual's sources of vulnerability and demonstrates how people often oversimplify the causal factors attributed to behavior.
	Group Dynamics Approach	Lewin	People change their attitudes because they are discrepant from those of their reference group. The group has power to reward or punish behavior, so when group effects are rewarding attitude changes in that direction, and when the effects are punishing, the opposite occurs. These changes are related to attempts to satisfy the individual's needs and motives. This theory emphasizes social pressures rather than persuasive communication.
	Adaptation-Level Theory	Helson	An application of perceptual theory to social behavior. All stimuli can be arranged on various bi-polar continua, each with a neutral zone called adaptation level. Focal, contextual, and residual stimuli are weighted and they interact. This accounts for the evaluation an individual gives to stimuli. The theory has not proved very applicable to social phenomena mostly because of its inability to handle complex situations and questions.

striving for a balanced personality, for balance between attitudes, between behaviors, between attitudes and behaviors, between cognitive elements, and even the search for a "unified world view." Inconsistency can occur because of discrepant social roles, illogical or misinformed cognitions, social or internal pressure, or environmental changes, to name only a few. All the models presented focus on the need for consistency; the variations occur both in the sources of inconsistency and how to establish and maintain balance.

Kiesler *et al.* (1969) list six criticisms of consistency theories. First, there are too many of these theories and none stands out as superior (with the exception of Dissonance Theory, which will be discussed in the next section). Second, the predictions that can be made from these theories are imprecise and they are not theoretically unique. Third, the amount or degree of consistency is not addressed (with the exception of Osgood's theory). Fourth, the complexity of an individual's consistency or inconsistency has not been adequately handled. Fifth, the need or striving for consistency is not universally accepted. Some theorists study the opposite motive, i.e., an individual's exploratory drive. These two theoretical views, Kiesler *et al.* (1969) say, may not necessarily be conflicting approaches. And, finally, little work has been done by these theorists on communication sources, the content of communications, and an individual's reaction to a communique. These are important variables and should be addressed experimentally. Kiesler *et al.* (1969) add, however, that even with these shortcomings, the consistency theories "appear to be the most exciting development in attitude change research in the last ten years" (p. 190).

The third group of theories, *Type or Functional Theories*, take the view that in order to alter an attitude you must first know what kind of attitude you are trying to change. Since attitudes are viewed as meeting different needs or performing different functions, it is incumbent on the change agent to understand the type of attitude to be changed. While this seems a plausible approach, the lack of agreement on types of attitudes and on category boundaries for identifying attitudes reflects how arbitrary attitude typologies are; this is a major weakness of these theories.

Following from this weakness is the major criticism of these theories; there is no adequate technology for assessing the function of attitudes (Kiesler *et al.*, 1969).

The final category of theories, labeled *Miscellaneous*, was included to show the range of approaches used for studying attitude change. We have included: (a) the Psychoanalytic theory developed by Sarnoff; (b) a cognitive theory, Attribution Theory; (c) a theory of socially-based needs, the Group Dynamic Approach; and (d) perceptual theory, the Adaptation-Level Theory by Helson. These theories have received little attention for a variety of reasons. For example, neither the Psychoanalytic nor the Adaptation-Level theory has been adequately tested. Attribution Theory is not included in the books by Insko (1967) and Kiesler *et al.* (1969) presumably because it is broader than an attitude change theory. The Group Dynamics Approach appears to be a front-runner of Social Judgment Theory; the latter will be discussed in the next section.

Selected Theories Having Instructional Implications

We have selected five attitude change theories to describe more fully because of the potential instructional implications that can be derived from each, shown in the section, Educational Implications. One theory, the Yale Attitude Change Program, is a behavioral theory. Social Learning Theory is a interactionist theory that uses many behavioral principles. Two are consistency theories: Dissonance Theory and Cognitive Balancing. The last theory is Social Judgment Theory; it offers yet another approach for determining instructional applications.

The Yale Communication and Attitude Change Program

This approach to attitude change, also called Reinforcement Theory, is actually not a theory but rather an empirically-based program or approach to studying attitude change. It is based on learning theory and has two central premises: (a) attitudes can be changed through reinforcement, and (b) in order to change an attitude, the cognitive elements, that is, beliefs and opinions, must be changed.

The Yale approach relies heavily on principles of learning to produce attitude change. "The principles of learning concerned with attention and comprehension are assumed to operate in persuasion in the same manner as they operate in ordinary instruction. Hence, many of the hypotheses which relate to effective instruction will also relate to persuasion" (Insko, 1967, p. 13). With this approach, the attitude to be learned comes in the form of persuasive communications where *one* proposition or conclusion (rather than many) is presented. Two key elements in the communication are that both a question (or an issue) is presented, and that an answer is provided. The focus is on changing the individual's beliefs or cognitions resulting ultimately in attitude change.

Drawing from learning theory, four important variables are emphasized. A communication must be *attended* to, *comprehended, accepted,* and *retained.* Acceptance is based primarily on reinforcement. Reinforcement occurs during the presentation of a persuasive communication where either the arguments themselves are reinforcing or expectations of reinforcement are aroused. Insko (1967) lists three major expectations that are critical and can be aroused: (a) Individuals expect to be right or wrong. Since expert sources are usually right, the opinion of a *credible source* will be more readily accepted. (b) An untrustworthy source is often seen as having manipulative intent. Usually, they are not accepted. (c) Social acceptance is important and rewarding, so when *social approval* can be highlighted, the possibility of acceptance increases. Prestigious sources can often be used for this purpose.

Other important variables in this approach are: (a) the setting or environment where the communication is presented and how the audience reacts to it, and (b) the actual content of the arguments or appeals. Since the intent is to change beliefs, resulting in attitude change, the content revolves around cognitive components, but questions remain as to whether a one-sided or two-sided argument is best or whether a rational or emotional appeal is most successful. With regard to one- or two-sided arguments, two-sided arguments show some advantages (Insko, 1967).

The major criticism of this approach is that an explicit

statement of what constitutes a reinforcing stimuli is not apparent or forthcoming. ". . . until some satisfactory theoretical statement of the nature of reinforcement is given, reinforcement theory will remain a rather primitive theory no matter how mathematically elegant it may be" (Insko, 1967, p. 62). Other criticisms include: (a) poorly worked out relationships between the attention, comprehension, and acceptance concepts, (b) the lack of an explicit description of the relationship between opinions and attitudes, and questions concerning whether opinion change can be facilitated through logical, quasi-logical, or emotional appeals, and (c) how a communication actually supplies incentives or reinforcement.

Regarding research, Brown (1965), quoted in Kiesler *et al.* (1969), says: "The work has been well done, especially the studies constituting the Yale series . . . but it lacks something of compelling intellectual interest because the results do not fall into any compelling pattern. They summarize a set of elaborate contingent, and not very general, generalizations" (p. 117). Kiesler *et al.* go on to say that the research is problem-oriented rather than theory-oriented and that variables related to this research were discussed years earlier by other researchers.

Dissonance Theory

Cognitive dissonance theory is based on the premise that inconsistency in an individual's cognitive system produces tension that must be reduced or eliminated. There are two basic hypotheses:

"1. The existence of dissonance creates psychological tension or discomfort and will *motivate* the person to reduce the dissonance and achieve consonance. . .

2. When dissonance exists, not only will the person attempt to reduce it, but he will actively attempt to avoid situations and information which would increase the dissonance" (Kiesler *et al.*, 1969, p. 193-194).

Cognitive elements and their relations are the basic features of this theory. Cognitive elements are defined as knowledge, e.g., facts, opinions, beliefs, and even statements of attitudes. There are three relations cognitive elements can have: consonant, dissonant, or irrelevant. Dissonance usually refers to the discrepancy or inconsistency between the cognitive elements. However, dissonance may occur in other ways, too, for example, when behavior and beliefs are discrepant or when present and past experiences or evaluations of experiences are not in accord. The amount or magnitude of dissonance depends primarily on how important the individual perceives the cognitive elements to be and the ratio of the dissonant to consonant elements. Once dissonance is aroused in a person, it can be reduced in one of three ways: the individual can (a) change his behavior, e.g., stop eating high sodium foods, (b) change his psychological or physical environment, and/or (c) add a new cognitive element.

Festinger has embellished his theory by discussing implications for specific events or situations that facilitate dissonance: decision-making, forced compliance, involuntary exposure to information, voluntary exposure to information, and social support. Table 4.3 briefly explains each situation and the associated dissonance-reducing techniques.

There have been several extensions of dissonance theory. The most notable one is advanced by Brehm and Cohen, and discusses the role of commitment and volition to the production and reduction of dissonance. "Dissonance is more likely to occur in a given situation if one *commits* oneself to some course of action while remaining aware of one's *volition* to do otherwise" (Zimbardo *et al.*, 1977).

While Insko (1969) says that judging from the amount of literature, dissonance theory is the most popular theory of attitude change, he states two major drawbacks of this theory: (a) the imprecise definition of dissonance and (b) the imprecise description of cognitive elements, i.e., when is a cognitive element a single component versus a cluster of elements? He goes on to say that with the exception of selective exposure and reward in forced compliance situations, the research is fairly supportive.

In addition to these criticisms, Kiesler *et al.* (1969) list several others: (a) the failure to address individual differences in both dissonance producing and reducing situations, (b) how to determine the discrepancy between cognitions, i.e., when does one's cognition "psychologically imply the obverse" of the other (p.

Table 4.3

Dissonance Theory and Implications

(Adapted from Insko, 1967)

Situation	What Causes Dissonance	Dissonance Reduction Techniques

Decision-Making (Free Choice)	1. Dissonance is a result of making a decision.
	2. Dissonance increases when:
	  a. the decision is very important
	  b. an unchosen alternative is seen as attractive
	  c. cognitive overlap between the elements is small.
		1. Revoke the decision.
		2. Make the chosen alternative more attractive.
		3. Make the unchosen alternative less attractive.
		4. Establish greater cognitive overlap.

Forced Compliance	1. Dissonance occurs when one complies to public pressure without a concommitant change in private opinion. 2. Magnitude is dependent on reward and punishment, specifically, the greater the reward or punishment, the less the dissonance. 3. If individual decides not to comply, the greater the reward or punishment, and the less important the opinion, the greater the dissonance.	1. Reduce the importance of the behavior or opinion. 2. Change private opinion to agree with public behavior. 3. Increase the reward or punishment used to invoke the behavior.
Involuntary Exposure to Information	1. Dissonance occurs when information is inconsistent with the cognitions already held.	1. Misperceive the information so that it no longer dissonant. 2. Avoid the information. 3. Change opinion.
Voluntary Exposure to Information	There are two conditions when dissonance may be aroused: 1. People may seek information to help in decision-making. or 2. People may seek information to help reduce dissonance.	1. Gather enough information to increase dissonance to such levels that a decision will be revoked. 2. Increase dissonance above the level of resistance for change by adding a cognitive element that may eventually reduce dissonance.

Table 4.3 (Continued)

Situation	What Causes Dissonance	Dissonance Reduction Techniques
Social Support	1. Agreement with people reduces dissonance, disagreement increases dissonance. 2. Magnitude of dissonance is dependent on: (a) ability to test the disagreement, (b) the number of agreeing and disagreeing people, (c) importance of the issue, (d) the attractiveness and credibility of the disagreeing person, and (e) the extent of the disagreement.	1. Agree with the disagreeing person by changing beliefs. 2. Persuade the disagreeing person to change beliefs. 3. Increase the possibility of comparing the two points of view.

235), and (c) several difficulties in measuring variables, e.g., importance of a cognition, amount of dissonance, etc. Although Kiesler *et al.* feel that these criticisms of the theory are important, they also feel that "the theory has been an extraordinary useful tool for the study of attitude and cognitive change" (p. 237).

Cognitive Balancing

This theory, also named Affective-Cognitive Consistency Theory, is not as well known as the two just discussed, yet it is of interest to us for three reasons. First, unlike other balance theories, it takes into account both the cognitive and affective components of attitudes. Second, Insko (1967) states that the later version of this theory "is one of the most sophisticated and compelling statements of the consistency point of view" (p. 197). Third, it seems to provide some insight into the development of value structures. Unfortunately, it is somewhat difficult to derive instructional implications from the theory, but the premises are interesting enough to include it.

There are two versions of the theory—an earlier version (Insko, 1967, cites Rosenberg, 1953, 1956, 1960) and a later version (Insko, 1967, cites Abelson and Rosenberg, 1958; Rosenberg and

Abelson, 1960). In the first version, there are two characteristics of attitudes that are important. First, attitudes are seen as having both cognitive and affective components, where the cognitive components relate to objects of affective significance in an *instrumental* way. For example, negative feelings toward an object, such as behavioral objectives, include negative affect for the object, and also the belief that the object is instrumental to some other outcome, for example, that behavioral objectives will lead to "fractionalized learning" and "unfair accountability standards." Second, attitudes have *psychological structures*, i.e., relationships exist so that changes in one psychological event will result in changes in another event.

Like other consistency theories, attitudes can be in a stable or balanced state or an unbalanced state. When attitudes are unbalanced, balance will be attempted. Rosenberg (cited in Insko, 1967) gives three ways reorganization of the attitude structure can occur: the individual can (a) reject the communication that forced the unbalanced state, thereby restoring balance, (b) fragment the attitude from other attitudes, and (c) form a new attitude by accommodation. Reorganization by accommodation is actual attitude change and can occur by a cognitive change followed by affective change, or the reverse.

In the later version of this theory, cognitive elements, i.e., actors, means, and ends, are related in one of four ways: by positive, negative, null, or ambivalent relations. Cognitive elements and their relationships are called cognitive units, specifically "each instrumental relation between the attitude object and another affective object involves a cognitive unit" (Insko, 1967, p. 180). All cognitive elements phenomenally related to an issue or attitude object form a *conceptual arena*. When a person thinks about issues or attitude objects in the conceptual arena, she/he uses "psychological" rules, such as A opposes B; B is directed toward C; therefore A opposes C.

The discovery of an inconsistent or ambivalent relationship can be restructured toward balance in one of three ways: the individual can (a) change at least one of the relations, (b) redefine an element or discriminate at least one element from the others, or (c) refuse to think about the inconsistency. The authors suggest that the chosen way of restoring balance will be the one requiring the least amount of effort.

Abelson (1959, cited in Insko, 1967) gives several other ways of restoring balance: denial, bolstering, differentiation, and transcendence. Of particular interest to us is differentiation, "splitting apart a cognitive element," and transcendence, creating a superordinate structure that encompasses the inconsistent cognitive elements. (While not stated as such in the theory, the development of this superordinate structure appears to be similar to the development of a new or differentiated value system.) Abelson states that denial and bolstering will be used first to reestablish balance because these methods are easier and a more simple means to the same end. However, while these two are ways of restoring balance, they do not necessarily influence attitude change; only differentiation and transcendence appear to involve accomodation and, therefore, actual attitude change. It is these two strategies that educators may want to use.

Social Judgment Theory

Social Judgment or Assimilation-Contrast Theory revolves around the concepts of anchors, assimilation, contrast, and latitudes of acceptance, rejection, and neutrality. In general, the theory states that people form reference scales, that is, they place social stimuli on a continuum, with anchors at the end points. These anchors can be either internal (attitudes) or external (persuasive communications). For each reference scale there are three regions: the latitudes of acceptance, rejection, and neutrality. The width of the various latitudes shifts in size depending on the individual's ego-involvement or personal interest in the attitude object. Attitude change occurs in two stages. First, the individual judges a persuasive communication according to his own position on the reference scale. Next, he judges the amount of discrepancy between the communication and his reference scale, specifically categorizing his position in terms of latitude regions.

When using this theory to address attitude change, the following predictions can be made:

    1. If a persuasive communication on a topic of low ego-involvement for the individual falls within his latitude of

acceptance (if it is not too discrepant), the individual will be favorably influenced.

2. If a persuasive communication on a topic of low ego-involvement falls within the latitude of rejection (if it is more discrepant), minimal or negative influence will occur.

3. Low ego involvement topics have larger latitudes of acceptance; therefore, communications on such topics are likely to be more persuasive.

4. As the discrepancy between the communication and the individual's own stand increases, attitude change is more likely as long as the position that is communicated remains within the latitude of acceptance.

5. In the latitude of rejection, more discrepancy produces less opinion change.

Since this theory predicts that most attitude change occurs within the latitude of acceptance, the wider the region, the more discrepant the persuasive communications can be, and, hence, the greater the change in attitude. Therefore, the use of successive approximations to increase the width of the latitude of acceptance combined with persuasive communications on the outer edge of that region should produce slow but successful attitude change (Kiesler *et al.*, 1969).

Although the experimental results, in general, support the theory in predicting attitude change, both Insko (1967) and Kiesler *et al.* (1969) report a lack of precision in the theory and in specifying causal relationships. Insko concludes that, ". . . in its present form, [the theory] is not a serious contender in the field of attitude change. This does not mean that judgmental principles have no relevance to attitude change. It just means that such relevance has not been adequately demonstrated" (p. 91).

Social Learning Theory

One basic premise of social learning theory is that behavior is determined and actually learned by the consequences one expects after the behavior has occurred. If the behavior is reinforced, it will probably occur again; if the behavior is punished, it is unlikely that it will occur again. While this sounds like a strict behavioral theory, it is not. Cognitive processes are seen as important because the individual must remember past consequences of a behavior in order for that behavior to influence future or present behavior. This plus the fact that cognition plays a large role in anticipating or predicting the consequences of behavior make this theory an interactionist theory.

Assuming that behavior change is a form of learning the consequences that follow actions, there are several strategies that can be used to alter behavior and change attitudes. First, an individual can *directly experience* the consequences of his/her own behavior. Second, a person can learn from watching the consequences of someone else's behavior. This is called *modeling* or vicarious learning. Third, one can *read* or *hear about* the consequences of a behavior and infer a causal relationship, for example, if X, then Y. Finally, one can learn through *associations* that arouse negative or positive emotions. For example, the term "behaviorism" may arouse negative feelings because it has been associated with other terms or ideas that are negative, e.g., the use of studies conducted with animals to predict human behavior is bad, therefore behaviorism is bad. As a behavior is learned, it is *discriminated* so that people learn to expect different rewards or punishments as the stimuli changes. It is also *generalized*, so that people learn to respond in similar ways to similar stimuli.

Bandura (1977b) suggests four major factors that influence an individual's behavior: performance accomplishments, vicarious experience, verbal persuasion, and emotional arousal. Associated with these are a variety of "modes of induction" for behavior and attitude change. Four general techniques are emphasized: (a) direct reinforcement including shaping by successive approximations, (b) extinction by removing the reinforcing or punishing consequences, (c) modeling, and (d) providing instructions, rules, or communications in the form of persuasive messages. (See a discussion of Social Learning Theory in Chapter 6.)

Gagné (1977) and Gagné and Briggs (1979) regard human modeling in attitude development as one of the most important and fundamental methods that currently exist. They list several characteristics of the model and its presentation to the learner that are important if the learner is to be influenced: the model must be credible, respected by the learner, and someone with whom the learner can identify. In addition, the learner must see the model's behavior being reinforced (or punished). The model need not be present or even alive to be effective. A model can be presented on film, by television, in a novel, or through other vicarious means.

Social learning theory is less concerned with attitudes and attitude change, per se, than are the other theories we have considered. The emphasis is on categories of behavior and how stimuli and consequences influence those behaviors. In a sense, social learning theory merely discusses attitude as one type of behavior. For example, agreeing that birth control is important and actually using birth control are different behaviors followed by different consequences (Zimbardo *et al.*, 1977). Zimbardo *et al.* summarize social learning theory by saying, ". . . a social learning approach discards the concept of attitude in its attempt to understand and produce changes in behavior. Instead, it determines a class of behavior that is to be changed (. . .). Then it tries to specify what the person has learned and what is therefore controlling his or her present behavior. Once these crucial bits of information have been found, the technique (modeling, direct reinforcement, persuasive communications, and so on) that is most likely to produce a change in such information is applied" (p. 121). Therefore, in social learning theory, attitudes have been redefined as behavior and are treated in the same way as any other behavior.

We have summarized these five theories in Table 4.4. We have listed each theory, the basic premises, instructional implications, plus a brief comment about the research efforts. In the section that follows, we attempt to synthesize the applications and specify major techniques for influencing attitudes.

EDUCATIONAL IMPLICATIONS

There are several important factors to consider when trying to derive implications from the attitude change theories we have described. First, the social psychologists' interest in attitude development and change constitutes basic theorizing and research. In general, the researchers have tried to develop a theory or an approach that allows for as much predictive power as possible. The

Table 4.4

Selected Theories with Implications for Instructional Planning

THEORY	BASIC PREMISE	MAJOR VARIABLES	INSTRUCTIONAL IMPLICATIONS	RESEARCH
Yale Program Hovland, Janis, Kelley (1953)	– Change the attitude by changing opinions or beliefs. – Use persuasive communication. – Individual must attend, comprehend, accept, and retain the message.	– Source – Communication or message – Audience – Audience reaction	– Provide both a question and an answer in the communication. – Individual must engage in *mental rehearsal* of the attitude. – Provide *incentives* for making a new response, that is, for bringing about acceptance of the new opinion. – Use a credible *source*. – Avoid high fear and manipulative communications. – Present two-sided arguments. – Provide for overt verbalization (possibly in the form of role-playing).	– Well constructed and conducted individual studies. – Conflicting findings. – No true patterns or firm generalizations have emerged. – Not a formal theory, rather a program of attitude change.

Table 4.4 (Continued)

THEORY	BASIC PREMISE	MAJOR VARIABLES	INSTRUCTIONAL IMPLICATIONS	RESEARCH

Dissonance Theory
 	
Festinger (1957)
Variations by a host of other researchers
	– When cognitions are dissonant, an individual seeks to reduce that dissonance by:
	1) changing his:
	  a. behavior
	  b. attitude
	  c. environment
	2) adding a new cognitive element
		– The magnitude of dissonance depends on (a) the *importance* of cognitive elements, (b) the *number* of the dissonant or consonant elements in each cognitive cluster and how equal they are, and (c) *cognitive overlap* between elements.	– Provide cognitive elements that reduce (or increase) dissonance (depending on desired attitude change).
			– Induce action dissonant with attitude so attitude will change.
			– Best results occur in *free choice* rather than complicant situations.
			– Provide alternatives for decision-making.
				– More experiental studies than any other theory of attitude change.
				– In general, data supports the postulates.
				– A number of substantive criticisms both of the theory and individual experiments exist.

Table 4.4 (Continued)

THEORY	BASIC PREMISE	MAJOR VARIABLES	INSTRUCTIONAL IMPLICATIONS	RESEARCH
Cognitive Balancing	– A variation of the basic balance model. – When attempting to resolve imbalance, the change requiring the least effort will be chosen.	– *Consistency* of attitude structure – *Predictability* of attitude – *Instrumentality* of related attitudes or attitude objects.	– Extend the conceptual arena of the individual by relating the attitude object to a variety of issues and/or other attitude objects. – Motivate the learner to think about elements in the cognitive arena by presenting communications that demonstrate imbalance. – Ask learner to explain his "psycho-logical" thinking, that is, how she/he is relating the elements. – Assist learner in (a) differentiating cognitive elements by redefinition of the cognitive and/or affective components, and (b) establishing a superordinate structure that relates the inconsistent units.	– Highly consistent and supportive findings. – Many elements of the theory are untested, e.g., degree and intensity of imbalance are not explained or handled satisfactorily. – "Cognitive relations" is not adequately defined

Table 4.4 (Continued)

THEORY	BASIC PREMISE	MAJOR VARIABLES	INSTRUCTIONAL IMPLICATIONS	RESEARCH

Social Judgment Theory
 	
Sherif & Hovland
	– The way in which an individual judges a persuasive communication and the amount of discrepancy between that and his own attitude will influence attitude change.
	  It is a two-stage process:
	  1) make judgment about the communication
	  2) judge discrepancy.
	– Internal factors and social factors influence judgment.
	– The individual's categorization of the communication is central for predicting change effects.
		1) *Involvement*: Personal attitudes revolve around three theoretical regions:
		  a. latitude of acceptance
		  b. latitude of rejection
		  c. latitude of noncommitment.
		2) *Discrepancy*: comparison of the position in the communication with one's own.
			– Make persuasive communication in the latitude of acceptance.
			– Within latitude of acceptance, make as large a discrepancy as possible for greatest change. Persuasion will succeed when it moves in small, modest steps.
			– Broaden latitude of acceptance by successive approximations.
				– The data on attitude change seem to mostly support the theory, but the central premise of the theory, i.e., judgmental responses mediate attitude change, remains an assumption.
				– Theory is very narrowly focused, e.g., only two major variables.
				– A number of unanswered questions.

Table 4.4 (Continued)

THEORY	BASIC PREMISE	MAJOR VARIABLES	INSTRUCTIONAL IMPLICATIONS	RESEARCH
Social Learning Theory Albert Bandura (1977b)	– Mechanism by which a person's behavior changes is a form of learning. – Theory addresses the interacting influences of the person, their behavior, and the environment. – Behavior is shaped by stimulus (antecedent) – response – consequence (feedback). – Consequences are reinforced or punished; individual learns "if-then" relationships. – The environmental influence is mediated by cognitive processes that help individual define, interpret, discriminate, and generalize, the environmental stimuli. – Pays particular attention to attention, remembering, and motivational processes.	– Four major factors affecting behavior: 1) performance accomplishment 2) vicarious experience (modeling) 3) verbal persuasion 4) emotional arousal.	– General techniques for changing behavior: 1) direct reinforcement 2) extinction 3) vicarious reinforcement and extinction through modeling 4) providing instructions, rules, or communications 5) social role modeling	– In general, the studies on performance accomplishment show that successful performance on a task increases the possibility of a successful performance of that behavior in future, similar situations. – The studies on modeling tend to demonstrate consistently that use of a model is an effective means for changing behavior. (A number of modeling studies have been done in theraputic situations. Others have used models in television commercials, and for the diffusion of innovations.)

quest for a formal theory is quite different from the search for applications; in the former, statements of the theoretical constructs and the relationships among them form the basis. This is an exceptionally difficult task for a concept like attitude; it is exceedingly difficult to operationally define the constructs and to specify important relationships among them. Kiesler *et al.* (1969) state, "Even the best developed of our current theories of attitude change do not adequately specify the conditions under which their predictions should hold true, and the conditions under which the theoretical processes are either not relevant or are cancelled out by some other process" (p. 43).

A second factor to consider is the tenuous link between attitudes and behavior. The best that can be said is that the relationship is weak. The evidence seems to suggest "that it is possible to predict behavior from attitudes but without a great deal of precision" (Kiesler *et al.*, 1969, p. 27). Depending on an individual's philosophy, this information may or may not be problematic for the educator. If one's assumption is that education *is* behavior change, then what these theories have to offer may be limited. The research as a whole suggests that there is a correlation between attitudes and behavior; however, questions such as which attitudes affect which behavior, how much influence is exerted, and under what circumstances behavior is influenced, are largely unanswered. It is also unlikely that these questions will be answered in the near future.

Another factor of interest is the "content" of most of the experimental studies. In general, the attitudes manipulated were of social significance, e.g., racial and ethnic prejudice, experimentation with drugs and sex, issues related to abortion, job satisfaction and absenteeism, capital punishment, suicide, community problems, politics, and leadership styles and roles. If one wanted to find out how to change attitudes specifically related to a particular attitude object, presumably he/she could review the literature for those studies and synthesize the findings. We have not done that because (a) the likelihood of finding consistent results is slim, but more importantly, because (b) educators, especially teachers, instructional designers, curriculum developers, and professors in state supported institutions must make careful decisions about the types of attitudes they attempt to alter and influence. For example, we might be perfectly safe in promoting negative attitudes about substance abuse, that is, persuading students not to take specific drugs or consume alcohol, yet be in treacherous waters when dealing with the issue of abortion. Educators in private industry, military training, and medical and nursing schools may have greater latitude in deciding what attitudes are important to change, yet the most important ones may not be those that were manipulated in the studies reviewed.

This factor, then, actually raises a twofold dilemma. The first is philosophical and political: what attitudes *should* we change or influence? The second is practical: *How* should we influence the attitudes we believe fall within our jurisdiction? We have partly addressed the problem by separating moral and ethical behavior from other attitudes and providing different conditions of learning for each (see Chapter 5). We have taken a developmental and, hopefully, non-judgmental perspective in discussing morals and ethics. The remainder of this chapter is devoted to summarizing the internal and external conditions that may influence the development of attitudes. It is up to each individual, in his own setting and situation, to determine whether the attitudes to be influenced fall inside or outside the realm of morals and ethics, and which, if any, influence strategies should be used.

One final point needs to be addressed. We have relied exclusively on attitude change theories because the bulk of attitude theories focus on alteration and modification. However, as educators we are also interested in attitude development or formation and attitude extension as well as attitude change. We believe the conditions outlined are suitable for formation, extension, and change. Attitude extension and change are more closely aligned than attitude development; similar strategies can be used for the former. Attitude development is viewed largely as a cognitive process (Zimbardo *et al.*, 1977), that is, building a set of beliefs based on knowledge, facts, and ideas. We assume the instances where attitude change or modification is desired outnumber instances where initial attitudes are being developed. However, when teaching a new subject or tackling a new issue, the attitude change strategies described here can be instrumental in helping an instructor present new information in such a way that the desired attitude is developed.

We now present the conditions of learning for attitude and value change and development. Refer to the Introduction to Part II for a definition of internal and external conditions of learning.

Internal Conditions

Attitudes are conceptualized as having three components: cognitive, affective, and behavioral. The internal conditions revolve primarily around the cognitive and behavioral components, i.e., being knowledgeable about the attitude object and about ways of acting or responding. Therefore, the primary internal conditions are: (a) intellectual skills in the form of concepts and rules, and (b) meaningful information.

Attitudes are highly dependent on one's beliefs and knowledge. In terms of intellectual skills, *learners must be able to identify the attitude object and comprehend information presented about it.* If the learner cannot identify the attitude object, it will have to be presented before the attitude change strategies can be effective.

Because many of the cognitive attitude change theories make use of dissonance or discrepancy, *learners must be able to identify relationships among cognitive elements.* In order to do this, use of rules of logic (such as A = B, B = C, therefore, A = C) may be important. Likewise, *learners must be able to identify alternative points of view and remember the differences.* This allows the learner to place himself on a continuum and establish latitudes of acceptance, rejection, and neutrality. Therefore, two additional internal conditions are: (a) *some minimal understanding of the rules of logic* or at least an understanding of causal relations, and (b) *the ability to place himself or herself on a continuum when provided alternative views.*

The importance of a human model in change strategies requires that the *learner recognize the model* and either identify his or her credibility and power or will accept information that establishes the model's important characteristics. Therefore, appropriate *characteristics of the source* must be known or established.

Finally, when the attitude is intended to produce a behavior change, the more alternative pathways that can be established for action, the higher the probability that the attitude will influence behavior. *Intellectual skills related to a desired course of action must be previously known and understood.* For example, if the desired attitude requires comparison shopping of foods or cars, the ability to make the correct computations for comparison is crucial.

Meaningful information is also an important internal condition for attitude learning and change. Often this information relates to situations where actions may occur, e.g., knowing the street names of drugs and in what social situation to find them (Gagné, 1977), but information may also be important for comprehending a message. For example, if a person does not know the slang terms for drugs, ethnic groups, or certain geographic regions, etc., he or she will not be able to evaluate a communication in the same way as someone who has that information.

These internal conditions, if not prerequisite to the learner, must be established before attitude change can be effective. However, intellectual skills and information are necessary, but not sufficient to influence attitudes. External conditions stimulate the change processes.

External Conditions for Attitude Change

We have arranged the external conditions in categories by type of change strategy, e.g., persuasive communications. However, there is one condition that supercedes all others: *use a variety of approaches.* We believe a multidimensional approach to attitude change and development will be most successful.

Persuasive Communications
Sources.
1. Use a credible source. Credibility includes both *expertise* (knowledge and skill) and *trustworthiness* (an unbiased approach).
2. The source should present some views already held by the target audience.
3. The more discrepant the views of a credible source and the

audience, the greater degree of attitude change likely. (Social Judgment Theory would maintain that the view presented must be within the latitude of acceptance.)

The Message.

1. Present only one side of the issue to a "friendly group," that is, a group who is not violently opposed to the desired position.
2. Present both sides if the audience is hostile or when the other side will be presented also.
3. Present the most important issue or argument last.
4. Present both a question or problem and a solution; that is, draw an explicit conclusion to your argument.
5. Fear often does not work; however, providing recommendations for action that are explicit and feasible increases its power.
6. Provide an opportunity for overt verbalization or action.
7. Delineate the *reasons* for accepting an attitude as well as providing the attitude itself.
8. Provide incentives for change within the communication.

The Audience.

1. Attempt to lower the ego-involvement of the attitude object, since communications are more readily accepted about low ego-involvement objects.
2. Provide for mental rehearsal of the attitude, or some form of active participation.

Dissonance Theory

Table 4.3 lists the five major conditions under which dissonance can be invoked and lists dissonance reduction techniques. We will list several general approaches that can be used to establish and/or to reduce dissonance. An educator may want to establish dissonance and then reduce it to produce the desired attitude change.

Establishing Dissonance.

1. Create dissonance by setting up decision-making instances. The decisions to be made should involve alternatives that are:
   a. important
   b. attractive, and
   c. with little cognitive overlap.

2. Provide information that is discrepant with already held views and beliefs.
3. Demonstrate the social acceptance (or disagreement) of the desired attitude. If establishing dissonance, the attitude to be formed and the attitude of the group supporting it would be opposite.
4. Induce action that is discrepant with already held views and beliefs.

Dissonance Reducing Techniques.
1. Provide cognitive information that is consonant with the attitude to be altered.
2. Provide alternatives for decision-making.
3. When making a decision, make the chosen alternative very attractive; the unchosen alternative less attractive.
4. Reward behaviors that are congruent with the desired attitude; punish or extinguish undesired behaviors or attitudes.
5. In social situations, use high credibility sources, and refer to groups whose attitudes are congruent with the desired attitude.
6. Make the issue(s) surrounding the attitude object appear important.
7. Provide for free choice situations as often as possible.
8. Establish wide latitudes of acceptance of an issue by using successive approximations.
9. Within the latitude of acceptance, make the persuasive communications as discrepant as possible without being in the range of rejection.

Modeling
1. Establish the model's credibility and reputability.
2. Be sure the learner comprehends and sees the model demonstrating the behavior *and* being reinforced.
3. Have learners role play the desired behavior using an imagined model (Gagné, 1977).

Other Techniques
1. Use group discussions.
2. Provide direct reinforcement for the desired attitude.
3. Set up contiguous situations, e.g., make the environment where the attitude is displayed pleasant and reinforcing.

4. Use the group norms of desirable groups to influence attitudes.

External Conditions for Values Development

The external conditions above refer primarily to attitude change; we have said little about the development of values. Using Cognitive Balancing Theory for this purpose, there are several important external conditions for establishing or altering value systems.

1. Extend the conceptual arena of the learner by establishing relationships between cognitive elements (i.e., actors, means, and ends) and/or issues and other attitude objects.
2. Ask the learner to explain how she/he relates or views the relationships among cognitive elements, issues, and relations.
3. Help the learner establish a superordinate attitude or value structure that links subordinate or inconsistent cognitive elements.

OVERVIEW OF THE EDUCATIONAL TASK

Attitudes and values are such a pervasive force in all our endeavors that the thought of not taking them into consideration during instructional planning and implementation seems absurd. Yet, they are often addressed only tangentially, if at all. It is not difficult to see why so little has been done to try to influence attitudes in instructional situations. There are philosophical considerations, e.g., Is it our job? If yes, which attitudes should we develop, alter, or change? There are practical problems, e.g., What strategies will be most effective? How does one influence an entire group? We have not attempted to answer all these questions, nor have we even posed all the questions that need consideration. What we have done is list a variety of internal and external conditions that may influence attitudes. We believe that an effective attitude change program could be established using these conditions as guidelines. The most effective strategy will surely be one that encompasses many approaches and is continued over time rather than tried once and discontinued. Repetition and delayed exposure will most likely prove to be useful techniques.

In general, the techniques for changing attitudes fall into four major categories: (1) persuasive communications, (2) reinforcement, (3) dissonance production and/or reduction, and (4) modeling. As we shall see in the next chapter, some of these same techniques are used for the development of moral and ethical behaviors.

Considering the complexity of attitude formation and change, summarized in this chapter, the problem of curriculum development for educational institutions appears even more formidable when one considers the following needs:

1. Acquisition of commonly needed information and intellectual and motor skills.
2. Establishment of attitudes, values, and moral and ethical behaviors for survival in society.
3. Development of cognitive strategies useful in continued schooling and in the more self-initiated life-long learning not supported by formal instruction.
4. Development of self-esteem and successful human relationships.
5. Maintaining health and recreational adequacy.
6. Economic and vocational self-sufficiency.
7. Contributing as a citizen to formation of a better society.

In Part III of this book, we make some small contribution by suggesting effective sequences of instruction for a variety of educational and training settings. Then, when designing such sequences and individual lessons, the reader may refer to the various external conditions of learning presented here.

Chapter 5

Developing Moral and Ethical Behavior

**A PLACE FOR MORAL AND ETHICAL BEHAVIOR
IN THE EDUCATIONAL PROCESS**

THREE IDEOLOGIES

The Cultural Transmission Ideology

The Romantic Ideology

The Developmental-Philosophic Ideology

Kohlberg's Theory

**EDUCATIONAL IMPLICATIONS FOR
DEVELOPING MORAL REASONING**

Internal Conditions

External Conditions

CONCLUDING THOUGHTS

Chapter 5

Developing Moral and Ethical Behavior

Unlike the concepts of attitudes and values that always appear in descriptions or taxonomies of the affective domain, the concepts of morals and ethics do not. In addition, while the development of attitudes has been described in at least some models of instructional design (Gagné, 1977; Gagné & Briggs, 1979), the development of moral and ethical behaviors has not. However, as instructional technologists and designers continue to move into instructional planning roles in the areas of medicine, law, and business, the development of professional ethics and moral behavior will require attention. Likewise, rational decision-making in the realm of morals and ethics is valued in schools, although the choice of which moral or ethical behaviors to develop is a difficult and unresolved subject. For these reasons, we have decided to include moral and ethical behaviors as one category of the affective domain and to separate them from attitudes and values.

In general, morality refers to the principles of right and wrong, a conception of right behavior, making a right decision, or conforming to the standards of right behavior. Principles of justice form the core of the concept of morality (Irwin, 1983; Kohlberg & Mayer, 1972; Rawls, 1971). Ethics refers to a set of moral principles, or a theory or system of moral values (*Webster's Dictionary*, 1965). Although the terms morals and ethics are used synonymously, ethics is actually a superordinate category; the relationship is much the same as that between attitudes and values.

145

Irwin (1983) gives three theoretical perspectives for studying moral development: (a) social learning theory stressing moral behavior, (b) psychoanalytic theory stressing moral feelings and guilt, and (c) cognitive-developmental theory stressing moral judgment and reasoning. In this chapter, we will describe a cognitive-developmental position on moral education, and we will derive some instructional implications and strategies for developing moral and ethical behaviors in learners from that perspective. Our focus here is upon two broad areas: (a) the developmental-philosophic ideology, and (b) internal and external conditions that can be derived from the developmental perspective.

First, there are several educational ideologies that suggest ways to enhance the development of moral and ethical behaviors. The one most likely to be used by instructional designers is sometimes referred to as the *Cultural Transmission* ideology (Kohlberg & Mayer, 1972) or a social-learning theory perspective (Irwin, 1983). This position supports direct, planned instruction and objective, testable knowledge. It also supports the transmission of the agreed upon social and moral rules and values of the culture. The diversity and lack of agreement about specific rules in today's society makes this position a difficult one to use, plan for, and implement.

Another ideology, the *Developmental-Philosophic* position, takes the stance that moral and ethical behaviors develop in a series of invariant stages; these behaviors cannot be directly taught, but they can be influenced. Kohlberg's theory of moral development (1969) is the best known theory from the developmental perspective. We here adopt the developmental perspective, and draw upon it for offering our implications for designing materials and learning experiences.

Second, without directly teaching particular values, the developmental-philosophic position suggests instructional conditions that enhance the development of moral and ethical behaviors. These conditions, coupled with conditions of learning from other theoretical perspectives (e.g., the cultural transmission ideology, information-processing theory, and humanistic and behavioral psychology), and from conditions previously established for the cognitive domain, may provide a more comprehensive scheme for instructional planning. In the final section of this chapter, we suggest some learning and instructional conditions that can influence development of ethical and moral behaviors derived from the developmental perspective.

A PLACE FOR MORAL AND ETHICAL BEHAVIOR IN THE EDUCATIONAL PROCESS

Two fundamental criticisms characterize the educational process today. The first is startling facts that reach the public almost daily about students who cannot read, write, compute, or think critically (Boyer, 1983). Some reports suggest that almost 13 percent of all 17-year-olds and approximately 40 percent of minority youths can be considered functionally illiterate (*A Nation at Risk*, 1983). Second, the educational system has been severely criticized by many because of its lack of attention to the overall development of students. This includes not only lack of provision for a climate of self-development, but a concomitant lack of concern about the development of the learner's attitudes, values, and feelings.

Included in the second category of criticisms are discussions about both the appropriateness of and the strategies for developing moral or ethical behaviors in learners. Shaver (1972) points out that schools are assumed to be responsible for improving students' thinking and decision-making abilities, and that this is as true in the realm of values as it is in mathematics and science. He describes three types of values important to schooling about which students should be engaged: esthetic values, instrumental values, and moral values.

Other educators (Bloom, Hastings, & Madaus, 1971; Krathwohl *et al.*, 1964; Scriven, 1966; Smith, 1966) agree that discussions about moral values have a place in schools. (See Johnson, 1982, for a history and review of moral education.) In fact, in many subjects, cognitive knowledge does not have full impact without reference to and discussion of moral values. For example, units on drug and sex education are generally found in schools, and issues such as capital punishment, nuclear war, and chemical warfare are often components of school curricula; discussion centering on moral values can hardly be avoided. At the same time, issues like cheating, stealing, and lying continue to demand both time and attention in schools.

Outside schools, educational programs in business, industry, medicine, law, and the military must also address ethics. In a recent article, Nelson (1983) stated that a major concern in the medical profession is the problem of lack of compassion among physicians in interactions with patients. One step taken to reassert the importance of compassion in medical practice is that educational programs "stressing humane values and ethics have recently been adopted in most of the nation's medical schools" (p. 28).

In other educational programs outside the K-12 curriculum, morals and ethics are being incorporated within courses or are receiving specialized attention. For example, remedial moral education is being conducted in prisons (Mabe, personal communication, November, 1983); some law schools include the philosopher John Rawls' book, *A Theory of Justice*, on reading lists and in classes; the military must educate soliders on matters of compassion to civilians during times of war; and business and industry programs grapple with how to reduce employee theft, graft, and other forms of dishonesty.

Clearly, then, the educational process can hardly avoid questions of morals and ethics. Two of the most important issues facing educators today are (a) what the goals and objectives of the educational process should be, and (b) how to determine the worth of these goals and objectives (Kohlberg & Mayer, 1972). Kohlberg contends that moral education is one of the critical functions of the school. His theory, described in the next section, comes from the developmental-philosophic ideology and from developmental psychology. He believes that his theory and its implications constitute an important and viable approach to the development of morals and ethics.

THREE IDEOLOGIES

Kohlberg and Mayer (1972) describe three streams of educational ideology that make different assumptions about psychological development and the development of values and morals. The three ideologies, Developmental-Philosophic, Cultural Transmission, and Romantic, are summarized and compared across some major dimensions in Table 5.1.

Since one purpose of this chapter is to describe alternative frameworks for conceptualizing the educational process, readers are urged to use Table 5.1 to compare and contrast ideologies. In the following sections, we present a summary of each of the three ideologies that we took from Kohlberg and Mayer (1972). Later on, we present our suggestions as to conditions of learning to be incorporated into instruction.

The Cultural Transmission Ideology

The cultural transmission ideology assumes that what is learned and valued is a collection of knowledge and rules that can be passed on or "transmitted" to learners. The instructor's role is to directly teach these rules and bodies of information. Educational technology is closely associated with this ideology. Although there are different groups within the cultural transmission ideology, i.e., those that emphasize knowledge and values that are central to the culture of western man versus those that emphasize outcomes that are appropriate for helping learners adjust to a technological society, both groups described what is to be learned in terms of a fixed body of knowledge and skills. Moral rules are also fixed, and the goal of educators is to help learners internalize them. External cultural "correctness" is used as the basis for establishing criteria for both cognitive and affective behaviors.

The Romantic Ideology

The basic assumption of the romantic ideology is that children grow and develop naturally and spontaneously into good adults. Educators inclined toward this view endorse increased respect for the rights of the child and great trust in the child's "goodness." Innovative school practices such as free-schools, open schools, humanistic educational programs and schools without walls are some of the outgrowths of this ideology.

There are a number of variations of this view, i.e., some educators focus on the mental health and happiness of the child,

Table 5.1

*Three Streams of Educational Ideology
as They Relate to the Development of Values or Morals*

	CULTURAL TRANSMISSION	ROMANTICISM	DEVELOPMENTAL-PHILOSOPHIC
GOAL OF EDUCATION	To transmit bodies of knowledge, skills, information, and the social and moral rules and values of the culture. Knowledge and values are located in the culture. It is a "culture centered" approach.	To develop the "inner" self; it is the self that gives standards to values and self-development. It is a "child-centered" approach.	To create conditions so that learners will mature and pass through successively higher stages of reasoning and moral development.
VIEW OF THE CHILD'S DEVELOPMENT	Development occurs by internalization of the values and knowledge of the culture.	An innate pattern unfolds; development occurs "naturally"; it is an inborn or hereditary pattern.	Development occurs by progression through an invariant ordered series of sequential stages where the higher stages are superior to the lower stages.
IMPLEMENTA-TION STRATEGIES	Provide adult models or develop through direct instruction; guided learning.	Create an environment for "healthy unfolding" of the individual.	Present resolvable genuine problems or conflicts to be solved; create cognitive conflict.
ETHICAL VALUE POSITION	Social-relativity Use given values of society as a starting point; "adjustment" to the culture is the educational end.	Value-neutral or value-relativity Whatever the child values, accept it.	There are successively higher stages of moral development. Stimulate the development of ethical principles in students.

Table 5.1 (Continued)

	CULTURAL TRANSMISSION	ROMANTICISM	DEVELOPMENTAL-PHILOSOPHIC
PHILOSOPHIES OF SCIENCE— WHAT IS KNOWLEDGE?	Stress knowledge that is "objective" testable, and measurable. Based on "sense-reality"	Existentialism or Phenomenological Based on "inner experience."	Pragmatic—knowledge is "resolved relationship between a human actor and a problematic situation."
PSYCHOLOGI-CAL THEORY OF DEVELOP-MENT	Associationistic-learning, or Environmental-contingency Theory	Maturationist Theory	Cognitive-developmental or Interactionist Theory
MAJOR THEORISTS	Locke, Thorndike, Skinner, Bereiter & Englemann	Rousseau, Freud, Gesell, A.S. Neill G. Stanley Hall	Plato, Hegel, Kant, Dewey, Piaget, Rawls, Hare

Adapted from Kohlberg & Mayer, 1972.

while others address self-actualization, self-realization, and spontaneity. Although natural growth in some direction is expected, a specific standard of development is generally not specified. Critics of this view ask whether the freedom to grow and develop naturally is necessarily a good thing. Dewey (1938) stated, ". . . Hence, it is agreed that 'growth' is not enough; we must specify the direction in which growth takes place and the end toward which it tends" (p. 75). This ideology, then, is viewed by Kohlberg and Mayer (1972) has a value-relative and elitist position because of a "refusal to impose intellectual and ethical values of libertarianism, equal justice, intellectual inquiry, and social reconstructionism on the child, even though these values are held to be the most important ones . . ." (p. 146).

The Developmental-Philosophic Ideology

Educators adhering to this ideology support *ethical universals* and reject socially traditional standards and value-relativity. This ideology is rooted in philosophy and takes the position that there are ethical principles, such as liberty and justice, that can and should determine both the ends and means of education. Unlike the cultural transmission ideology, this view is described as non-indoctrinative because the ethical principles are presumed to develop in a *culturally universal* series of stages that represent successively "advanced or mature stages of reasoning, judgment and action" (Kohlberg & Mayer, 1972, p. 149). Because people prefer higher stages and move toward them, they are not imposed. Moreover, since the stages are hierarchical and develop naturally, attainment of the higher stages is a valid aim of education.

Kohlberg's Theory

Kohlberg derived six (sometimes he reports seven) stages of moral thinking, each qualitatively different from the previous one. He identified these stages by studying how people (men) actually reasoned about moral questions or dilemmas. The six stages fall into three broad categories or levels defined by the "judging" framework the individual uses in responding to or reasoning about moral issues. The three broad levels are: preconventional reasoning, conventional reasoning, and postconventional reasoning.

Reasoning and judgments about moral behavior are reflected in statements the individual makes; these statements are composed of specific types of thinking. For example, at stage 1, the individual's reasoning revolves around the physical consequences of his behavior. At stage 4, the individual's reasoning reflects a desire to follow prescribed rules and laws regardless of the legitimacy of those laws. Below is a brief description of the type of reasoning at each stage. Table 5.2 gives a more complete description.

Stage 1— Statements/judgments are made in reference to avoiding pain and punishment.

Stage 2— Statements/judgments are made in order to get or do what is best for the self.

Stage 3— Statements/judgments are made so others will

know the individual is nice, conforms, and pleases others.

Stage 4— Statements/judgments are made in accordance with the laws and rules of the society. These include religious rules, such as The Ten Commandments.

Stage 5— Statements/judgments about laws or rules are made in terms of their applicability to particular situations; each situation must be examined in order to derive general *ethical principles* for governance.

Stage 6— Statements/judgments are made according to universal ethical principles, e.g., freedom, equal opportunity. These principles are not necessarily written down nor are they necessarily a system of formal laws, as they are in Stage 5.

In general, the research supports Kohlberg's theory, although the possibility of sex bias has been reported since Kohlberg utilized only male participants in his studies.* The cross-cultural studies indicate, however, that there is an invariant sequence of stages, from lower to higher, and that no stage is ever skipped (Sprinthall & Sprinthall, 1977). Moral reasoning, then, develops from the lower to the higher stages, that is, to stages that are more comprehensive and integrated. It is interesting to note that people generally prefer reasoning one stage higher than their own because the higher stage is seen as a more adequate and better system of thought.

Kohlberg's theory is linked closely to Piaget's theory of cognitive development (see Table 5.3). Kohlberg acknowledges that higher levels of moral reasoning are possible only when the cognitive capabilities of formal operational reasoning have been acquired, i.e., the individual has the ability to do abstract thinking and to take the perspective of others. Intellectual and moral development are viewed as parallel aspects of growth. This growth is actually described as a *reorganization* of psychological internal structures. Such reorganization leads to qualitatively different levels of cognitive and moral thought.

---

*Carol Gilligan has not found the same moral reasoning stages in females as Kohlberg found in males. See *In a Different Voice* by Carol Gilligan. Cambridge: Harvard University Press, 1982.

Table 5.2

Kohlberg's Stages of Moral Growth

Basis of Judgment	Stages of Development
Preconventional Moral value resides in the individual and is defined by good and bad acts, external happenings, or hedonistic notions. It is an egocentric level.	*Stage 0* — Premoral *Stage 1* — Punishment/Obedience orientation. Actions are judged in terms of their physical consequences. *Stage 2* — Instrumental hedonism orientation. What can I do for another to satisfy my own needs and desires, i.e., concrete reciprocity.
Conventional Moral value resides in performing the right roles or maintaining the traditional social order. It is an exocentric level.	*Stage 3* — Good person/bad person orientation. The motive is to be accepted and gain approval of others. Conformity to group norms and laws is important. *Stage 4* — Law and order orientation. The motive is on maintaining the social order and keeping the rules of society.
Postconventional Moral value resides in universally accepted principles. The principles are self-selected and directed; they can be applied universally.	*Stage 5* — Social contract, legalistic orientation. Judgment is based on majority will and rule; there are no absolutes. Society changes because it is best for the majority and it reflects the rights of others. It is the morality of contract and democratic law. The U.S. Constitution is written at this stage. *Stage 6* — Universal principle orientation. Judgments are based on an orientation to general principles, e.g., justice, equality, dignity of all people, rather than on specific social rules. Decisions are based on one's conscience, what is right for all people; these are more important than any given law. *Stage 7* — Cosmic or infinite morality. Judgment refers to the self in relation to the unity of the entire cosmos.

Adapted from Zimbardo, P.G., *Psychology and Life*, 10th Edition, p. 245.

Table 5.3

*The Relationship Between Cognitive
and Moral Development*

Piaget: Cognitive Development	Kohlberg: Moral Reasoning
Sensorimotor period (ages 0-2)*	
Preoperational, intuitive thought (about 2-7 years) —The child relies on perception over logic.	*Preconventional* Level (about 3-9 years)** Stages 1 and 2
Concrete Operations (about 7-11 years) —The child relies on. logic over perception. —The child deals in the here and now, i.e., the concrete world.	*Conventional* Level (about 9-14 years) Stages 3 and 4
Formal Operations (early adolescence) —The child can form hypotheses; handle abstract thought. —The child can systematically test hypotheses using combinatorial thinking.	*Postconventional* Level (about 14+ years) Stages 5 and 6

*The ages are approximate—there is considerable variability of development especially in movement from concrete to formal operations.

**Notice the time lag between cognitive and moral thought. Moral reasoning develops only after a given cognitive level is firmly established.

Some estimates indicate that only 50 percent of the adult American population ever fully reaches the final stage of formal operations (cognitive development) and only 5 percent reach the highest stage of moral development (Kohlberg & Mayer, 1972). This indicates that while it is possible to reach the higher stages of moral development without planned intervention, it is by no means inevitable.

EDUCATIONAL IMPLICATIONS FOR DEVELOPING MORAL REASONING

The most important distinction regarding instruction that separates the developmental-philosophic ideology from the cultural transmission ideology is that the developmental group does not believe direct instruction will move an individual from one stage to the next. They do believe that planned instruction can *stimulate* movement to the next highest level; however, this instruction is of a more general nature—it is not highly specific in content or meaning (Kohlberg & Mayer, 1972). Additionally, the developmental educator does not purport to accelerate stage growth, but rather to insure that all adults reach the highest stages.

In view of the fact that only about 5 percent of the population reach the final stage of moral reasoning, it may be possible for educators who support direct, planned instruction to incorporate ideas from the developmental position into instructional sequences for the explicit purpose of stimulating moral development to the higher stages. Rawls (1971), a philosopher who developed a three-stage theory of moral education closely resembling Kohlberg's three major levels, states: "Many kinds of learning ranging from reinforcement and classical conditioning to highly abstract reasoning and the refined perception of exemplars enters into its [moral learning] development" (p. 461).

While we have stressed the work of Kohlberg and Piaget in the preceding summary of the three ideologies, and have tended to take their work as our starting point, we seek now to draw from all ideologies in offering our recommendations for practice.

We now present conditions of learning for developing moral and ethical behaviors. The definitions of internal and external conditions of learning can be found in the Introduction to Part II.

Internal Conditions

The primary internal conditions leading to higher stages of moral reasoning appear to be (a) *cognitive reasoning capabilities*, and (b) *cognitive prerequisites in the form of intellectual skills and verbal information*. First, as described earlier, Kohlberg accepts the fact that higher levels of moral reasoning are dependent on certain cognitive capabilities as described by Piaget (see Table 5-3). Without these capabilities, the individual is unable to attain higher levels of moral reasoning and thinking. We do not describe or outline the development of cognitive reasoning from Piaget's perspective; however, a number of good books exist on the topic (see Flavell, 1963; Ginsberg & Opper 1969; Wadsworth, 1971, 1978).

A second major area of internal conditions includes the availability of necessary *verbal information and intellectual skills* in the learner's working memory. For example, one of the external conditions recommended by Kohlberg is discussions of moral and ethical questions that create cognitive conflict. The learner's *ability to engage in meaningful discussions is at least partly dependent on his knowledge and understanding of the issues at hand*. If a moral dilemma involves the issue of capital punishment or abortion, learners should have the cognitive prerequisites, e.g., facts, data, and perhaps understanding of biological principles and rules, that can influence their reasoning. In addition, they must have the capability to (a) *recognize different points of view including the different wants and needs of individuals*, (b) *identify definitive features of varying perspectives*, and (c) *be able to view things from a multiplicity of perspectives* (Rawls, 1971). Although moral development is based on the *structure* of moral reasoning, not on the *content*, accurate information and essential intellectual skills are important internal conditions that influence reasoning.

In addition to these two major areas of internal conditions, Rawls (1971) suggests that *young children must feel a sense of their own value and worth*. Self-worth, developed primarily by the unconditional love and trust of parents and significant others, leads eventually to self-regulated behavior governed by universal principles (Rawls, 1971). These include a sense of right and justice, a love of mankind, and self-command.

External Conditions

External conditions refer to those aspects of instruction that can be designed to support internal processes. There are several important factors that stimulate moral development; these have considerable bearing on the identification of external conditions.

First, a change in internal structures is dependent on *experience, reflection*, and *interaction* with the environment. Students must, therefore, be actively involved in the learning process and must have the opportunity to engage in a variety of discussions about genuine moral dilemmas or conflicts. Learners must also have the opportunity to examine their experience; it is the *examination* of their experience that is critical.

A second important factor is what developmental educators refer to as "*horizontal decalage*," i.e., the lateral generalization of the "reasoning type" across the range of the stage. The purpose of horizontal decalage is to explore the limits of the reasoning potential of the present stage and guard against partially adequate reasoning. Therefore, it is necessary to provide the learner with a wide variety of examples, conflicts, and problem-solving situations that can be discussed and examined.

A final factor to be considered in deriving external conditions is what developmental moral educators refer to as *+1-stage modeling*. Since students understand and prefer reasoning one stage higher than their present stage, instructors who present views one stage higher than the students' level will encourage understanding of that higher stage and facilitate development toward it. With a large group this is, at best, a difficult requirement since groups of adults and groups of adolescents are often at widely varying stages. However, if a general or common stage can be determined, the instructor or teacher should present ideas and responses one stage higher than the most common stage.

Using these general factors as a basis, the following is a beginning list of the major external conditions that can stimulate reorganization of internal structures and facilitate moral development.

1. Provide *genuine* dilemmas and problem solving situations that cause dissonance. Use newspaper stories, films, books, and everyday occurrences as stimuli.

2. Provide opportunities for role playing where students take another's perspective. Examine the experience by describing different points of view, and the features behind those views (e.g., wants, desires, opinions, etc.). This is particularly important to facilitate movement from conventional to postconventional reasoning.
3. Ask students to choose among alternative courses of action and to support their choices with reasons.
4. Point out discrepancies in the individual's reasoning.
5. Engage learners in a wide variety of moral dilemma discussions. Use as many different examples as possible.
6. Model appropriate behavior, and explain the underlying principles on which the behavior is based.
7. Demonstrate more adequate reasoning by +1 modeling.
8. Enumerate clear and intelligible rules adapted to the individual's level of reasoning and provide reasons for the rules (Rawls, 1971).
9. Create a supportive atmosphere for discussion.
10. Separate drill and practice periods involving basic or background information and skill learning from the discussion period. The former requires detailed feedback; the latter requires the safety of free expression, and a supportive atmosphere encouraging reasoning at a higher level.

These conditions reflect the major factors that stimulate moral development: experience, reflection, interaction, "horizontal decalage," and +1-stage modeling. It is also important to note the highly cognitive nature (as opposed to emotional nature) of these external conditions. Much of what is recommended is intended to increase the learner's ability to handle cognitive information, for example, supporting choices with reasons, and discriminating among situations or people involved in those situations.

Concluding Thoughts

The developmental educator's view of moral development is somewhat parallel to the treatment of cognitive strategies by Gagné (1977) and Gagné and Briggs (1979). They believe that cognitive strategies are not directly taught, but rather are influenced and developed over the course of years by experience and interaction with the environment. They have identified and explained learning conditions that can stimulate growth of cognitive strategies. Well-developed cognitive strategies are viewed as essential elements of the educated person.

In much the same way, influencing the development of morals and ethics is seen as an essential goal of the educational process; failure to attend to this aspect of learning represents a failure of the educational enterprise. The field of instructional design has some extremely worthwhile contributions to make toward planning educational practices (as differentiated from direct instruction) to influence moral development. One of these contributions is the identification of internal and external conditions of learning. Identifying and applying internal and external conditions of learning aimed at the development of moral and ethical behavior can provide a new depth to planned instruction. This contribution, coupled with well-developed media directed toward the same end, is a highly worthwhile task. Its accomplishment will expand the scope of educators by demonstrating how instruction can be designed to influence both the cognitive and affective capabilities of learners.

Chapter 6

Self-Development

ETHICAL AND PUBLIC POLICY ISSUES

PERSONALITY THEORIES

Overview of Personality Theories

Psychodynamic Theories
Behavioral Theories
Social Learning Theories
Humanistic Theories
Summary

Some Issues Related to Instruction

SELECTED PERSONALITY THEORIES OR CONSTRUCTS
HAVING INSTRUCTIONAL IMPLICATIONS FOR
SELF-DEVELOPMENT

The Individual Psychology of Alfred Adler

Student Centered Learning of Carl Rogers

Social Learning Theory

Self-efficacy
Self-regulatory Behavior
Locus of Control

Attribution Theory: Learned Helplessness

EDUCATIONAL IMPLICATIONS

Internal Conditions

External Conditions

CONCLUDING THOUGHTS

Chapter 6

Self-Development

In almost all descriptions of the affective domain or of affective education a concept like self-development appears. If it does not, as for example in the affective taxonomy proposed by Krathwohl *et al.* (1964), the researchers are criticized for excluding a most crucial dimension. Because of the importance of this aspect of the affective domain, we have devoted a complete chapter to self-development, or the personal dimension of the affective domain.

The constructs and terms associated with the personal dimension of the affective domain are as diverse as the researchers and theorists who describe them. In many cases, the term *self* is included as part of the descriptor. Examples include: self-concept, self-esteem, self-consistency, self-efficacy, self-realization, ideal self, creative self, self-system, real self, self-structure, self-confidence, and so on. But there are other terms and constructs that also refer to the personal dimension of the domain. Some of these include: mental health, ego development, personality, creativity, locus of control, personal growth, becoming, and style of life, to name only a few. Although our review of the various taxonomies of the affective domain in Chapter 3 leads us to believe that this essential dimension of the domain could not be overlooked, deciding how to address it from the point of view of instruction was difficult.

Humanistic psychology is largely responsible for the increased awareness of and interest in personal growth and development as a goal of education. The work of Maslow (1962) and Rogers (1969,

1983) was instrumental in highlighting the importance of self-growth and human potential in psychology and in education. Although there are many differences among humanistic psychologists and educators (for example, is self-growth a means to help students achieve greater cognitive growth, or is self-growth an end itself?), the one dominant concept that all humanists share is self-actualization (Allender, 1982). Allender (1982) gives the following definition, "Postulated as a need, [self-actualization] is every human's potential road to creative self-fulfillment" (p. 95). The emphasis, then, of all humanistic education is the development of the whole person, the movement toward self-actualization.

In addition to humanistic psychology, other theories and approaches have also addressed self-development. Many personality theories focus on self-development or some aspect of it (see Massey, 1981), and some of the recent literature from social learning theory and from attribution theory also addresses aspects of self-development.

In view of the fact that our task in this book is (a) to study domain interactions, and (b) close the gap between needs, curriculum, and instruction, we have made some very selective decisions about the theorists and concepts we will cover in this chapter. We have not attempted to give a complete review of the self-development literature; rather, we have selected only parts of the literature. Our choices are defensible primarily because of the instructional implications that can be derived from the few selected theories. However, a case could be made for the inclusion of other theories or constructs that we have omitted.

We have organized this chapter as follows. First, we briefly identify several issues related to the inclusion of self-development goals in any curriculum. Second, we give a very cursory overview of representative personality theories or theory groups; then we identify some basic issues, related to instruction, that influenced our choice of the theories or constructs to be considered further. Third, we describe several theories or constructs with important instructional implications. These include: (a) the individual psychology of Alfred Adler (1956), (b) the student-centered learning of Carl Rogers (1969, 1983), (c) the concepts of self-efficacy and self-regulatory behaviors defined by Albert Bandura (1977a; 1978), (d) the concepts of expectancy, value of reinforcement, and locus of control as discussed by Julian B. Rotter (1975), and (e) the concept of learned helplessness from attribution theory (Abramson, Seligman & Teasdale, 1978). Finally, we conclude this chapter by deriving and listing the internal and external conditions of learning for healthy self-development.

ETHICAL AND PUBLIC POLICY ISSUES

By including this chapter on self-development, we have made an assumption that this is an important aspect or goal of education. Perhaps most would agree. However, the decision to include explicit goals related to self-development in a curriculum raises a number of important issues. We mention only a few of these here.

The first issue concerns the content of the curriculum. If it is the duty of the school (or of training departments in non-school settings) to help students reach their full potential, how should this be accomplished? Should self-development goals be integrated with cognitive goals, or should a separate aspect of the curriculum be developed for this purpose? If a separate aspect of the curriculum is to be developed, what should be included in it, and what should be omitted from the existing curriculum? Our goal in this book is to demonstrate how affective and cognitive goals can be integrated, but even when cognitive and affective goals are integrated, additional classroom time may be required. Unless there are significant changes in the structure of the curriculum and/or the structure of schools (e.g., open classrooms, independent learning centers) some aspects of the existing curriculum may suffer.

A second issue relates to the amount of structure that individual students need or that is required for specific goals. As you will see later, some of the conditions of learning for self-development include opportunities for students to set goals, to evaluate themselves, and to work in independent learning environments. Teachers must certainly impose some limits on students while at the same time encouraging them to assume responsibility for learning. The amount of structure that is needed and that is desirable may vary across content areas, learning activities, individual students, and according to teacher preferences. Providing the right amount of structures places an enormous responsibility on teachers; they must strike a delicate balance between providing too much and too little structure.

Third, if students are to set their own goals, self-evaluate their work and assume responsibility for their learning, they must somewhere learn how to do so. Teachers may prefer to work with students individually to help them set goals, etc., or they may provide "training" in large or small groups. Whatever the choice, teacher and learner time must be devoted to helping students learn to be self-directed.

A fourth issue again involves individual differences. Should students who are low on the self-development dimension be given additional teacher time and energy at the expense of others? What is the best way to help such learners? Should other students be used as peer tutors or counselors to help low self-esteem students make progress both academically and affectively? What are the benefits for both peer tutors and those being tutored? How does a teacher determine when a student needs professional help? These are just a few of the many concerns related to individual differences, and the questions raised are not easily answered. Of course, a teacher should help all students develop to their potential, but this is not an easy goal to achieve.

A final issue relates to teacher training. Should teachers receive different training than they presently do to enable them to develop or foster self-development in learners? If yes, what kind of education should teachers have? For example, should teachers learn how to help students set goals, or should they learn how to adapt or develop and implement individualized programs? Should teacher training include how to teach in an open classroom, and/or how to state, evaluate, and execute affective goals and strategies? In addition, or instead of, the potential teacher training goals listed above, should teachers be taught how to express their own feelings more openly, learn how to be more empathic, and/or be asked to develop a personal philosophy or position concerning the major goals of teaching? Since teachers will themselves have to make value decisions when selecting and implementing educational goals, they will most likely be responsible for finding a personal balance between fostering the traditional goals of education and schooling, and developing more humanistic and affective goals.

There are other issues which could be addressed regarding self-development as a goal of education (e.g., what is the role of the home and church versus the role of the school?); however, we have listed only a few. We believe that teachers and instructors can and do have impact on the self-development of learners, although this goal is often implicit rather than explicit. The conditions of learning we list in the last section of this chapter should be helpful to those teachers who wish to be more explicit about fostering self-development; however, the issues raised above demand attention from individual teachers, teacher training institutions, schools and school systems, education departments in non-school settings, and the larger community. Notice, as you read this chapter, how many of the recommendations made by the various authors and those made by us are related to the issues we raised above. Some of the recommendations would require that significant changes be made in the current educational system and in teacher education programs.

PERSONALITY THEORIES

Overview of Personality Theories

Psychodynamic Theories

Freud's psychoanalytic theory is the oldest of the current personality theories (Draguns, 1982). Freud was primarily interested in the formative events of infancy and childhood, and the unconscious motives that influenced various acts. This orientation led him to link present behavior with past events. A key element in his theory was the explanation of sexual drives. He believed that personality was largely dependent on how important psychosexual experiences were handled and resolved in early childhood (Draguns, 1982).

Freud's theory plus the personality theories of Adler (1956), Jung (1968), Horney (1937), Sullivan (1953), Fromm (1947), and others form the group of theories known as the psychodynamic theories. All of these theories view unconscious determinants of behavior as very important, and they view behavior as guided by complex motivational sources. The particulars of the individual theories vary significantly from one another and from Freud's theory (1964), yet they are all clinically based and they focus on childhood experiences thought to be crucial for personality development (Draguns, 1982).

Behavioral Theories

The behavioral theories are typically concerned with learning theory rather than with personality theory; however, applications of classical and operant conditioning have been made to personality development. There are two groups of behavioral theories, and the primary difference between them revolves around whether one model of learning is sufficient to explain all behavior or whether there is a difference between the two kinds of conditioning. Draguns (1982) gives the following examples: Mowrer (1950) suggests that we learn feelings and emotions through classical conditioning; by operant conditioning we learn motor and other skills. Dollard and Miller (1950), however, suggest one model of learning—cue, drive, response, and reward—for both classical and operant responses.

Social Learning Theories

Social learning theory attempts to integrate behavioral and cognitive theories (Rotter, 1975). Four classes of constructs make up social learning theory variables: behaviors, expectancies, reinforcements, and psychological situations. The general notion is that the probability of a behavior occurring in a particular psychological situation is dependent on the individual's expectancy to receive reinforcement, and the perceived value of the reinforcer (Rotter, 1975). Bandura (1977b), also a social learning theorist, is best known for his hypothesis that learning occurs by imitation and modeling rather than by the trial and error method described by the behaviorists. Social learning theorists differentiate between learning to perform and actual performance. Reinforcement, they believe, is a key element in *eliciting* a performance. We will have more to say about social learning theory in the next section of this chapter.

Humanistic Theories

Draguns (1982) states that the humanistic approaches to personality are best exemplified by Rogers (1959) with his emphasis on the self, and the maintenance and growth of self-concept. We will discuss Rogers' theory in the next section. Other humanistic approaches include Allport (1955) and Maslow (1962). The humanists stress "consciousness, choice, growth to one's full potential, and attention to the total person" (Massey, 1981, p. 267). What mainly differentiates the behaviorists and the humanists is that the former stress the common elements of human beings and animals, whereas the latter focus on the distinctness and uniqueness of each individual (Draguns, 1982).

Summary

Like the attitude change theories discussed in Chapter 4, the results of most of the personality research are inconclusive; in addition, the theories themselves are twenty plus years old (Draguns, 1982). The move toward developing constructs such as locus of control and prosocial behavior, constructs that are outside the purview of traditional personality theories, is viewed by Draguns (1982) as a step in the right direction. These constructs may form the core of newer, more comprehensive, and presumably more useful theories. The movement toward studying personality as an interaction of the person and the situation is viewed as a promising line of inquiry, and most researchers agree that the two must be studied together. However, the relative weights of the two components (person and situation) still spark considerable controversy (Draguns, 1982).

Some Issues Related to Instruction

As we began our search of the personality literature, three issues arose that influenced our choice of which theories and constructs to include, and which to exclude. First, in much the same way that learning theoriess can be viewed as descriptive and instructional theories as prescriptive, personality theories can be described as descriptive or prescriptive. Although the case is not as clear-cut with personality theories as with learning and instructional theories, the distinction does exist. Draguns (1982) states that the psychoanalytic and the psychodynamic theories are primarily oriented toward explanation rather than prediction; social learning theory, on the other hand, emphasizes prediction over description and explanation. The applications of Skinner's radical behaviorism to personality theory are also predictive rather than explanatory.

A second issue we encountered that we deemed very important to our choice of which theories and constructs to select revolved around the nature of the constructs themselves. One primary distinguishing factor is whether a construct can be defined as a state or a trait. A trait is usually thought of as a relatively stable personality characteristic, whereas a state is more flexible and situationally based. Traits, sometimes referred to as dispositions, are the unique arrangement of personality structures and characteristics of an individual. Allport (1961) categorized dispositions as cardinal, central, or secondary depending on their pervasiveness in any given individual. Cardinal traits are highly generalized dispositions which characterize a person's life; central dispositions are less dominant but still influential; secondary traits are more limited and guide specific actions. The point here is that traits are less amendable to influence than are states; cardinal dispositions are more stable than are secondary dispositions. Because we are interested in influencing people during instruction, we are interested in personality constructs that are somewhat flexible.

The final issue, related to the above, revolved around the stability of personality constructs in children and adolescents versus adults. Since instructional designers develop instruction across many age groups, this seemed to be an important issue. Our real question was whether or not children and adolescents and adults require different instructional conditions for healthy self-development. We know, for instance, that their cognitive structures are different, and we know there are developmental differences, but how stable are personality differences under various conditions? We were not able to find much related to this question. Rotter (1975) however did suggest that children may be less influenced than adults by social desirability factors, especially as these factors relate to academic achievement. If this is true, instruction could capitalize on social desirability when it is designed to influence self-development of adults, and it could be minimized when the instruction is designed for children.

Three issues, then, influenced our choice of how to approach self-development, and our choice of which theories and constructs to consider: we wanted (1) *prescriptive* theories with somewhat (2) *flexible constructs* that were relatively (3) *stable across age groups*. The theories and constructs addressed in the next section were selected partly on these three bases.

SELECTED PERSONALITY THEORIES OR CONSTRUCTS HAVING INSTRUCTIONAL IMPLICATIONS FOR SELF-DEVELOPMENT

In this section, we have chosen relevant aspects of several theories to discuss in more detail. The authors of some of the theories make specific references to teaching, learning, or instruction for self-development. Where relevant, we have reported their ideas. For other theories, we have made leaps from counseling or therapy applications to instructional applications. We have adapted this work for our purposes. In still other cases, we used research findings that were not directly related to instruction and applied them to instruction.

Where possible we have also differentiated between implications for children and adults. This has been much more difficult to do than we hoped it would be.

The Individual Psychology of Alfred Adler

There are several basic tenents of Adler's theory (1956) that are directly relevant to our discussion of self-development. First, he believes that individuals strive toward perfection and totality. This is the basic driving force that characterizes all human activity. People tend to move from a position or feeling of inferiority to one of superiority by active adaptation to the outer world. Second, this striving is manifested in the form of a goal, created by the self, and unique to each individual. This goal may not be fully recognized or understood by the individual, but it is there. It is an ideal goal rather than a concrete, real one. This personal goal is the key to understanding each individual. Third, this goal forms the core of a self-consistent personality. Adler refers to this as *style of life*. Finally, the individual is embedded in a social context, and cannot be considered apart from it. Socialization is a key element in Adler's theory; he suggests that it is developed through innate human ability. He calls this ability social interest.

From these basic propositions, Adler makes logical and straight-forward applications to schooling. Adler believed that schools and educators have the enormous responsibility and opportunity to correct, if necessary, and to facilitate the child's adjustment to social life. Children must look positively and happily toward the future, and it is the teacher's responsibility to see that this is so by encouraging the child, and instilling in him faith in his abilities. "An educator's most important task . . . is to see to it that no child is discouraged at school, and that a child who enters school already discouraged regains his self-confidence through his school and his teacher" (Adler, 1956, p. 400).

Adler advises teachers to enhance self-confidence by making the child more independent; he suggests starting with one single accomplishment and encouraging and enticing the child with it. "One must put tasks in their way which they can accomplish, and from the accomplishment of which they can gain faith in themselves" (Adler, 1956, p. 400). He goes on to say that children who are behind can "catch up," and this must be shown to them so that they do not have the mistaken judgment that they cannot accomplish tasks throughout their lives.

Although Adler never explicitly uses the terms successive approximations or reinforcement, both concepts are implied. First, children must have the opportunity to succeed in order to maintain, enhance, or restore their self-confidence. This can be done by the teacher setting tasks which the child can handle. Therefore, breaking complex goals into manageable components might be a useful strategy. Second, Adler states specifically that if we continually tell a child he or she is bad or stupid, we will undermine his or her self-confidence. Reverse or avoid this trend by praising the child and insuring his or her successful attainment of academic subjects.

The key, then, to development of self-confidence, according to Adler, is to arrange the school environment so that children succeed. It is the duty of educators to both plan for children's success and to insure it.

In addition, Adler sees the school as a social organization, and the classroom as a community. He recommends that teachers stress cooperative learning environments and group activities, where the success of one individual benefits all. This, he says, increases the interest of all children and facilitates their development. He also recommends the use of tutors to further enhance cooperative learning among children.

Regarding education and learning, Adler discussed only children and school learning. Adult education, as we perceive it today, was not part of Adler's work. However, he does discuss the problems of old age when describing general life problems. Two points are relevant to education. Feelings of inferiority, he says, arise from a number of factors, one of which is "feelings of intellectual insufficiency." These feelings damage self-esteem, and curb the continued development of older people. Adler recommends two strategies to enhance self-development: (a) provide an opportunity for the aged to expand their interests and occupations, and (b) provide them with opportunities for self-expression.

Self enhancement, then, for Adler revolves around successful achievement and goal-directed behavior. The goal must be external to the individual, that is, it is not a goal of overcoming one's deficiencies, but rather a positive goal of striving for accomplishments. Additionally, the individual should strive to make a contribution for the benefit of all. Schools and other educational institutions are partly responsible for equipping the individual with the abilities to make a contribution, for enhancing self-development by arranging for success, and for developing social interest.

Student-Centered Learning of Carl Rogers

For Carl Rogers (1969, 1983), the aim and purpose of

education is to help students grow and develop into self-actualized individuals. Genuine growth is only possible when students are allowed to select their own goals and are responsible for the accomplishment of them. He believes that the process of goal selection and attainment promotes personal integration and realistic self-assessment.

Like Adler, Rogers believes that individuals gravitate toward growth, health, and adjustment. He also believes that emotions and feelings override intellectual responses, that the present has more influence over people than does the past, and that a therapeutic relationship contributes to the growth experience (Massey, 1981). Although Rogers originally concentrated the majority of his efforts, as a clinical psychologist, on therapy strategies, his background in educational psychology led him to write extensively about education and learning. Many of his ideas about self-growth, however, were first seen in his work with clients. The goal in therapy was primarily one of helping patients feel better about themselves and their adequacy; to promote feelings of self-acceptance and to help them move conceptually closer to their personal definition of "ideal self."

This orientation led Rogers to criticize teacher-directed learning and to propose student-centered learning:

> I have a negative reaction to teaching. Why? I think it is because it raises all the wrong questions. As soon as we focus on teaching, the question arises, what shall we teach? What, from our superior vantage point, does the other person need to know? ... Are we *really* sure as to what they should know? Then there is this ridiculous question of coverage. ... The notion of coverage is based on the assumption that what is taught is what is learned; what is presented is what is assimilated. I know of no assumption so obviously untrue (Rogers, 1983, p. 120).

From this stance, Rogers defines his view of teaching—the *facilitation of learning.* "To free curiosity; to permit individuals to go charging off in new directions dictated by their own interests; to unleash the sense of inquiry; to open everything to questioning and exploration; to recognize that everything is in process of change—here is an experience [facilitation of learning] I can never forget" (Rogers, 1983, p. 120).

For Rogers, the purpose of education is to facilitate learning in such a way that the whole person is developed. He believes that the educated person is one who knows how to learn, can adapt and change, and understands that knowledge is in a continual state of flux. The teacher, therefore, does not instruct, but rather arranges the conditions so that learning occurs. Rogers also believes that the content of learning is less important than the process of learning; however, he does not dismiss content as unimportant. It is merely secondary to the process of learning and to the process of becoming a fully-functioning individual.

Rogers offers concrete ways to "encourage self-initiated, significant, experiential, and 'gut-level' learning by the whole person" (Rogers, 1983, p. 121). He lists nine features of the person-centered mode of education. The first is essential and without it the others matter little:

1. The leader or facilitator must trust the learners to think for themselves, and to learn for themselves.
2. The leader must share with the learners the responsibilities for learning.
3. The leader must provide both human and material resources for sustaining the learning process.
4. The learner must develop his or her own learning plan, including both what to learn and what resources to use. (This can be done in cooperation with others.)
5. A climate of caring, sharing, and understanding must be provided.
6. The content of learning must be secondary to the process of learning.
7. The discipline for attaining one's goals must be the responsibility of the learner, not the teacher.
8. The evaluation of learning must also be the learner's responsibility.
9. A facilitative climate promotes deeper, more rapid learning, and is more pervasive in the life of the individual (Rogers, 1983, pp. 188-189).

To summarize, the key ingredients of Rogers' student-centered learning model are: (a) provision for self-initiation, self-direction, and self-evaluation, (b) unconditional positive regard for and trust of the learner, and (c) a facilitating climate.

Rogers gives several specific ways teachers can promote self-directed learning. These include providing real and meaningful problems to be solved, providing resources, using contracts that help students set goals and plan their activities, using the resources of the community, and encouraging peer teaching and tutoring. He also recognizes that not all learners can be initially self-directed and, therefore, recommends dividing the class into groups and directing those that choose to be directed. "If students are free, they should be free to learn passively as well as to initiate their own learning" (Rogers, 1983, p. 154). Programmed learning, he says, is a viable way to direct learning and is also a useful tool for students to use in filling the gaps in their knowledge bases.

Weil, Joyce, and Kluwin (1978) have adapted Rogers' work and refer to it as the Nondirective Model. Not only do they give an overview of the theory on which the model is based, they also describe the role of both the student and teacher in the nondirective interview. They list the skills teachers need to develop in order to use this nondirective counseling model, including: nondirective lead taking, nondirective responses to feelings, semidirected responses to feelings, and directive counseling moves (Weil *et al.*, 1978). Some specific skills teachers must learn are (a) to accept and reflect on students' feelings, (b) to help students choose and develop an interview topic, and (c) to ask open-ended questions. (See Weil *et al.*, 1978, for a complete discussion of Nondirective Teaching.)

In summary, the goal of education according to Rogers is the development of fully-functioning persons. There is never an end point as such; the learner is always in a fluid state. Such a person is self-directed, realistic, creative, and always in the process of self-discovery. Although Rogers recognizes this as an ideal, theoretical goal, he believes educators should help learners move in this direction. He believes that the facilitating conditions he prescribes for education—a climate for self-direction and growth—can be designed to help all people reach their potential. We assume that the goals of education and the facilitating conditions that Rogers describes are applicable for all learners—children, adolescents, and adults.

Social Learning Theory

Self-efficacy

Self-efficacy, according to Bandura (1977a), is "the conviction that one can successfully execute the behavior necessary to produce outcomes" (p. 79). He differentiates between self-efficacy and "outcome expectancy" by defining the latter as the prediction that a certain behavior will facilitate a particular result. The former is a *belief* that one can actually produce the necessary behavior that will lead to a desired outcome.

Other theorists have also defined and used the construct of self-efficacy; however, there are important differences between their conceptions and that of Bandura (Bandura, 1977a). In general, the social learning perspective views self-efficacy as: (a) a behavior of *choice* rather than as a drive motive; (b) a behavior that arises from an information base of direct or mediated experiences; and (c) a "coping capability" that takes into account the situation and the task; it is not viewed as a global personality trait (Bandura, 1977a).

The importance of self-efficacy to our discussion of self-growth is based on Bandura's hypothesis that self-efficacy corresponds closely to behavior change, that it enhances one's chances for success, and that it affects one's ability to cope once behavior is initiated. That is, as one's perceived self-efficacy increases, the probability for success at a task and the potential for maintaining effort toward a task also increases. Hence, self-efficacy in a classroom or other learning environment could lead to potentially higher performance, which in turn could lead to positive feelings toward the self. "Efficacy expectations determine how much effort people will expend, and how long they will persist in the face of obstacles and aversive experiences. The stronger the perceived self-efficacy, the more active the efforts" (Bandura, 1977a, p. 194).

Expectations of personal efficacy are based on four sources of information: (a) performance accomplishments, (b) vicarious experiences, (c) verbal persuasion, and (d) physiological states. Performance accomplishments are the most influential of the four sources of information (Bandura, 1977a). In general, performance accomplishment refers to personal mastery experiences, those experiences where the individual experiences success. Not only do these mastery experiences influence present perceptions of self-efficacy, they also tend to generalize to other situations.

Vicarious experiences are also useful for increasing self-efficacy, although they are not as successful as direct performance success. Vicarious experiences include a variety of forms of modeling. Models who are similar to the learner, who have salience, i.e., perceived value, and who are engaged in experiences that actually show the model's success at the task or behavior convey the most efficacy information.

Verbal persuasion has definite limitations because people are not readily persuaded to believe in their own success if they have a history of failure (unless that failure is attributed to external factors beyond their control). However, verbal persuasion can have some effect, especially if it is repeated over time and coupled with some performance mastery.

Emotional arousal can lead to decreases in efficacy because fear, high anxiety, and other stressful conditions can debilitate performance. Bandura (1977a) recommends a cognitive approach to relieving emotional arousal—change the individual's perceived self-competence by providing information related to his or her success, if it is possible; or simply acknowledge the individual's arousal.

The key to increased self-efficacy seems to lie in successful performances on tasks; these successes will have a greater chance of influencing the individual if they are perceived to be the result of skills, abilities, and personal effort rather than the result of luck. Efficacy will also be stronger if success is perceived to be the result of ability rather than effort unless high ability reduces the need to expend very much effort. Likewise, a challenging task, successfully completed, increases self-efficacy more readily than an easy task (Bandura, 1977a). Finally, graduated progress increases self-efficacy more than a success followed by a plateau or leveling off of performance.

Self-efficacy appears to be a powerful and useful construct to enhance self-development. Facilitating the belief that one can succeed, through performance accomplishments, and that the success is attributable to one's self, increases the possibility of future success, which, in turn, enhances self-development. Using techniques like successive approximations (graduated tasks) to ensure high performance on tasks of varying difficulties, and providing successful and salient models in cooperative learning environments are potential strategies for increasing efficacy. We believe that arranging the conditions for success is in the range of possibilities in most instructional situations.

Self-regulatory Behavior

Social learning theory emphasizes the interacting influences of cognition, behavior, and the environment in psychological functioning. The causal processes among the three influences are referred to as *reciprocal determinism* (Bandura, 1978). Because of these interacting influences, the "self-system" is viewed by social learning theorists as having considerable influence over self-regulating functions. Hence, individuals can plan, regulate, and control their own behavior. "By altering their immediate environment, by creating cognitive self-inducements, and by arranging conditional influences for themselves, people can exercise some influence over their own behavior. An act therefore includes among its determinants self-produced influences" (Bandura, 1978, p. 345).

Since people can influence their self-direction, they can direct their experiences and their lives by exercising some control over their behavior. We are assuming that such control is beneficial for self-development because it provides an avenue by which each person can attain his or her potential.

Cognition plays a major role in determining what the individual perceives, how he or she evaluates his or her behavior, and how he or she regulates behavior. Bandura says that the four processes of direct experience, vicarious experience, judgments from external sources, and logical verification of experiences influence self-directing behavior. For example, the way one judges his or her behavior is largely dependent on one's personal standards. Likewise, self-evaluations vary depending on how significant a behavior is for a given individual, and the degree to which an individual believes his or her behavior is dependent on his or her abilities and/or the effort expended (Bandura, 1978). Therefore, altering one's cognitions can change self-regulatory patterns.

There are several ways people can self-direct their own behavior. The primary means is through providing incentives for themselves. However, an application of modeling is also an important means. Seeing valued or salient others regulate their behavior is a viable way to increase one's own self-regulating behaviors.

Self-managed behavior can also be learned through instruction (Bandura, 1978). The major behaviors to be learned are: how to set realistic goals, how to evaluate one's performance, how to select incentives and rewards, and how to manage contingencies. Once these behaviors are learned and employed, and self-regulation is viewed as possible, the change in perceived self-efficacy influences further self-direction (Bandura, 1978).

By learning self-regulating behaviors, people can increase positive self-regard, gain and maintain control over their behavior, and direct, manage, and even determine their future. Such possibilities can have enormous influences on self-esteem and self-development. "Within the process of reciprocal determinism lies the opportunity for people to shape their destinies as well as the limits of self-direction" (Bandura, 1978, p. 357).

Locus of Control

Perceived locus of control is another construct from social learning theory that has implications for self-development. Rotter (1975) states that the original interest in the locus of control concept was to help explain how reinforcements altered expectancies.

External locus of control refers to those conditions in which an individual is reinforced for something over which he or she preceives little control, for example, when luck or chance occurrences intervened. Internal locus of control refers to those situations in which the individual perceives that his or her own skills, abilities, and efforts were the dominant influencing factor in receiving reinforcement. Studies have shown that those individuals who attribute their rewards to skill (internal) rather than luck (external), are more likely to alter their expectancies in a positive direction (Massey, 1981). The concepts of internal and external control, therefore, refer to an individual's *perceptions* about the reinforcements that he or she receives.

Locus of control is a generalized expectancy model. It has been used somewhat successfully to predict academic achievement/success in children (Rotter, 1975). Shama (1984) points out several issues that must be kept in mind regarding this model:

1. Expectancy *per se* is not affected by reinforcement, but rather the *magnitude of change* in expectancy is the variable that is influenced.
2. Greater changes in expectancy occur for individuals who perceive an *internal* locus of control.
3. The more *novel* a situation is (without it being perceived as random) the more likely it is that the individual will generalize the expectancy. Generalized expectancy plays a less important role in familiar situations.
4. An individual must *value* the reinforcement for it to be effective. Internal locus of control alone is not a sufficient predictor of behavior; an individual must perceive that the reinforcer is important and has value for him or her.

We included this section on locus of control for two reasons: (a) different age groups are differentially affected by preceived locus of control, and (b) if academic success does generalize to similar situations (which Rotter, 1975, claims it does), then a generalized expectancy for success may aid in healthy self-development. However, there is real concern by many educators and researchers that the locus of control model is not as adequate as are some other positions, e.g., attribution theory (see Weiner, Nierenberg & Goldstein, 1976).

First, regarding age differences, Rotter (1975) states that there is greater predictive power of academic success (using locus of control) with young children than with college age students. Presumably this is because younger children come into contact with more novel, ambiguous situations than do older learners. Even though a great many achievement situations may be novel for students of all ages, Rotter (1975) states ". . . by the time the student is in college, he knows pretty well what the relationship is for him between effort, studying, etc., and grades. What will differentiate his behavior from that of another student with the same ability is apparently the level of motivation or the value placed upon academic reinforcements versus other reinforcements that are competing" (p. 60). For the older learner, then, the value of the reinforcer and motivation may be more important than other factors (locus, expectancy, etc.) since these older students have had more experience determining how achievement, effort, and luck interact in personal learning situations. Younger students, on the other hand, are still learning to attribute their successes to internal and external factors.

Rotter also states that the effects of social desirability factors on academic success varies across age groups. It appears that social desirability factors are less important for younger children than for college students, although there is some evidence to suggest that even children are influenced by social desirability, particularly in the area of academic achievement. He further suggests that throughout the schooling experience, schools promote the social desirability of internal locus of control. Over time, the social desirability of internal control increases.

With respect to age differences, then, younger learners may be more influenced by internal attitudes and novel, ambiguous, and less structured situations, and less influenced by social desirability factors of internality than are college age learners. College age learners appear to be more influenced by the value of academic achievement rewards, and their individual level of motivation.

Second, if success is a factor in promoting self-development, then the fact that an expectancy for success can generalize across similar situations may aid in self-development. Rotter (1975) states that the more experiences an individual has with success the more that success experience will generalize to other situations that the individual perceives as similar. Therefore, with successful experiences, the magnitude of expectancy for success increases in similar experiences.

In summary, it appears, especially for children, that the perception that abilities (internal) are more influential than are luck or chance (external) in achievement performance leads to a generalized expectancy for success. Arranging instructional conditions so that children and adolescents succeed and can attribute success to their abilities and efforts, may therefore positively affect self-development. The reinforcing aspects of success may also generalize to other situations and may further influence healthy self-development. For college students, capitalizing on reinforcements of high value to them may be more influential than internality.

Attribution Theory: Learned Helplessness

Learned helplessness is an individual's belief that outcomes are uncontrollable. It is related to but conceptually distinct from self-efficacy and locus of control. All three constructs focus on expectancy to some degree; however, self-efficacy highlights social influences, whereas locus of control provides a psychological view (Massey, 1981). Learned helplessness also offers a psychological explanation; however, Abramson, Seligman & Teasdale (1978) state that locus of control and learned helplessness are orthogonal, or statistically independent, constructs.

Learned helplessness researchers have hypothesized that an individual's inability to control outcomes results in three types of deficits—cognitive, motivational, and emotional. The cognitive deficit revolves around expectancies and thus retards later learning; the motivational deficit revolves around failure to initiate a response; and the emotional deficit revolves around depressed affect (Abramson *et al.*, 1978).

A number of learned helplessness studies have been conducted on both animals and humans; many of the studies on humans have examined the relationships between helplessness and depression, i.e., depressed affect. Our interest in learned helplessness revolves around its effects on self-esteem, not depression, although low self-esteem and depression are often related. We therefore give an overview of learned helplessness only as it relates to lowered self-esteem.

Researchers have differentiated between personal and universal helplessness. Personal helplessness refers to situations in which an individual believes he or she has no control over outcomes, but that other people do have control over the same or similar outcomes. Universal helplessness, on the other hand, is the belief that neither he or she nor any other individual has control over an outcome. Personal helplessness is highly dependent on social comparison, that is, evaluating the self in relation to relevant others. If others succeed, where he or she has failed, an individual's self-esteem is diminished. Failing implies that an individual has been unsuccessful in performance output where others have been successful. It has been empirically demonstrated that lowered self-esteem occurs only in personal, not universal, helplessness (Abramson, *et al.*, 1978).

Another aspect of helplessness relates to the type of attributions an individual makes. There are four dimensions: internal-external, stable-unstable, global-specific, and controllable-uncontrollable. Internal, stable, global, controllable attributions produce the most lowered self-esteem effects in failure (but not in success) situations. For example, if a student believes his or her failure is due to lack of ability or effort (internal), self-esteem will be lowered. Likewise, if an individual believes that in most future situations (global), he or she will be unable to alter the outcome (stable), self-esteem will suffer. (Notice that none of the external attributions produce lowered self-esteem.) Internal, global, and stable attributions lead to an expectancy that increases the possibility that future self-esteem will be negatively affected. (We will discuss attributions again in Chapter 7.)

Fortunately, researchers believe that helplessness can be altered and prevented by providing an individual with success experiences (Abramson, *et al.*, 1978). Not only can success* (and even recalling successful experiences in some instances) reverse or alter helplessness, but initial success on a task can also prevent the individual from making global attributions. (In a failure situation in which an individual perceives that he or she has control, for example, the amount of effort expended, negative feelings such as self-blame, self-criticism, and guilt are more likely to occur.) When events are viewed as uncontrollable, self-esteem is not likely to suffer. Shifting the attribution from uncontrollable to controllable in success situations, and vice versa in failure situations, should help alleviate helplessness.

Abramson, *et al.* (1978) give four strategies or treatments for reducing depression based on the learned helplessness hypothesis.

---

*The success must be *perceived* by the *individual* as success and the success must be attributed to one's own abilities, skills, and/or effort.

We have adapted them for self-development in instructional and learning situations:

1. Arrange the environmental contingencies so that the probability of success is higher.
2. Help the learner set realistic goals and expectations and help him/her reevaluate goals that are unattainable. For example, the desire to be valedictorian or to go to Harvard is unrealistic for most students. Help the student find a suitable alternative goal.
3. Alter expectations from uncontrollable to controllable in success situations, and vice versa in failure conditions.
   a. When skills and abilities are not present in learners, provide them so that students have some measure of control over their performance on a task.
   b. When a student already has necessary skills, change the expectation from failure to success by: using graduated tasks, reminding the learner of previous successes, and focusing on effort expenditures rather than ability deficits.
4. Change unrealistic attributions.
   a. When dealing with failure, alter the person's unrealistic attributions toward those that are external, specific, and unstable. For example, help the learner see that his failure was due to a one-time poor performance on a test that was extremely difficult (of course, this must be true).
   b. When dealing with success, change unrealistic attributions toward internal, global, and stable attributions.

The learned helplessness literature gives another view of the effects of failure and success, attributions, and expectancies on self-development and self-esteem. In general, if a learner perceives that success is due to his or her abilities and effort rather than luck or chance, the learner's expectancies for future success will increase, and self-esteem will also increase.

EDUCATIONAL IMPLICATIONS

The similarity of prescriptions for healthy self-development and self-esteem across the theories we have reviewed are indeed striking. Regardless of theoretical base or philosophical position, the one outstanding and overriding condition for enhancing self-development is *providing for success.** Although this does not necessarily mean only academic success related to subject matter or content, we see this as an important factor in instructional and learning environments. Success in areas such as (a) setting and achieving both academic and non-academic personal goals, (b) having positive interpersonal relationships, and (c) successfully managing time and resources are also important and can be planned for and implemented in instructional situations.

Blocher (1982) reports the results of a six-year study that corroborates the importance of academic and social success. He states that one of the most important factors in promoting mental health in children lies in their educational competence, and its recognition and approval by the classroom teacher. "The implications of this finding clearly seem to be that a primary mental health function of schools is to insure that all children master basic educational and social tasks and are given warm and personal recognition for doing so" (p. 1215). He goes on to say that the ability to reason, solve problems, make decisions, and form judgments about social and moral issues are essential for self-satisfaction and satisfaction of life in general.

Maslow (1962) and Bloom (1976) concur. For Maslow, learning to choose wisely and direct oneself are essential components for healthy self-development. Bloom focuses on academic competence. He says that a low academic self-concept increases the probability that an individual will have a low general self-concept (see Chapter 3 for more about Bloom's conception of the development of a low self-concept).

Using the theories and ideas discussed above, we now provide

---

*A literal interpretation of Rogers' work would not allow us to make this statement as strongly as we have regarding academic success, *per se*; Rogers is more concerned with a learner's success in learning how to learn and with helping students develop feelings of personal adequacy. We maintain that learning how to learn is an important component of academic success, and that both lead to feelings of personal adequacy. Perhaps we have, however, put more emphasis on academic competencies, *per se*, than Rogers would.

internal and external conditions of learning for self-development. Refer to the Introduction to Part II for the definitions of internal and external conditions of learning.

Internal Conditions

The internal conditions for self-development are primarily cognitive. Since self-development is so highly dependent on success and performance mastery related to both academic and non-academic tasks, the most important internal conditions are the *intellectual skills and knowledge necessary for achieving success.* If these do not exist in the learner, instructors will have to provide for them.

Several categories of intellectual skills are necessary. First, *intellectual skills for academic mastery in the form of rules and concepts* are required. In the early grades, math and reading skills are essential for adequate performance on many school related tasks. If these skills are not mastered, older students and adults will suffer. The incidence of functional illiteracy and its related problems of unemployment, and dependence on governmental and social agencies is a case in point.

A second category of *intellectual skills are those related to setting realistic goals, self-evaluation, and managing time and resources.* Since independence and the belief that one can "shape his or her own destiny" are important for self-development, students must have the intellectual skills necessary to set goals and evaluate their own performance. In addition, students must possess *skills related to finding and using resources.* Library skills, research skills, and organizational skills are but a few examples.

Other intellectual skill areas include: (a) *skills related to interpersonal relationships,* such as listening, paraphrasing, sharing, etc.; (b) *skills related to self-management such as identifying rewards, and contingency situations;* and (c) *the ability to identify a relevant role model(s).*

Cognitive strategies and *meaningful information* are also important internal conditions. For example, students must be able to discern the relationship between their actions and the results of that action. Likewise, they must have the necessary prerequisite knowledge, e.g., information, data, and facts, to make good choices and to succeed.

External Conditions

Three major categories of external conditions seem to override all others. The first and most important is the *provision for success*; the second is *provision for self-directed behavior*; the third is *provision for social interaction*. We have listed these three below with some accompanying strategies, and we have listed a few other external conditions.

1. Provide the conditions for academic mastery and success.
   a. Stress the learner's abilities; skills and effort rather than referring to external variables not under the learner's control.
   b. Graduate tasks so that students achieve. Use of successive approximations is a possible strategy.
   c. Provide the human and material resources necessary to accomplish various tasks.
2. Foster independence by providing the conditions for self-directed behavior.
   a. Provide opportunities for students to set their own goals and evaluate their performance.
   b. Encourage students to use self-rewarding techniques, e.g., selecting rewards and managing contingencies.
3. Provide conditions for cooperative learning and social interaction.
   a. Use peer teaching and tutoring to promote academic success and interpersonal relations.
   b. Provide opportunities for interaction with the instructor and with other learners. Although independence in learning situations is an important goal, the ability to interact with others and to share and cooperate is also important.
4. Provide an atmosphere of acceptance of the learner; demonstrate positive regard and trust of the learner.
5. Praise and reinforce the learner and his abilities and effort.
6. Select and use models who are successful and self-directed. Also use models with whom the learner can identify.

7. Use real and meaningful problems for discussion and for solutions.

CONCLUDING THOUGHTS

The influence of cognition on the affective category of self-development is as pronounced as it was for the categories of attitude development and moral development. For self-development, cognitive prerequisites for mastery are essential. These include all varieties of intellectual skills and knowledge related to academic performance, interpersonal relationships, and self-development. The work of Derry (1984) on learner strategies training and the work of Sternberg (1983) on intellectual training may have important implications for helping students become independent and successful learners.

Although the conditions and strategies we have included are presumably applicable for both younger and older learners, we assume that early success strategies will have the most pronounced influence on self-development. Fortunately, however, as the learned helplessness literature has shown, low self-concepts and poor self-development can be altered, even reversed. There seems to be little doubt, therefore, that instructional designers can have an enormous influence on self-development by appropriately arranging for the internal and external conditions we have identified.

Chapter 7

Other Dimensions of the Affective Domain: Emotional Development and Feelings, Interest and Motivation, Social Development and Group Dynamics, Attributions

EMOTIONAL DEVELOPMENT AND FEELINGS

Teaching of Emotions

The Relationship of Cognition to Emotions

Cognitive Appraisal Theory
Gray's Theory
Child Development

Conditions of Learning for Emotional Development

Internal Conditions
Understanding one's own emotions
Understanding another's emotions
External Conditions

INTEREST AND MOTIVATION

An Overview of Topics, Theories, and Issues Associated with Motivation

Keller's Motivational Design Model

Conditions of Learning for Interest and Continuing Motivation

Internal Conditions
External Conditions

SOCIAL DEVELOPMENT AND GROUP DYNAMICS

Taxonomy of Social Purposes of Public Schools

Social Competence

Conditions of Learning for Social Competence

Internal Conditions
External Conditions

ATTRIBUTIONS

Some Issues Related to Attribution Theory

Educational Implications and Conditions of Learning

Internal Conditions
External Conditions

SUMMARY

Chapter 7

Other Dimensions of the Affective Domain: Emotional Development and Feelings, Interest and Motivation, Social Development and Group Dynamics, Attributions

The affective domain can be characterized by many different components as shown in Chapter 3. In Chapters 4, 5, and 6 we have described conditions of learning for three components of the affective domain that are important and dominant in the literature: attitudes and values, morals and ethics, and self-development.

In this chapter, we discuss briefly and provide relevant conditions of learning for four additional components of the affective domain. It is quite possible and likely that some of these dimensions are correlated with each other and with the components discussed earlier. We have, nevertheless, addressed them as separate entities.

To be consistent with the other chapters in Part II, we discuss each of the components in this chapter as goals or outcomes of instruction. So, like attitudes and values, morals and ethics, and self-development, we discuss emotions and feelings, interest and motivation, social development and group dynamics, and attributions as potential instructional goals. In later chapters, we will discuss the components of the affective domain as instructional means, inputs, supporting prerequisites, and/or learner entry characteristics. In this section, however, we address each component as an instructional end product.

EMOTIONAL DEVELOPMENT AND FEELINGS

Instead of separating feelings and emotions into two categories we have combined them because of our focus on integrating cognition and affect. Although emotion has been variously defined as a subjective feeling state, a motivational state, and a physical state, we have adopted the following cognitive definition of emotion: emotions are physical feelings coupled with cognitive evaluations. Emotions are the cognitive judgments or appraisals that an individual makes that relate to or give meaning to feelings. Our working definition is similar to the two-component theory of emotion, which states that emotions vary on two dimensions, intensity and quality. The intensity dimension refers to physiological arousal and is a necessary but not sufficient condition for emotion. The quality dimension is determined by cognitive clues taken from the environment and interacts with the physiological component to give meaning to the emotion (Schachter & Singer, 1962).

Emotions, then, according to the two-component theory, are complex cognitive processes (evaluations) coupled with physiological arousal. Both components are present (although the physiological dimension may be real or only believed to be real), and the components interact. The cognitive component, however, plays an essential role in emotional expression; it gives meaning to physiological arousal.

The number of terms associated with emotions and feelings is vast. Several basic emotions have been identified, although the exact number varies from researcher to researcher. Generally, at least these seven are considered basic emotions: fear, anger, happiness, sadness, surprise, disgust, and distress. Using the two-component theory, one can see through various terms used how the intensity dimension and the cognitive evaluation (quality) dimension interact. For example, associated with the emotion *happy* are the following words on some rough continuum from strong to mild: thrilled, overjoyed, elated, delighted, cheerful, wonderful, glad, pleased, and satisfied.

Teaching of Emotions

Two main issues arise when planners begin to think of emotional development as a goal of education or training. First, are emotions states or traits? Second, are emotions innate or learned?

With regard to the first issue, researchers think of emotions as both states and traits. On one hand, situations change, influencing how we feel (e.g., seeing a large snake frightens some people); however, once the situation changes, so does the emotion. This is the more transient state conception of emotions. On the other hand, a happy-go-lucky person is an example of the trait conception of emotion, that is, emotion as a more stable individual characteristic.

The prevailing notion with regard to emotions as innate or learned is that both elements are involved. "Recent analyses have moved away from an 'either-or' debate. . . . There may be genetic determinants of the basic emotions that are found universally, but differences in their expression may be due to experience, social setting, and culture" (Zimbardo, 1979, p. 403).

The position taken by Romiszowski (1981) is that it is a moot point whether or not we can teach feelings. What is important, he says, is that we can "transfer, or attach, certain specific feelings or emotions to certain specific objects, events, or people" (p. 225). By Pavlovian conditioning, i.e., pairing stimuli, we can and do evoke positive or negative feelings to learning, to specific subjects, specific events, and so on. Likewise, he says, educators can use operant conditioning principles to reinforce positive feelings and emotions.

We take the position that emotional development is amenable to instructional influence, and hence, deserves our consideration.

The Relationship of Cognition to Emotions

We here give briefly three different positions on the relationships between cognition and emotions. First, we describe cognitive appraisal theory; next, we discuss Gray's theory of emotional/cognitive structures; finally, we note the role of cognitive development in the development of children's emotions.

Cognitive Appraisal Theory

Cognitive appraisal theory is really two theories, one an extension of the other. The basic premise is that an individual evaluates or appraises the importance of a stimuli, and that it is this appraisal that determines the emotion. Arnold (1960, cited in Zimbardo, 1979) described a four-step process to explain his appraisal theory: (a) perception of the stimuli; (b) evaluation of the stimuli as good, bad, or neutral; (c) expression of the emotion (through facial features, gestures, etc.) sometimes organized as an approach or an avoidance; and (d) action.

Lazarus (1968, cited in Zimbardo, 1979) extended this theory to make the appraisal step more explicit. He described primary and secondary appraisal. The former refers to judging the stimuli; the latter to determining how to cope with the judgment made. In threatening situations, for example, an individual could cope by taking direct action or by reassessing the situation to reduce the negative emotional state.

Gray's Theory

William Gray is a psychiatrist who has proposed a theory that states that feelings and emotional nuances (complex feeling-tones) form, link, and code thought (Ferguson, 1982a). Gray contends that emotional nuances are the organizing structure for thought and knowledge, with cognitive structures having a much less important role to play. Paul LaViolette is a systems theorist who has translated Gray's theory into a brain theory that describes how information is handled. The Gray-LaViolette theory, called ECS (emotional/cognitive structures), integrates the role of feeling and thinking.

Sommers (cited in Ferguson, 1982a) has conducted research that gives some validity to ECS theory. Her research concluded that there is a correlation between an individual's range of emotions and his or her cognitive structures. Rather than the highly emotional individual being flighty and impulsive, Sommers' data indicates that highly emotional people have advanced cognitive organization.

With regard to learning and education, Gray suggests that ignoring feelings may actually retard efficiency in learning. He states that emotional codings are "more easily and rapidly dealt with than the information they represent" (Ferguson, 1982b, p. 4). Therefore, it is as important to be aware of the emotional nuances of thoughts as it is the informational aspects. Learners should be able to identify not only their feelings toward something they like or dislike, but also the variations in intensity and quality. Gray further links emotions and creativity by stating that "emotions are the hidden source out of which the creative process grows" (Ferguson, 1982b, p. 2).

The ECS model proposes that emotions may be the key to more advanced cognitive organization. An individual may therefore have to learn to respond with more emotion, rather than learning to control emotion. This can be accomplished by providing role situations where learners have to take many different perspectives and quickly alter their evaluations and emotions. "To respond with more emotions may thus require particular cognitive endeavors: to recognize the [limits] of one's own viewpoint and to search for further information by which to evaluate a situation" (Ferguson, 1982a, p. 3). New information provides a different basis on which to appraise a situation and thus facilitates the transformation of an emotion.

Child Development

Several authors have linked the emotional development of children to Piaget's stages of cognitive development (Fogel, 1982). Hoffman (1975, cited in Fogel, 1982) states that emotional maturity requires formal operational thinking. In order for children to understand their own emotions and feelings, and those of others, they must have the ability for abstract thinking; without these abilities, children are unable to conceptualize emotional experiences. Similarly, the emotions of shame and guilt require the ability to represent oneself and to associate one's actions with the self (Fogel, 1982). Therefore, complex emotional states require as prerequisites formal operational thinking.

Gilbert (1969) conducted a study in which she asked children to talk about their affective states, and she asked their teachers to rate each child's emotional expressiveness. She found that *affect-aware* children were more verbal, more imaginative in play, more expressive in the number of emotions displayed, and more empathic. Perhaps this corroborates the propositions of Gray and LaViolette that a wider range of emotional nuances is strongly linked to more highly organized cognitive structures.

Conditions of Learning* for Emotional Development

The information we have presented on the relationships between emotions and cognitive development is certainly not conclusive, yet there is some evidence to suggest that emotional development and cognition are linked. Unless one is thinking of a purely physiological response, cognitive understanding and appraisal have a role to play in emotional expression if not in emotional development. Since our interest is in instructional situations, we will focus on emotions as learned states, not as innate traits.

Internal Conditions

We have separated the internal conditions into two categories: understanding one's own emotions and understanding another's emotions.

Understanding one's own emotions. The internal conditions include:

1. A cognitive developmental level commensurate to the complexity of the emotion(s) under consideration (e.g., multi-emotional states can best be understood by formal operational adolescents and adults).
2. The ability to differentiate intensity and quality of an emotion (if the emotional expression requires such discrimination).
3. As emotions become more multidimensional, the ability is needed to cognitively evaluate both the negative and positive components of events, stimuli, and emotions.
4. The cognitive representations (intellectual skills, verbal

---

*The definitions of internal and external conditions of learning are given in the Introduction to Part II.

information) involved in acting on an emotion (approaching-avoiding) must be present.

5. The ability to recognize one's own viewpoint and to express (verbally or non-verbally) one's emotion (changing the viewpoint and the emotion when necessary).

6. The ability to associate one's emotions to one's self.

Understanding another's emotion. The internal conditions include all the above, plus:

1. The ability to take another person's point of view.

2. The ability to conceptualize the self as separate from others.

External Conditions

Some external conditions to facilitate emotional expression and perhaps development include:

1. Provide experiences for role playing in which different emotional expressions are required or can be used.

2. Use classical or operant conditioning to transfer or attach emotions to particular objects, events, and learning situations.

3. Model appropriate and varied emotional states. (Studies have shown that even small children learn emotional responses and expressions by seeing how others respond; Fogel, 1982).

4. Strive to develop positive emotional bonds between learners and instructors.

5. Match learning tasks to the individual's ability so that positive rather than negative emotions are associated with learning (Fogel, 1982).

6. Provide opportunities for learners to evaluate situations and to verbalize their emotional responses.

7. Provide opportunities to change the informational base on which an emotion is made, and therefore, to change the emotion.

8. Provide opportunities to discuss ways of coping with negative emotions.

9. Encourage learners to express a range of emotional reactions to situations (e.g., anger, frustration, fear, etc.), altering the intensity and/or the quality dimensions.

10. Provide examples of other's emotional responses through films, audiotapes, video, television, etc.
11. If not disruptive, allow and encourage emotional expressions.

Interest and Motivation

Interest and motivation have often been linked to academic achievement as causal influences in an individual's success or failure on a task. In fact, some educators have argued that an individual's failure to work up to his or her potential is largely due to lack of interest and/or lack of motivation. To remedy the effects of failure caused by lack of interest or motivation, educational planners often provide incentives to increase motivation (e.g., rewards and praise), provide educational settings that are "motivating" and conducive to learning, and develop materials that are stimulating and enjoyable. The end product of such planning is to increase academic competence by increasing an individual's levels of interest and motivation.

Interest and motivation, viewed in this way, are means to ends. Both interest and motivation, however, can also be addressed as important educational end-products themselves, as important as academic achievement. Krathwohl *et al.* (1964) recognized this when they developed their Affective Taxonomy. They included Responding as one of the five categories of outcomes. "At this level we are concerned with responses which go beyond merely attending to the phenomenon. The student is *sufficiently motivated* that he is not just willing to attend, but perhaps it is correct to say that he is actively attending" (p. 118, italics added). The authors suggested that this is the category where most "interest" objectives could be found.

Continuing motivation is also being recognized as an outcome of instructional planning. Continuing motivation refers to sustained effort, the tendency for an individual to work on a particular task or a similar task when not under the direct influence of an instructor, or away from the instructional context. Continuing motivation implies that an individual voluntarily chooses to maintain or sustain activity toward a task over a period of time.

After a brief overview of the more encompassing theoretical aspects of motivation, and a review of Keller's Motivational-Design Model (1983), we will return to our discussion of interest and continuing motivation as outcomes of instruction. We will also present relevant conditions of learning.

An Overview of Topics, Theories, and Issues Associated with Motivation

Motivation is a hypothetical construct that broadly refers to those internal and external conditions that influence the arousal, direction, and maintenance of behavior. Definitions of motivation are unusually wide and diverse, and the theoretical constructs associated with the term are equally varied and diverse. Ball (1982) states, "No current theory or research covers and integrates all the concepts that have been proposed under the umbrella term of 'motivation' " (p. 1256). The following is a list of some of the topics that have received considerable attention related to motivation; it aptly shows the breadth of this "umbrella term": interest, curiosity, self-esteem, anxiety, achievement motivation, attribution, level of aspiration, reinforcement theory, locus of control, power motives, learned helplessness, self-efficacy, and expectations.

The terms above relate to the study of motivation from the perspective of the individual, for example, how motivation is influenced by the way an individual characterizes the causes of his or her success and failure, or according to his/her expectations for achievement. Other researchers, however, have examined how the school's social structure, climate, and size influence personal motivation. Garbarino (1981) suggested that smaller schools facilitate active participation, encourage a sense of self-responsibility, and tend to be more personalized. Teachers have more direct contact with learners, expect them to succeed, and encourage students more directly. The school context factors, he contended, have a positive influence on motivation.

From the brief overview given, it is clear that the study of motivation takes into account a vast number of theories, topics, and constructs. Some are directly related to motivation at the

individual level; others relate more directly to social and environmental influences on motivation.

In addition to the concepts and topics associated with motivation are a number of issues related to the study of motivation. For
example, is motivation a personality trait, or is it a state that is
influenced by situational factors? In this age of life-long learning,
this question may be a critical one. Are older people stable in their
motivational levels, or do these levels increase or decrease with
age? The answer to this question will have direct implications for
the design of instruction for various groups of people. Other issues
revolve around value-questions. For example, is it ethical to
establish interest and sustain motivation when the eventual object
of that interest and motivation may not be desirable to all
segments of the population? More specifically, if we can directly
influence motivation, toward what ends do we want to motivate
learners? Who decides what it is important to be motivated
toward? Should all people be motivated toward the same or
similar ends? If not, how does one make the necessary selective
decisions? Clearly, these are not easy questions to answer.

We have very briefly touched on some of the modern
theoretical bases of motivation, and on some issues that arise when
studying motivation. We made no attempt to discuss any of the
theories or to relate them to instructional design. Keller (1983),
however, has developed a theory of motivation, performance, and
instructional influence that integrates numerous theory bases and
prescribes motivational strategies. We encourage readers to take
advantage of the work he has done and become acquainted with
his theory and his motivational-design model; we will address only
selected parts of it in the next section. We discuss it further in
Chapter 14.

Keller's Motivational Design Model

Motivation, according to Keller (1983) "refers to the magnitude
and direction of behavior ... it refers to the *choices* people make
as to what experiences or goals they will approach or avoid, and to
the *degree of effort* they will exert in that respect" (p. 389).
Keller's theory of motivation, performance, and instructional

influences uses these two concepts, choices and effort, to illustrate (a) the reasons a person approaches or avoids a task and (b) how to design instruction to make a task more interesting. He differentiates between effort, performance, and consequences in the following way: performance is an actual behavioral response or accomplishment; effort is action directed toward task completion or accomplishment; consequences are the intrinsic and extrinsic outcomes coupled with cognitive appraisal that influence continuing motivation. We are particularly interested in this concept of continuing motivation.

Keller's theory draws heavily from expectancy-value theory, i.e., how an individual's needs, beliefs, and expectancies influence his or her choice of behavior. He also addresses the role of reinforcement on motivation. He represents reinforcement as the combined effects of consequences and evaluation on motivation.

Accompanying Keller's theory is a motivational-design model. It has four categories: interest, relevance, expectancy, and satisfaction. He also provides strategies for accomplishing the goal of each category. These are briefly summarized next.

Interest refers to establishing and maintaining curiosity and achieving optimal levels of learner arousal. Keller provides specific strategies to increase curiosity, such as using novel problems, guiding inquiry into unfamiliar but not totally unknown areas, and using personal examples about which learners have some emotional attachment.

Relevance refers to linking the learning situation to the needs and motives of the learner. He provides strategies for power needs, affiliation needs, and achievement needs; he also gives conditions for instrumental-value strategies and cultural value strategies. Some strategies related to relevance include opportunities for success as a result of effort; opportunities for cooperation and personal choice; helping learners see the relationship of one goal to the next; and providing peer and cultural group support.

Keller uses many of the concepts and theories we used in our chapter on self-development to discuss his concept of expectancy. Expectancy refers to the causes one attributes to his or her behavior and to the potential for repeating or at least approaching similar tasks. The goal is too develop confidence for success. The concepts of locus of control, attribution, learned helplessness, and personal causation play central roles in the expectancy category, and are clearly seen in the strategies. For example, he suggests attaching success to personal, internal attributions, and increasing the number of success experiences.

The concept of outcomes is the one of most interest to us, since it is most closely associated with continuing motivation, defined as "motivation to continue pursuing similar goals" (Keller, 1983, p. 422). Keller suggests that developing intrinsic motivation is the key to sustaining motivation, and that external reinforcement capitalizing on the information rather than the controlling aspects of reward can aid in this endeavor. He lists five important strategies, and includes an explanation of each. We have included only the strategies:

1. "To maintain intrinsic satisfaction with instruction, use *task-endogenous* rather than task-exogenous rewards . . .

2. To maintain intrinsic satisfaction with instruction, use *unexpected, non-contingent* rewards rather than anticipated, salient, task-contingent rewards (except with dull tasks) . . .

3. To maintain intrinsic satisfaction with instruction, use *verbal praise* and *informative feedback* rather than threats, surveillance, or external performance evaluation . . .

4. To maintain quality of performance, use *motivating feedback* following the response . . .

5. To improve the quality of performance, provide *formative (corrective) feedback* when it will be immediately useful, usually just *before* the next opportunity to practice" (p. 424-427).

We have presented a capsule version of Keller's motivation theory and his motivational-design model. We applaud his fine efforts on this important and nearly untouched area of instructional design, and we encourage researchers and practitioners to read his original works. In the next section we use several of Keller's concepts and strategies to derive conditions of learning.

Conditions of Learning* for Interest and Continuing Motivation

Both Keller (1983) and Krathwohl *et al.* (1964) use the concept of interest in relationship to continuing or sustaining motivation. Krathwohl *et al.* suggest that all objectives from first being aware that some phenomena exists (the first level of Receiving) to avidly pursuing a phenomena (the second level of Valuing) represent "interest" objectives (see Figure 3-1). The authors present the following interest objectives at various levels of the Taxonomy:

- "Recognition that there may be more than one acceptable point of view" (p. 100) (1.1—Awareness)
- "Develops a tolerance for a variety of types of music" (p. 108). (1.2—Willingness to Receive)
- "Listens for rhythm in poetry or prose read aloud" (p. 113) (1.3—Controlled or Selected Attention)
- "Willingness to comply with health regulations" (p. 120) (2.1—Acquiescence in Responding)
- "Voluntarily looks for information books dealing with hobbies or other topics in which he is interested" (p. 125) (2.2—Willingness to Respond)
- "Personal satisfaction in carrying out sound health practice" (p. 132) (2.3—Satisfaction in Response)
- "Continuing desire to develop the ability to speak and write effectively" (p. 141) (.1—Acceptance of a Value)
- "Interest in enabling other persons to attain satisfaction of basic common needs" (p. 145) (3.2—Preference for a Value)

The above objectives represent interest objectives in the schema developed by Krathwohl *et al.* Although it is possible to argue that in some of these objectives students are not truly demonstrating interest (e.g., 1.1 and 2.1), we believe the objectives taken together do illustrate a growing or continuing involvement in phenomena. At the upper level of interest, 2.2 through 3.2, students voluntarily deepen their involvement with a thing or event; they are interested in and motivated toward a phenomenon.

---

*The definitions of internal and external conditions of learning are given in the Introduction to Part II.

Unfortunately, the Taxonomy authors provide no strategies for helping students attain these objectives.

Keller (1983) also uses the term interest in his motivational-design model. It is the first of the motivational concepts he discusses. He describes epistemic curiosity as a key element of interest. Epistemic curiosity "refers to information-seeking and problem-solving behavior that occurs as a result of the stimulation of curiosity" (p. 399). This concept seems to be closely related to or a first step in sustaining or continuing motivation; it also parallels, in part, some of the Krathwohl *et al.* objectives in which students voluntarily engage in pursuing or seeking out a phenomenon. One strategy Keller gives for arousing and maintaining curiosity is to provide opportunities for students to learn more about topics they already know about or believe in, and to give them some experiences with the unfamiliar and unexpected. This is in some ways similar to the "range of acceptance" attitude change strategy we described in Chapter 4. That strategy involves providing information within a learner's range of acceptance, and by successive approximations, moving the individual outside the range of acceptance, i.e., give them "moderate doses of the *unfamiliar and unexpected*" (Keller, 1983, p. 402).

Other strategies Keller gives for sustaining curiosity are:
1. Provide examples of real people and real-life problems.
2. Provide a personal or emotional component to exercises and materials.
3. Use ambiguous, paradoxical, and novel situations or events.

Keller also discusses instrumental value as it relates to continuing motivation. Instrumental value "refers to the increases in motivation to accomplish an immediate goal when it is perceived to be a required step for attaining a desired future goal" (p. 408). He suggests that clearly explaining how one goal is connected to another and how accomplishment of one goal leads to the accomplishment of a desirable future goal will have an impact on continuing motivation.

Expectancy for success also leads to sustained motivation (Keller, 1983). Students who feel they have personal control over successful completion of a learning task and who believe their success is related to personal ability and effort will tend to persist longer than those who feel they have little control, or those who believe their success is due to external factors.

Finally, intrinsic satisfaction is a key to developing and maintaining motivation (Keller, 1983). This coupled with reinforcement aimed at providing information rather than controlling the learner may lead to sustained motivation. Earlier, we listed several key strategies given by Keller to maintain intrinsic satisfaction. They are paraphrased in the section below that lists the external conditions of learning.

To summarize, the educational implications of most concern to us in this section revolve around maintaining interest and continuing motivation. We focused on the concepts of epistemic curiosity, instrumental value, expectancy for success, and intrinsic satisfaction. Using these concepts, we now present conditions of learning for interest and continuing motivation.

Internal Conditions

The internal conditions for interest and continuing motivation include:

1. Intellectual skills and verbal information necessary to achieve success on tasks in which the objective is to increase motivation for further learning.
2. Cognitive capabilities that enable learners to differentiate between internal and external causes. For example, young children sometimes are unable to distinguish between ability and effort.
3. Ability to distinguish between rewards and non-rewards, and/or the ability to give examples of personal rewards.

External Conditions

The external conditions include the following:

1. Teach learners how to reward themselves for task accomplishment.
2. Demonstrate how to match tasks to present and future personal needs and values.
3. Discuss ways to motivate oneself to do unpleasant tasks. For example, show learners how to link undesirable tasks

to future needs, desires, and wants; show learners how to break large tasks into smaller units, and to reinforce each step.

4. Use the classroom as a way to demonstrate to learners how to apply the Premack principle to their own study, by rewarding themselves with a preferred activity after completing a non-preferred activity.

5. Provide opportunities for students to continue a task at a time and place away from the original learning environment. Reinforce future task attempts.

6. Use rewards and reinforcement that follow naturally from the task rather than ones unrelated to or minimally related to the task (i.e., use task-endogenous, not task-exogenous rewards; Keller, 1983).

7. Use the informational rather than the controlling aspect of a reward (Keller, 1983).

8. Use unexpected rewards and verbal praise to maintain motivation.

9. Link success to personal attributes (ability and effort).

10. Provide opportunities for control of success over the learning situation.

11. Provide opportunities to further involvement with topic(s) which students already know about or believe in.

12. Increase dissonance to stimulate interest and continuing motivation by (a) providing information slightly outside the "range of acceptance"; (b) using novel and unexpected situations or events, and (c) using personal and emotional materials and situations.

SOCIAL DEVELOPMENT AND GROUP DYNAMICS

The fact that we have included this category, social development and group dynamics, as a component of the affective domain shows our bias concerning its importance in education and training, but we are by no means convinved it is truly a component of the affective domain. Rather, it may be a separate domain, as Romiszowski (1981) has suggested, and as Joyce and Weil (1980) imply by categorizing the social interaction family as distinct from the other families of teaching models, i.e., information-processing, personal, and behavior modification. We have chosen to include it here because it does have important interdomain relationships, related, for example, to self-image, academic competence, and self-control.

We selected the category label, Social Development and Group Dynamics, because it is a somewhat inclusive title and because it hints at the complexity of the category. For example, all of the following could be included in this category as subcategories: social competence, social behavior, social relationships, interpersonal skills, peer relationships, socialization, interactive skills, social influence, leadership, social roles, cooperation, friendship, group development, participative skills, and skills related to living and working in a democracy. Of course, the subcategories we have listed are not independent from each other; however, there are nuances of meaning associated with each that imply particular behaviors or competencies.

We have chosen here to concentrate on a limited aspect of social development and group dynamics, social competence. We have used Oden's (1982) definition of social competence, "the ability to initiate and maintain interaction with adults and peers and to build relationships with others in group and dyadic contexts" (p. 1719). Her definition was used to define children's social competence; however, we use it for both adults or children. In adopting this definition, which is still quite broad, we focus our discussion on only one aspect of social development and group dynamics.

Throughout this section, we have omitted infant and preschool children from our discussion, and have included adult learners. New arenas of social competence are being required for adults due to the changing fabric of our society and, therefore, adult social development, or perhaps social adjustment, may be an important focus for educators. For example, divorce, early retirement, career changes, increased amounts of leisure time, longer life spans, and unstable financial futures may require new and different coping strategies, dependence on support groups and community agencies, new friendship patterns, and new uses of time. These, in turn, may require new or adjusted social skills and group relationships.

A number of authors have suggested that instruction in social skills has proved an effective means of increasing social competence (Joyce & Weil, 1980; Oden, 1982; Romiszowski, 1981; Runkel & Schmuck, 1982).

Taxonomy of Social Purposes of Public Schools

We digress from our discussion of social competence to briefly describe a taxonomy of social purposes for the public schools developed by Derr (1973). We believe this taxonomy gives an adequate overview of the category, social development, and although it is related to schools, it can be adapted to non-school settings.

Derr developed his taxonomy because he believed that the taxonomies developed by Bloom (1956) and Krathwohl *et al.* (1964) failed to explicitly take into account objectives related to the social dimension, for example, economic efficiency, civic responsibility, worthy use of leisure time, and interpersonal relationships. "In essence, the taxonomy would serve the function of identifying each type of social purpose, making it possible for professional educators and the public to assess systematically the advantages and disadvantages of schools' adopting each type" (Derr, 1973, p. 36).

Derr makes it clear that his taxonomy refers to categories of school purposes, not objectives. He says, however, that objectives can be developed from the social purposes. For example, the purpose: "Perpetuate democracy by developing a commitment to it among youth," may have the following objectives:

> Participates in school elections.
> Contributes to discussions of contemporary political events.
> Evaluates the performance of elected representatives.
> Appraises both majority positions and minority positions on political issues in terms of objective standards" (p. 146).

The classification of school purposes proposed by Derr is shown in Figure 7.1.

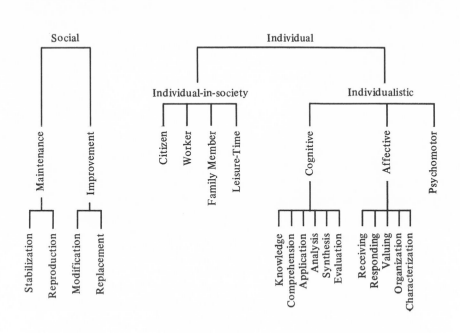

Figure 7.1. Tentative Classification of School Purposes (Derr, 1973, p. 125).

The main division is between social and individual school purposes. Social purposes refer to instances in which the intended effect is on social conditions in the community or society. Social purposes is further divided into maintenance purposes, e.g., "preserve democracy as a way of life" (p. 90), and improvement purposes, e.g., "eliminate prejudices and provincialism wherever they exist" (p. 90). These categories are further subdivided. Examples of the subdivisions are:

> "Stabilization: Insure that citizens continue to vote whenever possible.
> Reproduction: Develop the next generation into adults who vote whenever possible.
> Modification: Induce citizens in the community to vote more frequently.

Replacement: Develop the next generation into adults who vote more frequently than adults typically do today" (p. 91).

The other main division, Individual, includes two categories: Individuals-in-society and Individualistic. "Reference is being made, of course, to those values which pertain to the rights of the individual and those which pertain to the obligations which society may impose upon its members in the interest of its progress and preservation" (p. 121).

This taxonomy, while geared to school purposes, could certainly be used in any instructional or training setting to facilitate discussion about the social purposes of that institution or setting. For example, the focus in the individual category is related to types of effects schools have on cognitive, affective, and psychomotor behavior changes. In individual-in-society category, the effects might relate to possible careers that an individual has or could have, or to an individual's social position.

Relating this to our previous discussion about social competencies, it is possible that this taxonomy might prove useful to planners in setting aims and goals for education and training. For example, social studies teachers might at times focus on social purposes such as the improvement of citizenship skills; adult community educators might develop goals related to the use of leisure time for specific groups of individuals-in-society; trainers might develop instructional units on the cognitive and affective aspects of good interpersonal relationships or salesmanship.

Social Competence

Several researchers have found that increased competence in social skills has produced important affective and cognitive outcomes. Several examples follow. Competence in emotional expression may promote intimacy due to self-disclosure (Oden, 1982). Ability to cooperate and knowledge of conflict resolution strategies increase one's ability to maintain and sustain peer relationships and provide some measure of self-control. Self-control has been found to relate to achievement (de Charms, 1972, cited in Oden, 1982; Runkel & Schmuck, 1982). Students who have a chance to participate in decision-making and, hence, feel some degree of power and influence, tend to have better self-images (Runkel & Schmuck, 1982). In addition, academic achievement, friendship and interpersonal relationships, positive self-esteem, an individual's liking of school, and race relations have all been influenced by cooperative learning situations (Slavin, 1980; cited in Runkel & Schmuck, 1982).

Oden (1982) has subdivided social competence into three major categories, each with further subcategories. We have listed them here to show the range of behaviors related to developing social competence, and where necessary, we have given a brief description:

1. Social-affective competence
   a. Attachment (ability to establish bonds with others)
   b. Expressiveness (to express one's emotions and feelings so others can comprehend them)
   c. Self-control (self-regulated behavior)
2. Social-cognitive competence
   a. Social knowledge
      1. Knowledge of persons
      2. Knowledge of the social self
      3. Knowledge of social situations
      4. Knowledge of social interaction processes
      5. Knowledge of social relationships
      6. Knowledge of social roles
   b. Perspective-taking (to take the perspective of others)
   c. Attribution (determining social causation)
   d. Moral judgment (ability to reason at higher levels; see our Chapter 5).
3. Social behavior (categories of observable skills)
   a. Communication (verbal and non-verbal)
   b. Cooperation (sharing)
   c. Support (to give emotional, physical, psychological help)
   d. Inclusion and participation skills (initiating and sustaining peer interactions)
   e. Conflict management (negotiation)
   f. Achievement (to develop and demonstrate one's uniqueness and accomplishments)

g. Autonomous social self (knowing how to maintain one's uniqueness, and to sustain a degree of independence in thought)

We have adopted this list to provide a framework for the category, social competence. These skills, abilities, and knowledge related to social competence are widely diverse. Many are amenable to direct intervention strategies. With children, however, their cognitive levels of development are important prerequisites for developing social competence. For example, children who are not able to make abstractions and not cognitively able to take multiple perspectives may be unable to ascertain the effects of their behavior on another child, and may be unable to understand the emotions and feelings of another in a group learning activity or in social situations. Adults, on the other hand, may begin to increase their social competence at all levels through direct instruction. This, in turn, may also produce marked benefits in other aspects of cognitive and affective development.

Conditions of Learning* for Social Competence

Internal Conditions

The internal conditions for social competence include:

1. A positive or neutral attitude toward the worth and necessity of social interaction and interpersonal relationships.
2. Ability to express basic emotions and label them.
3. Cognitive developmental levels suitable to perform specific social or interpersonal skills. For example, the ability to take another's perspective or to make abstractions.
4. Necessary intellectual skills and verbal information to:
   a. Perform academic tasks in cooperative learning groups.
   b. Take some action, e.g., to vote (knowing polling places, how to register to vote, etc.).
   c. Participate in discussions about social issues and prob-

---

*The definitions of internal and external conditions of learning are given in the Introduction to Part II.

lems, or to understand issues related to the individual, the individual-in-society, and social conditions.

External Conditions

The external conditions include the following:

1. Provide direct skill training in social skill behaviors, e.g., conflict resolution and management, cooperation skills, groups dynamics, etc.
2. Provide opportunities to work in groups.
3. Use simulations, role plays, and games to give learners a chance to take another's perspectives.
4. Provide opportunities for shared decision-making.
5. Model good interpersonal skills and cooperative behaviors.
6. Pair students to work together. Pairs might include a low self-esteem and a high self-esteem learner, a popular and an unpopular student, a student with good interpersonal skills and a student with poor interpersonal skills, etc. Such pairings have been found to have some positive effects; however, they are usually short term (Runkel & Schmuck, 1982).
7. Give students opportunities to set and pursue their own goals, that is, to increase self-responsibility.
8. Reward effort, participation, and cooperation.
9. For young children, provide opportunities for mixed-age group interaction. Oden (1982) reports two studies (Hartup, 1978; Shatz & Gelman, 1973) indicating that both age groups benefit.
10. Provide opportunities to interact with various social and ethnic groups, and with handicapped people. Where this is not possible, use audio-visual media that depict good relationships among all groups of people.
11. Have discussions on current events, social conditions and problems, government, etc.
12. Where not disruptive, encourage self-expression.
13. Encourage learners to identify their strengths and weaknesses in situations involving academic, social, personal, and physical skills.

ATTRIBUTIONS

Attribution theory is an umbrella term for several theories that investigate causal perceptions. An attribution is an *inference* an individual makes about the causes of his or her own behavior or the causes of another person's behavior.

In Chapter 6 we described one of the attribution theories, learned helplessness, and its relationship to self-development. In this chapter we discuss attribution theory as it relates to achievement behavior.

Rather than being a direct component of the affective domain, attributions appear to be an underlying factor that influence many different cognitive and affective behaviors. For example, attributions have been shown to correlate with intensity of performance (Weiner, 1972), to influence feelings of pride or shame (Weiner & Kukla, 1970), and to correlate with task persistence (Dweck & Reppucci, 1973).

Weiner's attributional theory of motivation makes a basic assumption that "search for understanding is the (or *a*) basic 'spring of action' " (Weiner, 1979, p. 3). People want to understand the causal events of their environment. Although other factors may have an influence, Weiner states that there are four main causes of expectancy for success or failure in achievement-related contexts: ability, effort, difficulty of the task, and luck (Bar-Tal, 1978). Other important attributions include mood, chance, bias, help, fatigue, illness, etc., but the four causes listed above have been the ones generally studied.

To account for the almost infinite number of attributions, Weiner (1979) proposed a three-dimensional taxonomy of causes based on the properties of the cause. The dimensions are: (a) internal-external causality, (b) stability, and (c) controllability. Theoretically, examples of internal causality are effort, ability, and mood; examples of external causality are luck, difficulty of the task, and whether a teacher likes or dislikes a student. Stability refers to the potential situational fluctuations of the attribution. Weiner hypothesized that stable causes include ability, typical effort, and bias. Unstable causes include immediate effort, fatigue, mood, and luck. Controllability refers to an individual's perceived control over an outcome. Weiner suggested that uncontrollable causes include ability, task difficulty, and luck. Controllable causes include bias and effort.

Weiner (1979) classified each attribution on each of the three dimensions, and within each dimension on two levels: locus of causality (internal or external), stability (stable or unstable), and level of control (controllable or uncontrollable). For example, Weiner classified ability as internal, stable, uncontrollable; typical effort as internal, stable, controllable; and luck as external, unstable, uncontrollable.

The theoretical assignment of attributions to the various dimensions and within dimensions on two levels (see examples in previous paragraphs) has not been fully supported by research. Data gathered by Chandler and Spies (1984) indicated that five of the original eight attributions were classified differently by subjects than Weiner (1979) did. Of particular interest to us in discussing achievement are two attributions: ability and effort. Effort was found to be internal, unstable, and controllable as hypothesized. However, Weiner classified ability as stable, internal, and uncontrollable, whereas Chandler and Spies found ability to be classified as somewhat unstable (they used a continuous rather than discreet scale), internal, and controllable.

Although all three dimensions are important, Weiner (1979) contends that the stability factor is the most influential for expectancy of success or failure in achievement related situations; he refers to the magnitude of expectancy. Therefore, this change of ability from stable to unstable and from uncontrollable to controllable has implications for expectancy of success or failure. If a student perceives that his ability is unchangeable (stable), she or he is not likely to alter his or her expectations for success. If however, ability is unstable, then an individual's expectation for success has the potential for change. Regarding controllability, if a student perceives ability as controllable, then his or her expectation for success is amenable to modification.

Some Issues Related to Attribution Theory

There are three issues we want to raise briefly with respect to attribution theory. The first is concerned with the general attribution construct. The second and third concern attributions and achievement-related behaviors.

With regard to the attribution construct, it is not clear how or whether attributions are different from more generalized psychology constructs such as ego-structure (Shama, 1984). It may be that an individual's concept of self is influential in determining the attributions the individual makes. Study of attributions then might account for less of the variance than other dimensions of ego, for example, achievement needs and rigidity. Some research has been conducted along these lines, but the findings are inconclusive.

A second issue concerns whether or not attributions can be modified. Bar-Tal (1978) reported several studies suggesting that intervention strategies are successful in changing the attributions one uses to account for success or failure. The assumption is that attributional reassignment is possible. This assumption has been challenged (Shama, 1984), yet there appears to be more data supporting attribute modification than not supporting the assumption.

This brings up a third issue related to intervention strategies. If attributions are amenable to alteration, what are the associated ethical and moral implications of intervention? For example, what attributions should we modify in low ability students? Is it fair to change the task difficulty for individual students in order to alter his or her attributions when in life (outside the learning environment) that may rarely occur, if ever. How would religiously devout individuals feel about altering attributions toward internal causes and away from external causes like God's influence in man's life? These are just a few of the moral and ethical questions related to attribution modification. There are many others.

We have raised three issues related to altering an individual's attributions. It is with these in mind that we present the next section, educational implications and internal and external conditions of learning.

Educational Implications and Conditions of Learning

Weiner (1972) and Bar-Tal (1978) suggest that changing the cognitive structures associated with the attributions learners make may influence future expectancy for success. Since they believe these cognitive structures can be learned, and since environmental factors also alter the inferences made about success (Weiner, 1972), specific intervention strategies may be used. Bar-Tal (1978) gives the following:

1. Teacher should use individualized tasks to match abilities so that success will be attributed to ability.
2. Teacher feedback should emphasize internal attributions for success, i.e., ability and atypical effort, and point out that failure is caused by lack of effort.
3. Teachers should use direct positive reinforcement when students who do not normally attribute their success to internal causes do so.
4. Teachers should provide adequate instructions for a task so students have good chances for successful task completion.

In addition, associating situational factors with success may also alter attributions. For example, time on task and social norms may influence attributions and expectancy for success or failure.

We now provide our list of internal and external conditions of learning.*

Internal Conditions

The internal conditions of expectancy for success include:

1. The necessary intellectual skills and verbal information to accomplish the given task.
2. The ability to differentiate between internal and external attributions, stable and unstable attributions, and controllable and uncontrollable attributions. Shama (1984) stated that children are sometimes unable to make these distinctions.

---

*The definitions of internal and external conditions of learning are given in the Introduction to Part II.

External Conditions

In general, Bar-Tal (1978) concluded that it is desirable to emphasize effort and ability with success experiences and lack of effort with failure experiences. Weiner would concur and in addition would suggest emphasizing attributions related to stability; that is, demonstrate to the learner that effort and ability continue, over time, to contribute to success.

Based on these recommendations and our literature review, we provide the following list of external conditions:

1. Match task difficulty and learner ability.
2. Provide multiple experiences for success, and identify internal, stable, and controllable attributions as causes for success.
3. Reinforce successful experiences, and reinforce learners who attribute success to their own abilities.
4. In failure situations, provide feedback related to lack of effort, not to lack of ability.
5. Provide opportunities to "test out" the effects of expending more or less effort on a variety of different tasks matched to ability levels. Relate success experiences to controllable attributions, generalized across tasks.
6. Break difficult tasks into manageable, less difficult components where multiple instances of success can be attained.
7. Use audio-visual media that demonstrates the effects of persistent effort, for example, in athletic accomplishments and scientific discovery.

SUMMARY

In this chapter we have discussed four dimensions of the affective domain: emotional development and feelings, interest and continuing motivation, social development and group dynamics, and attributions. Each of these dimensions is a field of study itself, so our coverage is cursory at best. We selected specific aspects of each dimension and stressed the affective and cognitive aspects of particular behaviors. For emotional development, we emphasized emotional expression as both a physiological response and a cognitive evaluation of a situation. For social development and group dynamics, our focus was on social competence in personal understanding and interpersonal relationships. We also presented a taxonomy of the social purposes of public schools (Derr, 1973). For interest and motivation, our emphasis was on sustaining interest and motivation in learning situations. We presented Keller's (1983) motivational-design model, paying particular attention to interest and intrinsic satisfaction and motivation. For attributions, we briefly described Weiner's (1972) attribution theory as it pertains to academic achievement.

With this chapter, we have concluded Part II of this book, the overview of the research background and our listing of the conditions of learning for each component of the affective domain. In Part III, we demonstrate how to sequence instruction to integrate the two domains, and we provide examples from elementary and secondary education, undergraduate education, and education for the professions.

Introduction to Part III:
Sequencing Instruction from
Needs to Lessons (Audit Trails)

In the chapters of Part III, we present the technique of "audit trails" as a mechanism for accomplishing the dual purposes of this book: (a) integration of instructional sequencing in the affective and cognitive domains, and (b) closing the gap usually existing between the broad, life-long goals of education, curriculum, and instruction.

Audit trails work "from the top, downward." They begin with the most complex life-long needs and goals in people's adult lives, and they work downward through the entire curriculum, including objectives for courses, course units, and lessons. Audit trails thus cut across the traditionally separated functions of needs assessment, curriculum development, and instruction. Audit trails contain both affective and cognitive objectives, thus facilitating the design of instruction which integrates the two domains.

In Chapter 8, we discuss the complexities of planning curricula for the elementary and secondary schools, but we also present an illustrative audit trail for the broad goal of "effective citizenship," attempting to show how these complexities may be handled. We recommend making one audit trail for each broad goal of education, as identified by consensus panels of concerned citizens and educational professionals. Our illustrative audit trail plots out the major citizenship objectives for a K-12 curriculum, terminating with pre-school learning. Just as an audit trail works "from the top, downward," instruction is to be sequenced "from the bottom, upward," using the audit trail as a guide for development of instructional sequences.

In Chapter 9, we discuss the peculiarities of curriculum design for undergraduate education, and again, we present an audit trail for "citizenship," but this time for a person majoring in political science in college. The life-long objectives for this person are more complex than those for the high school graduate.

In Chapter 10, we discuss education for the professions, using the profession of instructional design for our illustrative audit trail. In this case, the audit trail for "designing instructional materials" is addressed to one of twenty-two competency areas listed in the needs assessment. Our audit trail adds affective objectives, including those related to professional ethics, to the original list of cognitive competency areas.

We chose to place Chapters 8, 9, and 10 before Chapter 11, which (a) shows how audit trails help implement our entire proposed model of instructional design, and (b) gives directions for how to do an audit trail. We assumed that you, the reader, would prefer to see examples of audit trails (Chapters 8-10) before you read about how they are developed (Chapter 11). However, you have an opportunity to pursue the reverse order by reading Chapter 11 first, in case you believe you would understand the material better in that order. Our chapter sequence represents an inductive approach to learning about audit trails. Reading Chapter 11 first would represent a deductive approach to learning. You may have previously decided which approach is best for you.

In Part IV, we do not present audit trails, but we do continue to discuss them in the context of applications of our model to industrial and military training, and other settings.

Chapter 8

Elementary and Secondary Education

LIFE-LONG LEARNING GOALS

The Concept of Needs

An Illustrative Audit Trail

Life-Long Citizenship Goals
Curriculum Goals and Objectives
Course Organization
Unit Organization
Lesson Organization

NEEDED RESEARCH

SUMMARY

Chapter 8

Elementary and Secondary Education

Continuing the overall dual themes of this book, (a) the integration of the affective and cognitive domains, and (b) closing the gap between needs, curriculum, and instruction, we turn now to recommendations pertaining to elementary and secondary education. The two chapters that follow deal with recommendations for higher education and education for professions.

A basic recommendation in this and following chapters is: *Design from the top down; teach from the bottom up.* The details of our rationale for this recommendation will be made apparent in these chapters.

A second recommendation is also illustrated in this group of chapters: *Design an "audit trail" connecting all levels of goals and objectives, from life-long goals to lesson objectives.* This recommendation is offered as a mechanism for (a) connecting goals and objectives from general to specific, and for (b) integrating affective and cognitive outcomes.

In the illustrative audit trails in this and the next two chapters, we have not adopted any single style or form for writing goals and objectives, such as the three-component form by Mager (1975), the five-component form by Gagné and Briggs (1979), or the four-component form by Romiszowski (1981). Rather, we have chosen to use common, non-technical language to express our intent, so that it could be read by both laymen and educational professionals. We do, however, recommend use of one of the three forms just mentioned when a professional team effort in instructional or curricular design is underway, or when measures of learner performance are being developed. This is discussed further near the end of Chapter 11. In our audit trails in Chapters 8, 9, and 10, we have tried to vary our forms of expression to present a variety for your consideration and use.

LIFE-LONG LEARNING GOALS

The purpose of elementary and secondary schools is not only to help the children learn and develop during these formal schooling years, but also to prepare them for adult life. Since most elementary and secondary schools in the United States are not intended to prepare learners for specific careers, we have focused on the most generally applicable goal of education. We do not treat separately here schools with a vocational orientation, but we intend our comments to apply to such schools as well as to schools offering general and college-preparatory programs.

Since life-long goals are almost indistinguishable from "needs," we next examine the concept of needs.

The Concept of Needs

It may be said the long-range purposes of elementary and secondary education are to prepare students for adult life as marriage partners, parents, citizens, and workers, all within their own specific choices. In more general terms, we could mention quality of life and contributions to society.

Kaufman and English (1979) define a need as a gap between the present state of affairs and the desired state of affairs. They go on to identify the minimal acceptable outcome of schooling as consisting of preparing people to at least *survive* in the society as it is expected to be when they legally leave school. Beyond this minimal level, there is the possibility that some people will *contribute* more to society than they benefit from it—that they will produce more than they consume. People performing below these two levels are *dependent* upon society for survival. Another level might be suggested—those who make *outstanding contributions* to the welfare of society. Kaufman and English also stress the importance of working from life-long needs, back to the design of curricula which will enable people to experience the fulfillment of needs. Kaufman further states (1983) that the failure to decide upon educational goals (ends) before legislating the means to the end has already risked failure in the current move to achieve educational excellence. He sees efforts to lengthen the school year, increase content, pay teachers more, and invest more money in specified curriculum areas as tinkering with the process before the goals are specified. We sympathize with this view, as is reflected in our recommendation to "design from the top down"—from life-long needs, to curriculum goals, and then to instructional objectives.

Burton and Merrill (1977), citing Bradshaw (1972), have illustrated five kinds of needs: (a) normative needs, (b) felt needs, (c) expressed needs or demands, (d) comparative needs, and (e) anticipated or future needs. Both pairs of authors, Kaufman and English, and Burton and Merrill, offer procedures for conducting needs assessments, whether done by lay and professional groups, at a national, state, or local level. Both sources emphasize the desirability of forming consensus groups from a broad spectrum of people concerned with education, the individual, and society. These ideas will be encountered again in the section of this chapter dealing with setting curriculum goals.

Once life-long needs are identified, the authors cited above have provided suggested procedures for setting goals and arranging them in order of priority. Next, resources and constraints are considered, and then curricular decisions are made. Only after these steps have been taken can relevant instruction be designed, according to their models. As we will see in the section on curriculum in this chapter, many present ways of designing curricula run counter to the recommended models. As we will see, confusion arises when different sets of people take leadership or exert political influence for determination of (a) needs, (b) curriculum goals, and (c) instruction. This separation of responsibility for the three functions arises partly because of the differing influences of federal, state, and local agencies. Another problem, of course, is the lack of general agreement on how needs, goals, and objectives should be determined and a lack of agreement on who should make the decisions.

An Illustrative Audit Trail

By "audit trail" we refer to our recommendation to derive needs, goals, and objectives "from the top down"—that is, to design from complex life-long needs, to curriculum goals, to design of courses and units of courses, and on down to lesson objectives.

Let us suppose that a needs assessment has been made, as recommended by Kaufman and English (1979), in order to identify the major areas of competence required to enable people to be survivors and contributors to society as they will encounter it after high school graduation. Let us further suppose that a curriculum for elementary and secondary education has been implemented for the students to help them fulfill the life-long needs identified. Suppose these broad areas of needs have been organized under the following major categories: (a) enjoyable and orderly human relationships; (b) occupational and financial self-sufficiency; (c) effective citizenship; (d) healthy and satisfying use of leisure time; (e) ability to adjust to rapid changes in society; and (f) ability to foresee problems and to contribute to problem solution. (Such categories of needs would not be greatly unlike the *Cardinal Principles of Secondary Education*, developed by National Education Association Commission on Reorganization of Secondary Education, 1918.)

How can the broad areas of need identified above become the basis for curriculum development, and how can courses and lessons be designed to help learners achieve such far-off competencies for adult life? What is to connect together each school day's lesson objectives with curriculum goals upon graduation and the achievement of needs over a lifetime? Our suggested mechanism for achieving such a formidable task is to design an "audit trail" for each major need area. Each audit trail represents a curriculum strand, running vertically through all years of schooling, designed to enable students to achieve the life-long need. Then the design of curricula, courses, and lesson objectives cuts across these strands to relate horizontal groupings of objectives for specific instructional sequences. Figure 8.1 summarizes these relationships.

In Figure 8.1, each vertical arrow represents an audit trail consisting of a list of goals and objectives which support one of the six needs. The portion of each audit trail representing elementary and secondary education may be referred to as a "curriculum strand." The portion of the audit trail which extends down to preschool life represents desired home and family experiences. Course and lesson sequences are designed by selecting one or more objectives from one or more audit trails, thus representing linkage across audit trails in some instances.

We next illustrate the above ideas in the following sub-sections, going from adult goals to home experiences. In our illustration, of course, we cannot show a complete curriculum. We intend only to illustrate the three principles of (a) designing from the top down, (b) integrating affective and cognitive objectives throughout the audit trail, and (c) closing the gap between needs, curriculum, and instruction. We will provide also a few examples of sequence of objectives for instruction which cuts across audit trails.

We do not know of a curriculum that has been designed according to our recommended scheme, but undoubtedly similar intents and concerns have been reflected in actual curriculum development projects.

For our illustrative audit trail, we have selected the need of "effective citizenship." In the following sub-sections we deal with the vertical time segments shown in Figure 8.1. As mentioned earlier, we follow no particular formal style for expressing goals and objectives. Note also which expressions of objectives suggest the affective domain, which the cognitive domain, and which appear to combine elements of both domains. In general, we have intended to arrange the goals and objectives in the audit trail from complex down to simpler skills, thus illustrating designing from the top down.

We have arranged our objectives in a vertical linear format rather than in the form of hierarchies, discussed in earlier chapters. We have done so for two reasons: (a) we only intend to suggest the sequential order of major objectives in an approximate fashion, and (b) we believe the readers may find such a format easier to use. The general principle is the same in our vertical linear sequence and in hierarchical arrangements: for each higher objective, ask: "what would the person need to be able to do before being able to perform this objective?"

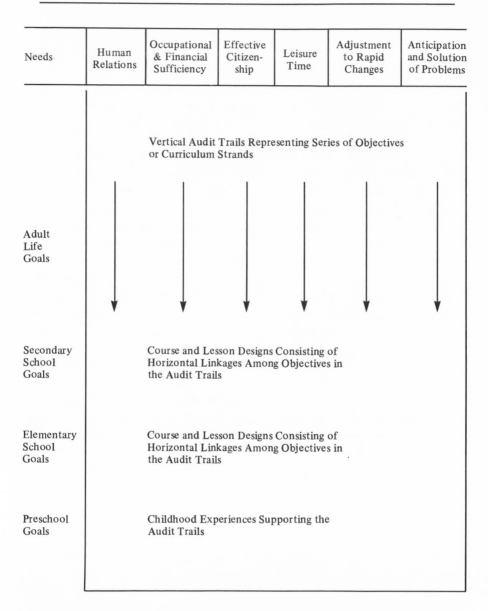

Needs	Human Relations	Occupational & Financial Sufficiency	Effective Citizen- ship	Leisure Time	Adjustment to Rapid Changes	Anticipation and Solution of Problems

Vertical Audit Trails Representing Series of Objectives or Curriculum Strands

Adult Life Goals

Secondary School Goals

Course and Lesson Designs Consisting of Horizontal Linkages Among Objectives in the Audit Trails

Elementary School Goals

Course and Lesson Designs Consisting of Horizontal Linkages Among Objectives in the Audit Trails

Preschool Goals

Childhood Experiences Supporting the Audit Trails

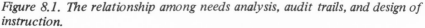

Figure 8.1. The relationship among needs analysis, audit trails, and design of instruction.

We have numbered the objectives in the audit trail to show the continuity intended even though we break in for introductions to each level of objectives.

Life-Long Citizenship Goals
1. To contribute more to society than one receives from it.
2. Commitment to action or leadership roles in solution of social problems and in alleviating societal ills.
3. Chooses to become a knowledgeable participant, if not an expert, in group actions for the civic good.
4. Values various methods for bringing data to bear upon solutions of civic and social problems.
5. Seeks to receive and respond to such information sources as science, technology, futurism, history, finance, etc.
6. Chooses to respond to opportunities to participate in civic, social, or political group efforts.
7. Devotes time to study of information and problem-solving techniques concerning selected areas of service, such as in church, school board, city council, or other areas of interest and belief.
8. Through study of information sources or participation, seeks to learn the concepts and rules pertaining to chosen areas of citizen participation.
9. Chooses to vote and participate in elections concerning issues and candidates for public office.
10. Seeks information about public issues and candidates.
11. Accepts appointment or election to groups responsible for solutions to problems in one's area of interest, information, or expertise.
12. Abides by laws, and participates in achieving changes in laws when convinced of the desirability of changes.
13. Models observances of laws.
14. Expresses publically and privately the values and ideals held, and is willing to debate them.
15. Encourages the dissemination of information on public issues and problems.

Curriculum Goals and Objectives
We interrupt our audit trail regarding citizenship to introduce

some background about curriculum for elementary and secondary schools.

Short (1982) has outlined some profound changes in the control of curriculum over the last two decades. While the authority for curriculum is still placed at the local level, there are also multiple sources of mandate over the curriculum. Short summarizes (a) the actions in courts to protect First Amendment rights to access to schooling; (b) federal legislation concerning access and support for special areas, such as language education and education for the handicapped, all tied to specified conditions for federal spending; (c) mandates by state legislation concerning curricular areas and evaluation of outcomes; (d) pressures from unions regarding such matters as class size and resources for various curriculum areas. The result of these mandates has been the diffusion of authority among federal, state, and local government.

In our view, the diffusion of authority, sometimes involving conflicting mandates, is further made a problem by the tendency to mandate means before ends, as Kaufman (1983) has pointed out. Governmental agencies and the general public appear to offer solutions to problems that have not been identified—a tendency to place the cart before the horse, when manipulating processes as the solution to poorly identified problems. A third complicating factor is that different groups of people tend to work independently on three aspects of education which should all be handled by a single procedure in order to achieve congruence and harmony among (a) needs, (b) curriculum goals, and (c) instruction. And, finally, the production of instructional materials often takes place independently of the other three educational functions.

There appears to be no easy solution to the above dilemmas; a first step would appear to be to convince everybody concerned that we should identify the needs and goals before we specify curriculum content and teaching processes.

Short (1982) has set forth criteria for choosing between locally developed curricula, called site-specific curricula, in which the developing agency is also the educational delivery agency, and generic curricula, developed by an outside agency not having jurisdiction over implementation. He favors the former, when both local and outside talent are used and when there is local control over adoption.

Tanner (1982), reviewing the history of curriculum development, places its beginning as a self-conscious field of study in 1918 with the publication of the *Cardinal Principles of Secondary Education*, referred to earlier in this chapter. Tanner believes this report ended the domination of colleges over secondary curriculum, and ushered in the emphasis upon making education more democratic. Even so, there immediately arose conflict over whether the curriculum should focus upon (a) the learners' needs, (b) society's needs, or (c) subject-matter areas. This conflict has never been resolved; the pendulum swings from one to another emphasis. Current models of teaching (Joyce & Weil, 1980) also reflect these differing viewpoints.

Tanner (1982) credits Tyler (1949) with making clear what a curriculum should cover: (a) purposes, (b) learning exercises, (c) organization of experiences, and (d) evaluation of the attainment of purposes. He also emphasizes that development of a curriculum should (a) heavily involve teachers and curriculum specialists, (b) avoid dominance by subject-matter scholars, and (c) bridge the gap between subject matter and the learner. We consider our idea of audit trails to be consistent with the above, with the added emphasis upon integrating affective and cognitive objectives more directly in both curriculum and instruction (and also research).

Schubert (1982) has discussed some choices to be made in curriculum development. It is interesting to note that we have made the choice for each pair of alternatives he names: (a) we have chosen to differentiate among needs, goals, and objectives, as opposed to treating them as interchangeable terms; (b) we have chosen to organize our ideas by statements of objectives rather than by content of materials; (c) we have chosen a psychological, hierarchical way to define objectives rather than making a logical arrangement of content items; and (d) we have attempted to bridge the gap between curriculum and instruction by our examples of audit trails.

We now resume our example of an audit trail for the citizenship need, which now becomes a strand in the elementary and secondary curriculum. We resume the numbering system for our illustrative objectives where we left off in the previous section of this chapter. We do not attempt to specify the grade level to which each objectives belongs, nor to show the break point between elementary and secondary schools. We leave that to curriculum people. Otherwise, our purpose is to attend to the "design from the top down" rule that we have been following.

16. Volunteers to participate in mock legislatures and other simulations of government functions.

17. Generates position statements on civic and political issues.

18. Learns the concepts and arguments of others regarding public policy issues.

19. Receives and responds to information sources relating to alternate solutions to selected problems of society.

20. Develops own value systems regarding issues raised by study of history, government, and current events.

21. Can summarize the guarantees provided by the Bill of Rights.

22. Can generate alternate solutions to simulated or actual conflicts among the three branches of the federal government.

23. Can explain the concept of "balance of power" among the branches of federal government.

24. Can trace the history of development of roles of the three branches of federal government.

25. Given the electoral college tally of votes for President of the United States, can determine whether a person has been elected or whether the vote will be cast by the House of Representatives.

26. Can summarize the method of election or appointment of Congressmen, judges, and Cabinet officers.

27. Can summarize the process by which a bill becomes a federal law.

28. Can list ten factors considered in making foreign policy decisions, and can demonstrate how those factors were apparently weighted in making historical decisions.

29. Chooses to participate in elections of class and school officers.

30. Accepts opportunities to participate in school government.
31. Is active in class discussion of civic affairs.
32. Seeks to gain information on current events and to participate in discussion of them.
33. Is willing to reveal own value systems in discussion of moral and ethical issues.
34. Organizes own value systems and responds in terms of them.
35. Is committed to the deliberate process of forming personal value systems.
36. Demonstrates concern for others in personal relationships.
37. Responds to opportunities to learn about history, government, and social problems.
38. Responds to study of local, state, and world government as summarized in objectives 16-20 in this list.
39. Can summarize cultural differences for selected nations of the world.
40. Seeks to understand the role of cultural differences in international relations.
41. Can generate rationales for favoring or not favoring selected elements of culture among nations.
42. Can generate arguments to support positions on simulated or real instances of conflict between individuals and society.
43. Participates in efforts of teachers to introduce democratic classroom procedures.
44. Is willing to serve as a "judge" in democratic classroom management procedures.
45. Is willing to abide by rules of the school and the classroom.
46. Participates in making pupil-developed rules.
47. Is willing to serve on faculty-pupil councils concerning school government.
48. Observes and discusses local, state, and national elections.
49. Participates in pre-election discussions with family, peers, and teachers.

50. Questions parents concerning their views about election issues.
51. Seeks information from parents as to their reasons for decisions made about what is right or wrong for children to do.
52. Begins to develop own code of conduct, and to give reasons for choices made.
53. Begins to reason with parents and peers about incidents of interpersonal relationships.
54. Begins to describe feelings of pleasure or frustration rather than relying entirely upon screams of rage or pleasure.

Course Organization

Up to this point in this chapter we have presented some brief comments about curricula for elementary and secondary schools. In Figure 8.1 we suggested that first needs assessments should be undertaken, resulting in identification of major groups of needs to enable high school graduates to be survivors and participants in society. Then we suggested that an audit trail be developed for each major need. Such an audit trail was illustrated for the "effective citizenship need." This audit trail began with life-long objectives, both affective and cognitive, and ended with objectives for preschool children.

Our illustrative audit trail, of course, only "hit the high spots," because it is only an audit trail, *not a curriculum*. We must have overlooked some of the high spots, but our main purpose was to show what we mean by an audit trail—*a list of objectives arranged in descending order of complexity*—roughly, a hierarchical order.

The matter of designing a curriculum would require completion of an audit trail for each major need, then designing "cross links" among audit trails, ending up with objectives organized by each year of school (elementary school) or each "course" (secondary school).

Since we have presented an audit trail for only one need, we can only present suggestions for course design and lesson design.

We have said earlier that curricula and courses have often been organized around a major emphasis on either (a) learner needs, (b) society needs, or (c) subject matter or discipline. Ideally, a curriculum would aim for all three emphases, but this is difficult if the basic orientation intended is to be maintained.

An alternate suggestion, attempted perhaps a few times in the past, is to organize the total instruction around "problems." The familiar "project method" of past years is an example of this approach. In modern times, such an approach might center around these "problems": (a) a pluralistic society, (b) rapid change, (c) war and threat of war, (c) pollution, (e) world hunger and thirst, and (f) space and oceans. Then lessons in mathematics, science, and so on, would all draw subject matter from the problem area.

Still another approach, but only for the science and mathematics portion of the curriculum, is illustrated in *Science—A Process Approach*, (AAAS Commission on Science Education, 1967). In this approach, a long series of lessons was developed for each major process used by scientist—observing, measuring, forming hypotheses, etc. Each lesson on observing might draw content from a different discipline, and the observing lessons were interspersed with the other groups of lessons for each level of instruction in science.

Our recommendations have points of both similarity and difference to the above approaches. But note that our audit trail, above, drew upon an identified need, and upon the needs of both the learner and society, all while using content of social and political science.

We now turn to suggestions on "course" organization, or, in the case of elementary schools, organization of a "level" or year of study.

A course is typically divided into "course units," each requiring perhaps three or four weeks of instruction. It is conceivable that an entire unit or course would utilize only one audit trail, such as twelfth grade American Government, which would draw mainly from the "citizenship" audit trail. On the other hand, a course or unit in elementary school social studies might cut across all the audit trails shown in Figure 8.1, plus other audit trails resulting from a needs analysis different from the hypothetical one represented in Figure 8.1.

Taking first the case of the American Government course, one could conceive of a course based almost exclusively on objectives 16-30, from our audit trail. Some of those objectives might become unit objectives; others might become lesson objectives. Objective 16, for example, might become the terminating activity of the course. Alternatively, the twelfth grade course might be broadened, with perhaps a change in title, to include some objectives from our audit trail but many others from other audit trails. Ways to express the organization of a course might include: (a) a list of objectives, as in our audit trail, (b) learning hierarchies, discussed in earlier chapters, or (c) instructional maps, illustrated by Briggs and Wager (1981).

Turning now to the elementary school, we first observe that some schools are organized around "subjects," such as language arts, mathematics, science, social studies, etc., while others may employ the "project" method, which cuts across those subject areas. (Ideally, according to our model, the results of the need analysis would help determine the form of curriculum and school organization.)

Unit Organization

We will use as our example of one unit for a course, a sixth grade social studies area of study. The "citizenship" strand of such instruction might draw upon objectives similar to objectives 30-48. However, objectives from other audit trails or curriculum strands would also be employed. We give here an illustration of objectives for a unit of such instruction. The "unit objective" is taken from our audit trail. The other objectives were derived from this unit objective, or were assumed to appear in other audit trails shown in Figure 8.1.

1. Our audit trail objective 42: Can generate arguments to support positions on simulated or real instances of conflict between individuals and society.
2. Can identify sources of conflict among individuals, special groups, and society as a whole.
3. Can give examples of how the need to make a living enters into conflicts (from the occupational strand or audit trail).
4. Can locate information on which occupations are increasing or decreasing in demand, and what future trends have been predicted (from the occupations audit trail).

5. Can summarize the impact of automation upon demands for various occupations (from rapid change strand).
6. Can predict some occupations or professions which should survive the "replacement by automation" threat.
7. Can relate leisure time to demands of unions (from leisure time strand).

Lesson Organization

A series of "lessons" makes up an instructional "unit," just as a series of units makes up a "course."

We use the term, lesson organization, to refer to the selection of objectives for a lesson. The broader term, lesson design, the subject of chapter 15, refers to both the selection of objectives and the plan for teaching and learning activities for the lesson.

As will be noted by referring back to our audit trail, the objectives listed there are broader than lesson objectives. Our approach of designing from the top down has the following implications (among others): (a) each lesson objective should contribute to a unit objective; (b) each unit objective should contribute to a course objective; (c) each course objective should contribute to a curriculum objective; and (d) each curriculum objective should contribute to a life-long need. (For those readers who regard the above statement as too rigid a view of education, we will state that we do believe in the value of "expressive objectives"–unforeseen and thus unplanned outcomes of schooling. Our suggestion is to observe these unexpected outcomes, and when appropriate, incorporate them as objectives in the redesign of the overall instruction. We do not mean to imply that all students will achieve the same unexpected outcomes.)

Referring back to our illustrated set of objectives for a unit in social studies, just preceding, we will use objective 5, "can summarize the impact of automation upon demands for various occupations," as a lesson objective. The eight objectives shown below are subordinate to this lesson objective. (In practice, one would have to determine whether this lesson objective requires more or less study time than is usually meant for a "lesson.")

1. Can demonstrate the significance of costs, income, and profit and loss to a business.

2. Can demonstrate the effect of unemployment upon a person and society.
3. Can classify examples of costs, income, budget, profit, loss for a family and for a business organization.
4. Can locate information on demand for various occupations, and can identify which have been most affected by automation.
5. Can define automation, and classify examples and non-examples of it.
6. Can interpret graphs and charts. (Probably a previously learned skill, or "entry skill.")
7. Chooses to seek information about occupations expected to be in good demand in the future.
8. Shows increasing awareness and receptivity to the role of work in quality of life.

Again, we have probably overlooked some helpful lesson objectives, or wrongly sequenced some of them. Also, we cannot predict the entry skills of the learners, nor the exact amount of learning time required. We have intended only to suggest what a completed audit trail might be like, when working downward from life-long needs to lesson objectives.

NEEDED RESEARCH

There has been little or no research or evaluation of the usefulness of an audit trail as we have dealt with in this chapter. The idea of an audit trail, however, fits into much of the research and prior practice in curriculum, instruction, and instructional design. Our treatment of audit trails also is consistent with the rule to identify needs and goals before proposing specific objectives or instructional methods.

The research areas most closely related to this chapter include needs assessment, curriculum, instruction, and instructional design. Research on the idea of audit trails could well be integrated with these on-going research areas. New research could include further study of the integration of affective and cognitive objectives at all the levels of planning illustrated in this chapter.

It is an interesting dilemma that we know more about objectives at the micro level than at the macro level. For example, Briggs and Wager (1981) offered much more explicit illustrations of how to organize courses, units, and lessons than could be offered on how to organize curricula.

A similar dilemma exists in the area of instruction. We know much more about how to teach information and intellectual skills than we know about attitudes and cognitive strategies. It is understandable, of course, that we know more at the micro level in both analysis of objectives and in teaching, but all too often we have shied away from tackling the macro problems. It is also understandable that a doctoral student selects a micro problem for dissertation research, because it is appropriate for a short-term research effort, and the methodologies are well established. *Now we need methodologies for tackling the macro problems.* We hope this book will stimulate such research.

SUMMARY

In this chapter we have illustrated our meaning of audit trails as a technique for designing curricula to meet life-long needs. In Figure 8.1 we related needs to audit trails, or curriculum strands, for elementary and secondary schools. Then we demonstrated the construction of an audit trail running from objectives for adults to objectives for preschool children. We also discussed and briefly illustrated how units and lessons can be designed by cutting across audit trails, each intended to meet a different adult need. Our illustrative audit trail contains both affective and cognitive objectives.

We briefly discussed trends in curriculum history and development, and related this chapter to some of the persistent problems in curriculum theory. We called for more research at the macro level in design of objectives, and for more research in the more complex forms of learning, which include problem solving, cognitive strategies, and the affective domain.

The following chapters further demonstrate the idea of audit trails in instruction beyond elementary and secondary education, and further illustrate the integration of instruction in the affective and cognitive domains.

Chapter 9

Undergraduate Education

THE UNDERGRADUATE CURRICULUM

An Illustrative Audit Trail

Life-long Citizenship Goals
Curriculum Goals and Objectives
Course Organization
Lesson Organization

NEEDED RESEARCH

SUMMARY

Chapter 9

Undergraduate Education

It is a curious fact that college level (undergraduate) schools have no self-conscious specialty in "curriculum" corresponding to curriculum theory and development for elementary and secondary schools, as described in Chapter 8. There is also for the college level nothing, that we have discovered, to parallel the *Cardinal Principles of Secondary Education* (National Education Association Commission on Reorganization of Secondary Education, 1918). As a consequence, we do not have major curriculum strands or goals such as "citizenship," "vocational competency," etc., as discussed in Chapter 8 for elementary and secondary schools. Why is this?

Our supposition is that one reason is historical. In the early periods of United States culture, few persons attended college. Those who did attend were largely headed for the ministry, law, or medicine. The undergraduate curriculum consisted primarily of the classical studies—history, mathematics, languages, and rhetoric. The curricula were not designed for the masses, but were intended for the wealthy, the elite, and those heading for the professions. Secondary schools were also more exclusive than at present, and their curricula were for the college bound.

As college became less exclusive, high school curricula tended to diversify, offering choices of academic, vocational, and general education. As the number of persons attending high school increased, and as compulsory attendance laws came into effect, interest increased in identifying broad goals (curriculum strands) for secondary education. Thus, not only were national commissions established to set major goals for secondary education, but also colleges of education began to train curriculum specialists. So the "discipline" of curriculum appeared in the training of teachers and school administrators. But this emphasis did not appear for undergraduate education in general.

A second reason for the lack of a parallel to the "cardinal principles" for undergraduate instruction is the strongly discipline-oriented nature of college faculty. Whereas the teacher in the elementary school is expected to help develop "the whole child," and whereas high school teachers are expected to be interested in cardinal principles (goals) as well as in their subject specialties, college professors must be professors of some academic discipline. Although college faculties do work together to establish the required courses or areas for the first two years, leading to the A.A. degree, their loyalties and their promotion and tenure are centered on their respective disciplines and academic departments. So while required courses are prescribed for the liberal arts and science curriculum of the first two years, these requirements are not based on a needs assessment, as discussed for elementary and secondary schools, in Chapter 8. Rather, they are based on perceptions of what the educated person should know about the arts and sciences, and the capacity to enjoy life, to think, and to solve problems.

A third influence is the perceived mission of the college. Private and public colleges perceive somewhat different missions, but with considerable overlap, of course, among colleges.

In summary, college curricula for the first two years are not based on a systematic needs analysis; and, in the second two years, the students specialize in a "major." The second two years of the curriculum are thus even *more* discipline centered. We will not discuss in this chapter the curriculum for juniors and seniors who switch from liberal arts to a professional college, such as education or nursing. This will be touched upon in Chapter 12. In the remainder of this chapter we have in mind students who attain an undergraduate degree in disciplines other than professional schools.

THE UNDERGRADUATE CURRICULUM

At this point, we again pick up the idea of an "audit trail," which, as seen in Chapter 8, expresses the curriculum in terms of goals and objectives, not in terms of the subject-matter content of a discipline. In the absence of anything approaching a set of "cardinal principles of undergraduate instruction," and in recognition of the general situation in undergraduate curriculum, discussed above, we are working within the existing framework of college and university organization.

While we would like to see something like the "cardinal principles" develop in undergraduate curricula, we do not expect this to happen, and we would foresee problems in converting colleges from the discipline orientation to the "curriculum strand" orientation. Theoretically, however, we can visualize a university which takes the needs assessment and curriculum strand approach. The strands might resemble the strands shown for elementaty and secondary education in Table 8.1, but the objectives for each strand would reflect higher levels of performance of the learners. A similar set of strands would then be prepared for graduate instruction. Both the graduate and undergraduate set of strands would allow specialization in a discipline by the use of different linkages across strands, as shown also in Table 8.1.

A final note about the undergraduate curriculum; some students change majors from undergraduate to graduate school, and some do not. For example, a student first majoring in chemistry may be likely to keep that major through the Ph.D. degree; but a few with that major may change.

Other examples: consider new Ph.D. programs, such as adult education or instructional design. Most students who receive the Ph.D. in these two areas did not have that major in undergraduate school. Also, present chemistry professors probably received the Ph.D. in chemistry, while the professors in adult education, especially the older ones, may have been trained in agriculture or home economics. Many of the present older professors of instructional design were trained in psychology, media, management, or engineering.

Our point is that an undergraduate curriculum oriented to

problem-solving in various strands might make such career shifts more easily accomplished as changes in society create new needs, calling for new majors at both graduate and undergraduate levels.

An Illustrative Audit Trail

Here we take as our example a student majoring in political science at the undergraduate level. We will assume that one strand in the curriculum is "citizenship"—the same strand chosen for our audit trail for a high school graduate in Chapter 8. Other strands might pertain to objectives concerning various levels of government, both in the United States and in other countries. Still other strands might pertain to international law and economics. So specific sequences of lessons in various courses might cut across strands, as illustrated in Chapter 8. Since we have illustrated the idea of links across strands in Chapter 8, here we confine our illustration to the citizenship strand.

Note that for the terminal high school curriculum in Chapter 8, we began with life-long goals and objectives, and worked downward through the secondary and elementary school curriculum. So in Chapter 8 we stated life-long citizenship objectives that we thought could be attained on a basis of no college education. In this chapter we show *additional* citizenship objectives for our hypothetical person holding an undergraduate degree in political science. So in the following audit trail, we intend that you, the reader, will assume that our college graduate can do everything listed in the audit trail for the high school graduate in Chapter 8, plus the following objectives.

Life-Long Citizenship Goals
1. To use the undergraduate degree in political science to have more than the normal impact upon government, politics, and society.
2. Exhibits concern for the welfare of less fortunate people.
3. Selects an area of government to develop personal leadership roles for the betterment of society.
4. Becomes an expert in some aspect of governmental solutions to special and political problems.

5. Actively seeks election or appointment to full-time or part-time roles consistent with the above goals.
6. Exerts leadership in coordination of efforts of local, state, and national government.
7. May choose to develop expertise in world needs and international relations.
8. Develops an organized self-education program in the area named above.
9. Develops both working and lobbying skills to enhance the above activities.
10. Models responsible citizenship for other adults and children.
11. Chooses to participate in public forums to advocate personal values regarding government and society.
12. Organizes time to meet responsibilities to family, work, society, and personal welfare.

Curriculum Goals and Objectives

As stated earlier, the curriculum for the undergraduate major in political science may formally be expressed as "courses" in local, state, and federal government; international law; economics; sociology, etc. However, the faculty of such a program could well develop curriculum strands within courses and across courses, as in the curriculum strands and linkage illustrated for elementary and secondary schools in Table 8.1.

Based on such a curriculum, we assume one strand to be something like "citizenship applications to political science," and we resume our audit trail with that strand in mind.

13. Seeks to participate in class simulations, such as mock trials, mock legislatures, and the like.
14. Volunteers for debates or discussion panels on government and social issues.
15. Practices government and political skills by participating in school elections, student committees, etc.
16. Visits local courts, councils, and legislatures, and seeks internship roles there.
17. If eligible, participates in elections.
18. Studies new sources to compare on-going government functions with principles taught in courses, and seeks interchange between the two.

19. Studies systematic and practical methods for analyzing issues in order to arrive at personal values and related actions.
20. Studies diligently to establish the needed knowledge base for the above activities.
21. Volunteers, as time permits, to work for the welfare of students and others, both for its own sake and to gain experience for citizenship activities after graduation.
22. Seeks to relate history and culture to current international problems and conflicts.

Course Organization

We will assume the existence of a course in local and state government within the political science undergraduate curriculum. This is the reference point for the following objectives for the citizenship strand.

23. Can summarize the various structures and functions of state and local governments.
24. Can summarize the structure and functions of the branches of government in the resident city and state, and show how they resemble that of other cities and states.
25. Can summarize the structure of resident local and state courts, legislative bodies, and executive departments.
26. Conducts interviews and observations of proceedings of local and state government entities, and compares observations with formal descriptions of functions.
27. Compares the actual basis for decisions reached by government entities with theory of government.
28. Keeps current on local and state government functions, and relates them to the course.
29. Volunteers for arranging guest appearances of government officials to the class, as coordinated with the instructor.
30. Is active in directing questions on political and economic issues to government officials.
31. As a project, develops a stand on a local or state issue, and discusses the stand with relevant officials, students, citizens, and the local newspaper.

Lesson Organization

For a lesson in a unit, forms of local governments, within the course just discussed, the following objectives might be adopted.

32. Reports his or her view as to which of the two forms of mayor, "strong" or "weak," the city has adopted, after interviewing the present mayor.

33. Presents the arguments for and against the "strong mayor" option.

34. Presents conclusions about the "strong mayor" option in general, and in respect to this city.

35. Outlines a program to be presented to citizens to bring about any changes believed needed in the role of the mayor in this city. Presents a rationale for the proposed changes.

36. Compares the mayor's function to that of the city manager.

NEEDED RESEARCH

We have said that the matter of curriculum is handled much differently in undergraduate schools than it is in elementary and secondary schools. We have offered some possible explanations for this. We also said that curriculum is viewed as a discipline in colleges of education, and it is a specialty in elementary and secondary school staffing. There is no corresponding discipline of curriculum in colleges and universities. Actual decisions are made by faculty, faculty senates, and administrators.

There is a relatively large body of research on the affective needs of children. Research in child development has provided some guidelines for teachers in helping develop "the whole child." This book offers further recommendations on how to integrate instruction for cognitive and affective objectives.

There is less research on the affective needs of college undergraduate students, and the recent tendency to consider them adults may tend to discourage such research. At the same time, colleges have abandoned the "parental" stance of former years, perhaps further lessening a preceived need to consider "development of the whole adult." Yet we know that undergraduates have affective needs, and we know that this period in their lives may be as stressful as the much heralded period of adolescent "storm and stress." We also know little about the problems of "middle life" as compared to knowledge about children and old people.

Have we turned over the responsibility for the affective welfare of college students to advisors? We know that many college instructors, as persons, are concerned with the total welfare of their students. But as an institution, do colleges formally identify this role as a requirement of faculty positions? Is this role reflected in the curriculum?

We appear to need two kinds of research related to undergraduate instruction. First we need research in the development of college students, and second we need research on the affective aspect of teaching. We cannot undertake here a detailed discussion of the first kind of research, but many of our recommendations in Chapters 14 and 15 about teaching of affective objectives are relevant for both children and adults.

Some research on undergraduate instruction has been conducted so as to deal with attitudes of students toward various teaching methods. Conrad (1982) has summarized this area of research. Some of the conclusions are listed briefly here:

1. Discussions bring about greater changes in attitude and beliefs than do lectures.
2. Discussions enhance problem solving more than do lectures.
3. Lectures are effective for learning facts and for overview, orientation, and summary.
4. While individualized instruction programs may yield superior achievement on the average, there are many drop-outs and incompletes, especially among less academically capable students.
5. Adjustment of method to individual learning modes is recommended, but often is difficut to implement.

Future research is needed to determine, among the recommendations made in this book for integrating affective and cognitive objectives, which are effective for all age groups and which are especially effective for college students.

SUMMARY

We have shown how the concept of curriculum is handled

differently in colleges than in elementary and secondary schools.

We have, nevertheless, seen how the concept of the "audit trail" is as possible for undergraduate instruction as for children.

We have pointed to the need for research on the affective needs of college students, both in their total lives and in their attitudes toward instruction. We have suggested research to verify which of our recommendations for conditions of learning for the affective domain (Chapter 14) are especially applicable for college students.

In this chapter we illustrated further the principles of "design from the top down—teach from the bottom up," and the principle of including both affective and cognitive objectives for college instruction.

Chapter 10

Education for Instructional Designers

RESEARCH IN TRAINING OF INSTRUCTIONAL DESIGNERS

Discussion of the Research

AN ILLUSTRATIVE AUDIT TRAIL

Life-Long Objectives

Objectives to Be Achieved During Pursuit of the Doctorate

Comments Regarding the Illustrative Audit Trail

AUDIT TRAILS AND CURRICULUM DESIGN

SUMMARY

Chapter 10

Education for Instructional Designers

We have chosen not to present a chapter on graduate education in general. We have chosen rather to discuss education for the professions, believing this topic to be of greater interest to the readers. However, for documentation of the continuing great growth in number of graduate degrees awarded, see the summary by Pelczar (1982).

As our illustrative profession for the purpose of this chapter, we have chosen the profession of instructional design. This seemed to be a convenient choice for several reasons:

1. Instructional design is a new profession for which university graduate education and training programs have been established only during the past 20 years or so.

2. Instructional design is a growing profession in terms of number of masters and doctoral degrees awarded and in terms of employment in industry, the military, and higher education and research organizations.

3. We know more about this profession because we, the authors, are members of that profession, and we are engaged in training of students for the profession.

4. As a sub-area of the broader field of education and training, instructional design deals directly with the subject matter of this book, which cuts across education and training.

5. Instructional designers have part of their training in research, and part in practice, making this profession ideal for the purpose of this chapter. This profession also

requires dealing with students, colleagues, clients, and organizations, making possible a wide range of both technical and ethical objectives for an illustrative audit trail.

6. Unlike training for some other professions, practically all faculty members hold the Ph.D. degree, and are proficient in both research and practice. This differs from dental schools, for example, in which many of the faculty members are part-time teachers and part-time practitioners (Zumeta & Solomon, 1982). This leads to concern for sufficient emphasis upon research to improve practice, and creates conflict between academic and professional faculty.

7. While instructional design is a new field for professional training, the curriculum for this field has been based upon procedures recommended by instructional design models for all curricula. Faculty members responsible for training of instructional designers have practiced what they preach; they have seriously worked to define the training needed by practicing professionals, and they have applied formative evaluation procedures to improve on-going training programs. Some of these efforts are described next.

RESEARCH IN TRAINING OF INSTRUCTIONAL DESIGNERS

Faculty members who train instructional designers have initiated graduate training programs on the basis of their own experience as designers and upon their collective estimates of skills needed in various kinds of organizations which employ professionals in instructional design. Boutwell (1977) has described this early phase in the program at Florida State University (FSU). Subsequent to this early state in operating that curriculum, after a sufficient number of students had graduated and been in professional positions for several years, even more intensive efforts were made to evaluate and improve the program at FSU. These later efforts have been described by Redfield and Dick (1984). These more recent efforts included: (a) faculty-developed review of a list of skills needed by instructional designers, (b) cross-checking that list of skills with similar lists developed across several universities (Bratton, 1981; Silber, 1982), (c) conducting a mail survey responded to by 50 graduates working in a variety of settings, (d) convening a group of 10 former students to give additional written and oral recommendations, and (e) revising the curriculum on the basis of the data generated by these means.

The results of the study by Redfield and Dick strongly affirmed the usefulness of the skills in the original curriculum, suggested some areas for added emphasis, and became the basis for further fine-tuning of the curriculum.

It may be noted that the above efforts could be classified as a "demand type needs assessment" (Burton & Merrill, 1977), and a real-life application of formative evaluation (Dick, 1977a). By "demand" is meant that the skills in the curriculum are those thought originally by the faculty to be needed on the job, and these needs were confirmed by graduates on the basis of their more recent job experiences; thus there is a market demand for the skills identified.

The areas identified as requiring even added emphasis in the curriculum, according to the reports from graduates of the curriculum, included: (a) dissemination and diffusion of ideas and products, (b) formative evaluation of instruction, (c) program evaluation, and (d) basic management skills (Redfield & Dick, 1984).

The competency areas identified by the faculty and confirmed by the graduates were broken into two categories: core skills and specialty skills. The core skills were found needed in all career areas, whereas the specialty skills were required more in some career areas than in others.

Eight career areas were identified. These include, among others, working in R & D organizations, military and industrial organizations, universities, state departments of education, and teacher education centers. The report by Redfield and Dick lists all eight areas, and the number of FSU graduates working in each.

Sixteen competency areas were identified, of which seven were specialty areas and nine were core areas. There was remarkable agreement between the areas on the FSU list and other lists referred to earlier.

Discussion of the Research

First, it is reassuring to note that the needs assessment represented in the FSU list of competency areas agreed so well with lists which crossed university boundaries. Thus it can be said that the faculty members and former students in several instructional design programs agree well upon the skills needed by instructional designers. There is an interesting parallel finding that textbooks recommended by both faculty members and design practitioners nationwide are in general agreement (Braden & Sachs, 1983).

Second, we observe that training programs for other professions might well benefit from adopting the research procedures just summarized.

Third, we note the curious absence of reference to the affective domain, particularly the absence of reference to professional ethics. While the recommendation to offer more training in dissemination and diffusion of ideas and products might include how to bring about changes in attitudes on the part of prospective adopters (the need for which was mentioned in Chapter 1), it is curious that neither faculty nor students included attitude objectives and professional ethics for training of instructional designers. While we know by personal contact that the faculty members at FSU consistently model ethical behavior for their students, this emphasis has somehow not attained notice, much less prominence, in the formal list of curriculum competency areas. It is partly because of this curious oversight that we have decided to focus our illustrative audit trail for this chapter upon a small segment of cognitive skills represented in the identified cognitive competency areas, and to show how affective components might be integrated with cognitive ones for that limited area.

We have elsewhere drawn attention to the need to integrate affective and cognitive components in professional training. The possibility of doing this, and support for that possibility, were presented for an area of teacher training (Hurst, 1980b). Also, the need for such an integration of domains has been noted both for materials used to train instructional designers (Briggs, 1984), and for the training materials that designers produce (Briggs, 1982a, 1982b).

It is instructive to add an historical note about the program at FSU, as it illustrates a principle of formative evaluation: "in trying to fix one problem in curriculum design, we sometimes create other problems." Back in about 1974 a course in professional ethics, particularly relating to the conduct of research, *was* taught in the FSU program. Then, due in part to one of the several cycles of program evaluation and revision, that course "dropped through the cracks." Later, a unit on ethics was incorporated into another course, which was also dropped during still another evaluation and revision cycle. Thus, in concentrating upon responding to evidence of need for new curriculum areas, some old ones were dropped. This may be due in part to problems encountered when the entire program faculty participated in curriculum changes, even though one person was designated to implement the curriculum by assigning courses to faculty members. We do not mean to say that the dropped ethics course or unit is more important than the additions that were made by the revision process, nor that formal courses are a substitute for modeling of ethics by faculty members. An important part of the program at FSU is student participation in research and development projects conducted by faculty members and in internships in organizations outside the university. So we do not assert here that ethics are best learned in a formal course. However, we seize upon this historical accident to show how affective objectives, including ethical principles, could be built into *any* course in the curriculum.

In the above context, we next select only one competency area from the list of competency areas, in the article by Redfield and Dick (1984), to use for our illustrative audit trail. We do this by adding affective objectives, and cognitive skills subordinate to the ones listed there.

In spite of the above historical accident, the several cycles of evaluation and program revision unquestionably did more good than harm. New needs *were* identified, and we have no evidence that graduates of the program have not managed to learn professional ethics somewhere. Nevertheless, for the purpose of this book, we choose to illustrate how affective objectives can be included along with cognitive ones in *any* course in the curriculum.

In closing these comments on the research in training of instructional designers, we point to the vitality exhibited by faculties which train these professionals. The attempt to build the curriculum on a sound conceptual and theoretical base has been complemented by a continuing effort to update the curriculum in order to be responsive to real-world needs as reflected in the market place. We feel fortunate to be members of this new and ever-changing profession. We further believe that this book should be a contribution to achievement of some of the future directions of the profession as we attempted to foresee them earlier (Briggs, 1982a). It may be hoped that such vitality continues, and that the present state of the art does not become a cherished tradition not to be questioned in the future.

AN ILLUSTRATIVE AUDIT TRAIL

In the report by Redfield and Dick (1984), previously discussed, nine core competency areas and seven specialty competency areas were listed as used by instructional designers in the performance of their duties. These same areas were also listed in more detail as 22 separate competencies, ranging from conducting and interpreting research, to needs analysis, defining objectives, developing instructional materials, assessment procedures, and general management skills. For the purpose of this illustrative audit trail, we have selected the competency, "developing instructional materials." There is one course by this title in the FSU program for doctoral students, and a course entitled "modular design" for master's students. Other courses and internship experiences also relate to this competency. This competency is a core competency, needed in all career fields which graduates enter.

For the purpose of this audit trail, we will assume that a student completes the doctoral program and enters the job market as a professional instructional designer. So, again, we open our audit trail by stating life-long objectives for this competency, and then go on to objectives achieved during the doctoral program by our hypothetical person. We do not know the sex or color of our hypothetical person, as graduates have included students of both sexes and all races, and they work throughout most parts of the world.

Life-Long Objectives

1. The person will seek to utilize the most appropriate model of instructional materials development, considering the nature of the learners, the setting, and the nature of the objectives to be achieved by use of the learning materials.
2. The person acquires knowledge about a variety of materials development models by reading the professional literature, by participating in a variety of materials development projects, and by conducting research in developing new models or testing old ones. The person also may develop new models or adaptations of existing models to accommodate special learner groups or situations.
3. The person receives, attends to, and internalizes information, criticism, and evaluation of a variety of models. The person uses this information to select models for given situations, or designs unique models when no existing model appears fully appropriate.
4. The person uses formative evaluation to revise and improve the materials developed by the person.
5. When conducting formative evaluation or any research concerning materials being produced, the person exhibits ethical behavior.
6. If an experiment involves assigning learners to alternate versions of the learning materials, and one version consequently proves to be superior to others, the person subsequently arranges for all learners to use the most effective version after the experiment is over.
7. If deception of learners is necessary and justified by the importance of an experiment, the person subsequently conducts a full debriefing on the nature and purpose of the deception, and assists in removing any stress that may have resulted from the deception.
8. The person conducts all tryouts of materials or experiments relating thereto so as to minimize deception or stress.
9. In reporting results of evaluation of materials or research related thereto, the person takes steps to ensure objectivity and freedom from personal bias.

10. In reports relating to materials development and evaluation, the person acknowledges the contributions of colleagues, including students and teachers, and the prior contributions by persons whose research aided in the design of the work. The person also avoids plagiarism in any form, and makes general acknowledgments of major concepts borrowed from others* and specific acknowledgment of source details quoted. Permission for lengthy quotations is sought, following professional and publishing conventions.

11. If the person is a faculty member or supervisor of others, the person models professional ethics in teaching, research, and development activities.

12. The person avoids using a teaching or supervising role to deny others full rights to their own work, within working agreements. The person does not reproduce or publish the work of students or others without their permission, and special acknowledgment of the source.

13. If the person is a faculty member or supervisor, the superior position is never used in a coercive manner to deprive others of their rights by exploiting them sexually, financially, or otherwise.

14. After receiving the doctorate, the person seeks to improve upon the state-of-the-art by scholarly pursuits and design practice.

15. As a life-long endeavor, the person seeks to improve upon the work performed and to maintain high ethical standards. The person consults with colleagues as one means for achieving this objective.

---

*In this section of the chapter, the authors have made use of some of the ethical principles appearing in the code of ethics developed by the American Psychological Association (APA, 1967; 1973). However, we have rephrased and reinterpreted them to apply to the competency area addressed (development of instructional materials). We have not used any other printed professional code of ethics; we have relied upon our own experience and discussion with colleagues in the past. Our faulty memories do not permit more explicit acknowledgment. Readers may wish to consult codes developed by their own professions.

Objectives to Be Achieved During Pursuit of the Doctorate

In continuing our audit trail, to cover the learning of the person during doctoral training, we have maintained our "top down" approach, discussed in previous chapters. Thus we have worked from more general to more specific or subordinate objectives. If you, the reader, prefer to follow the probable sequence of learning these objectives, merely read them in the reverse order.

16. The person will be able to utilize a number of models for developing instructional materials.
17. The person will be able to summarize the features of several "systems models" for designing learning materials and activities, such as models described in the book edited by Reigeluth (1983a).
18. The person will be able to summarize the features of several models of teaching other than systems models, such as the models described by Joyce and Weil (1980).
19. The person will generate a script for a lesson, following an assigned design model, such as the one described by Gagné and Briggs (1979) and by Briggs and Wager (1981).
20. The person will choose to search out techniques to employ in making a script more interesting, motivating, and effective.
21. The person will exercise the time, care, and attention to detail and accuracy required for a script.
22. The person will develop an appropriate achievement test for use in formative evaluation of the script. In so doing, the student will choose to review basic techniques for insuring validity and reliability. The student will write a plan for how the test is to be used during formative evaluation of the script.
23. The student will prepare a set of prescriptions for the script to be developed. This will include a statement of the lesson objective, the media to be used for each event in the lesson, and a script summary or storyboard, for each instructional event.
24. The student will choose to review and incorporate appropriate conditions of learning for the prescriptions to be written for a script.
25. The student will choose to read available material on how to select media for the script to be written.

26. The student will choose to determine the characteristics of the students for whom the designed script is intended, and to describe how this influenced decisions made in planning the script.
27. The student will design an audit trail which is the basis for identifying objectives to be grouped in the planning of the course, its units, and individual lessons within units.
28. The student will choose to attend to and utilize information provided on how to employ instructional curriculum maps, learning hierarchies, and other sequencing aids for the design of a course.
29. The student will demonstrate several methods for writing objectives.
30. The student will originate and explain a value system which he or she has adopted in order to select a preferred method of writing objectives.
31. The student will receive and attend to information provided as to the advantages and disadvantages of several methods of writing objectives. The student will choose to seek out arguments for and against the practice of writing objectives, and will take a position on the issue. (Note: The course requirements will probably oblige the student to write objectives, in any systems-oriented curriculum for training of instructional designers. The student should know this at the outset, and be free to seek another program if the practice conflicts with personal values.)

Comments Regarding the Illustrative Audit Trail

Notice that the above audit trail intersperses cognitive objectives with attitudinal ones. The cognitive objectives represent "the requirements" of the course, in terms of what the student must produce during the course. Although the attitude objectives state that "the student will" take various actions reflecting attitudes, the student may in fact not take all those actions. This choice may reflect either a lack of motivation or a deliberate choice, showing a contrary view to that expressed in the attitude objective. It is possible that not taking some of these attitude-based actions may downgrade the evaluations made of the student's work on cognitive objectives, although it would be best if affective objectives were unobtrusively measured and not used as part of a grading system. This could reflect real hierarchical relationships between cognitive and attitude objectives, so that performance on cognitive objectives is really inferior if the attitude-based objectives are not met. Or, it could reflect the evaluator's reaction to the rejected attitude objective. However this may be, in practice the student would probably opt out of the program if personal values strongly conflict with systems oriented practices.

In any event, we face here the same issue raised in Chapter 1: "should attitude objectives be stated or required?" We pause here to separate this instance into separate issues:

1. As more alternative models for development of instructional materials arise, the practices deemed acceptable by faculty members may be broadened. This would perhaps be considered a lowering of standards by some, and a desirable degree of open choice by others.

2. Students often find out what the cherished practices and values of the doctoral program are before they enroll in it. This enables a freedom of choice which probably no person would wish to remove.

3. Practitioners in all professions define the range of acceptable and unacceptable practice by anyone studying or practicing the profession. Within these limits, there are disagreements among members of a profession, and these should be considered when evaluating a trainee's performance.

4. Instructional systems practices are being well publicized, and open debate between the "systems" approach and other approaches is to be encouraged. This information can assist students in deciding what kind of program they wish to enter.

5. Many instructors welcome debate with students over philosophical differences. This offers the opportunity for modification in the views of both instructor and student.

6. Instructional designers do attempt to seek empirical data in relation to their practices. Models, theories, and

philosophical positions are harder to test by empirical means. Free choice of positions, and hence training programs and professions, is to be encouraged.

7. As philosophical positions shift within a profession, practices will be modified. The present practice of instructional design reflects largely the behavioristic and the information-processing positions. Gradually, perhaps, more concepts from other positions may further influence changes in practice.

8. The market place can influence professional practice. We have mentioned, early in this chapter, how feedback from persons in various employing agencies has influenced the training of instructional designers.

9. Choices about attitude objectives in a professional curriculum involve some issues different from those encountered in curriculum planning for children. In basic education, values held strongly by parents may clash with attitude objectives in the school. These clashes relate to fundamental differences within a pluralistic society on very basic issues. Differences of opinion within a profession hold different implications relating to a narrow range of responsibilities to specific clients or constituencies.

AUDIT TRAILS AND CURRICULUM DESIGN

The preceding example of an audit trail was restricted to one of 22 competency areas listed by Redfield and Dick (1984), in a curriculum for training at the doctoral level in instructional design.

The implication is that 21 more audit trails could be developed for that curriculum. In a broad sense, this has been done. Each instructor for each course in the curriculum conveys the objectives of the course to the students. Usually, however, *only the cognitive objectives are stated.* One value of this is to avoid the problem of dealing with affective objectives in a direct way. Instructors, of course, model and discuss attitudes in a rather incidental way in many courses, and attitudes may be dealt with in a real-life setting during internship experiences.

We do not have a clear idea of whether inclusion of attitude objectives has the same impact for children as for adults in a professional training program. Nor do we know clearly how these differ from learning by adults in non-professional settings. Each of the three settings deserves more thought on this matter.

In any event, our illustrative audit trail demonstrates the feasibility of listing both cognitive and affective objectives, including those pertaininng to professional ethics.

SUMMARY

In this chapter we reviewed research concerning a curriculum for training of professionals in instructional design. This research related to identifying training needs, and formative evaluation and revision of a training program.

From that total curriculum, we selected one of 22 competency areas, and we developed an audit trail for that area, consisting of both cognitive and affective objectives, including those relating to professional ethics.

We briefly discussed the matter of dealing with affective objectives, and we suggested that the issues may be somewhat different for educating children, for professional education, and for non-professional adult learning.

Chapter 11

Audit Trails: Purposes and Procedures

THE FUNCTION OF AUDIT TRAILS

In Existing Conventions

In Our Recommended Model

Relationship to Other Components
Variations Among Situations
  In education
  In education for the professions
  In industrial and military training

HOW TO DO AN AUDIT TRAIL

USES OF AN AUDIT TRAIL

Going from Audit Trail to Curriculum

Going from Curriculum to Instruction

SUMMARY

Chapter 11

Audit Trails: Purposes and Procedures

We have placed this chapter where it is in this book because we wanted you to see the three examples of audit trails in Chapters 8, 9, and 10 before we presented this chapter on how to do an audit trail. In this chapter we first discuss the place of audit trails in the overall context of this book and in the overall activities of needs assessment, curriculum development, and instruction.

THE FUNCTION OF AUDIT TRAILS

The primary function of an audit trail is to serve as a connecting link among needs, curriculum, and instruction. This function is discussed first in terms of existing conventions, then in terms of the overall strategy recommended in this book.

In Existing Conventions

As pointed out in Chapter 8, there is at present a discontinuity among needs, curriculum, and instruction. In conventional practice, one group identifies needs or goals of education, another group designs the curriculum, and still another conducts instruction. To make matters worse, yet another group produces the instructional materials. We observed this separation of responsibilities of the several groups some time ago (Briggs, 1970). One result of this separation of responsibilities is a discontinuity among (a) the broad life-long goals identified by a consensus group through a needs assessment effort, (b) the intermediate goals stated by curriculum developers, and (c) the lessons designed and conducted by teachers.

The discontinuity is reflected in several ways: (a) it is not clear how the curriculum could result in the intended long-term goals, (b) it is not clear how each lesson contributes to either the curriculum goals or the life-long goals, and (c) there are often no suitable instructional materials for some lesson objectives.

The above problem is often exacerbated by a conflict among the four groups (needs assessors, curriculum specialists, teachers, and material developers) as to the purposes of education. The pendulum in curriculum swings from emphasis upon society's needs, to emphasis upon the person's needs, to emphasis upon subject matter areas. At the same time, various persons or agencies interested in education call for emphasis upon basic skills, self-actualization, solving society's problems, earning a living, life-long learning, and general problem solving skills.

So, one kind of discontinuity is disagreement among the groups on the purposes of education. This problem is most complex for the education of children, but even in job training programs similar confusion arises as to the exact purpose of training, such as job skills versus human relations. While the above discontinuity varies in degree, perhaps, between education and training, it is usually present in all cases.

In education, one reason for the federally funded curriculum development projects was to reduce such discontinuity by having one group responsible for designing the goals, curriculum, and teacher training. Other reasons for these projects were to explore alternate curriculum philosophies, to provide for more emphasis upon evaluation, and to serve as a stimulus for curriculum efforts. Federal policy on this matter has shifted, so this method of bringing more continuity may not be promising.

Our recommendation is that audit trails be developed as a means for bringing about better continuity among life-long needs, curriculum, and instruction.

Even when all the groups mentioned above agree upon the purposes and goals of education, so that there is no disagreement upon *intent*, there is still discontinuity, in *practice* at least, in the form of "gaps." That is, there may be some instruction relating to a goal, but not enough to enable students to *reach* that goal. In other words, the instructional objectives do not, collectively, appear adequate for the related need and curriculum goals.

The use of audit trails would enable each group responsible for education or training to perceive what all the groups are planning. At present, goals and objectives are stated at three levels, going from general to specific: (a) life-long needs, (b) curriculum goals, and (c) instructional objectives. It is now more difficult to perceive existing discontinuity than if all goals and objectives were stated as continuous audit trails.

Our suggestion is that when a consensus group has identified the needs, each need results in construction of an audit trail. Then curriculum developers and teachers could design sequences of instruction which do address the identified needs and which do not leave gaps in instruction, and which cut across audit trails when desirable to embrace objectives from more than one audit trail in many instructional sequences.

In summary, within the context of present conventions, the construction of audit trails could be a basis for closer coordination of all the concerned groups to the end that discontinuties are reduced among needs, curriculum goals, and lesson objectives. Thus conflicts between means and ends are reduced, and a mechanism is provided for integrating instruction for cognitive and affective objectives.

In Our Recommended Model

In Chapter 2, we gave an overview of our approach to (a) assuring continuity among needs, goals, and objectives, while at the same time (b) blending affective and cognitive objectives in instruction. We now review the place of the audit trail technique in implementing our recommended approach or model of instructional design.

Relationship to Other Components

In Chapters 1 and 2, we gave an overview of the major components recommended for implementing our model for designing instruction for affective and cognitive objectives. We now review those components to further clarify the purpose of audit trails. Each component in our model is <u>underlined</u>.

A <u>needs assessment</u>, according to Kaufman and English (1979), reveals gaps between present outcomes of education and desired outcomes. Such an assessment is usually made by a group of citizens representing the broad spectrum of persons who are interested in the outcomes of education. Consensus techniques are employed to identify the needs, and to set goals and priorities among goals, so that educators can then develop curriculum and instruction.

Procedures for accomplishing a needs assessment have been presented by Kaufman and English (1979) and by Burton and Merrill (1977) among others. Notice that needs assessment is restricted to <u>ends</u>, not <u>means</u>. This distinction not only emphasizes the different responsibilities of citizen groups, which set the goals (ends or desired outcomes of education), and educators who determine the means of reaching the goals, but also reminds us not to mix up ends and means. Otherwise, people begin to discuss solutions to problems (means) before they are clear about the desired ends. Mixing up problems and solutions at the same time merely adds confusion. It is noteworthy that state legislatures often prescribe means without having first identified a problem (Kaufman, 1983). The result often is a whole array of conflicting legislative proposals for "improving education," each proposal, perhaps, addressing a different perceived but unannounced problem or need.

In the case of industrial training programs relating to a new product or service, one need not belabor the definition of need as a gap between present and desired performance of employees; rather, one can focus on defining the desired outcome of the new training program. Also, in industrial and military settings, one often has the choice of three major ways to meet a new human performance need: selection, training, or on-the-job experience. Some needs might be met by a change in policy or company procedures rather than by developing a training program. We will assume here, however, that education or training is the correct way to meet a new performance need.

The end product of a needs assessment is a set of goals and

priorities among them. These are bases upon which education or training programs are developed.

Our proposed mechanism for connecting up the needs assessment outcomes with a curriculum or training program is the audit trail.

An audit trail is a series of objectives, listed in descending order of generality and complexity, which are to be achieved by instruction and incorporated into the subsequent life and behavior of the learner. Thus an audit trail begins with life-long objectives relating to a need, and goes on through objectives for all levels of the curriculum or training program down to the point of identifying skills already possessed by the intended learners.

An audit trail, in our model, consists of both affective and cognitive objectives, and in many applications would also include psychomotor objectives. The audit trail represents an outline of objectives for curricula, courses, course units, and lessons. Different segments of the audit trail may pertain to several different courses or years of study in a curriculum. Sometimes several objectives in a segment of an audit trail become objectives for a series of lessons. On other occasions, a lesson may draw an objective from several audit trails, as shown in Chapter 8.

An audit trail is constructed for each need resulting from the needs assessment. It is for the curriculum builders and the teachers or instructors to decide when a sequence of lessons should follow only one audit trail and when a sequence of lessons should cross over audit trails.

The audit trail thus becomes the basis for the sequencing of instruction. An audit trail may be broken up into courses, course units, and lessons. Sequences of objectives are taken from one or more audit trails, and arranged so as to enhance the interaction among affective and cognitive objectives.

In the process of arranging sequences of objectives for lessons, one will often need to further analyze some of the objectives in the audit trails, in order to break up an objective in the audit trail into smaller components. Constructing a learning hierarchy (Gagné, 1977) is one way of doing this for cognitive objectives. To enhance interactions between affective and cognitive objectives, one may employ the kind of hierarchy illustrated by Hurst

(1980b), and discussed in Chapter 3. If you refer to the audit trails in Chapters 8, 9, and 10, you will note that the sequencing of affective objectives often follows the taxonomy by Krathwohl *et al.* (1964), also discussed in Chapter 3.

Now we note the relationship of taxonomies of outcomes to audit trails. Chapter 3 mentions several uses of taxonomies. These include checking audit trails for completeness. Also each objective in an audit trail is classified as to type of outcomes listed in a taxonomy, to remind the designer to incorporate appropriate sets of conditions of learning into the instructional events when designing lessons.

So the final relationship of audit trails to other components in our model is in designing and evaluating instruction.

The audit trail is thus an important connecting link to all other components in our design model.

Variations Among Situations

In the previous section we have shown, in general terms, the relationship of the audit trail to other components in our design model. We now discuss audit trails as used in various situations.

In education. We have shown in this chapter and in Chapters 8, 9, and 10 that audit trails are applicable to elementary and secondary education, to undergraduate education, and to education and training for the professions. We now focus more on the situation rather than the purpose of audit trails.

When a consensus group has delivered a list of needs, goals, and priorities to the public for verification and to educators for implementation, audit trails would next be developed, one for each need or goal. We recommend that the first draft of each audit trail be accomplished by one person. The first draft could then be reviewed by the consensus group to see if the intent of that group has been preserved. The first draft would be reviewed by educators and teachers to see if the audit trail could be implemented. If agreement is reached to this point, educators and teachers would study the several audit trails to construct a curriculum scope and sequence plan to be implemented by teachers. This plan would show, year by year, how the curriculum objectives would meet the needs. Then teachers who are responsible for instruction would design lesson sequences for various segments of the curriculum. Hopefully designers of instructional materials would use the lesson objectives as the basis for their work.

In education for the professions. In Chapter 10 we showed how an audit trail was developed for one of 22 competencies identified for a curriculum for a profession. In that situation, the needs assessment was established by faculty members and graduates of the curriculum. Each of the 22 competencies was treated as an established "need." We also demonstrated how affective objectives could be interwoven with the purely cognitive objectives resulting from the needs assessment. The next cycle of formative evaluation and improvement of that program could begin with construction of the remaining 21 audit trails. Note that doing this would provide a much more detailed basis for fine-tuning the program, since perhaps 30 objectives, on the average, would be stated for each of the 22 "needs." This degree of detail would be easier to handle for a professional program of three or four years than for an entire K-12 curriculum. The professional program is not only shorter in duration but also more restricted in scope, as compared to a K-12 curriculum. It also has the advantage of focusing upon training for a professional curriculum whose success is demonstrated by the job performance of the graduates. The success of high school graduates in living and performing in a wide variety of job and life situations would be more difficult to evaluate.

In industrial and military training. In education, the school undertakes responsibility for the child's learning up through high school graduation. In contrast, an industrial or military organization may first offer limited training for newly entering personnel.

In industry, an employee may be hired because he or she can already do the job (meeting needs by personnel selection), or because he or she is judged to have potential for profiting from either formal or on-the-job training and experience. In either event, the person may not be retained if an initial period of service is disappointing. If the initial period goes well, the person may be retained and may receive additional training interspersed with job experience up until the person's retirement.

A similar situation exists in the military. An initial enlistment period is for a limited number of years, and retention beyond that can rest in part upon performance in this initial period.

Due to the above circumstances, an audit trail having life-long goals would be applicable only to retained personnel, but more limited audit trails would be relevant for short-term personnel.

Unlike the situation for elementary and secondary education, the needs assessment for military and industrial personnel will not be a matter of interest or participation beyond the managers of the organizations. Thus, consensus is needed only within the organizations, and with their higher headquarters.

The details of the audit trails would be left to training managers and their staff and instructors. The audit trail functions to guide sequencing of instruction and lesson design, just as in education.

An audit trail is probably easier to conduct for restricted jobs in industry and the military than for public education. They would often contain more psychomotor objectives than would be the case for most educational applications.

HOW TO DO AN AUDIT TRAIL

It is assumed that the person undertaking a draft audit trail understands the purpose of an audit trail as outlined in this chapter. It is also assumed that the person is an expert in the subject matter related to the need for which the audit trail is developed. If these two assumptions are not met in any available person, a team of one instructional designer and one subject matter expert may undertake the task.

The illustrative audit trails in Chapters 8, 9, and 10 are first-draft audit trails. They were developed in a relatively short time without use of any reference documents of any kind. The audit trail in Chapter 8 required about 10 hours to draw up, and the one in Chapter 10 required about two hours. We thus think audit trails are well worth the time they require to draw up, so we believe this is a practical way to achieve the purpose we have described in this chapter.

We next record the rules of thumb we kept in mind in drawing up our illustrative audit trails for Chapters 8, 9, and 10.
1. Determine a starting point representing a single need or goal from the needs assessment. In Chapters 8 and 9, we began with the need "effective citizenship" suggested long ago by a

consensus group (National Education Association Committee on Reorganization of Secondary Education, 1918). We judged this need just as valid today as when it was first proclaimed. In Chapter 8, we drew an audit trail intended for the high school graduate. In Chapter 9, we drew an audit trail for the college graduate who majored in political science.

2. Put aside all textbooks, course outlines, lecture notes, lesson plans, or existing curriculum scope and sequence statements. Do not refer to any such materials while working on the draft audit trail. Referring to them might lead you to mix up objectives, teaching methods, and course content, thus confusing ends and means. Also, our purpose is to avoid the gaps and discontinuities in existing documents which we discussed earlier in this chapter.

3. Begin to write objectives which describe what the person can and will do as an adult after completing all formal education or training. Begin with the most general, complex objectives the person will reach at the peak of his or her adult life or professional career. These are the ultimate life-long objectives for this need or curriculum strand.

4. In focusing upon describing what the person will be doing to show that each objective has been achieved (ends), avoid any reference to how the person learned to do it (means).

5. Include actions resulting from decisions or choices (affective objectives) as well as actions reflecting knowledge and skills (cognitive objectives).

6. If relevant to the need, also include psychomotor objectives (which do not appear in our audit trails because they are not relevant). To decide whether a performance of a special motor skill is needed, ask: "Could any adult with normal physical and manual dexterity do this without motor skill training *if only he or she knew what to do*?" (We call a TV repairman not because he is more clever with his hands than we are but because he *knows* things we do not know.)

7. State each objectives in common language, not in technical terms. Both laymen and subject-matter specialists have a reason for later reviewing your audit trail. Write it so that any educated adult can read it.

8. Do not worry about using any of the several available formal models for writing objectives; we referred to several such models in Chapter 8. Save the models for a later use among education and training professionals, to be mentioned later in this chapter. However, you may find it useful in clarifying your own intent and to convey that intent to others, to use some of the "standard verbs" suggested by Gagné and Briggs (1979) and adopted by Briggs and Wager (1981). More about this later.

9. Do not worry if you seem to include both a cognitive and an affective component in the same objective.

10. Try to arrange related cognitive and affective objectives in such a sequence that learning in one domain will enhance the other.

11. Write the objectives "from the top down." Start with the most general and complex life-long objectives and work in supporting objectives next in the sequence. Then take up less complex life-long objectives before turning to objectives to be demonstrated at the end of education and training. Then list objectives to be achieved *during* education and training. Keep this descending order until you begin to state objectives people presumably have mastered *before entering* education and training. Look at the last few objectives in the audit trail in Chapter 8. They were presumably learned in the home before entering school. Leave these objectives in your draft audit trail so that teachers can check to see whether children have achieved these objectives. This aids in planning any needed "catch up" or "remedial" instruction.

12. Don't worry about when or how the objective will be learned. Later on, curriculum specialists and teachers will decide upon this. While some of your objectives will later become "end-of-curriculum" objectives, or "course" objectives, or "unit" objectives, or "lesson" objectives, leave that aside for now. We discuss this later.

13. Don't worry too much about the completeness of your audit trail, but do be concerned about its comprehensiveness. If there are some gaps between or among general and supporting objectives, these are the responsibility of curriculum and

instruction personnel. So attend to the scope of your major objectives, and do the best you can to avoid large gaps. Cover a reasonable number of supporting or enabling objectives for the more general or complex objectives. To illustrate these considerations, our audit trail for "developing instructional materials" in Chapter 10 listed only 31 objectives. Each of these 31 objectives represents a rather "large step" in learning. When this audit trail is converted to a "course syllabus," it may contain some 200 objectives, because the syllabus will break down skills in the audit trail into subordinate skills, and many more "information" objectives would appear in the syllabus. (The syllabus for such a course taught by one of the authors consists of 15 pages of both "information" and "intellectual skills" objectives, plus "criteria for evaluating the students' products" for the course. Honestly, we checked this *after* we drew the audit trail.)

14. After you write each major objective, ask yourself "what would the person previously have had to learn in order to demonstrate ability to do this objective?" This will give you a clue for some of the enabling objectives. This is the same question asked when doing a more limited learning hierarchy for a single intellectual skills (Gagné, 1977). One also asks "what affective objectives would either *facilitate* learning of this cognitive objective or *result from* learning it" (Hurst, 1980b)?

These, then, are the "rules of thumb" that we can recall from *our first experience* in writing draft audit trails. We hope these rules and examples will lead others to use this key technique in our model for achieving two major goals: (a) integrating instruction for affective and cognitive objectives and (b) overcoming the present discontinuity, disagreement, and gaps among needs, curriculum, and instruction.

USE OF AN AUDIT TRAIL

After the draft audit trail has been completed, it can then be both put to use and revised.

It can be checked by the consensus group which generated the need. But the major use is in constructing a curriculum or a course (depending upon the complexity of the need and the amount of learning time estimated to be needed). The audit trail in Chapter 8 is for an entire K-12 curriculum, and it represents "one curriculum strand" among perhaps a dozen needs and resulting audit trails and curriculum strands. The audit trail in Chapter 9 represents one curriculum strand in a college undergraduate major in political science. The audit trail in Chapter 10 represents a one-semester doctoral level course plus use of skills from other courses and internship experiences. Due to the differences among these three situations, different sets of people would be involved in converting the audit trail to a curriculum strand and the resulting instruction.

Going from Audit Trail to Curriculum

To take the most complex situation as an example, we discuss the use of the audit trail in curriculum construction or revision for elementary and secondary schools. So our audit trail in Chapter 8 is one of, say, 10 strands, each responsive to a different identified need. After the first draft of each of the audit trails has been completed and checked for consistency with the intents in the 10 needs identified by the citizen consensus group, the curriculum and instruction personnel meet the administrators and the authors of the draft audit trails. This group then develops a scope and sequence plan, showing which segments in each audit trail are to be accomplished during each year of schooling.

The next step is to arrange instructional "units" within each year of instruction. Some of these units may consist of several objectives in sequence from one audit trail. Other units may cut across two or more audit trails, using one or more objectives from each audit trail selected for the unit. We illustrated this in Chapter 8. The group which accomplishes this step may or may not be the same group which first checked the audit trail.

The completion of this step usually would represent the end of the curriculum development work. Just how this step and the next step merge would vary among educational organizations.

Going from Curriculum to Instruction

The work completed in the above phase would become the basis for designing the instruction. Again, just who are involved in this varies among organizations, as well as where one stage ends and another begins.

During either the previous step or this one, in any event, the objectives from the audit trails, in the original or revised form, become expressed as course or end-of-year objectives. Examples of designing instruction by making three levels of curriculum maps (for courses, units, and lessons) have been presented by Briggs and Wager (1981). The curriculum map is a convenient way to divide the objectives into the three levels of specificity appropriate for course objectives, unit objectives, and lesson objectives. There is nothing sacred about using three levels rather than fewer or more levels. These three levels are convenient for a course of five months, but they may not be convenient for a two-week training course. In any event, the purpose of arranging objectives into levels is to preserve the degree of generality or specificity of various objectives, so that superordinate and subordinate relationships among the objectives remain clear. The implication of this relates to the sequence of objectives for instruction, and to time allocations for instruction.

During this phase of work, some of the gaps in the audit trails are filled by writing more subordinate objectives. It is at this stage that the language in the objectives from the audit trails may be revised, even when the original intent is to be maintained. We refer back now to earlier comments to the effect that adopting one of the several formal models for writing objectives may be worthwhile when all members of a working group are educational or training professionals. The purpose of using one of these models is to clarify intent of objectives by using a more precise language and format for expressing objectives. If all members of the group can agree to use the same model for writing objectives, communication is improved. We have listed in Chapter 8 only three of the many models for defining objectives (Mager, 1975; Gagné & Briggs, 1979; Romiszowski, 1981). We add now a fourth reference source (Briggs & Wager, 1981), which offers practice exercises for learning to use the model by Gagné and Briggs.

For this book, we have adopted the model of writing objectives by Gagné and Briggs and continued by Briggs and Wager. One advantage of this model is that it employs two verbs for each objective: a capability verb and an action verb. The action verb expresses the *observable overt performance* of the learner, such as on a test over the objective. The capability verb expresses the newly learned *capability that we infer* has been demonstrated by the overt performance. Many examples of objectives written according to this model and discussion of them appear in the two references cited above. In the model by Gagné and Briggs there is a *standard capability verb* for all objectives within a sub-domain in a taxonomy, while the action verbs may vary among objectives within the same category.

The use of these standard capability verbs does seem to enhance communication among those who use the model, and it therefore helps reaching agreements among member of the working group. Any disagreements then are over the intended outcomes of instruction, not disagreements in interpreting the meaning of an objective. This improved communication facilitates reaching agreements on the objectives desired, how they will be taught, and how the learners' performance will be assessed following relevant instruction.

In Chapter 15, we list the standard capability verbs offered by Gagné and Briggs (1979), as well as some new verbs for new taxonomy categories, especially in the affective domain.

The end product of this phase of work is the identification of sequences of objectives pertaining to desired course outcomes, unit outcomes, and lesson outcomes.

Individual teachers assigned responsibility for specific sets of objectives then proceed to design lessons and to conduct them. After this, student achievement is assessed at appropriate points, both to improve the instruction and to evaluate learner progress. The design of each lesson is the subject for Chapter 15.

SUMMARY

In this chapter we have shown the important functions served by audit trails in the design of curriculum, courses and course units, and lessons, and in evaluation.

We described how audit trails can be used to solve two important problems addressed in this book: (a) the artificial separation of instruction for affective and cognitive objectives, and (b) the discontinuity, disagreement, and gaps among needs, curriculum, and instruction.

We next traced the connection between audit trails and needs assessment, curriculum, the sequencing of instruction, the design of lessons, and the assessment of learner performance. Audit trails serve as an important connecting link among the components in our design model.

Having provided examples of audit trails in Chapters 8, 9, and 10, in this chapter we offered rules of thumb for doing first draft audit trails, and we have described how audit trails are then used in curriculum and instruction.

We closed by discussing models for writing objectives, and we referred to more information about one of the models, presented in Chapter 15.

Introduction to Part IV:

Other Applications

In Part IV, we give two additional applications of our work: (a) Industrial and Military Training, and (b) Education for the Professions. We continue to discuss audit trails, and the integration of the affective and cognitive domains; however, we address these applications more generally than we did in Part III.

In Chapter 12, we trace some of the origins of instructional technology, and we discuss the special features of planning of training for industrial and military applications. We focus on audit trails as a way to plan for career progression. We draw some sequencing implications from Part III and some training principles from Part V. We discuss motivation and self-monitoring behaviors in relation to computer-assisted instruction. We do not pretend, however, to review the literature in industrial and military training. We do discuss the relationships among morale, motivation, and proficiency.

In Chapter 13, we discuss a variety of issues relating to education for the professions, especially the health professions. We call attention to several curricular issues related to the affective domain, paying particular attention to medical ethics and to the training of health professionals in interpersonal skills.

We do not offer illustrative audit trails in Part IV, as we did in Part III. This is the major distinction between Parts III and IV, both of which deal with special applications of our overall model.

Chapter 12

Industrial and Military Training

293

Chapter 12

Industrial and Military Training

In Part I of this book, we called attention to two major problems in research and in instructional practice: (a) the separation of the affective from the cognitive domain, and (b) the discontinuity among needs, goals, and objectives.

In Part II, we reviewed research in the affective domain because we need a clearer view of what that domain embraces before dealing with how to integrate it with the cognitive domain. We also reviewed briefly, however, the status of research in the cognitive domain.

In Part III, we presented three audit trails as examples of how to address both problems mentioned in the first paragraph, above, especially for education in elementary and secondary schools (Chapter 8), in undergraduate education (Chapter 9), and in education for the professions (Chapter 10). In Chapter 11, we showed how audit trails help integrate the affective and cognitive domains and help bring continuity among needs, curriculum, and instruction. Audit trails thus address the *sequencing of instructional objectives* in such a way as to enable learners to achieve the life-long goals of education. Later, in Part V, we will turn to the second major component in our approach to solving the problems we identified in Part I, namely the design of lessons which incorporate appropriate *conditions of learning*. Thus, sequencing of instruction and lesson design are the two major integrating mechanism for handling the total complex of issues addressed in this book.

Turning now to industrial and military training, we find that the magnitude of the two major problems appears somewhat less than is the case in education. There are several reasons for this:

1. Education is responsible for learning during the formative years, approximately from ages 5 to 18. So a longer period of learning must be planned than is the case in most industrial and military training programs.
2. Education is for all children, regardless of their initial competencies or their eventual careers. Education thus must plan for long-range periods, for a variety of types of life stations, for the entire range of entry status of children.
3. Education covers the period when both cognitive and affective learning shape the entire personalities of children.
4. Education must be oriented to the total adult roles and responsibilities the children will later undertake. Industrial and military training programs are more narrowly oriented, can exclude ineligible persons, and begin with already fixed sets of adult attitudes, values, and skills.

For the above reasons, the problem of discontinuity among needs, curriculum goals, and instructional objectives is less severe in industry and the military than in education. Also, a narrower range of persons is responsible for the goals in industry and the military. For these and other reasons, we do not present audit trails for industrial and military training. Rather, we discuss sequencing of instruction within a more narrow context.

On the other hand, the problem of integrating affective and cognitive objectives during instruction is present for all formal learning, but again, it is a more narrow problem in training than in education. Education is concerned with the development of "the whole child," including citizenship, morality, and social development during formative years. Training is concerned with morale, motivation, and proficiency *within the interest of the employing organization*, not necessarily related to the adult's total role in society.

In general, the *principles* of sequencing of instructional objectives and the design of lessons are the same for education and training, but the *setting* and the *missions* are different. Therefore, in this chapter we concentrate on setting and mission, since other chapters contain the principles.

THE ORIGINS OF INSTRUCTIONAL TECHNOLOGY

This is an appropriate chapter in which to mention briefly the origins of instructional technology because they lie, in large part, in industrial and military training research.

Industrial Contributions

For nearly a century industrial psychologists have played a prominent role in selecting, training, and evaluating personnel. In some cases they were, or worked with, "efficiency experts" or "time and motion" study people. In the early days their entire loyalties were to the company which employed them. But as they began to work with safety measures and the morale and motivation of workers, benefits began to accrue for both workers and management. Some of the first applications of statistical regression techniques focused upon tests for the prediction of job success of applicants for employment, and of trainees. Later psychologists engaged in management training, interpersonal relationships, screening for management personnel, and similar functions.

Many of our present educational media had their origins in industrial training. Industry first produced the hardware, such as television and computers, and then in the natural course of affairs entered the software development field. Now industry tends to acknowledge instructional technology as the production of both hardware and software for training. In some companies, the only training interest is for company employees, but in a growing number of cases industry markets hardware, software, and *training*.

While the bulk of industrial training and research is practice oriented, many companies continue research and development (R & D) to improve the state of the art in instructional technology. A few, such as Bell Laboratories, conduct basic research in learning even when not associated with a product or planned product.

As instructional technology became a field and profession of its own, the work which was formerly the province of the industrial psychologist attracted engineers, managers, and others.

With the growth of computers, microcomputers, videodiscs, and the like, industry has taken a prominent leadership role in the field now known variously as: instructional systems design, educational technology, instructional technology, instructional design, etc. Many former "media specialists" have joined instructional technology.

At present, training is big business, as mentioned in Chapter 1. Professional instructional designers are employed in industry. Many of these people earned advanced degrees in university programs such as those described in Chapter 10. At present, the job market for such persons is promising in industry.

Military Contributions

Branson (1977) places the beginning of instructional technology with the "testing machine" developed by Pressey (1926). Work with teaching and testing machines was continued by Pressey (1950) for many years, in educational settings. So Pressey's first work in this area predated Skinner's article on teaching machines (1958) by 32 years. Pressey advocated the "large step" multiple-choice form of practice questions used as an adjunct to the textbook. Skinner advocated the "small step" for each learner-constructed response in a special text separate from a textbook. Both researchers encouraged a combination of print materials and machine-contained materials for both instruction and testing (Briggs, 1960).

Aside from the above origins within education, instructional technology had its largest early surge in the military. During World War II, psychologists were pressed into work to develop personnel selection, classification, and training for the military. A part of this work included research and development of training films. Another effort was for selection and training of flight crews (the Air Force was a part of the Army at that time).

After World War II, psychologists continued to work for all the military services, continuing research and development relating to personnel, including training.

During the post-war period up to 1958, probably the largest single group of psychologists working in any single organization was employed as civilians in the several laboratories of the Air Force Personnel and Training Research Center, within the Air Research and Development Command. These laboratories, under the leadership of Arthur W. Melton, centered upon training of pilots and other aircrew members and upon training of personnel for maintenance of electronic equipment. It was in that organization that many of the concepts and techniques of present instructional technology were developed. For example, Briggs (1980) traced how his own later contributions to a model of instructional design (Briggs, 1970, 1977; Briggs & Wager, 1981; Gagné & Briggs, 1979) grew out of his experience relating to training of maintenance technicians for an electronic system. Concepts and techniques developed then for a specific job application were only later recognized by him as generic—relevant for any instructional purpose.

Many of the research reports written in the Air Force during that period were since reproduced or summarized in the form of books (Finch, 1960; Gagné, 1962; Lumsdaine, 1961; Lumsdaine & Glaser, 1960). Some of the reports produced by the organization during that period were placed in the library of the University of Denver when the group was disbanded.

Apart from training of personnel to operate and maintain equipment then in the field, the Air Force Personnel and Training Research Center, under the leadership of Robert M. Gagné, also developed techniques for forecasting job requirements for new equipment still in the planning and design stages. This strikes us now as an early form of futurism. Psychologists worked with design engineers to learn about plans for the new equipment so that personnel could be trained to handle that equipment *before it was delivered to the field*.

Other groups of workers similar to the Air Force organization just described have engaged in similar activities in all the Armed Forces. Many of the training programs developed either in the Armed Forces or by contractors in industry naturally centered around jobs relating to operating and maintaining equipment. Thus, part of the training plans related to use of training aids, training devices, and simulators (Branson, 1977). Some of these kinds of training equipment not only facilitated realistic practice of jobs or job tasks but also contained teaching and feedback features (Briggs, 1959).

It is apparent that early work done in military organizations contributed significantly to the invention and use of concepts and techniques which are now recognizable in generic form in present instructional design models and practices. Some believe (Swanson, 1982) that the private sector may replace military training as a major contributor in the advancement of theory and practice in instructional technology. Be that as it may, both industrial and military organizations have made major contributions to the field. Many present academic personnel (professors in universities) were former members of industry and the military; they continue to provide conceptual leadership in the field, but they do not have the resources to do the applied work needed to implement new ideas. Many, of course, continue contact with military and industrial organizations as consultants.

THE DESIGN OF TRAINING PROGRAMS

As we have seen, many of the origins of present-day instructional technology were in industrial and military training. So it is not surprising that instructional technology continues to flourish there. Branson (1977) has outlined many of the reasons for this, contrasting industrial and military management conventions and traditions with those in universities. Wager (1977) also has summarized university practices which create barriers to applications of instructional technology in higher education.

If instructional technology were only a matter of interest in machines and equipment employed for learning purposes, the greater interest in them in industry and the military, as compared to education, would be easy to comprehend. But since it is widely recognized that software and the entire process for developing it are *just as important as the hardware*, we have to look further to understand the slow acceptance of the technology in universities. Also, there is increasing awareness that the processes of instructional design technology are just as applicable to conventional teacher conducted, group instruction, as to highly structured, pre-packaged instruction. Martin (1984) has made the point that when the designer has really internalized the principles of instructional design, he or she can implement them by either highly structured, individualized materials or by highly flexible group processes.

These major factors appear to lie at the heart of the more ready acceptance of instructional technology in industrial and military training than in universities:

1. *The management structure.* Training decisions are made by relatively high levels of management in industry and military organizations, and instructors abide by those decisions. In universities, the professors chart their own course and tend to "teach as they were taught."

2. *The instructional model.* Business and military training is concerned with efficiency—the greatest amount of learning in the shortest time, because training is an overhead expense. Training time is viewed as non-productive time when the trainees are not carrying out their job duties. In universities the time unit is semesters or quarters—*time to be filled*.

3. *The criterion of learning.* In training, the interest is "can the trainee perform the required tasks or not?" Especially in critical skills where errors could result in damage to equipment, injury to persons, or failure of the mission, a high level of precision in trainee performance is required for a "pass" on the test. In universities, grading is typically "on the curve," a "C" being the average (and acceptable) grade.

4. *Vested interests.* Most instructors in training programs would rather be out in the field performing the job than in the classroom teaching the job to trainees. If machines can replace them as instructors or at least reduce their time in the classroom, they will be happy. Teachers and professors, on the other hand, spent years acquiring their knowledge of subject matter, whether they have been through teacher training programs or not. They have an interest in maintaining the status quo in teaching methods. They are professional teachers. Of course, there are exceptions to all of this. Some training organizations

provide instructor training to make the undertaking more professional, and some professors seek assistance from educational technology faculty members to improve their teaching.

5. *Traditions in teaching methods.* Training is largely "job oriented," so the instructor demonstrates how to do the job, and requires the trainee to practice it. Much of the job requires following fixed procedures established by others. Precision, accuracy, and speed are often required. Discovery of new solutions or procedures by the trainee is usually discouraged. Demonstration and practice are the usual methods of training. University teaching follows the patterns set in German and English universities—lectures, seminars, and laboratories to encourage both the acquisition of present knowledge and the discovery of new knowledge.

The above circumstances, taken together, tend to favor highly structured, pre-packaged, individualized, and if possible *automated* instruction for training purposes. Instructional design models appear to be highly compatible with training purposes, especially when the objectives consist of information, intellectual skills, and motor skills. Due to the origin of those models, they pay more attention to design of instructional materials than to group processes. We have a long way to go in analyzing the role of the teacher and group processes (Briggs, 1982), especially for the affective domain, and for development of cognitive strategies. This book is intended to help redress the imbalance into which instructional design models have drifted.

Having addressed some of the differences between training and education, we now turn to more specific matters in military and industrial training—matters relating to the theme of this book.

Industrial Training

While we have said that industrial training is largely directed toward the performance of specific jobs, we now need to add that jobs vary greatly in nature, and so the nature of training also varies greatly. For example, an industrial firm might classify jobs as follows: assembly line jobs, technical jobs, sales jobs, and management jobs. This immediately suggests several kinds of training and varying amounts of that training for different employees. In this chapter, we will focus upon determining training requirements and sequencing of instruction, since the matter of lesson design is addressed in Part V.

Determining Training Requirements

We need to distinguish between employees who will probably hold the same job at a company for the duration of their employment and those who will progress through an entire series of jobs. If a person takes an assembly line job of narrow scope, a minimum of training is necessary at the outset, and only very small amounts of retraining as the product or assembly line procedures are changed. On the other hand, a person may start on the assembly line, then go to a technical job, say, in product redesign, then go into sales, then sales management, and then general management. The two career patterns are very different, and the training requirements are different.

For a career ladder. In a large company it may be practical to develop audit trails (Part III) for employees who may follow a "career ladder" going from a simple job to a complex one. Just as we presented an audit trail for citizenship behavior from elementary school through adulthood in Chapter 8, it would be possible to develop audit trails for employees who start in routine jobs and progress on to high management positions. Different segments from appropriate audit trails would then be used as the basis for designing the formal training programs the employee would receive over a period of years, and on-the-job training which may be required, all interspersed with periods of performing in the various jobs in a career ladder. Even knowing that such career progression and training for it are possible and do exist should be a morale builder for those who wish to achieve career progression. This might be a profitable plan for many companies to follow, and it would result in a publicized policy for career progression for those new employees who have the ability and interest to pursue such a plan.

The technique of audit trails could thus become a management tool for planning for career progression and for notifying employees that promotion is not a matter of luck or favoritism. The mixture of training programs for such a career progression might include technical training, sales training, human relations training, and management training.

For specific jobs. An advantage in planning training for a specific job is the possibility of using "job analysis" as the mechanism for identifying the training objectives. This is a much less complex problem than designing a curriculum for public education. A job analysis is developed by watching skilled workers perform the job, and noting each action on a job analysis form. As Branson (1977) has described, job analysis is sometimes followed by an occupational survey, in which a questionnaire is sent to a large number of people performing the same job, even perhaps in different industries. The incumbents indicate which specific tasks they perform, how long each task takes, and how often it is performed. Trade associations often cooperate in such surveys, and they may even pool resources to design the training.

It is important to distinguish between a *job analysis* and a *training analysis.* The order in which skilled personnel perform the various tasks in a job is not necessarily the order in which trainees should learn the tasks. Nor should each task necessarily be taught initially just as it is performed on the job. While a job analysis assures the *external validity* of training—the extent to which training corresponds with actual job requirements—it does not assure effectiveness and efficiency of learning during training. Training analysis studies reveal subordinate competencies for each job task which are not apparent by watching the skilled worker perform the job. Also, consideration is given to transfer of learning—how learning of one task or subordinate competency may facilitate the learning of another task or competency. Such a training analysis may include constructing hierarchies for intellectual skills (Gagné, 1977) or constructing instructional maps (Briggs & Wager, 1981) to show relationships and implied teaching sequences for objectives in the cognitive and affective domains.

Instructional sequences are then designed for the training program, listing detailed objectives in the order in which they are to be taught. Some entire sequences may be for information learning or intellectual skill learning, and so on, for each category in cognitive and affective taxonomies (Part II). Our concern here is for *integrating* the two domains when designing learning sequences.

Sequencing of Objectives for Instruction

We could not find many examples of education or training programs which systematically intermix cognitive and affective objectives. Thus the need for this book. Most models of teaching focus on one domain or the other, but not on both. The same is true of training programs.

In industry, job skill training tends to be separated from management training. Only the latter may bring in interpersonal relationships, and this is usually done in separate courses, such as T-group training. So the separation of the two domains persists. Yet we have reason to believe from the research by Hurst (1980b) and by Young (1984) that our recommended mixing of the two domains in the sequencing of instruction is a sound one. So we next summarize a few examples which are first steps toward the kind of sequencing recommendations that we are advocating.

The study by Markle. Markle (1977) has described the development of a First Aid and Safety Course developed by the American Institutes for Research for AT&T. We now comment on several remarkable aspects of that project.

1. Since first aid training was required for all employees of AT&T and its then associated Bell Telephone Companies, the different companies pooled resources to fund the development a new programs. Previously, each company had developed its own programs, of unknown effectiveness.

2. The contractual requirement was to reduce training time from 10 clock hours to 7.5 hours, at no loss of effectiveness as compared to previous courses.

3. The American National Red Cross First Aid Manual was to be the authoritative source from which the training content would be derived, and medical personnel approved by the Red Cross were to be the final authority on the correctness of the course content. Note that we usually recommend stating course objectives first, then producing relevant training materials (content). But in this

instance the Red Cross Manual was the authoritative source from which were developed the training objectives and the content of the materials. Another instance of this sort is represented in the study by Pantelidis (1975), who used state laws and regulations to design training in supervision of state employees. In both instances, the authoritative source was sound as to content but could not be read and used by trainees to insure dependable learning.

4. Markle employed tryouts and revisions (formative evaluation) for every design step from evaluating the objectives to evaluating the complete draft program and its component parts. Normally formative evaluation is conducted only after first-draft instructional materials have been developed.

5. Markle employed a "bare bones" approach to designing instructional materials. First, test questions were administered to tryout personnel, with automatic recording of the reading time and response time for each test question. The test items were resequenced with feedback to each response, and both response accuracy and response time were recorded for another tryout group. *Only when the tryout people failed a test item was instruction added.* This keeps unnecessary material from creeping into the instruction, and thereafter response times as well as response errors were used to add instruction, delete already known material, or to revise test items.

6. No formal media selection model was followed. Rather, instruction was designed for each objective remaining after identifying the previously known material. The resulting program consisted of films, workbook print material, and manual practice (for bandage wrapping and resuscitation).

7. The results were impressive. After three tryouts and revisions (and more revisions for specific parts of the program), the average score for the new program was 270, compared to a mean of 85 for untrained personnel and 145 for graduates of the standard course, on a test having a possible score of 326 points. Markle did not report the standard deviations in the document cited, but our recollection is that the distributions of scores for the new program and the old program *did not overlap.* That is, the lowest scoring person in the new program outscored the highest person in the old program. No test of statistical significance is needed. Also, the time limit of 7.5 hours was met.

8. Due to the success of the program when routinely used for AT&T personnel, other industries began to request permission to use the new course. As a result, AT&T made the program available to the American Red Cross for outside distribution. From 1970 through 1975, over 2.5 million persons were trained with the new program. The resulting time saving adds up to many times the cost of developing the program.

9. As a dedicated empiricist, Markle has since further revised the program, and he has developed other first aid programs for special group of people, such as a program for non-readers.

10. Affective elements in the program began with a series of filmed accident vignettes. Six frequently occurring situations were used. These vignettes begin the program with drama; each situation is carried to the point where the film stops and a critical question, relevant to the instruction, is posed. It is assumed that these vignettes arouse interest, provide a set for what is to follow later, and help state objectives. Each vignette is encountered again at the opening of the related instructional segment. Each relates to a critical decision to be made for each type of accident, injury, or illness.

The program by Paulsen. Paulsen has conducted a human relations program for managers and supervisors at IBM. His major strategy is to keep the training simple and practical, and to get the trainees to use it both in training simulations and immediately on the job. He described his program at a seminar at Florida State University in January, 1984. In response to our request, he supplied three examples of the kind of behaviors he asks the trainees to practice on the job. These "represent modifications of learning points originally written by Mel Sorcher." Paulsen kindly granted permission to use these three lessons for this book (Personal Communication from John R. Paulsen, February 6, 1984).

The three sets of behaviors, each related to a different management function, are presented next. Note the mixture of cognitive and affective language, as in our audit trails in Part III.

Handling an Employee Complaints
1. Listen, without arguing, to the full story.

2. Ask questions, if necessary, to understand the details.
3. Restate the employee's concern, recounting each step of the story.
4. Let the employee know you understand the reason for his/her concern.
5. State your position.
6. Arrange a follow-up meeting, if appropriate.

Giving Verbal Recognition

1. Choose a current incident to be recognized.
2. Tell exactly what the employee did and why it deserved recognition.
3. Express your personal appreciation to the employee.
4. Ask if there is anything the employee needs on the job.

Discussing Personal Work Habits

1. Tell the employee, without hostility, what you have seen and explain why it concerns you.
2. Ask for and listen to reasons for the behavior.
3. Ask for the employee's ideas on how to solve the problem.
4. Offer your help in solving the problem.
5. If appropriate, write down the ideas agreed upon and plan a specific follow-up date.
6. Express your confidence in the employee.

Consulting experiences. Industry meets training requirements for its own personnel by four different means: "in house" development of training by company personnel; purchase of training packages; arrangement for training development contracts; and use of outside consultants. In this section, we report two examples of the use of a consultant.

One of the authors served as a consultant for a telephone company on several occasions. We report here experiences with two such projects, training of "station installers" and training of salesmen for yellow page advertisements in the telephone book.

Station installer was the job title for men (they were all men, at that time) who place telephones in homes or offices. This involves determining a new number, stringing wires from underground cables or poles to the building, drilling holes, installing the telephone, etc. The company wished to utilize its own experienced installers as the course developers for an improved course. The consultant was engaged to train these men in course development and to oversee the development project. The course developers were able with assistance to list the job tasks required and to participate in discussion of how to design the training. However, when the manager reviewed the task list, he said: "This is fine for the technical part of the job, but where is the training on customer relations and sales?" The course developers disclaimed ability to specify behaviors representing that aspect of the job. They prided themselves on being "technicians," not "public relations men" or "salesmen." But management personnel said it was company policy for station installers to volunteer to answer any customer questions about service available anywhere in the company, and to attempt to sell additional phone lines or extensions when appropriate for the size of the house, the family, their telephone needs, etc. The manager also said there were two evidences of need for improved training: (a) customers were complaining that the installers seemed uninterested in anything but getting the order filled, and (b) few orders for additional service were placed after initial installment.

The consultant asked for a more detailed statement of company policy regarding the public relations and sales aspect of the job. The managers replied, "we all know what it is," but they could not be more specific. So the consultant decided to apply the "critical incident technique," earlier developed by John C. Flanagan, for such an instance. Groups of supervisors of installers were convened and handed two sheets of paper. One sheet contained a request for the supervisor to describe one installation by one man representing an example of "good public relations and sales" behavior. The directions stressed "describe exactly what the installer said or did that made his actions good company policy." The second sheet requested a similar description of an incident representing poor performance on this aspect of company policy. All these "critical incidents sheets," numbering about 300, were collected, sorted, and studied. Using these, the consultant wrote a set of course objectives for this aspect of the job. The manager was delighted. "This is exactly what I meant," he said. The consultant then designed a self-instructional booklet and a test over the new objectives. As a result of studying the booklet, trainees were able to choose the correct responses to almost all of about 50 "problem situations" presented on the test. So it was known that the trainees *knew* what to say or do, but would he *choose* to do it on the job? This question was then addressed by making recommendations for supervisors who observed the actual installations to enable them to monitor this behavior in the field.

In the above project an attempt was made to provide trainees with information and simulated practice in exhibiting decisions and actions reflecting the desired attitudes, including willingness to learn and to execute approved company policy. Thus, cognitive learning was used to support attitude development, and managers deemed it appropriate for supervisors to reinforce appropriate job behavior. This reinforcement of behavior desired by the company was not challenged by anyone. This incident of course does not involve some of the ethical issues encountered in dealing with controversial values in public education.

Yellow page salesman was the job title for telephone company employees who call on business people to sell advertisements for their businesses in the yellow pages of the directory. Again, all these people were men at the time of the consulting activity.

The sales manager reported to the consultant the fact that the sales volume of yellow page salesmen *dropped* with length of experience on the job, following training for the job. The consultant was asked to review the training course to see if training in the approved company sales approach was inadequate. Both the manager and the consultant suspected at once that training was not the problem. However, as a first step, the consultant analyzed the program and found it to present a clear and consistent set of guidelines for the job. Two hypotheses had to be considered: (a) the training was valid, but not designed to achieve long-term retention, or (b) the drop in performance with increased job experience was due to attitudes acquired on the job conflicting with knowledge and attitudes acquired during training.

To test both hypotheses, it was arranged that the consultant would "ride with the man" as he called on his customers or potential customers. The consultant spent one day observing each salesman. The men were selected from high, medium, and low sales records and from varying degrees of service following the training program.

Oral interviews with the men revealed that they had not forgotten what they learned in the training program. They could answer questions about the approved way of preparing for a call and for making the call upon a customer. So the training program did not appear to result in poor retention of information.

Spending a day with each man also revealed that those who followed company policy in reference to library research and use of the available artists and draftsmen to prepare sample advertisement proposals made the highest sales records. The men were trained to use the sales library to learn about the industry represented by the customer, and to prepare alternate proposals and layouts to discuss with the customer. Men who followed these practices made the most sales, and they were the men with less experience after training.

Men who did not take the above steps in preparing for each call made more calls per day but with poor results. They tended to call on customers at random or by convenience of location. They also complained more about the company.

The consultant's report contained some 30 recommendations, all having to do with attitudes and reinforcement of the desired sales behaviors. Some principles of reinforcement from operant conditioning theory were recommended to be built into a revised reward system.

In both industrial and military situations, the "old hands" in the field often tend to develop shortcuts contrary to the way they were trained, and they tend to teach or try to influence recently trained personnel in that direction. They often say to the person just out of training, "Forget what they taught you in school, and watch me."

Conclusion: (a) while proper cognitive training is important, the needed attitudes may not be established firmly, leading to later problems; (b) some problems do not require training changes as the solution—they require changes in management practices relating to the reward system for employees; and (c) "if the training program ain't broke, don't fix it."

Military Training

Military training, like industrial training, is largely oriented to the performance of specific jobs. However, for both officer and enlisted personnel, provisions are made for career progression. Such progression could involve higher degrees of skill in a given job, but it often relates to performing an increasing variety of jobs with increased levels of responsibility.

After basic training in military customs, field practices, and the like, most enlisted personnel receive some form of individual, technical training for various jobs. This is often followed by team training for situations in which coordination of action among team or crew members is important (Branson, 1977).

To illustrate career progression for enlisted personnel, we refer to the training of maintenance personnel for electronic equipment. Often such personnel are trained for a specific kind of equipment, such as fire control systems (consisting of a computer and a radar system) for fighter interceptor aircraft, or for a missile guidance system. The first technical course may require, for example, 17 weeks of training. During the first field assignment, the person would perform a limited array of maintenance tasks at a flightline location. After some experience, the person may be returned to a school for advanced maintenance training, after which a second field assignment involves more advanced technical skills. With added experience, the person may be promoted in both rank and responsibility to a supervisory position. By such a career ladder, individuals progress, and a complex mission can be performed.

Each military service faces the choice between initial broad training in the theory of electronic systems, to enable people to perform at a high technical level on their first field assignment, or a more progressive series of experiences from simple tasks to more complex ones. An engineer, for example, may be capable of performing maintenance on *any* electronic system, while a mechanic, having more narrow training, may work on a single system or a limited array of systems.

A service may opt for the first choice above, say, in training submarine crew members, who are few in number and isolated from other military resources. So each crew member must be an expert. The second option may be taken by a large Air Force base, where narrowly trained persons in the proper mix with experts provides effective and economical maintenance. The first option would be more appropriate for long enlistment periods, and the second for shorter periods. So personal turnover is an important factor in developing strategy for a maintenance mission.

The above principles apply to some extent for officer personnel, although the service periods and types of duties vary between enlisted and officer personnel. Some officers may be trained for increasingly complex technical roles, but the more frequent direction in career progression is broadening the scope of duties and increasing levels of responsibilities and command.

Determining Training Requirements

Military conventions speak of quantitative and qualitative training requirements. The former refers to how many people should be trained for each military job, and the latter refers to what should be taught for each job. The terms MOS (Military Occupational Specialty) and billet are often used to refer to what we call "jobs" here.

Each military service has its own way of classifying and organizing jobs and career progression provisions, just as it has its own rank structure. Each service revises such personnel systems as circumstances require.

Military mission requirements determine the personnel skills and the equipment needed to meet the mission requirements. The nature of the equipment required, in turn, dictates the kinds of skills needed to operate and maintain the equipment so as to meet mission requirements. The equipment and the tactical and strategic contexts determine the cognitive and affective behavior required of the personnel. We have mentioned earlier that a study of the equipment design plans can permit the training of personnel before the equipment is delivered to the field.

Within this broad context, job analysis can be employed, for existing jobs and anticipated jobs, to spell out the training objectives, as discussed earlier in this chapter. For maintenance training, these training requirements call for cognitive and affective behaviors, and motor or manual manipulations which may or may not require "motor skills training." Any aircraft pilot does require motor skills training, but many maintenance tasks can be performed by any person with normal manual dexterity once the person learns what to do (cognitive skills).

As indicated earlier, instructional technology is generally well received in both industrial and military training situations. Course designers of military training are often aware of some of the systems design models found in textbooks about instructional design. Contracts have been awarded to university-based instructional designers both to develop models of training design for the military and to develop specific training programs. An example of an overall training design model is that developed by Branson *et al.* (1975), and summarized by Branson (1978). A special model for media selection was developed by Reiser and Gagné (1983). Like industry, military units develop their own training, often in conjunction with contractors and consultants.

Present training practices in the military usually reflect careful attention to job analysis data, but as in industry, more attention probably needs to be paid to attitudes in course design. So we will devote most of this section of this chapter to the affective domain. However, to close this introduction to military training, we suggest that audit trails could be used, both to restudy career progression ladders and to improve training.

Morale, Motivation, and Proficiency

Military organizations are highly interested in the morale, motivation, and proficiency of personnel, both during training and after training. We present here a few relevant studies.

Morale. Morale has traditionally been considered a determiner of willingness to behave in such a way as to enhance the performance of military units. It is also assumed to be a determiner of reenlistment rates. Morale has been studied in relation to job satisfaction and reenlistment rates (Zeleny, 1951). Studies have been made of the relationship among various measures of morale (Smith, 1951).

Briggs and Roe (1953) used a morale survey as the dependent measure in an experiment. The independent variable was encouragement to register complaints. The morale survey was administered to the total trainee population of each of three Air Force technical training squadrons; the survey was administered both before and after the experimental treatment. The experimental conditions were as follows. The Commanding Officer of each of three squadrons held a squadron formation. Squadron A was told that complaints would be welcome, and that each week a period would be set aside for the men (all trainees were men) to register annonymous written opinions or complaints about the technical training they were receiving or about Air Force life in general. Squadron B was told that a "no gripping" policy exists. Gripping was a waste of time, and trainees were not to complain to the Commander or any of his subordinates. In Squadron C, the control group, no mention of complaints was made.

The results were that in all three squadrons there was a decrease in morale score from the first administration of the morale survey to the second administration six weeks later, but the decrease was greater for Squadron B (the "suppressed" group) than for Squadron A (the "encouraged" group). The decrease for the control group was greater than for the encouraged group and did not differ markedly from the decrease of the suppressed group. Two shortcomings of the research were noted in the report: (a) a large loss of participants over this six-week period, and (b) a difference among the three groups on the first administration of the morale survey.

It may be noted that several studies in educational settings note a drop in student effort and achievement during the middle portion of a school term. Apparently, course designs should include measures for alleviating this.

Motivation. The distinction between morale and motivation has never been clear, either conceptually or empirically, in the military as well as elsewhere. In an effort to work toward clarification, Briggs (1954) derived an empirical measure of student motivation. There were two forms of the measures, A and B. Each form listed *observable* behaviors of trainees in the classroom. The items for each form were developed by use of the critical incident technique discussed in the previous section of this chapter. Instructors were asked to write down *observed* behaviors of trainees which indicated high or low motivation in the classroom. Other instructors then used the items to rate each one of their current group of trainees. A motivation score was derived for each trainee. The trainees also were given the morale survey, and their grades in the course were noted. Motivation scores were found to correlate

-.21 with the morale scores. The motivation score correlated (positively) higher with course grades than did the morale scores. It was suggested that motivation scores taken early in training might predict future success better than would morale scores. It was also suggested that motivation scores be studied in relation to specific items of premilitary personal history in an attempt to predict military proficiency.

The negative correlation between motivation and morale scores, while not large, is interesting. It is at least consistent with these results to suppose that some trainees, at least, while complaining about military life, nevertheless go at their assignments with a will. Further study of different attitude components of morale and motivation, as well as study of personal history, might be rewarding.

Personal Characteristics and Learner Strategies

McCombs (1981-82) has reported a four-year effort to improve the performance of military personnel who did poorly in training conducted by computers. She attempted to evaluate the affective and cognitive entry state of these (remedial) students. She points out that since the end of the draft in 1972, enlistees have come in with lower aptitudes and less education. She found her student population to possess inadequate basic reading skills and motivational problems, poor decision-making skills, vocational immaturity, and lack of clear goals and values.

McCombs set out to first identify specific cognitive and affective skills deficiencies, then develop special learning modules which consisted of: (a) materials for helping students become aware of the requirements of self-paced individualized, and computer-managed instruction; (b) materials for developing active learning strategies and effective study skills; and (c) materials for developing motivation, personal responsibility, and effective life coping skills through positive self-control strategies.

The report does not present data showing the results of this effort, but it does discuss research designs which might be used to conduct a summative evaluation.

Derry (1984) has reported seven types of learning strategies that might be taught to academically deficient adult trainees: mood management, attentional management, memorization strategies, reading strategies, problem-solving strategies, test-taking skills, and vocabulary learning strategies.

Her overall plan is to first teach the study skills, so that when beginning subject-matter instruction, the students are required to invoke and use the previously taught learning strategies. She recognizes the need to continue this kind of training at least over a six-month period, as strategies take time to acquire and use well.

Derry outlined four approaches to strategy training: student controlled, conscious; student controlled, subconscious; lesson controlled, conscious; lesson controlled, subconscious. She then discussed these four approaches in terms of pre-packaged instruction, as with a computer, and in terms of the more "normal" teaching situation having less built-in structure. One of these approaches might be best for short-term achievement using highly structured material, but another might offer more long term pay-off when less structured learning situations are encountered.

It would appear that a combination of work like that of McComb and Derry should be considered. Between them they have identified important cognitive and affective components. One can visualize a program, perhaps either on a computer or teacher-managed, which includes: (a) diagnosis and remediation of needed entry skills; (b) strategy training; (c) mood and other self-control strategies; and (d) effective programming of the materials to meet the content objectives of the course.

SUMMARY

In this chapter, we first briefly traced the origins of instructional technology, noting contributions by industrial and military organizations.

We then discussed, in turn, industrial and military training settings and procedures, covering how training requirements are derived for careers and for specific jobs. We also discussed sequencing of affective and cognitive components in training.

We described some specific research and development projects and some consulting efforts, all designed to alleviate affective problems in job or training performance.

We discussed the relationships among motivation, morale, and proficiency, and we ended with two efforts designed to improve the self-management of learning, through work with affective and cognitive self-directed strategies.

Throughout, we referred to the acceptance of instructional technology, and need for improvement in the state of the art.

Chapter 13

Education for the Professions

EDUCATION FOR THE PROFESSIONS

Content Changes

Continuing Education

Delivery Systems

HEALTH, MEDICAL, AND NURSING EDUCATION

Health Education

Medical and Nursing Education

Preventive Health Care and Medical and Nursing Education
Curriculum Issues in Medical and Nursing Education
Medical ethics
Interpersonal skills

Uses of Educational Psychology and Technology
in Medical and Nursing Education

SUMMARY

Chapter 13

Education for the Professions

We have included this chapter on education for the professions because education for professional fields such as medicine, nursing, dentistry, law, engineering, and industry is becoming a big business in the United States. Professional instructional designers often find employment in these fields designing, or assisting in the design and development of, relevant educational and instructional programs. As these fields shift away from complete adherence to a scientific base and toward a more balanced study of science and the problems of society and humankind, the issues we have previously discussed in this book have some relevance.

Specifically, in this chapter, we: (a) provide a general overview of education for the professions, and we discuss a few related issues and concerns; and (b) provide a more in-depth coverage of health education in general, and education for the medical fields in particular. In general, we omit discussion of education for business and industry and for the military, since these fields were addressed in the preceding chapter.

EDUCATION FOR THE PROFESSIONS

Education for the professions is a generic term used here to describe education for the professional fields—medicine, nursing, dentistry, veterinary medicine, law, engineering, architecture, etc. As Zumeta and Solomon (1982) have noted, it is impossible to do justice to all professional fields in a general survey because there is so much variance among them; it is, however, possible to identify some trends. We include here basic trends and issues facing all professional fields; we pay particular attention to curricular and instructional issues.

Perhaps the most striking trend is the surge in enrollments and the number of degrees awarded. Zumeta and Solmon (1982) state that with the exception of the field of education, all the professional fields have grown substantially and that most have a surplus of qualified applicants. As growth in education for the professions has increased, the growth of education in liberal arts fields has decreased.

This growth of education for the professional fields is not altogether a welcomed change, since growth brings with it a number of problems. Among the more important non-curricular problems are: (a) lack of qualified faculty members, (b) cost constraints, (c) accreditation issues, and (d) how to select students for admission into professional schools (Zumeta & Solomon, 1982). For example, employment of qualified faculty is often difficult because professionals can make more money in the private sector, and because practitioners are often not adequately trained for the research demands of academic positions (Zumeta & Solomon, 1982). These problems are closely related to issues surrounding accreditation, e.g., the use of part-time faculty and of training programs at branch and regional campuses. Questions about the adequacy of such training and the quality of the students leaving such training are just a few of the issues facing many professional fields.

In addition to the concerns cited above, several curricular and instructional issues have emerged. We address two of these: (a) content changes, and (b) continuing education programs.

Content Changes

Two content related issues require attention in most all the professional fields. First, the knowledge explosion, especially in the medical and health fields, has increased so rapidly that hard decisions must be made about what to include and what to omit in professional training. As an example, Gershen (1982) states that the "increasing prominence of dental specialties has inflated curriculum content beyond the basic requirements of training the general dentist" (p. 440). Not only is the growth of specific fields problematic, but also some professional fields have begun to examine the scientific knowledge of related fields and include various aspects in training programs. In law education, for example, criminology, psychology, sociology, ethics, and economics have been influential (Zumeta & Solomon, 1982). This trend can also be seen in other professional schools.

A second issue revolves around increased attention to the humanities and social sciences in the training and development of education for the professions. The whole area of medical ethics (to be discussed in a later section in this chapter) is a well-known example. A less well-known example from the field of engineering serves to clarify our point. ". . . since each engineer must live as a person and a citizen as well, a substantial component (about 15 to 20 percent) of the undergraduate curriculum must be reserved for instruction in the liberal arts and social sciences. Indeed, recent social concerns about the impact of modern technology are reflected in even greater stress on the non-technical aspects of the engineering curriculum" (Marlow, 1982, p. 559). So while the emphasis in many professional fields continues to be on the scientific aspects of the respective fields, the role of the arts and the social sciences is becoming increasingly important. The need to broaden a curriculum to include, for example, health economics in medical school and professional ethics in law schools raises issues about what topics are most important to include, how to integrate curricular content, and even questions about expanding schooling to include more years.

These content issues are vitally important. The choices professional schools make will have significant impact on how the professions are practiced in years to come. Inclusion of content areas like interpersonal skills training and ethics can hardly be disputed as important, yet to include them requires revamping curricula. How and toward what ends this revamping is done demands attention in many of the professional fields.

Another dilemma facing most professional fields is the balance between the academic and practical side of professional education (Zumeta & Solomon, 1982). Although the health fields have included clinical work experiences in the curriculum for years, fields such as law and business are beginning to use practicums and internships to help balance the theory and practice aspects of professional education. How field work and how apprenticeship programs are organized and supervised will be watched carefully both in terms of the effect on academic rigor and in terms of faculty involvement (Zumeta & Solomon, 1982).

Continuing Education

The need to keep abreast of new developments in professional fields is one of the main reasons for continuing education programs. Many practitioners use continuing education to keep updated on scientific knowledge and practice, and to keep their certifications up-to-date. However, as Zumeta and Solomon (1982) state, continuing education may not be living up to the expectations for it. "It has not been clearly shown that continuing education for professionals protects the public from incompetent practitioners, which is ostensibly one of its primary purposes. But it has been and continues to be the most convenient method of seeking to satisfy the public interest in having qualified practicing professionals" (p. 1466).

As continuing education programs increase, curricular issues will need clarification. Marlowe (1982), reporting Klus and Jones (1978), estimates that over a five-year period at least 50 percent of all engineers enroll in at least one formal continuing education program. The same issues we raised earlier, e.g., the balance between the hard sciences and the humanities, and between theory and practice, will require attention when developing continuing education programs. Likewise, in continuing medical education (CME), the topics addressed must take into account issues related to relicensure and recertification of physicians as well as the needs of practice. The two areas do not always represent a one-to-one correspondence (Abbett, Bridgham & Elstein, 1982).

Continuing education both formally and informally (e.g., reading professional journals) is here to stay. Hard decisions must be made by universities and other organizations about what is most important to offer; equally hard decisions must be made by practitioners about what is most beneficial to take. Professional instructional designers may have a valuable role to play in helping professional schools make or carry out such decisions.

Delivery Systems

The professional schools are increasingly using advances made in educational psychology and educational technology to design and develop instruction for both pre- and in-service practitioners. Individualized instruction, use of audio-visual aids, including substantial uses of video systems, simulations using computer-based data banks, criterion-referenced measurement strategies, and the use of learning objectives are just a few of the educational innovations that are used consistently and with great promise in education for the professions.

The emphasis on clinical education has prompted the use of educational technology to provide quality education experiences. The emphasis on problem-solving skills and "contact" with professionals outside the university has increased the use of video systems, computers, and interactive video systems (systems that combine the capabilities of the computer with video). These technological advances have had a profound effect on instruction. As an example, Gershen (1982) states that most dental schools have video monitors in classrooms and labs, where they are used extensively for demonstrations of clinical and laboratory techniques. Additionally, simulations of dental office interactions and interactions between patients and dentists have been used. One series of videotapes was developed that provided insight into the thoughts and feelings of both patients and dentists (Gershen, 1982).

We do not attempt to address all the educational psychology and technology advances having an impact on professions education, but we do acknowledge their importance. The reliance on objectives, criterion-referenced measurement, and media matched to objectives are important developments, and are used extensively. (We will have more to say about this in a later section of this chapter.)

HEALTH, MEDICAL, AND NURSING EDUCATION

We have included this section on health care education as representative of education for the professions. These fields show as clearly as any the need to integrate affective and cognitive learning. We do not attempt an exhaustive review of these fields. Many of the issues we have discussed in the previous section relate directly to the health care fields, so we omit them here. What we include here is (a) an overview of preventive health education, (b) some affective outcomes of preventive health education, (c) how the preventive model might influence medical and nursing education, and (d) several important affective outcomes of medical and nursing education.

Health Education

Most definitions of health education today pay particular interest to the positive changes that an individual makes in life style and habits to increase the likelihood of a healthy life. In general, health education strives to motivate an individual to *use* health information—to do something with what is learned to promote and maintain health. Health education, viewed in this way, has a strong affective orientation. Jaccard (1975) states that health education programs must be aimed at influencing the beliefs and attitudes of people so they will perform behaviors directed toward health.

Baranowski (1981) differentiates between health and wellness. "Health is defined as the physical capacity of the body to fulfill personal expectations and perform social role tasks. Wellness is defined as the other capacities of the person to fulfill these same ends" (p. 246). This broadened definition of health and the related term, wellness, move the notion of health into the psychosocial sphere and away from a strictly biological definition. Although health is related to biological functioning, the goal of health is to facilitate functioning in social roles related to a person's family, occupation, and community. As an example, Baranowski states that increased oxygen intake is associated with physical fitness, but that this capacity enables an individual to perform better and to do more rigorous work, and hence is associated with his or her occupational role. Health, then, relates to biological functioning and the ability to fulfill social roles. Wellness, on the other hand, may include all the intellectual, social, physical, moral, and aesthetic aspects of personal functioning (Baranowski, 1981).

Motivating people to change their behavior patterns is perhaps the biggest issue in health education. Of course, people must have necessary cognitive knowledge to make changes, but in a free society, choice of life style and health behaviors is largely a personal choice. Individuals must, therefore, modify their own behaviors to maintain health and wellness. Some health behaviors that are most clearly related to health (and illness) are: nutrition and diet, exercise, accident prevention, smoking control, alcohol consumption, limited use of over-the-counter and prescription drugs, control of stress, wise choice of medical care, sex education, and dental health.

Intervention strategies designed to promote health require that the health educator organize health education around three areas: cognitive factors, affective factors, and skills (Ross, 1981; Parcel, 1976). In general, Ross (1981) states that the cognitive skills involve those behaviors related to making rational decisions which require information. She cites the Health Belief Model, which states that individuals will seek preventive measures if they believe a disease is serious, and if the benefits of the preventive measure outweigh the costs. The information a person seeks is basically in the realm of cognitive knowledge; it is often provided by physicians and nurses who give specific medical information to individuals about their specific problems (Ross, 1981).

The affective factors, according to Ross (1981), greatly influence personal action. Ross says that health educators should (a) encourage emotional responses that facilitate the use of preventive measures, and (b) personalize information rather than give it in clinical terms. In addition, health educators should provide specific recommendations for preventive health behaviors/care, and they should use interpersonal communications to provide a positive emotional climate so people can express their fears and concerns. The importance of interpersonal skill in health education and patient care cannot be overestimated (Ross, 1981).

Ross (1981) gives three categories of skills that enable individuals to carry out their intentions to alter their health behavior. These categories are (a) utilization skills, e.g., finding an appropriate medical care provider, making an appointment; (b) medical consumer skills, e.g., evaluating treatment options, keeping individual medical records; and (c) assertive skills, e.g., asking for a second opinion, asking for explanation of procedures.

Parcel (1976) provides a similar framework for health education. He states that there has been an increased focus on affective health education; this focus has also been coupled with an approach which emphasizes the integration of the cognitive and affective domains. Parcel suggests that skills such as the ability to communicate feelings, and activities that emphasize self-confidence and self-esteem should be included in health curricula, along with more traditional health concepts and skills.

The move in health education toward wellness and health and away from illness and disease takes into account both the affective and cognitive dimensions of behavior in significant ways. Examples of affective content that are recommended for inclusion in health care programs (along with cognitive information) include: interpersonal skills training, self-confidence and self-esteem building, emotional expression and development, and continuing motivation for health. It seems that health care curricula at all levels, i.e., patient care, community health care programs, school health programs K-12, and college health programs, are being developed to include the affective components of health education.

Medical and Nursing Education

The issues we have addressed in the previous section on health education have direct and indirect implications for education in the medical and nursing fields. We will briefly discuss those implications. There are, however, content and skill areas related more exclusively to the affective components of medical and nursing education, e.g., medical ethics, empathy training, and interpersonal skills development, that we will also address.

Preventive Health Care and Medical and Nursing Education

Both the medical and nursing education curricula have their bases in the biomedical model. Although there have been some attempts to alter the curricula away from this model, the attempts have largely been unsuccessful (Abbett, Bridgham & Elstein, 1982). In general, the curriculum for most medical schools is organized around disciplines such as pathology, anatomy, physiology, etc., although a few schools organize courses around major organ systems, and others structure course content around patient problems (fever, jaundice, etc.) (Abbett *et al.*, 1982).

Similarly, in the past, nursing education curricula were mostly organized around medical specialties or body systems, referred to as a "blocked" curriculum; more recently an integrated curriculum organized around concepts is emerging (Layton, 1982). The Neuman Model is an example (Bower, 1982). This curriculum model includes concepts such as intrapersonal, interpersonal, and extrapersonal stress, modes of prevention, levels of defense, etc.

Both medical and nursing curricula give a predominant place to the biological sciences. They promote an understanding of illness and disease coupled with clinical diagnosis, prescription, and treatment of diseases and disorders (Abbett *et al.*, 1982). This, of course, is in direct opposition to the health and wellness orientations that we discussed earlier. There have, however, been some challenges to the biomedical model. Abbett *et al.* (1982), citing others, give four prominent "ideals" for the practice of medicine that challenge the biomedical model: (1) "promote community medicine and preventive care, (2) ambulatory, primary care medicine, (3) caring and skillfulness in personal interaction, and (4) medical ethics" (p. 1204).

In nursing education the biomedical model has also been questioned. For example, a panel of expert consultants was convened to project national and state nursing requirements. The panel presented a number of specific recommendations but one is of particular interest. "The present problems in health care delivery and the requirements projections clearly point to the need for . . . increased emphasis on preventive care, including community health services" (Elliott & Kearns, 1978, p. 97).

Although new directions in the curricula of both nursing and medical education have been suggested, the biomedical model still dominates. With respect to medical education, Abbett *et al.* (1982) state that the four "ideals" listed earlier (e.g., preventive care, medical ethics, etc.) will probably have little impact on the curriculum. "Their place in the curriculum is likely to be limited and uncertain, however, until the profession resolves its uncertainty about how crucial each area is for the conduct of medicine" (p. 1204).

Perhaps there is a continuum of roles of the health care professional ranging from preventive health care on one end to emergency surgery on the other. Given such a continuum, the curriculum for each role, and for health care professionals in-between, may vary widely. On the preventive health care side the curriculum might include the cognitive, affective, and skill areas earlier identified in the section on health education. On the emergency surgery end of the continuum, the biomedical model may be the most logical and best way to organize a curriculum. At this end, however, medical ethics may also have an important part to play in the development of competent physicians. We will have more to say about this in the next section.

Curricular Issues in Medical and Nursing Education

The suggested move away from a curriculum organized around the biomedical model could include any number of new topics and content areas. We, of course, are not prepared to suggest what these should be, nor are we prepared to rank-order suggested areas in degree of importance. We were, however, struck by the vast number of recommendations by health care professionals to include affective components in both medical and nursing education. Two particular affective components were repeatedly suggested: medical ethics and interpersonal skills. We briefly address each area.

Medical ethics. Anyone who currently reads a newspaper or watches a television news broadcast must be aware of the ethical and moral questions that face physicians, health care workers, and the general public about health related issues. Some of the issues that come immediately to mind include human experimentation with organ transplants, and organ transplants from animals to humans; euthanasia; abortion; rising medical costs; the role of the medical community in developing countries; environmental health hazards; and optimal use of scarce health resources. *As society becomes more and more complex, the ethical and moral questions will no doubt multiply exponentially.*

Medical ethics, along with other content areas, has been recommended by some for inclusion in medical education, yet this poses problems for already packed curricula. Hiatt (1976) states, "Let me stress that the need for medicine to encompass broader missions in no way implies diminished emphasis on fundamental research in biomedical sciences and on applying the fruits of that research to clinical problems" (p. 36). Some of the courses that Hiatt recommends for physicians in their role as responsible members of society include: ethics, quantitative methods including epidemiology, statistics, decision analysis, and health management.

Continuing medical education either formally or informally may help alleviate the potential deficits in medical education. We addressed some of the problems of professionals continuing their education earlier. Many physicians informally continue their education through journals and interpersonal contacts.

One publication that addresses ethical concerns of the profession is the *Journal of Medical Ethics* published by the Society for the Study of Medical Ethics. "The Society aims to influence the quality of both professional and public discussion of medico-moral questions; to promote the study of medical ethics; to ensure a high academic standard for this developing subject; to encourage a multidisciplinary approach to the discussion of the consequences of clinical practice; to stimulate research in specific problems; to remain non-partisan and independent of all interest groups and lobbies" (*Journal of Medical Ethics*, inside front cover). Some of the issues addressed in recent issues of the *Journal* include: abortion, the physician as technician or statesman, the permissibility of torture, self help in health care, transsexualism, death and dying, homosexuality, ethical considerations of psychosurgery, i.e., pre-frontal lobotomy, the place of faith in the medical profession, and a philosophy of clinically based ethics.

No doubt medical ethics is a content area that deserves

consideration in medical education. Where it should be included in a curriculum and how it should be taught are beyond our sphere of knowledge. Perhaps, however, some of the recommendations we have made in earlier chapters, specifically providing the conditions of learning for moral and ethical behaviors, may be useful to medical educators.

Interpersonal skills. There is growing acknowledgment of the importance of interpersonal skills for all health care providers. "It is increasingly recognized that participation in treatment, compliance, and continued willingness to turn to the health care systems for assistance is affected by interpersonal communication between medical provider and patient" (Ross, 1981, p. 198).

A number of studies have been conducted assessing the effects of interpersonal skill training on patient satisfaction, medical provider satisfaction, and quality of health care. Ross (1981) reports several such studies, all of which produced positive results. For example, Werner and Schneider (cited in Ross, 1981) evaluated an interpersonal skills course and found improvements in student (a) self-assessment, (b) ability to empathize, and (c) an increase in exploratory and affect related questions. Layton (1982) also reports a study by Kalisch (1971) which compared an experimental group (given 12-1/2 hours of empathy training) with the control group (given lecture-discussions on human behavior) in an attempt to increase empathy in nursing students. The experimental group made statistically significant gains on four of seven empathy measures and showed retention of the behaviors six weeks later.

Again, we note the problems of all educators who build curricula: the knowledge explosion, the need to include more content areas in a curriculum, and the difficulties of adding, omitting, prioritizing, and integrating topic areas. The medical and nursing curricula are no exception. Yet, there does seem to be a need for interpersonal skills training and attention to medical ethics (to name only two) in educating physicians and nurses. We hope the work of integrating the cognitive and affective domains that we have done will assist these educators in some small way when they tackle these most difficult curricular and instructional problems.

Uses of Educational Psychology and Technology
in Medical and Nursing Education

Medical and nursing educators have embraced many principles that educational psychologists and technologists have proposed. The *Journal of Medical Education* and the *Journal of Nursing Education* regularly include articles on issues related to the systematic design of instruction and on new technologies for increasing the effectiveness of instruction. Some examples include articles related to objectives, taxonomies of objectives, criterion-referenced assessments, program evaluation, measurement of clinical problem solving, team teaching, computer-assisted instruction, and simulation gaming. (All of these topics came out of one *randomly selected* copy of each journal.) In addition, studies have been conducted assessing the effects of videotape, micro-teaching, computer-assisted instruction, programmed instruction, mastery learning, and other student-centered instructional strategies on the increased competence of nursing and medical students. The results of these studies are mixed, as they are with any of the comparative media studies. Our point, however, does not relate to the effects of these studies; rather, we include the studies and the journal topics to demonstrate the breadth of topics and concepts related to educational psychology, educational technology, and instructional design and development. We believe that our field has much to offer medical and nursing education, and more broadly education for the professions in general.

SUMMARY

In this chapter, we have addressed applications of our work to education for the professions. We have focused on the integration of affective and cognitive outcomes, and on specific areas of the affective domain.

Regarding education for the professions, we noted several content changes that have been proposed in fields such as engineering, law, and dental education. We described the inherent problems of adding more content versus insuring a well-balanced curriculum. We also briefly addressed continuing education, and the use of new technologies to deliver instruction in many of the professional schools.

We then discussed several issues related to health education. We began by describing preventive health care and contrasted this with present practices in medical and nursing education. We noted the need for cognitive, affective, and skill outcomes for health, medical, and nursing education. We next discussed two affective areas requiring attention in medical and nursing education: medical ethics and interpersonal skills training. Finally, we addressed the impact of educational psychology and educational technology on medical and nursing education.

Introduction to Part V:

Conditions of Learning and Lesson Design

In Part V we come to the culminating phase of instructional design—the design of individual lessons and sequences of lessons for a unit of instruction. By "lesson design" we include both conventional instruction led by a teacher or instructor and pre-packaged instructional materials, such as computer software and other media presentations.

In Chapter 14, we first briefly discuss the nature of 10 outcome categories for the cognitive domain. For each category we list a set of external conditions of learning totaling 98 conditions for the entire domain. These conditions are numbered serially from 1 to 98, each set arranged under the appropriate sub-domain outcome category. Next we list 14 outcome categories for the affective domain. Each of these 14 categories was discussed in some detail in Part II. For the 14 affective outcome categories, we list 132 external conditions of learning. In total, for both domains, we list 24 categories and 230 conditions of learning. Chapter 14 is thus a reference source for lesson design, the subject of Chapter 15. We close Chapter 14 with an explanation of how categories of outcomes and their associated conditions were discovered.

In Chapter 15 we open with a discussion of alternate ways of making decisions about delivery systems and media—whether these decisions should come before or after lesson design. Then we discuss the roles of teachers and computers in providing the relevant conditions of learning for lessons having either cognitive or affective objectives, or both.

Next we present four examples of lesson design, covering a

range of types of objectives, learners, and learning situations. We employ there the nine events of instruction discussed earlier in the book and selected external conditions of learning from Chapter 14.

We close Chapter 15 by additional suggestions for lesson design.

Chapter 14

External Conditions of
Learning for Instruction

TAXONOMIES AND CONDITIONS OF LEARNING

CONDITIONS FOR THE COGNITIVE DOMAIN

Learning of Intellectual Skills

Discriminations
  Conditions of learning for discriminations
Concrete Concepts
  Conditions of learning for concrete concepts
Defined Concepts and Writing Objectives
  Writing objectives
  Conditions of learning for defined concepts
Rule Using (Principles)
  Conditions of learning for rules
Problem Solving (Higher Order Rules)
  Conditions of learning for problem solving

Learning of Information

Verbatim Information Learning
  Conditions of learning for verbatim information learning
Learning of Facts
  Conditions of learning for learning of facts
Substance Learning
  Conditions of learning for substance materials

Learning of Cognitive Strategies

General and Specific Strategies
Immediate and Long-Term Strategies
A Dilemma: Highly Structured Learning or Strategy Learning?
Cognitive Strategies as Course Objectives and as Tools for Learning
   Conditions of learning for cognitive strategies as course-related
      objectives
   Conditions of learning for cognitive strategies as tools

CONDITIONS FOR THE AFFECTIVE DOMAIN

Conditions of Learning for Acquisition and Change of Attitudes

Short-Term and Long-Term Objectives
Alternate Positions on Teaching of Attitudes
Objectives and Measurement in the Affective Domain
   Concrete, short-term objectives
   More complex, long-term objectives
   Attitude scales
Conditions of Learning for Attitudes
   Persuasive communications as a strategy
   Establishing dissonance as a strategy
   Modeling as a strategy
   Other techniques as strategies

Other Components of the Affective Domain

Conditions of Learning for Values
Conditions of Learning for Moral Development
Conditions of Learning for Feelings and Emotions
Conditions of Learning for Self-Development
Conditions of Learning for Social Competence
Conditions of Learning for Attributions
Conditions of Learning for Motivation
   Interest
   Relevance
   Expectancy
   Outcomes

CONDITIONS OF LEARNING FOR DIFFERENT PEOPLE

THE ORIGIN OF OUTCOME CATEGORIES
AND CONDITIONS OF LEARNING

Gagné's Work

Our Work

For the Cognitive Domain
For the Affective Domain

SUMMARY

Chapter 14

External Conditions of Learning for Instruction

TAXONOMIES AND CONDITIONS OF LEARNING

In Chapter 3 we introduced the idea of taxonomies of instructional outcomes, and we reviewed research relating to evidence of the validity of the different categories of outcomes in each taxonomy for the cognitive and the affective domains. Our reason for stressing the importance of taxonomies was that each category of outcomes in taxonomies requires somewhat different sets of internal conditions of learning and also somewhat differents sets of external conditions of learning. So the chapters after Chapter 3 in Part II, each discussing a different category of outcomes for the affective domain, closed with a statement of appropriate internal and external conditions of learning for a category. In Part II, then, we attempted to do for the affective domain what Gagné (1977) had already done for the cognitive domain—identify conditions of learning for each category in the domain.

In this chapter we present a condensed summary of the external conditions of learning for all categories in both the affective and cognitive domains. We have chosen here to concentrate upon the *external* conditions because those are the conditions which are *most directly under the control of the teacher and the designers of instructional materials.* The external conditions which we identify in this chapter are essentially teaching rules or principles upon which teachers and materials developers can draw when designing lessons. The *internal* conditions, listed in Part II for the affective domain and in Gagné's work (1977) for the cognitive domain, have to do mostly with *prior* learning and learner strategies which help the learner profit from the external conditions incorporated into *new* instruction. In this chapter we concentrate on the *external* conditions themselves; in Chapter 15 we show how to operationalize these conditions when designing lessons.

The above paragraphs have simplified one matter which we now will clarify. In the first edition of *The Conditions of Learning*, Gagné restricted his coverage primarily to the "domain" of intellectual skills. By the third edition of his book, Gagné (1977) extended his coverage to include information learning and cognitive strategies, thus completing his coverage of what we call here the cognitive domain. He also covered learning of attitudes (which he calls a domain but which we refer to as one component of the affective domain), and learning of motor skills. Unlike our Chapter 4, which covers several methods of establishing attitudes, Gagné dealt only with the method of modeling. We make these explanations, not to imply that our terminology is better, but to clarify our intent. As a further clarification, we offer this key to the possibly confusing difference in terminology.

Gagné's Terminology	Our Terminology
Information learning domain	
Intellectual skills domain	Cognitive domain
Cognitive strategies domain	
Attitude domain	Affective domain: Attitudes and Values Moral and ethical behavior Self development Emotions and Feelings Social development Motivation Attributions
Motor skills domain	(not covered by us)

In this chapter we make use of Gagné's terminology for what we call the cognitive domain because he has arranged his conditions of learning accordingly. We also adopt his breakdown of information learning and intellectual skills learning into subcategories. We follow our own terminology for the affective domain.

In earlier chapters we introduced another important concept of Gagné: instructional events. The distinction between instructional events and conditions of learning will be discussed in Chapter 15. Both of those concepts, along with the concept of taxonomies, are central to our discussion of lesson design in Chapter 15. But, for now, you may simply think of external conditions of learning as principles to be incorporated into lessons. Just *how* the conditions may be built into lesson plans (and their instructional events) is the subject of Chapter 15.

In the major portion of this chapter, then, we relate sets of external conditions of learning to categories in taxonomies of the cognitive and affective domains. Near the end of the chapter we give some history of how these conditions of learning were derived, and we raise the questions of whether conditions of learning should vary according to the nature of the learner, as well as according to type of outcome sought.

CONDITIONS FOR THE COGNITIVE DOMAIN

In this section of this chapter we draw upon several sources for listing the external conditions of learning for the cognitive domain. These sources include two books (Gagné, 1977; Gagné & Briggs, 1979), and our own observations. For the section on cognitive strategies (learner strategies) we also borrow from Derry (1984) and from McCombs (1981-82). The actual wording of the conditions listed were derived from our experience in teaching these conditions to graduate students and from experience in designing instruction. As did Gagné, we also draw from research and reasoning and inference. Our wording of the various sets of conditions is largely our own, as drawn from our own course materials. We have not knowingly used direct quotations. However, we do wish at the outset to acknowledge that we have borrowed heavily, conceptually, from the work of Gagné in the areas of categories of outcomes and their associated conditions of learning.

Learning of Intellectual Skills

Gagné (1977) has distinguished among five categories of intellectual skills: discrimination, concrete concepts, defined concepts, rules (principles), and problem solving (higher order rules). The conditions for learning of specific objectives representing these categories have been discussed in more detail by him. The actual use of the conditions in design practice was further elaborated by Gagné and Briggs (1979). See Gagné (1977) for a discussion of the hierarchical nature of these five subcategories; see our Chapter 3 for research relating to these hierarchical relationships. We take up each category, in turn, briefly giving examples of objectives for each category, then listing the external conditions of learning to be incorporated into instruction. For formal definitions of categories, see Chapter 3.

In the remainder of this chapter we list the external conditions of learning for each component or category of both the cognitive and the affective domains. We number these conditions consecutively throughout the entire chapter. This numbering system should facilitate the reading of the sample lesson designs in Chapter 15. By inserting condition numbers in Chapter 15, we show how the lesson utilizes the conditions. This numbering should also facilitate group discussions based on this book.

Discriminations

Discriminations are exhibited by the learner's ability to say whether two stimuli are the same or different. Example: saying whether two tones sounded are the same or different in pitch; saying whether two shapes (e.g., squares and circles) are the same or different; saying whether two objects lifted are the same or different weight; saying whether odors from two test tubes are the same or different; saying whether two tasted liquids are the same or different.

Discriminations are thus sensory matters. The learner does not need to know the *names* of the shapes, liquids, etc.; being able to say (or otherwise correctly indicate) "same" or "different" is the point. Note that this technical meaning of discrimination is different from common parlance: racial discrimination (attitude) or telling the difference between a liberal and a conservative editorial (defined concepts). In test situations, several pairs of objects, drawings, or substance would be used in order to reliably infer that the learner has mastered a particular discrimination.

The following is a sample discrimination objective in the five-component form of Gagné and Briggs (1977): "In a classroom individual testing situation, and given a series of cut out cardboard circles and rectangles arranged in random order on a table, upon request the learner will point to all the shapes that are the same as the one the teacher points to."

Conditions of learning for discriminations. Here are some elements in lessons for teaching discriminations:

1. Point out distinctive features, such as rounded or straight edges of the object.
2. Use a variety of examples which range in non-relevant features, such as using shapes of many colors and sizes.
3. Group objects for the learner, saying "same" or "not the same."
4. Provide practice and feedback.
5. Avoid saying the names of objects or asking the learner to say them, unless you are trying to teach discriminations and concrete concepts simultaneously.
6. Remember that young children have to *learn* discriminations that are "obvious" to adults.

Concrete Concepts

Concrete concepts are demonstrated when the learner can name or otherwise identify a number of objects or positions belonging to the same class. Examples: chairs, test tubes, cars, cats, dogs, up, down, left, right, horizontal. Notice that the learner must first be able to discriminate among the objects or positions before identifying them (capability verb) by saying the name (orally; action verb). To do this, again the learner must respond in spite of irrelevant features such as color or size of object. Of course, a learner can demonstrate mastery by grouping objects as well as by saying their names.

Sample objective in five-component form: "In a classroom individual test situation and given a variety of shapes (circles, rectangles, triangles) of different sizes and colors drawn on paper and cut out of cardboard, upon request the learner will name each shape orally as the teacher points to it."

Notice that when a concept has been learned, the person could correctly identify *thousands* of examples of objects falling into the same *class* of objects. Note also that young children take considerable time to learn to ignore irrelevant properties of the concept—thus a young child may at first call a small dog a "cat," and a large cat a "dog."

Conditions of learning for concrete concepts. Here are some of the principles or teaching rules (conditions of learning).

7. Present a variety of examples varying in their nonrelevant features.
8. Point out relevant and irrelevant features or attributes.
9. Provide practice with a variety of examples.
10. Provide feedback.

Defined Concepts and Writing Objectives

In this section we have chosen to further illustrate the five-component method of writing objectives by using defined concepts as examples.

This category of intellectual skills (defined concepts) is some-what poorly named, because the purpose is *not* for the learner to memorize formal definitions of concepts, but to be able to *classify* previously unencountered examples and non-examples of concepts. While learning a definition of a concept (information learning) may help the learner acquire the capability of classifying examples and non-examples of the concept (an intellectual skill), the former is not an essential prerequisite for the latter. For example, a student may be able to classify each of several editorials as either "liberal" or "conservative," but the learner may not be able to give a satisfactory definition of the two "defined concepts." A deductive teaching method may begin by offering a definition early in the lesson, so we list offering of definitions as one condition of learning. An inductive method may enable learners to classify examples as indicated by saying "liberal" or "conservative" for each example without ever memorizing or discovering a definition. This distinction between the two capabilities, memorizing and classifying examples, is important because so much learning involves defined concepts.

To illustrate our point, consider the various defined concepts which are category labels in a taxonomy. You have encountered perhaps 20 such defined concepts for the affective domain in Part II, and you will encounter another 10 for the cognitive domain in this chapter. We believe you "understand" these even when we do not give formal definitions. You have also encountered the concepts of instructional events, internal conditions of learning, and external conditions of learning, and many other defined concepts.

In summary, we consider the learning of a verbal definition of a concept to represent "information learning," while ability to use a concept to classify correct and incorrect examples (thousands of them) to be an intellectual skill. Further, some concepts might be "discovered" by use of cognitive strategies.

Writing objectives. You have read earlier in this book of the five-component method of writing objectives, and in this chapter you encounter an example of this form of writing objectives for each category in the taxonomies. All these technical terms are defined concepts. Do you learn the categories and components better by seeing formal definitions (some were given in Chapter 3) or by reading explanations and seeing examples? Could you now classify examples of "capability verbs" and "action verbs?" We now give an example (referring to five defined concepts) of an objective referring to learning of the five components in the five-component method of writing objectives.

"In a written test situation, and given several examples of 'scrambled' five-component objectives, upon request the learner will classify each of the five components presented in random order by writing the names of the five components in blank spaces opposite each component."

We will present only one sample test question for this objective.

In a real situation, several such items would be presented as a test.
test.

Components of the Objective	Answer Key
1. without any reference materials	Tools and constraints
2. by writing	Action verb
3. in a written test, and given several editorials	Situation
4. the name of the appropriate defined concept opposite each editorial	Object
5. the learner will *classify* each editorial as "liberal" or "conservative"	Capability verb

The normal sequence of writing the scrambled objective used for the above test item objective would be:

"In a written test, and given several editorials (upon request), the learner will classify each editorial as 'liberal' or 'conservative' by writing 'liberal' or 'conservative' opposite each editorial without the use of any reference materials."

Probably you have now learned the five components of this method of writing objectives, if you hadn't learned it previously. If so, you could classify the five components of an objective for a large number of provided objectives, indicating that you have learned the five "defined concepts," even though we haven't given definitions of these five components. For less sophisticated learners, we would use all the conditions of learning noted below. You could probably also *generate* your own objectives, calling for the intermediate skill of rule using, in which you *demonstrate* ability to write your own examples of each of these five components. So a sophisticated learner may not need all the conditions of learning for the three types of capabilities: defined concepts, rule using, and problem solving. Yet we will list these sets of conditions for teaching less sophisticated learners.

We admit that the five-component method of writing objectives often results in stilted, inelegant language. Often it would be more natural to rephrase the objective, either for team efforts in designing instruction or for communicating the objective to the learners. Here is how we could rephrase the objective when speaking to the learner: "In Chapter 4 of the textbook (Briggs & Wager, 1981), you can learn about writing objectives by the five-component method. On Friday I will give you a test in which I will list some objectives in which the five components are in a scrambled sequence, and you are to classify each of the five components by writing its name in blank spaces." The following week, after returning the test and giving feedback to the students, you might say: "Now you have learned to classify the five defined concepts (components) in this method of writing objectives. On the next test, I will give you some abbreviated objectives and I will ask you to *demonstrate* the rules for writing each of the five components by rewriting the objectives in five-component form. After that you will *generate* your own five-component objectives for the lessons you are designing."

The textbook chapter referred to above also covers the design of tests for the objectives. This task, also, follows the plan for teaching in this order: defined concepts (classifying), rules (demonstrating), and problem solving (generating).

Conditions of learning for defined concepts. Here is the set of conditions of learning for this category of outcome:

11. Stimulate recall of component concepts. (Often there is a whole hierarchy of defined concepts, from simple to complex.)
12. If necessary, provide remedial instruction for component concepts.
13. Give the definition and an explanation of it.
14. Provide examples and non-examples of the concept, and if relevant, examples of opposing or confusable related concepts. (Concepts are often taught in pairs, such as "liberal" and "conservative.")
15. Give practice in classifying *new* examples of the concept, along with non-examples (irrelevant examples), and opposing examples.

16. Ask learners to explain the concept in their own words.
17. Ask learners to paraphrase the definition.
18. Ask learners to develop their own examples and non-examples, and to coach and test each other.
19. Ask learners to explain why their responses are correct.
20. Provide feedback.
21. Provide, at first, clear-cut examples of the concept and gradually move to less clear-cut examples.
22. Broaden the context of use of the concept, as across subject areas or application areas.
23. Provide for periodic review. (This may be less necessary when related rules and problem solving objectives immediately follow.)
24. If appropriate for the learners and the context, point out that the students are learning defined concepts, and that the purpose of this is to enable them next to learn related rules so they can then generate solutions to problems. This was illustrated in the preceding section on writing objectives. One study (S. Young, 1981) went beyond this in using the instructional design model as a study guide for students. Young made a learning hierarchy for a textbook chapter; the hierarchy listed three levels of objectives: defined concepts, rules, and problem solving. These three levels of objectives were color coded. Students were given three colored markers for underlining parts of the textbook chapter relating to each level of objectives. Such techniques reveal the designer's strategy to the students for their study purposes. This may be an example of metacognition. This seems especially appropriate in training teachers and instructional designers, and we have employed such efforts to relate the students' learning to the course content and objectives in an instructional design course. This presumably should be motivating as well as helping the learners "experience" what is being taught. So general learner strategies may at times be supplemented by strategies related to course content.

Rule Using (Principles)

As was the case for defined concepts, for rule learning it is essential to distinguish between being able to recite a rule and demonstration of the rule for appropriate examples. The former is information learning; the latter represents rule governed behavior. It is one thing to be able to say "warm air rises"; it is another thing to use that rule in deciding how to heat a room or design an air conditioning system.

Many rules describe a procedure to be followed—a set of rules to be applied. Formulas are verbal or symbolic statements of rules to be followed. For example, we can express the (complex) rule for finding areas of circles as A = pi r^2 (A = πr^2). Applying this rule requires recall of several prerequisites; some of these prerequisites represent information learning (recalling that A stands for area; pi stands for 3.1416; r stands for radius). Other prerequisites are intellectual skills (more simple rules: recalling how to square a number, and recalling how to multiply two numbers, (pi and radius^2). Notice also that area and radius are concepts the understanding of which makes more meaningful the significance of the computation done to find the area of a specific circle. Thus we have an example of "domain interaction"—the interaction of prior learned information and intellectual skills when demonstrating the area rule to find the area for a specific circle. Notice also that if the test circle gives the radius directly (r = 2 inches), the problem is simpler than if the test items gives the diameter (4 inches). In the latter case, the learner must either *recall* or *infer* that diameter = 2 X radius. If this relation of diameter to radius has not been taught, the learner may need to employ a cognitive strategy to infer it, thus enlarging the amount of domain interaction. If the learner previously formed a favorable attitude toward applying formulas, then there is a further interaction involving the affective domain.

The *capability verb* for the example of finding areas of circles is *demonstrate* (the rule or formula). One infers successful demonstration of the capability when the learner can give the correct answer for a number of examples, and can show how the answer was reached.

We now state the five-component objective for this example of rule learning: "On a written test presenting either the diameter or the radius of several circles, the learner can demonstrate the rule for finding areas of circles by computing the answers, in writing, without assistance." A teacher may also ask the learner to explain the process of finding the answer in order to rule out chance success, and to be sure the learner "really understands" about areas of circles. A separate objective and test could involve giving the learner only the circumferences of articles and asking for the diameter, radius, and area. If this were not directly taught, it would require application of cognitive strategies. If it were directly taught, it would represent further rule learning.

Conditions of learning for rules. Here are some relevant conditions to be incorporated into lessons to teach rule use.

25. State the rule, and provide demonstrations of its application (alternative: have learner discover the rule).
26. Explain the relationships among subordinate rules and defined concepts.
27. Use game-like examples to enhance interest and positive attitude.
28. Provide for early success on simple examples to enhance self-esteem.
29. Stimulate recall of related concepts and rules.
30. If an inductive method is used to encourage learners to discover the rule, provide a safe environment for making errors without risk during the discovery phase. If a deductive method is used (the teacher gives the rule), avoid penalty for errors in student practice of the rule.
31. Provide feedback without punishment. One way to do this is to make practice private by use of computers or other individualized techniques.
32. Make sure the learners realize that errors are often made during learning, as distinct from testing.
33. Make a game in which learners present their own practice examples of the rule (a form of peer teaching).
34. Have students present their own explanations of the rule, how it works, and the relationships among subordinate rules and concepts.
35. Encourage the learners to verbalize the rule and its significance in several ways.

36. Present problem-solving examples from real life in which use of the rule is necessary, in order to show the larger significance of the rule for solving more complex situations.

Problem Solving (Higher Order Rules)

Throughout this chapter we are offering our own interpretations of the various categories of outcomes, since interpretation and usages vary greatly in the literature. The category of problem solving is probably more murky than is the case for discriminations and concepts. There is no standard or widely agreed upon interpretation of just what constitutes problem solving.

Because of this, we are offering four situations that could be construed as representing problem solving. We cannot say whether all four must be present, or only one or two, to justify classifying an instance as problem solving. But we do illustrate each of the four situations for your consideration.

First, a problem situation usually requires the learner to decide which of all rules, previously learned, are applicable. For example, if one has a flat tire, but no jack for raising the tire off the ground, one has to search for rules or principles that would suggest another way for lifting the tire. One solution, of course, is to call for assistance. Another solution would be to ask "what ways are there to raise a heavy object?" This might lead to recall of rules involving a fulcrum and a lever. One might find a board or a tree limb, and an object such as a large rock. This might suggest a solution, if another person is there to retain pressure on the lever while the tire is being changed. The person has thus selected previously learned rules about fulcrums and levers, and has discovered that a tree limb can be a lever. The person also may have discovered a rule about the length of the lever and its proper placement on the fulcrum.

A second characteristic of problem solving, then, is that the solution requires selection and use of several subordinate rules plus discovery of a new rule.

A third characteristic of problem solving is suggested by the capability verb, generate. If the problem is to write a short story involving strong emotion, the learner generates his or her own story rather than rearranging a story given to the learner. After one learns to *classify* the five components in an objective, and to *demonstrate* writing components for abbreviated objectives given by the teacher, one is then asked to *generate* objectives for a course different from the one from which the teaching examples were drawn.

A fourth characteristic of problem solving is the requirement to simultaneously generate new content while also observing many rules of grammar and punctuation during writing of the required theme, or objectives, or what-not. There is thus an *integration* of skills from several areas while producing novel content.

We admit that it is sometimes difficult to decide whether an objective represents rule using or problem solving, but the above four criteria should help. If, for example, students are directly taught all the *rules* for solving linear equations, and the *order* in which the rules are applied, a test over this is probably a rule using test, not a problem solving test. Contrast this to the following objective.

Here is an example of a problem solving objective. "Upon request, the learner will generate five-component objectives, in writing, representing each category of intellectual skills for a subject area of his or her own choosing, without assistance."

Conditions of learning for problem solving. Here are some principles for teaching problem solving.

37. Present a previously unencountered problem.
38. Ask learner to generate a solution.
39. State criteria for a successful solution.
40. Ask learners to seek help only if they are "stuck," but assure them that help will be given when needed.
41. Inform learners that when help is needed, you will at first give a minimal clue, and increase the clues as necessary. Challenge them to try to finish without help or with minimal help.
42. When help is requested, examine the effort that has been made, and choose a minimal appropriate clue (such as "what rule might help with this part?" Other such clues: "Which of the five components is missing?" "Does this have anything to do with the concept, capability?" "Where is the action verb?")
43. If several clues, hints, and prompts are necessary for the

learner to reach a correct solution, provide reward and encouragement, and then challenge the learner to try to do another problem without help. (Example: "It was a struggle, wasn't it? But you finally wrote correct objectives. For you to be sure you have mastered this, why don't you now pick a favorite hobby and write another set of objectives for that? I will be glad to look at them and give you my comments. Then you will be sure you can do this task for many other subject areas in the future—this is a highly marketable skill.")

Learning of Information

We distinguish among three subcategories of information learning: verbatim memorization, learning of facts (non verbatim), and substance learning. Each will be discussed, in turn, in separate sections.

Learning of information is legitimate in its own right whether learned because it often needs to be recalled (such as a telephone number), or is useful for learning intellectual skills and other outcomes (domain interactions), or is enjoyable (a poem). The major instructional decisions are to choose *what* information should be learned, and *why* it should be learned. Learning of information is thus desirable, but it should not be overdone so as to crowd out learning in other domains and categories of domains. One way to avoid this is to draw up instructional maps (Briggs & Wager, 1981) which have intellectual skill and attitude objectives as terminal objectives for a lesson, unit, or course, but which include information objectives that are *supporting* (but not necessarily *essential*) prerequisites for the terminal objectives (Gagné, 1977). As we have seen earlier in this chapter, intellectual skills, such as rules, have other intellectual skills, such as defined concepts, as essential prerequisites and information as supporting prerequisites.

While in general the person who has learned much information probably also tends to have learned the most intellectual skills, this correlation is not perfect. Exceptions include people who can recall vast amounts of information but who otherwise are not very competent in terms of intellectual skills. Some competent people know little information as compared to other people, but they are inventive. Thus information is knowing *that*, while intellectual skills represent knowing *how to do.*

It is no small feat to attain a good balance between information and intellectual skills in the planning of instruction. But use of learning hierarchies, taxonomies, instructional maps, and audit trails helps us to deliberately examine the balance between the two, and to achieve relevance among objectives. This seems to us to be a better course of planning than to leave the choice of objectives entirely up to the learners or to replace *performance* objectives with course content as a planning device. While we have earlier presented the views of those who advise leaving choice of objectives almost entirely up to the learner (Part II), our inclination is to advocate *systematically designed instruction which includes affective objectives.* We do not agree that highly structured instruction by nature has to be authoritarian and repressive. We seek here to take clues from social interaction and humanistic theorizing when designing systematic instruction. We believe that making learners aware of objectives facilitates an open and honest relationship between teacher (or designer) and learners, and helps learners see how the instruction and evaluation of learner performance are congruent with the objectives. But we do believe that the objectives should include development of learner strategies and affective goals. Also, breaking learning tasks into smaller tasks leads to success which can be rewarded, thus enhancing self-esteem.

Verbatim Information Learning

This category includes learning of poems, symbols for defined concepts, and memorization of essential and frequently needed information.

Learning of poems can be handled so as to contribute to affective objectives. Learning of symbols for chemical elements can facilitate both classroom and laboratory learning of objectives in the area of intellectual skills. Insuring success in both of these can enhance self-esteem.

Conditions of learning for verbatim information learning. We include here mainly conditions supported by research. We do not include specific training in memorizing. A useful chapter on the latter is found in Joyce and Weil (1980).

44. Provide or ask the learner to invent memory devices, or memory bridges, either as words or images.
45. Provide a meaningful context. (Examples include recognizing the theme of a poem before memorizing it; learning the properties of a chemical element as the symbol is memorized in association with the name; learning the total meaning of a printed passage before learning specific portions verbatim.)
46. Provide practice, with prompting as necessary, and spaced reviews and feedback.
47. Break up large memory tasks (such as a lengthy poem) into small units (stanzas) for practice.
48. Employ backward chaining; e.g., learn the last stanza or sentence first, then work backwards to the opening portion (research is conflicting on this technique; it may work better for learning to recite the alphabet than for learning to recite a poem).
49. For lengthy tasks, rehearse in increasingly large units, repeating learned parts while learning a new one.
50. Distribute practice over time.
51. Provide direct prompting. (If the learner fails to recall the next line of a poem beginning with "the river," prompt by supplying "the river," not "a body of water." This is in contrast to problem solving, for which we advised indirect prompts.)

Writing objectives for memorizing tasks is usually straightforward. Here is an example: "In an individualized (private) oral test situation, the learner will recall verbatim (capability verb) the poem, 'Old Ironsides,' by reciting it, without reference to the printed poem."

Learning of Facts

This category refers to learning of isolated facts, but it does not require verbatim memorization. A poem must be recited exactly as it is printed; no paraphrasing or word substitution is permitted. On the other hand facts can be correctly stated without using the exact language of the source. Examples of facts are: this book costs $25; this book has a blue cover; this event in history occurred on this date; the current President of the United States is..........; it rained in Chicago yesterday.

A test over such facts could be worded in several ways; the student could therefore respond correctly in several ways. Because of this, we use the standard capability verb of "state" (meaning in the learner's own words) rather than "recall verbatim" as for the previous category discussed.

A sample objective: "On a written test, the learner will state in writing the number of innings in an untied baseball game, without use of references."

Conditions of learning for learning of facts. Here are the relevant conditions:

52. Provide a meaningful context.
53. Ask practice questions in several ways, preferably requiring different responses.
54. Provide rehearsal and spaced reviews.
55. Encourage verbal or pictorial encoding.
56. Reverse the stem (the practice question asked) and the required response. (This is to provide what has been called S-R reversal; e.g., in one question have the learner supply an event in history; in another question have the learner supply the date or person concerned.)
57. Encourage learners to state the answer in several ways.
58. Have the learner recall related facts.
59. Have the learner recall other things he or she knows related to the fact.

Substance Learning

This category is often imprecisely called "meaningful" learning. The goal is to recall the main ideas of a passage without having to recite verbatim or to state specific facts. The capability verb is *summarize* (in your own words, the main ideas). This category does not require making inferences beyond the information source; it requires only summarizing, not analysis, critique, or evaluation of the information.

One criterion for distinguishing (not discriminating) this category from memorization and factual learning is that the test questions must not be capable of being answered on basis of a single sentence in the text.

Substance learning is remarkably resistant to forgetting without later rehearsal, although spaced reviews do tend to result in holding retention high. A few studies even showed evidence of "reminiscence"—students scored higher on a delayed retention test (without planned intervening rehearsal) than they did on the test immediately following initial learning (English, Welborn & Killian, 1934). However this finding has sometimes not been substantiated by others (Briggs & Reed, 1943). Neither of these studies could control for unplanned rehearsal during the delayed testing intervals; both studies used multiple-choice recognition tests rather than free recall tests implied by the capability to "summarize." Other studies are needed using essay type tests.

Briggs and Reed (1943) discussed possible explanations for their findings as compared to the contrasting findings of English, Welborn, and Killian (1934). For now the conclusion about reminiscence of substance learning is "now you see it, now you don't." However, both studies showed higher levels of retention for substance learning over a period of up to 90 days than levels of retention reported previously for facts. All these levels of retention were higher than retention of nonsense syllables (Briggs & Reed, 1943), the favorite task of one branch of experimental psychology for a century.

A sample objective for this form of learning follows: "On an essay test, the learner will summarize in writing the main protections provided by the Bill of Rights, without references."

Conditions of learning for substance material. Appropriate conditions are as follows:

60. Provide materials that are well organized and interesting, with highlights of the main ideas.
61. Ask the learner to read with the intent to remember the main ideas.
62. Provide metaphors and analogies.
63. Tie in and cross reference among parts of the passage.

64. Teach learners to read, recite, and review each section of the passage.
65. Provide a "set" to look for the main ideas.
66. Provide an advance organizer.
67. Suggest to learners how to relate the new material to their existing schemata.
68. Use material having typographical clues.
69. Use questions designed to promote integrative reconciliation (see Ausubel, 1963).
70. Provide for spaced reviews.
71. Provide feedback to practice questions to help learner do selective rereading, if necessary.
72. Show how the information relates to skill objectives to be learned.
73. Tie in attitude and skill objectives with the recalled material.

Learning of Cognitive Strategies

We are treating cognitive strategies as a category of the cognitive domain, not as a separate domain.

At this point the reader may wish to glance back to Chapter 12, in which we discussed the relationships among morale, motivation, proficiency, personal characteristics, and learner strategies. We reported there the work of McCombs (1981-82) to improve the learning performance of military personnel who had done poorly in prior training. We also reported the work of Derry (1984) in teaching learning strategies. These two persons have attacked the problem of helping students develop systematically designed learning strategies in a more concrete way than is true of much other research on this problem.

General and Specific Strategies

Much earlier research relates to encouraging learners to discover their own general strategies. Other research has focused on general study skills, such as how to read a chapter in a textbook.

In contrast, the work of McCombs includes first diagnosing the learner's skills, then taking remedial actions relating not only to "objective" skills, such as memorizing and other study skills, but also to personal self-concept and self-management.

Derry also includes specific training which cuts across cognitive and affective strategies.

So some work has been addressed to very general strategies, such as applying the scientific method for solving problems and how to read effectively, while the work just cited centers on more specific strategies.

Immediate and Long-Term Strategies

There is a dual goal here: (a) learning cognitive objectives from the current study program in which learners are engaged, and (b) learning strategies which will enhance life-long learning capability. It is therefore legitimate that some research focuses upon learning of strategies to master the objectives of the present course and that some focuses upon the longer-term goal of life-long learning.

A Dilemma: Highly Structured Learning
or Strategy Learning?

We now introduce a dilemma: to what extent should we lead the learner by the hand through the course by carefully designed, highly structured, small-step instruction by whatever media and methods are being employed, and to what extent should current instruction be designed to enhance learner strategies for later learning situations that place learners on their own? Most of the conditions of learning we have listed up to this point in this chapter focus most clearly upon highly structured learning of the objectives currently being taught in a course rather than upon development of learner strategies. In this section we address the longer term problem of how adults will continue to learn without systematic instruction. In our opinion, both the programmed instruction movement (now almost extinct, *per se*) and the instructional systems movement have focused on the former problem to the neglect of the latter. *Both have also almost entirely ignored the affective domain.* Thus we felt the need for a systems-oriented book that addresses learners strategies, self-development, the affective domain, *and* an attempt to integrate needs assessment, curriculum, and instruction. Much research has been done on each of these, taken separately; it has been our goal to try to address the integration of all of them in instruction and in research.

One position that could be taken is that information and intellectual skills should be learned by deductive, highly structured, didactic, direct instruction, and that cognitive strategies and affective objectives should be taught by self-directed, loosely structured, inductive, permissive, inquiry learning.

Another position that has been taken under the humanistic philosophy is that learners will best fulfill their destinies by nondirective instruction (Chapter 6), regardless of the types of outcomes under discussion.

Traditional instruction leans toward direct instruction with little attention to strategies and affective outcomes.

When one examines the many models of teaching summarized by Joyce and Weil (1980), one finds some examples favoring direct didactic instruction, some favoring inductive learning, some favoring strategy training, and some favoring affective outcomes. But we could not find one model which embraces all of these.

To be sure, it is a formidable task to plan instruction embracing all the above goals. We have essentially accepted highly structured approaches for learning of information and intellectual skills, fairly highly structured approaches for cognitive strategies, and a less structured approach for the affective domain. We have tried, both in Part III on sequencing of objectives, and in this chapter on conditions of learning, to suggest the appropriate degree of structure for various desired outcomes. At the close of this chapter we also suggest varying degrees of structure for different learners, as Joyce and Weil (1980) also have suggested.

Cognitive Strategies as Course Objectives
and as Tools for Learning

In our review, "cognitive strategies" has meant two separate matters in past research: (a) originating novel solutions to *specific* problems related to a course, and (b) acquisition of learner strategies applicable to future new learning. Following the practice of Gagné and Briggs (1979), we adopt the standard capability verb *originate* when we refer to the former (a specific objective); we will use the verb *devise* when we refer to the learner's own development of a new strategy for learning new material or learning how to learn from a new medium. We believe that the other categories we have discussed (under the section of this chapter on learning of intellectual skills) cover the situation in which the learners are being *directly taught* new strategies for learning.

Example of an objective in the curriculum referring to solving a *specific* problem: "the learner will originate a novel way to write performance objectives and will explain in writing how to use the novel method."

Example of an objective referring to a learner's own discovery of a strategy for learning new materials and for learning by a new medium: "In a course in statistics being conducted via computer-assisted instruction, the learner will *devise* a way to learn to calculate the standard deviation (without a computation machine) by accessing the specific information needed for mastery."

Example of an objective for applying a mood-management strategy that was previously *directly taught* to the learner (this is a problem-solving objective): The learner will detect a need for use of the mood-management strategy during a session with computer-assisted instruction on a new topic, and will generate for himself or herself the appropriate self-task to overcome his or her lethargy, resulting in successful completion of study on the topic."

Conditions of learning for cognitive strategies as course-related objectives. These conditions appear appropriate for strategies as course-related objectives:

74. Present a problem and make clear the meaning of a novel solution.
75. Provide a stimulating environment which encourages exploration without penalty for false starts.
76. Encourage multiple modes of attack upon a problem.
77. Ask learners to discuss solutions attempted to encourage both team and individual effort.
78. Encourage divergent thinking before convergent thinking.
79. Provide information on models of problem solving.
80. Provide startling departures from common expectancies and relationships.

81. Use group brainstorming.
82. Make the familiar unfamiliar, and the reverse.
83. Use analogies. Example: Harriman (1984) reports a solution to a corporate problem of how to raise oil from extreme depths by use of an analogy of how to calm a cat (an example of the use of "synectics" in a brainstorming session). (See also Joyce & Weil, 1980, and the August, 1984 issue of *The Futurist*.)

Conditions of learning for cognitive strategies as tools.
84. Provide suggestions on study skills particularly appropriate for the objectives to be learned and for the media or method being used.
85. Teach self-management skills, including making schedules of study.
86. Encourage learners to report to each other about study skills used for a lesson or unit.
87. Teach specific but generalizable strategies, such as those developed by Derry (1984): mood-management, attentional management, memorization strategies, reading strategies, problem-solving strategies, test-taking skills, and vocabulary learning strategies.
88. Intersperse instruction on strategies with course content learning over a period of time, as strategies take some time to learn and use well.
89. Encourage students to discuss how they study and learn, and to exchange suggestions with other students.
90. For substance learning, teach students to read, recite, and review.
91. For problem solving, ask students to apply models from science or other disciplines.
92. Encourage divergent thinking before convergent.
93. Encourage reading about how great discoveries and inventions came about.
94. Invite community members to tell how they solve problems.
95. Encourage learners to set aside specific times for devising strategies as distinct from studying course materials.
96. Ask students to give examples of inductive and deductive thinking.

97. Refer students to books on effective study techniques.
98. Provide opportunities for practice varying the situations as widely as possible.

CONDITIONS FOR THE AFFECTIVE DOMAIN

In the preceding portion of this chapter, which lists conditions of learning for the cognitive domain, we have discussed the nature of each category in that domain because, except for Chapter 3, no review of these categories has previously been offered in this book.

In contrast, for the affective domain, each category has been discussed in detail, in Chapters 4, 5, 6, and 7, including research to validate each category, and lists of appropriate sets of both internal and external conditions of learning have been offered. In summary, in Chapters 3 through 7, we have presented, for the affective domain, the kinds of information that have earlier been presented by Gagné (1977) for the cognitive domain.

For the above reason, in this section on the affective domain, we offer no further discussion to validate the categories. Instead, we summarize the external conditions listed in Part II, adding a few conditions not found earlier in this book.

Conditions of Learning for Acquisition and Change of Attitudes

Short-Term and Long-Term Objectives

We distinguish between attitudes which can be established or changed in an hour or a week of instruction from those which require longer periods. An objective such as willingness to receive information on a fairly non-controversial, limited topic, such as soccer as a hobby or elective physical education activity, may be quickly established. On the other hand, taking a studied position on a complex, highly controversial topic, such as abortion, may require a long period of information learning, debate, soul searching, and position taking. Also, an attitude toward study of a single topic in a course may be taken quickly, while it would take longer to form an attitude toward the entire course, toward the school or other organization, or toward a newly encountered culture or form of government. Consequently, one attitude objective may be appropriate for a lesson objective, while another may be appropriate for an end-of-course or end-of-curriculum objective.

Alternate Positions on Teaching of Attitudes

Unlike many basic skill (cognitive) objectives, which are generally regarded as needed for students and thus the duty of teachers to insure, attitude objectives are more controversial as having a place in schools. Here are some different positions that might be taken:

1. The school has no mandate to try to establish or modify attitudes. It should stick to cognitive objectives.
2. The school should present all sides of controversial issues, leaving the learners to decide whether they wish to take any position, and if so, what position to take.
3. The school should require that *some* position be taken, but not dictate the position.
4. The school should pass on to students the prevailing attitudes of the local community.
5. The school should promote attitudes approved by the state or federal government.
6. Because of a pluralistic society, the school should air information about the full range of attitudes but treat this as information learning, without debate or encouraging that positions be taken.
7. Because of a pluralistic society, all positions should be aired and debated, with each person encouraged to take a position.
8. Same as No. 7, but with position dictated.

It appears that a given citizen or teacher might take different positions from among those just listed, for different potential attitude objectives. For example, one might favor teaching a positive attitude toward the U.S. Constitution, encouraging debate about unicameral legislatures, but not discussing religion at all, considering that the province of the church or synagogue and the family.

Years ago it might have been possible to achieve a broad

consensus about specific attitudes toward a range of issues to be taught in the schools. Now it would probably be difficult to reach such a consensus. For these reasons we believe the duty of teachers is now more difficult to determine than was true in the past. Since a determination on these matters should rest with the community which supports the school, we cannot suggest an ideal policy here. We do believe there should be public discussion on such matters, with citizens, teachers (including instructional designers), and children taking part. So we will focus on the conditions of learning for attitudes without attempting to say which attitudes should be taught. But to avoid reducing the role of either teachers or designers of materials to that of mere technicians, we believe that these people should participate actively in debate on policy issues and needs assessments. *Instructional designers, like scientists, have a moral responsibility, we believe, to be concerned with the ends toward which their techniques are applied.*

While industrial and military training have a different role in society than does the school, similar issues could be raised. In what areas, for example, could the aims of private industry and the military conflict with those of the society as a whole? When should a salesman sell a product known to be harmful to the consumer? When should a soldier protest against an order which has been issued? We cannot address these issues here, but we raise them to acknowledge the moral and value aspects of our topic, teaching of attitudes. And we stress that no single stance is likely to be equally defensible for all potential attitude objectives. We encourage all instructional professionals to ponder these issues while practicing their art. (One of the authors has turned down consulting contracts which required designing of instruction for objectives which the consultant found personally unacceptable.)

So we proceed to offer our summary for conditions of learning for attitudes, without saying which attitude objectives should be taught directly, which should be discussed, and which left out of the curriculum. But for specific instances we would face our responsibilities as citizens and as professionals.

Objectives and Measurement in the Affective Domain

For the reasons discussed in the preceding three sections of this chapter, no single pattern can be offered for writing objectives and for measuring outcomes for attitudes (or for other categories of the affective domain). Because of this we do not offer sample objectives and their corresponding test items for each affective category as we did earlier in this chapter for cognitive categories. Rather, we will use a range of examples for attitudes to reflect the situation for the entire affective domain.

Concrete, short-term objectives. For this kind of affective objective, it is convenient to use the same five-component method of writing objectives that we used for the cognitive categories, and to use an explicit form for assessing the outcomes.

Here is a sample objective: "Given a free play period and a wide choice of games, the learners will *choose* to play soccer as evidenced by their joining in the soccer game in the field."

The measurement of this objective, as implied in the action verb in the objective, is simple—merely observe where the student goes and observe which game he or she joins.

Here is another example having more cognitive components: "After the readings and discussions of bicameral and unicameral legislatures, the learners will *choose* one type and will write a position paper reflecting their personal opinion, giving arguments to support the chosen position." The evaluation consists of rating the facts and logic presented in the position paper, as well as the position taken; however, either choice is acceptable.

Here is an objective we have used in one of our courses: "After reading the chapter in the textbook on Carl Rogers' model of teaching, the student will prepare a position paper stating whether that model would be chosen for a course and group of learners to be described in the paper." Again, the evaluation refers to the learners' correctly interpreting Rogers' model and to the arguments presented in light of the specific course and the specific learners; the student is not evaluated as to the actual position taken for or against the use of the model generally; however, a position is required.

If a teacher can justify attempting to influence the learners for or against a specific idea, issue, or choice of action, then the choice itself could be a part of the evaluation. For example, if honesty of students in grading their own test papers is a behavior sought by the teacher, then that behavior would be reinforced.

More complex, long-term objectives. For this type of affective objective, unobtrusive observation of students over a lengthy period of time is often the method of assessing outcomes. Here is an example of a long-term attitude objective: "Between September and April the learner will exhibit an increase in incidents of helping other students." The teacher may keep a cumulative anecdotal record of observed occurrences of helping behavior on the part of each student.

The above kind of situation is likely to exist for other components of the affective domain: moral and ethical behavior, value formation, self-development, social development, attributions, and motivation. For these outcome categories, objectives may or may not be stated to the learner. The teacher would have such objectives in mind all during the school year; the teacher may or may not keep records in writing. Both the teachers' guidance or teaching efforts and the evaluation of learner progress might consist more of a clinical procedure than of formal written testing.

Attitude scales. The measurement of behavior in the affective domain is a complex research area in itself. Precision in measurement is difficult to attain for complex affective behavior. We will not delve into the kind of measurement needed for research in the affective domain, but we do comment here on the practical uses of attitude scales. (See Henerson, Morris & Fitz-Gibbon, 1978, for ways of measuring attitudes.)

Attitude scales are often in the form of a series of statements to each of which the student responds by marking degree of agreement or disagreement on a five-point scale presented with each statement. Alternatively, questions can be asked to be responded to by either a multiple-choice or open-ended format. Often attitudes of students toward a course are expressed on some form of structured or unstructured questionnaire, as one method of evaluation of teaching effectiveness.

Attitude scales or questionnaires may be used to assess specific attitudes desired as outcomes of instruction, or they can be used by teachers as a basis for course improvement (formative evaluation of instruction).

Thus, teachers may attempt to foster specific attitudes, or to encourage students to choose their own positions on issues. In some cases, then, there will be affective objectives for the course, whether or not they are communicated to the learners. In other cases, teachers will hope to establish a favorable attitude toward the entire course through the manner in which the total instruction is offered.

In the larger area of self-development, teachers will attend to instruction and to personal contact with students as means of promoting desired development.

In summary, for this section on the affective categories, we do not give sample objectives and test items. Instead we list at once the external conditions of learning for each category. The reader may wish to refer back to the chapters in Part II for more background about each category to follow.

Conditions of Learning for Attitudes

In Chapter 4 we listed conditions of learning for each of several strategies for attitude change. We follow the same organization of conditions here.

Persuasive communications as a strategy. Relevant conditions are:

99. The source of the communication should display credibility, expertise, and a balanced view, presenting some views already held by learners.
100. The message should be discrepant from the current view of the learners, but not excessively so.
101. Present the side of the argument preferred to a group already leaning toward that side, but present both sides to a group opposed to the target view.
102. Save the best argument for the end of the message.
103. Present a problem and proposed solution.
104. Urge explicit and feasible action, and evoke verbal or action responses.
105. Give reasons and incentives for attitude change.
106. Present distant (third person) examples of action to change opposing attitudes, but use direct (first person) appeal for action not opposed by the audience.
107. Provide for mental rehearsal or overt action on the position and arguments offered.

Establishing dissonance as a strategy.

108. Create dissonance by setting up decision-making instances.
109. Provide information discrepant with present beliefs of learners and show why it is socially acceptable.
110. Induce action that is discrepant with present views.
111. If excessive dissonance exists, make the presented view attractive logically and consequentially.
112. Show high credibility sources acting in agreement with the target view.
113. For excessive dissonance, use successive approximations—presenting actions working gradually toward the target view.
114. Make persuasive communications that are as discrepant from the learners' view as possible without encountering outright rejection.

Modeling as a strategy.

115. Establish the credibility or reputation of the model.
116. Show the model exhibiting the desired behavior and being rewarded for it.
117. Have learners role play the desired behavior of an imagined model.

Other techniques as strategies.

118. Use group discussions, especially when *some* position is desired of the learners, but not a prescribed one.
119. Use group discussion for controversial issues on which it is inappropriate to urge a particular position.
120. Use direct reinforcement for desired attitudes upon which there is citizen consensus.
121. Use group norms and activities which are enjoyable and reinforcing.

Other Components of the Affective Domain

Conditions of Learning for Values

122. Review specific attitude components of more complex values.

123. Lead learners to construct a value or value system which is superordinate to related specific attitudes.
124. Help learners integrate previous learning about events, people, ideas, and goals, in order to form a cognitive framework for value development.
125. Help learners cluster established attitudes into value areas on such topics as government, health, human relations, work, social life, etc.

Conditions of Learning for Moral Development

In Chapter 5 we discussed a lack of agreement among theorists and researchers as to whether moral development can be taught or merely encouraged as a development process. We also listed the internal conditions necessary for reaching decisions on moral and ethical issues. Many of those internal conditions represent examples of domain interaction—how cognitive learning must be accomplished as a prerequisite to making informed moral decisions. Without repeating the matters covered in Chapter 5, we go at once to listing appropriate external conditions of learning.

126. Engage learners in discussions about genuine moral dilemmas or conflicts. Use newspaper stories, films, books, and everyday occurrences as stimuli.
127. Provide learners with opportunities to act out the perspectives of other people.
128. Encourage learners to gather facts, discuss issues relating to the facts, take positions, and give logical reasons for their positions.
129. When appropriate, ask students to take actions consonant with their positions.
130. Point out discrepancies in reasoning.
131. Use a wide variety of issues and examples of each issue when planning for discussions.
132. Model behavior appropriate for positions consistent with the responsibilities of an instructor.
133. Demonstrate reasoning at the next higher level than that displayed by the learners.
134. List rules for reasoning at levels appropriate for the learners, and give reasons for the rules.

135. Provide an atmosphere encouraging of expression of opinions and supporting arguments; correct learners on faulty facts and logic but do not punish position-taking.
136. Separate sessions for drill and practice with feedback for information and skill learning from discussion of related moral and ethical issues.
137. Use classroom or work related (for non-school settings) behavior as an opportunity to relate moral principles to actions.
138. Encourage learners to agree upon classroom behaviors and rules of conduct related to issues discussed for other contexts. For example, call attention to intellectual honesty of a student or teacher as deserving of attention as financial honesty. Relate classroom and student government to civil government.

Notice that the conditions of learning listed above have strong cognitive involvement (information, intellectual skills, and cognitive strategies) even though we classify moral behavior as a component of the affective domain (another example of domain interaction). We have not dealt directly with feelings and emotions related to moral issues and decision making, although in practice these often are involved as either antecedents or consequences of discussion of some moral issues. Feelings and emotions were addressed in Chapter 7.

Conditions of Learning for Feelings and Emotions
In Chapter 7 we presented our general discussion of feelings and emotions. Here we present only the external conditions of learning.

139. Provide role playing experiences permitting expression of a variety of feelings and emotions.
140. Use classical or operant conditioning to transfer or attach emotions to objects or events.
141. Model appropriate and varied emotional states.
142. Strive to develop positive emotional bonds between learners and instructors.

143. Match tasks to each learner's ability so that positive emotions are associated with learning.
144. Provide opportunities for learners to evaluate situations and to verbalize their emotional responses.
145. Provide opportunities to change the information base of emotions to shift them to a more positive direction.
146. Provide opportunities to discuss ways of coping with negative emotions.
147. Provide ways to alter stimulus situations to permit changes in the intensity and/or quality dimension of emotions.
148. Provide examples of others' emotional responses through films, audiotapes, video, television, etc.
149. If not disruptive, allow and encourage emotional expression toward both course content and the learning environment.

Conditions of Learning for Self-Development

Earlier in this chapter we raised the question of whether teachers should avoid teaching of attitudes, should encourage discussion of attitudes and position taking, or specify actual positions which learners should take. We said the choice would probably vary among potential attitude objectives, for a given teacher, and among teachers. We also mentioned disagreement on whether morals and ethics result from teaching or from natural development. We believe the answer is "both."

Similar issues can be raised about self-development. It is a responsibility of schools, of parents, or of the learners? Is it teachable, or a natural aspect of human development? Separate aspects of self-development were discussed in Chapter 6: personality, self-esteem, self-efficacy, self-regulatory behavior, locus of control, and learned helplessness.

One could ask, "Is it the duty of schools to foster self-development (whether by direct instruction or by the environment provided)?" We assume that the answer is "yes."

A separate question is: "How well prepared are teachers for guiding self-development?" This is a tougher question. At first glance it would appear that teachers would have to be trained in human development, clinical psychology, and perhaps even psychiatry. But when we list the conditions of learning (next page), we again see the strong cognitive component and the rather concrete actions that teachers can take in fostering self-development. Our conclusion is that between selection and training of teachers, it is realistic for the schools to exert strong influence on positive self-development. Of course, individual children or adults who have severe problems will require the service of counselors or mental health specialists. In those cases, the teacher and the specialist may need to coordinate their actions.

We have chosen, in this chapter, not to list separate sets of conditions for the subcategories of self-development discussed in Chapter 6. We therefore offer a consolidated list.

150. Do everything possible to enable the learners to experience success. This means that careful pretesting may be needed to determine an appropriate starting point, in the course, for each learner. Also, complex tasks must be broken down into simpler component tasks, carefully sequenced and taught to insure a whole series of success experiences. Alternately, if a discovery method is used, point out and reward instances of success.

151. Teach learning strategies, both general ones such as how to use a library, and specific ones for particular types of objectives and media.

152. Teach learners how to learn from each other, including interpersonal skills such as listening, paraphrasing, sharing, and group projects.

153. Teach scheduling of work and other self-management skills.

154. Use parallels, such as relating the components of success on a job with success in school.

155. Encourage social interaction as a means for solving complex problems.

156. Use highly structured methods for basic skills, and reward successful learning of these skills.

157. Focus upon mastery of prerequisite skills and personal effort as the keys to success; do not focus on luck or the influence of other persons.

158. Provide the necessary resources for each learning task—instruction, references, materials, etc.

159. For prerequisite learning provide either highly structured teaching and learning materials or provide opportunity for self-direction and discovery, with access to help when needed.

160. Beyond required or core objectives, provide opportunities for independent goal setting, independent learning, and self-evaluation of progress.

161. Use peer tutoring to provide social interaction and to pair learners having complementary skills.

162. Strive for a mixture of solitary independent learning, peer interaction, and interaction with teachers and other adults.

163. Provide an atmosphere of acceptance of the learner, demonstrating positive regard and trust.

164. Cooperate with the learner in assessing present status, and in planning the next goals, and means for achieving them.

165. Provide reinforcement for success even on simple accomplishments, and challenge and help prepare the learner for achieving success on more complex objectives.

166. Provide models of successful performances and people, showing how success was achieved and what the rewards were.

167. Conduct discussions of sources of success for various areas of school, life, work, and leisure.

168. Graduate tasks so that learners become more competent and are successful on more difficult tasks.

Conditions of Learning for Social Competence

169. Provide training in conflict resolution and management, cooperation skills, group projects, etc.

170. Use role playing and simulation to provide learners with experience in taking the perspective of others.

171. Provide opportunity for shared decision making.

172. Model interpersonal skills and cooperative behaviors.

173. Pair students of unlike characteristics, academic and social, to work together.

174. Allow goal setting and self-responsibility in some class undertakings.

175. Reward effort, participation, and cooperation.
176. For young children, provide opportunities for mixed age group interaction.
177. Provide opportunity to interact with various social and ethnic groups, and with handicapped people.
178. Select films showing people with diverse characteristics working together effectively.
179. Conduct discussions on current events, social conditions, social problems, government, etc.
180. When not disruptive, encourage self-expression.
181. Encourage learners to identify their strengths and weaknesses in situations involving academic, social, personal, and physical skills.

Conditions of Learning for Attributions

182. Match task difficulty and learner ability.
183. Provide many success experiences, and identify internal, stable, controllable attributions as the cause of success.
184. In failure situations, provide feedback related to lack of effort, not ability.
185. Reinforce successful experiences.
186. Provide opportunities to "test out" the effects of expending more or less effort on a variety of tasks matched to ability levels. Relate success experiences to controllable attributions, generalized across tasks.
187. Break difficult tasks into manageable, less difficult components when multiple instances of success can be attained.
188. Use audio-visual media that demonstrate the effects of persistent effort, as for example in athletic accomplishments and scientific discovery.

Conditions for Learning for Motivation

In Chapter 7 we discussed some theoretical conceptions of motivation, and we briefly outlined the instructional design model of motivation by Keller (1983). In Chapter 7, the conditions of learning which we listed referred primarily to "continuing motivation."

We now turn to the broader view of motivation as both a *cause* and an *effect* of learning and achievement. Almost everyone would agree that an initial state of motivation increases subsequent learning, and that recognition of success in learning further increases motivation for continued learning. So we have a circular effect between motivation and learning. This effect builds up in cumulative spirals or episodes over a period of time. Thus, motivation refers to both *ends* and *means*—to both cause and effect (outcome) of learning. Various writers stress either the cause or the effect: reinforcement theorists stress the design of effective instruction so that the learner's success can be reinforced, thereby emphasizing motivation as an *outcome* (effect; end) of instruction; writers who stress the arousal of interest at the beginning of instruction are focusing upon motivation as the cause (means) of promoting learning.

In summary, it is reasonable to attend to two alternate conceptions of motivation:
1. Motivation should be established at the *beginning* of instruction as a *causes or means* of promoting learning. This emphasizes arousal, interest, and relevance.
2. Motivation is an *effect or end (outcome)* of effective instruction, provided that the learners perceive their efforts as successful. This emphasizes reinforcement and expectancy.

More complex interactions of these two major aspects of motivation were offered by Keller (1983) in both a flowchart form (p. 392) and in his discussion of four components of motivation: interest, relevance, expectancy, and satisfaction (outcome).

We have chosen in this chapter to arrange our conditions of learning in accordance with Keller's four components of motivation. So a separate sub-heading is given to each. We have borrowed heavily from Keller's chapter (1983), but we have adopted our own wording. Some of the conditions listed below are our own, and some are Keller's. We hereby make a general acknowledgment of our liberal use of his chapter. The wording and interpretations are our own. We have tried to cast all the conditions in as concrete a form as possible.

Interest. We include here both conditions for gaining attention (arousal) and conditions for establishing and maintaining interest.

189. Use some novel and unexpected stimulus to gain attention. The stimulus may be either relevant or irrelevant to the lesson content (a loud noise, a puff of smoke, a striking picture).
190. Pose a paradox or incongruity, a dilemma. Present a perplexing question or a puzzling object to arouse curiosity.
191. Use brainstorming questions and problems; encourage divergent thinking. Remove risk by withholding criticism of responses.
192. For later parts of the lesson, provide a moderate level of risk.
193. Use abrupt changes in content, context, or hypotheses to maintain attention and curiosity.
194. Present unusual perspectives of a problem.
195. Use anecdotes of a personal emotional element; use personal language and concrete stories about real people.
196. Give opportunity to learn more about something of which learners already have some knowledge, and add the unfamiliar and unexpected. Begin with something they already believe in, then introduce a paradox or different point of view.
197. Use analogies to arouse and maintain interest and to make the abstract more concrete.
198. Deliberately use analogies which are partly not applicable to the concept being taught; make the strange familiar, and the familiar strange.
199. Pose puzzling situations to encourage inquiry and to increase curiosity.
200. Use a mixture of the familiar and the unfamiliar, with reference to real people and real problems, to make the abstract more concrete and emotional.

Relevance. In some adult training situations, the learners may come to the training already convinced of the relevance of the instruction for their personal needs, goals, values, and career plans. In academic situations, on the other hand, considerable attention is needed to show the learners how the objectives of instruction relate to their needs and goals. The following conditions are offered for the latter situation.

201. Encourage learners to discuss their long-term goals, and when appropriate, show the relevance of the instruction to those goals.
202. On goal-relevant objectives, provide opportunity for achieving standards of excellence under conditions of moderate risk.
203. Use performance contracting tasks relevant to goals, agreeing upon standards the learner perceives as fair and realistic.
204. Maintain interest by use of non-zero-sum scoring systems based on predefined standards rather than normative standards.
205. Make use of small group work as a way of meeting standards.
206. To make use of the personal power motive, provide opportunities for personal choice, responsibility, and interpersonal influence.
207. Engage learners in setting tasks and standards to avoid power struggles with the instructor.
208. Agree upon ground rules to establish trust between instructor and learners, and among learners. Provide opportunity for no-risk, cooperative interaction. Adhere carefully to the ground rules to maintain trust.
209. Use self-study for learners with high achievement need and independence, and an internal locus of control.
210. Use group methods for students needing affiliation or power, or for those with external locus of control.
211. Vary instructional strategies over a prolonged period of instruction.
212. Begin a session with personal introductions, anecdotes, or responding to simple questions, to relax learners and avoid fear of social rejection.
213. When using group activities, ensure a clearly defined role for each learner and a recognition that each role is important.
214. Attempt to establish a cultural value of the activities by learners' communication with family, friends, and adults.

Show the cultural relevance of the accomplishments of the learners and of public figures.

Expectancy. Here we refer to both the learners' expectations of the results of their efforts and how their performances are viewed by others.

215. Insure success on carefully chosen tasks as a means of establishing and continuing the expectancy for continued success.
216. Insure success on each task by (a) being sure the learner is ready for it, (b) carefully sequencing tasks and lesson components, and (c) defining the indicators of success.
217. Communicate objectives to the learners to reduce anxiety, to focus the study effort, and to increase success expectancy. This also contributes to trust between instructor and learner because it establishes an open relationship (there are no hidden agendas or discrepancies between pre-announced standards for success and post-study evaluations).
218. Help learners associate success with their personal efforts.
219. Establish the experiences of success on easy tasks to establish expectancy of success on later, more difficult or complex tasks.
220. Discuss ways to motivate oneself to do unpleasant tasks, by linking them with desired success on a later task.
221. Teach learners to apply the Premack principle on themselves by rewarding themselves with a desired activity after finishing a less desired task.
222. Teach students to continue a task at a time and place away from the original learning environment. Reinforce those future attempts.

Outcomes. Here we deal with the goal of providing sufficient reinforcement and feedback to indicate success to the student, while not overdoing it and so decrease intrinsic motivation.

223. Try to make rewards directly related to the task. (Use of tokens for rewards not intrinsic to the task have been found to reduce self-initiated effort and solution quality.)

224. To maintain intrinsic satisfaction with instruction, use unexpected noncontingent rewards (except with dull tasks).

225. At the beginning of a session, ask easy questions, and reward the act of responding, regardless of the quality of the response.

226. At the close of a session, reward effort and task completion; withhold critical feedback.

227. In the second session (or practice trial) on a task, open with critical feedback designed to improve performance. (Note that 226 is a reward for effort, not quality of work, while 227 is a reward for quality and a corrective for any lack of quality).

228. Use verbal praise and informative (corrective) feedback as just described above; avoid sarcasm, threats, or other punishing feedback.

229. Use written performance standards, answer keys, and the like, to enable learners to evaluate their own performance and to revise work if necessary, before submitting work for corrective feedback from the instructor.

230. When a task has been satisfactorily completed, but only after repeated efforts and corrective feedback from the instructor, compliment the learner for the satisfactory performance, and then give an opportunity for the learner to repeat the performance in a new context (a new set of relevant problems or repeating the competency with new material, etc.).

CONDITIONS OF LEARNING FOR DIFFERENT PEOPLE

In his first edition of *The Conditions of Learning* (for intellectual skills), Gagné (1965) acknowledged that not all learners require exactly the same events of instruction and external conditions of learning. This idea was retained through the third edition of the book (Gagné, 1977), and was further expanded upon by Gagné and Briggs (1979), who placed more emphasis upon adult learning. Also in his third edition, Gagné directly related his nine instructional events with stages in information processing theory.

In this connection, Gagné and Briggs (1979) emphasized variations in the sophistication of the learners in providing some of their own events of instruction. For a child facing learning of a new task, all nine of the events of instruction and all of the external conditions of learning listed in this book (for a given outcome category) might be incorporated into a lesson for an objective falling into a given category of outcome. For a doctoral student planning a dissertation, the dissertation advisor provides mainly two events of instruction: (a) guidance to thinking, and (b) feedback. Intermediate degrees of learner responsibility for various instructional events could be expected, depending upon the age and degree of sophistication of learners.

Joyce and Weil (1980) have addressed three related questions: How can we match how we teach to the characteristics of our students? How can we combine teaching methods or models for maximum effectiveness? What kinds of learning outcomes does each model of teaching promote? The first question is the one we now address, but we rephrase it as "how might conditions of learning vary among learners?" The second question we have already addressed as "how can we promote domain interactions?" The third question we have addressed as "how do conditions of learning vary among categories of desired outcomes?" So we have used the terminology of instructional design models to address the three questions about models of teaching raised by Joyce and Weil.

On the first question, how to match models of teaching to learner characteristics, even within a single age level of learners, Joyce and Weil (1980, Chapter 25) describe some work by David Hunt, who proposed that learners can be classified according to their levels of conceptual complexity. Joyce and Weil then proceed to present a table (p. 437) which lists 16 models of teaching, each rated as to amount of structure it provides. Then they indicate whether each model is most appropriate for learners of high, moderate, or low levels of conceptual complexity. They suggest that the more highly structured models are most effective for learners of low complexity, and that the models of lower structure are most appropriate for learners of high complexity. Our suggestion is similar in intent, but it is more analytical, since it is expressed in microterms (selecting appropriate instructional events and conditions of learning to match both the type of outcome and the learner), while their own is expressed in the more macroterms of selecting intact teaching models. We agree with Joyce and Weil that degree of structure in teaching might well be varied to match the learner. Our suggestion is that to the extent practically feasible, the teacher may select, from among the conditions of learning offered for a *given type of desired outcome*, the conditions most appropriate for a learner's characteristics.

Another area of research having a similar practical purpose is known as research in "trait-treatment interactions." We shall not pursue either of these research areas here because in both cases (a) the research is in an early stage requiring further verification of findings, and (b) the findings would be difficult to put into practice, especially under conditions of conventional group instruction. Even under a one-to-one tutorial method, or even using a sophisticated computer, the task of always varying instruction according to the learner would raise serious problems in economy and efficiency.

Nevertheless, continued efforts to match teaching to the learner is to be encouraged. Bloom (1984) posed a similar question as "the 2 sigma problem," referring to data showing mastery learning to result in achievement one standard deviation above results for conventional group instruction, and one-to-one tutoring to result in achievement two standard deviations above conventional instruction. His question is "how can we make conventional group instruction as effective as tutoring?" He makes some encouraging suggestions toward such a goal, such as (concerning the intermediate effectiveness of mastery learning) one can turn to the literature on "individualized instruction" which is actually handled by about the same teacher-pupil ratio as conventional instruction. For a discussion of three such individualized approaches used fairly widely in schools, see Talmage (1975). Gagné and Briggs (1979, Chapters 13 and 14) have compared the degrees of *precision* in implementing the events of instruction for tutoring, individualized instruction, and instruction for various sizes of groups. It is these differences in precision in teaching which may account for the data reported by Bloom.

We do not pursue the problem of matching instruction to learners here. We merely encourage teachers and designers to employ flexibility in choosing conditions of learning appropriate for the learners, from the total set of conditions offered in this chapter for the relevant outcome category. Some authors have outlined conditions appropriate for the adult learner who has long been out of school. Other authors have addressed conditions for the handicapped or other special category of learners.

In Chapter 15, we present sample lesson designs for a variety of types of learners and types of outcomes.

THE ORIGIN OF OUTCOME CATEGORIES
AND CONDITIONS OF LEARNING

As a historical note, we now address the question, "what was the origin of the outcome categories and associated sets of conditions of learning listed in this chapter and in Part II of this book?

Gagné's Work

We asked this question of Gagné, especially in reference to the cognitive domain, and we have asked this question to ourselves in reference to the affective domain.

Actually, we asked Gagné a series of questions. The questions and Gagné's replies follow. (The replies were contained in a personal communication from Robert M. Gagné, January 23, 1984; they are quoted with his permission.)

Question No. 1. "How did you arrive at the various categories of learning outcomes?"

"I arrived at the categories of learning outcomes by thinking, but with continual attention to the research literature. There is, I think, an APA symposium paper on the subject, in the early fifties. . . . Some ideas on the subject are in my chapter in the book, *Psychological Principles in System Development* (Gagné, 1962). Another effort is in the chapter, "Problem Solving," in Melton's book, *Categories of Human Learning* (1964).

"In the first edition of *The Conditions of Learning* (Gagné, 1965), the categories of learning outcome are mainly intellectual skills, plus a little about verbal information, and less about motor skills. Comments on the book by students and colleagues, plus my own thinking, led me to see that when school instruction is considered as a whole, one must deal with verbal information, motor skills, cognitive strategies, and attitudes, as well as with intellectual skills. The result was the address, "Domains of Learning," and the reflection of these ideas in subsequent editions of *The Conditions of Learning.*

Question No. 2: "Which came first, the "conditions" or the categories?"

"As indicated by the chapter in Melton's book (as well as by even earlier unpublished efforts) the categories of learning came first (before the associated sets of conditions of learning). That is, the sub-categories of intellectual skills came first (Gagné, 1965). However, when I considered how to deal with the *learning* of such different entities, the idea of describing the "conditions" necessary for their learning emerged.

"When I later set out to deal with the five categories of my later work, the idea of "conditions" was already established as a framework (i.e., in the first edition). So I continued it, depending upon my own thought and upon research findings to the extent possible. The difficulty with research literature, of course, is that it almost never comes with these categories in its title, and seldom even internally in the paper. This is still true today, although the situation has improved somewhat."

Question No. 3: "How would one validate the categories?"

"I think the way to validate the categories is to perform studies which test the differential effectiveness of differing conditions. Such conditions differ from each other primarily in (a) what prior knowledge, and what kind of prior knowledge is of aid to new learning; (b) what features of the content are distinguished in the presentation of the learning task; and (c) what encoding strategies work best for learning and retention.

"Because of the difficulty of equating tasks in the different categories, the design of empirical studies appears to me to be a puzzling problem. One cannot legitimately (I think), make direct comparisons of conditions between one category of outcome and another. The tasks are different. Apples and oranges. Perhaps the approach to the answer will be somehow making comparable the measurement of one outcome and another. I am reminded of the problem of "comparable work," which we hear about these days."

Question No. 4: "Are the information processing activities the same for all categories of outcomes?"

"I think the information-processing activity is basically the same for all categories, with the exception of "manner of long-term storage." Is verbal information stored in the same form as an intellectual skill? I doubt that it is, but there are some theorists who argue strongly for this.

"Obviously, that must mean that the major difference among the categories is in the content. It is a matter of *what* is processed; but in the case of long-term memory, it is difficult to distinguish 'how' from 'what,' as stated in the previous paragraph."

The above quotations from Gagné referred to a series of questions primarily concerning the origin of the various categories of outcomes. In a previous exchange of notes, we had asked about the origins of the conditions of learning for each type of outcome. Again, our question and Gagné's response are quoted. The responses are from a personal communication from him, November 20, 1983, and are quoted with his permission.

Questions: "When you were first deriving the conditions of learning for each type of learning outcome, what were the **sources***? Would it be possible to estimate the proportions of the total set of conditions that were derived from the different sources, e.g., research and theory, practical experience, sheer brain power?"*

"The specific answer to your questions, as best I can remember, is as follows: The sources for what I describe as "external" and "internal" conditions came first in general outline by reflection on what research findings I remembered . . ." (Gagné then cited some examples of research findings.)

"Having set out upon that course, I reviewed what I took to be key research articles pertaining to each category. However, it should be noted that these articles were not written so as to conform to my purpose. Each had to be interpreted.

"As for practical experience, it had a good deal to do with *identification* of the five categories of outcomes. Primarily the experience was unobtrusive classroom observation. But once the categories were identified, the description of conditions (which is your specific question) did *not* rest upon practical experience to any notable degree.

In sum, I would estimate the contribution as follows:
research (not theory)—50 percent
reason and inference—50 percent
practical experience—a trace
"Interesting question!"

The above, then, represents Gagné's summary of the origins of his work related to our questions.

Our Work

We now turn to our own experience in preparing for the portions of this book relating to the origins of the categories we list, and the associated sets of conditions of learning.

For the Cognitive Domain

For the cognitive domain, as shown earlier in this chapter, in general we adopted Gagné's categories. However, whereas he uses the terms "information domain," "intellectual skills domain," and "cognitive strategy domain," we call all of these, collectively, "the cognitive domain." We have just changed word usage, not the categories themselves, for the most part. However, we did break up "cognitive strategies" into categories, as noted earlier.

As to the external conditions of learning for the cognitive

domain, as listed in this chapter, we drew heavily from Gagné's work, but we did much paraphrasing, restating, and adding of conditions. Like Gagné, we relied upon research, when possible, but also upon our own thinking, our experience in teaching courses in instructional design, and upon some project experiences. We also recalled examples of our observations in classrooms. We did not knowingly or intentionally quote verbatim directly from Gagné's work, but we make a general acknowledgment of our heavy reliance upon his work. We consider his relating of types of outcomes to instructional events and conditions of learning a monumental contribution to instructional design. So we did not here review the literature which he has already reviewed for the cognitive domain. We added our own knowledge of this literature to his, and we adopted or adapted all his categories and most of his conditions of learning. We worked from summary handouts prepared for our students. We did not intentionally use any verbatim quotations.

For the Affective Domain

Our work on the affective domain is a far different story from our work on the cognitive domain. We had no integrating and consolidating reference for the affective domain, as we had for the cognitive domain through Gagné's work. We did utilize Gagné's limited treatment of attitudes, and the modeling technique for influencing them.

In Part II of this book, we summarized the research literature for the affective domain. There we discussed several existing taxonomies for both domains (affective and cognitive). We then quoted research in validating domain categories, and we listed conditions of learning for each category in the affective domain.

We cited, in Part II, a surprisingly large body of research from which we derived, in part, our conditions of learning for the affective domain. But, like Gagné, we had to *interpret* the research to *derive* the conditions of learning—they were not directly spelled out in the literature.

In this chapter, we have consolidated the conditions of learning which we presented in Part II for the affective domain, and we have added our thinking to Gagné's for the cognitive domain.

When we first began thinking about integrating the cognitive and affective domains, we knew that the area requiring the most attention would be the affective domain. The only taxonomy that we knew of or could find in the literature that had identified outcomes or objectives was the taxonomy by Krathwohl *et al.* We adopted it knowing that there were only three research articles on the structure of the taxonomy, and that none of the research completely validated the structure. Parts of the taxonomy, however, were supported (see Chapter 3).

In an empirical study conducted before this book was planned, Hurst (1980b) adopted two categories of Gagné's types of learning—intellectual skills and verbal information. Using the categories from both the taxonomy by Gagné and the taxonomy by Krathwohl *et al.*, she hypothesized an integrated sequence of the two domains, and conducted a validation study. Her goal was to see if the domains interacted in any important way, not to determine the precise relationships between the two taxonomies. The findings indicated that there were meaningful interactions, so she decided that the study of domain interactions was a viable research effort. She continued her study of the literature in the affective domain. Then she noticed an article by Briggs (1980a) which also called for the need to apply domain interactions in practice. The two authors then decided to write this book.

Our next step was to derive categories of outcomes in the affective domain. This has been a crucial and difficult issue to address from the beginning. We ran into three problems repeatedly in the literature search:

1. Definitions of the domain and categories and definitions within domain taxonomies varied widely.

2. Most of the work on taxonomies was theoretical and had a limited research base (the Krathwohl *et al.* taxonomy is the exception).

3. Most categories of the domain (such as motivation) can be described as both an outcome and as an entry characteristic (or in Gagné's terms, an internal condition.).

With these problems in mind, we attempted to synthesize what we had read by mentally noting how often a particular category was referred to, and the importance (dominance or prevalence) of a category in the literature. So the actual selection of categories of outcomes in the affective domain was determined primarily by reasoning and inference (60-75 percent). Theory (not research) and literature reviews (opinions, position papers, some research) from knowledgeable authors accounted for the remaining contribution.

The final step was to derive conditions of learning. Here, research, or more truthfully reviews of research, and theory contributed most heavily to defining the conditions of learning. For the category, attitudes, we reviewed and interpreted a number of attitude change theories, and then synthesized the findings. The original intent was to provide one combined list of conditions. However, the theories and the supporting research were so diverse that we categorized the external conditions so that researchers and practitioners with different beliefs could select conditions based on preferred theory (e.g., behavioral, cognitive).

For the category of morals and ethics, we selected one theory and the associated research, and derived conditions directly from that literature. Because the theory for morals and ethics is a developmental theory, growth can be facilitated, but not directly taught. Therefore, much interpretation had to be done.

For the category of self-development, we used portions of theories relevant to self-development. For example, we used research based aspects of social learning theory, plus other theoretical positions that were not research based (e.g., Rogers, Adler). There was amazing similarity among various positions concerning external conditions of learning. The most notable condition, *expressed in all the literature*, is the necessity of success experiences. Some research suggested that learners who perceive that their success is due to internal, stable, controllable attributions tend to expect more future successes.

For the remaining categories, the conditions were derived primarily from theory, inference, and reasoning, drawing where possible on research.

Like Gagné, the categories came first, then the conditions. Also, as noted by Gagné, the research literature rarely used consistent terms and descriptions across categories. Much extrapolation, inference, and synthesis had to be done. While theory, and to some extent research, provided the background and basis, our own thinking and reasoning "pulled the pieces together."

We have thus interpreted the research literature as best we could, and we phrased our conditions of learning in terms of practices that teachers and other instructional designers can understand and apply in practice. In addition to drawing upon the literature, we added our own experiences in teaching instructional design courses and in designing actual instructional materials for a variety of educational and training situations.

SUMMARY

We opened this chapter by restating the important connection between categories of outcomes and their associated sets of conditions of learning.

Next, we briefly described the nature of each category of outcome, giving sample objectives and test items for each category of the *cognitive* domain. Then we listed the external conditions of learning appropriate for each category. We covered five categories of intellectual skills, three categories of information learning, and two categories of cognitive strategies, for a total of 10 categories of the cognitive domain. We listed 98 conditions of learning for the cognitive domain. With only a few exceptions, we adapted Gagné's categories and conditions for the cognitive domain.

For the *affective* domain, we first discussed positions that can be taken as to the propriety of teaching attitudes in the schools. Then we discussed long-term and short-term affective objectives, and how to state them and how to measure the outcomes. We illustrated a variety of ways to state desired affective outcomes, using the attitude category as an example of the affective domain. We also discussed unobtrusive observation of outcomes as well as attitude scales and questionnaires. We discussed measurement as a way to note pupil progress and as a way to improve instruction. Then we listed 132 conditions of learning for 14 categories of the affective domain. Thus we indentified a total of 24 categories and 230 conditions, for the two domains combined.

We next observed that conditions of learning have usually been related to categories of outcomes. We raised the additional question of whether conditions should be matched to learner characteristics, and we referred to several lines of research on that question.

Finally, we presented a brief history of how categories of outcomes and associated sets of conditions of learning were derived. We quoted Gagné's responses to a series of questions we had asked him about his work on categories and conditions. His responses pertained mostly to work in the cognitive domain. We then added a summary of our own work on these questions—the process by which we arrived at categories and conditions for the *affective* domain.

In the chapter that follows, we present a number of examples of lesson design, illustrating how conditions of learning and instructional events may be incorporated into lessons. Our examples include both long-term and short-term objectives for both the affective and cognitive domains. We illustrate lessons having a single objective and lessons having multiple objectives. We also offer a set of 20 principles for integrating instruction for the two domains, while achieving course-related objectives at the same time that long-term learner strategies are being developed.

Chapter 15

Delivery Systems, Media, and Lesson Design

SELECTING DELIVERY SYSTEMS AND MEDIA

Alternate Points for Selecting Delivery Systems and Media

Deciding Delivery Systems First
Deciding Media First
Intuitive Decisions
Size of Chunk in Selections
Media Selection Models

Comparing Group Instruction to Use of Packaged Materials

Closing Gaps Between Goals and Objectives
Domain Integration
The teacher's role
The computer's role

PLANNING SEQUENCES OF LESSONS

LESSON DESIGN

A Lesson for a Single Cognitive Objective

Discussion of the Example

A Lesson for Teacher Training

Discussion of the Example

A Lesson for Value Development

Chapter 15

Delivery Systems, Media, and Lesson Design

SELECTING DELIVERY SYSTEMS AND MEDIA

Gagné and Briggs have defined a "delivery system" as "the total of all components necessary to make an instructional system operate as intended" (1979, p. 175). Thus, a delivery system includes the physical plant, the teacher, instructional materials, and all media and activities related to instruction.

"Instructional media" includes all sources of communication to the learners. This includes any instructional hardware, such as computers, television, and slide projectors, and the associated software for them. By this definition, the teacher is a medium, and so are the learners who constitute a group.

Gagné and Briggs (1979, pp. 176-177) have presented a table which lists six delivery systems: group instruction; individualized instruction, small group instruction, independent study, work-study programs, and home study (as through correspondence schools). Opposite each delivery system in the table, they list probable associated media, the nature of the learner activity, and the methods and roles of the teacher or instructor.

The term delivery systems is thus broader than the term media of instruction. In this chapter we discuss these two aspects of instruction, and we relate them to many of the key concepts encountered earlier in this book: needs, goals, objectives, audit trails, curriculum, and sequencing of instruction. We then add the new element, lesson design, which in turn brings us back to instructional events and conditions of learning.

This chapter, then, serves to bring us to the culuminating stage of instructional design—lesson design. It is at the lesson design level that we reach the "pay off" for all the review of theory and research discussed in Part II, along with categories of learning outcomes and their associated sets of conditions of learning. It is also here that we are ready for the micro level of detail in planning that began with the macro level of needs assessment and audit trails in Part III.

To recap some of the above, lesson design follows from all these previously accomplished design stages:

1. Needs assessment, to determine life-long goals.
2. Audit trails, to trace the learning objectives needed to achieve life-long goals.
3. Curricula, to organize the entire learning experience.
4. Courses, to implement major parts of the curriculum.
5. Course units, to build toward end-of-course objectives.
6. Sequences of lessons for course units.
7. Design of individual lessons, using appropriate instructional events and conditions of learning.

But where do selection of delivery systems and selection of media fall in the above scheme of events? Why aren't they listed? The answer is that practices differ, and so we next discuss alternative plans for where these two design stages may fall in the total design procedure.

Alternate Points for Selecting Delivery Systems and Media

Up to this point in this book, we have consistently followed the rule, "design from the top downward." Thus, in Part III, we recommended that the life-long goals be determined first, after which audit trails work downward to curriculum, then to courses, then to course units, then to lessons. So it has been possible to stick to this rule in ordering goals and objectives from broad, long-term goals, to narrow, short-term objective. We maintain that this rule is the best for deriving objectives at the various levels.

We now raise the question as to whether the design of *instruction* should follow this same rule that we have applied to the design of the *objectives* for instruction. That is, should delivery systems be chosen before media of instruction, or just the reverse? Should media be selected before lessons are designed, or should the process of lesson design identify the media? We thus seek the desirable sequence for lesson design, media selection, and delivery system selection. We next discuss the pros and cons of several alternative ways of proceeding.

Deciding Delivery Systems First

Gagné and Briggs (1979, Chapter 2) presented a case for determining the delivery system early in the design process. They listed 14 stages into which the design process might be arranged. The first stage is determining needs, goals, and priorities among goals. The second stage is analysis of resources, constraints, and consideration of alternate delivery systems. The third stage is determination of curriculum scope and sequence and course delineation, then selection and design of the delivery system. They leave media selection to the later lesson design stage. This plan in itself suggests two things: (a) selection of a delivery system is closely tied to resources and constraints, and (b) there is great flexibility in "working media into the selected delivery system."

Suppose, for example, that the basic choice is between two delivery systems: conventional group instruction or individualized instruction. One could choose either system but work in almost any media for separate parts of the instruction. But under either delivery system choice, there must be a way to access, use, and store media and related materials, a way to monitor learner progress, a way to assess attainments, etc. It is interesting that since three widely used systems of individualized instruction, Individually Prescribed Instruction (IPI), Individually Guided Instruction (IGE), and Program for Learning in Accordance with Needs (PLAN) (Talmage, 1975) are of fairly recent origin, they make more specific plans, *in advance*, for how all of the components of the system work together, including how media are provided and used.

Making the delivery system choice early has practical advantages in that all components of the system can be jointly planned for in advance. Also, under the plan suggested by Gagné and Briggs, media choices are made later during lesson design, thus avoiding "force fitting" of lessons to pre-selected and possibly unsuitable media. This sequence also follows the "design from top down" rule.

Deciding Media First

An interesting alternative, feasible perhaps only when there is a long lead time between planning of instruction and the installation of that instruction, would be to design all lessons, then note the ideal media for each lesson, then design the delivery system. This approach would seem ideal for planning an entirely new course or curriculum before there are any students already "in the pipeline." Normally, however, a new approach to instruction is designed while the old approach is still operating to serve learners already in the system. Both these first two alternatives would appear to be systematic ways to select delivery systems and media.

Intuitive Decisions

In the rather unsystematic way in which instruction has traditionally been designed, there has been a tendency to select both delivery systems and media without much analysis of the objectives and learner characteristics. Instead, schools may tend to adopt what other schools or colleges are using and recommending. We thus encounter fads and bandwagon effects. Also, delivery systems brought in by outsiders tend to disappear when those outsiders leave. Media producers provide instructional materials in whatever media happens to be their business. Also, one often uses whatever is available, or in the case of hardware purchased without software, much of what is "available" gathers dust on the shelf.

Not all intuitive decisions are poor ones. For example, the need for "distance learning" has been established by several institutions, leading to use of media and delivery systems matching the resources and constraints of the distance learning commitment.

Other intuitive decisions are based on media and delivery systems choices with which the teachers feel comfortable, or with which the learners feel comfortable.

In sum, the choices of delivery systems and media may rest primarily upon (a) analysis of resources and constraints, (b) analysis of lesson designs, (c) popularity, or (d) intuitive choices.

Size of Chunk in Selections

A delivery system may be designed for a single classroom, a school, or school district. For example, individualized instruction systems are sometimes found in isolated classrooms, but more often they flourish only when supported by administrators. In this case, most classrooms in a school are using the same system, except for teachers who elect not to use it. Actual *systems* of individualized instruction (as distinct from informal efforts most teachers make to pay attention to individuals as needed) require a support system that is distinctly different from that of the traditional group instruction. This is why both administrative support and teacher training are needed to make those systems function well. Usually individualized instruction systems are first adopted for reading or mathematics, not for the entire curriculum. In some cases, the system is adopted only for slow learners or at the option of the teacher. So in the same classroom some instruction will be on an individualized system and some on a group system.

Media selection, also, is made in varying chunk sizes. In the model proposed by Gagné and Briggs (1979) and Briggs and Wager (1981), a medium is selected for each instructional event in a lesson, resulting often in use of several media for a single lesson. In other plans, a whole course may be conducted by one medium, for example, by computers. There are all degrees in between these two extremes in "size of chunk."

Media Selection Models

Reiser and Gagné (1983) reviewed nine media selection models. They prepared a table (p. 15) listing the models and noting which factors were taken account of for each model: learner, setting, and task characteristics, including categories of outcomes and events of instruction; physical attributes; and practical factors. They also classified the model as to how the media selections were made and displayed: by use of (a) flowcharts, (b) matrices, or (c) work-sheets. For their own media selection model, Reiser and Gagné selected the flowchart because it is easier to use and requires only one simple decision at a time rather than simultaneous consideration of several factors. They present a series of flowcharts which enable the user to focus upon only one factor at a time, still reaching media decisions quickly. Their model appears especially appropriate for designers without extensive training in instructional design. Other models might permit more precision in analysis if used by highly trained designers.

Factors in media selection, in addition to those cited by Reiser and Gagné, as noted above, could include: (a) the capability of the proposed producers to provide the needed hardware and software; (b) the suitability of various media for the planned learning environment; (c) the features of the economy and the culture in which use is intended; (d) the capability of the media for teaching cognitive and affective objectives; (e) the capability of learners to use the media with enjoyment and mastery; (f) the capability of the media for enhancing success, self-esteem, learning strategies, and satisfying study conditions; and (g) the capability for contributing to the four aspects of motivation discussed by Keller (1983), by providing conditions of learning listed in Chapter 14.

Comparing Group Instruction to Use of Packaged Materials

Teachers traditionally have employed large-group instruction, in which they usually *select* rather than *develop* appropriate instructional materials whether print, non-print, or physical objects such as for physics and chemistry. They also design learning activities as a part of lesson planning. The traditional delivery system is group instruction, conducted by the teacher, with use of chalkboards, books, and other media. With little time for planning and lesson design, teachers often "design while they teach." They do not have a paid interval for designing courses and developing instructional materials before they begin teaching. They must maintain discipline and keep the class moving as their first priorities. They have little time for theorizing about *why* they teach as they do. Consequently, they must make many "on the spot" decisions, which have the advantage of spontaneity in adjusting to unexpected student responses, but which cannot always be carefully thought out in advance.

Even the university professor, with a lighter class load than teachers in elementary and secondary schools, is often hard-pressed for time for adequate planning of instruction. He or she must "publish or perish," and money and time are more readily available for research than for instructional design and development (Wager, 1977). Neither level of schools is likely to provide the course development time that is provided by industrial and military training practices (Branson, 1977). It is standard in industry and the military to provide instructional development funds and other resources separate from instructional delivery resources. Even two different groups of people are often assigned the two distinct functions.

As a consequence of the above, most recent graduates trained in instructional design and development tend to find jobs in military or industrial training rather than in educational institutions. Since it is their function to develop training to be delivered by others, and since some of the instructors have minimal training in teaching, instructional designers usually produce highly-structured, pre-packaged, material-(media) dependent instruction. They deliberately make the instructional packages the least instructor dependent as possible. They seek packaged, self-instructional materials, usually presented by computers or other "non-teacher" media. The many consequent differences between traditional teacher-designed instruction and team-designed (systems) instruction have been described by Hannum and Briggs (1982).

In summary, teachers tend to use group instruction, and professional instructional designers tend to develop self-instructional packages of material. What are the implications of this for the two main themes of this book—(a) audit trails to close gaps between goals and objectives, and (b) integration of instruction for the affective and cognitive domains? We discuss these two implications in turn.

Closing Gaps Between Goals and Objectives

In Part III we illustrated how audit trails can be used for school curriculum and instructional development in order not to leave large gaps or other discrepancies among needs, goals, and objectives. In Part IV we discussed audit trails for use in other than school settings. We indicated that developing audit trails is a larger task for education than for training. It would take cooperation among more groups for the larger instructional tasks for education than for training, but we believe the technique is equally applicable to both situations.

Audit trails deal with deciding *what* to teach; delivery systems, media selection, and lesson design deal with *how* to teach.

Domain Integration

The problem of how to utilize domain interactions to achieve domain integration should be faced in both group instruction and packaged, "mediated" instruction.

The conventional wisdom is that the human teacher can foster affective development better than any other media can. This might be true if each teacher had only one student. But with normal teacher-pupil ratios, it would take an unusually wise, energetic, and efficient teacher to monitor and nurture optimal self-development for each of 30 students per class, and up to 150 per day in secondary schools. It has been shown elsewhere (Gagné & Briggs, 1979, Chapters 13 and 14) that even for cognitive objectives, group instruction lacks the *precision* of individualized instruction in implementing the nine events of instruction. We believe the task for affective development is even more difficult and complex. So we recommend trying to obtain the most help possible from packaged mediated instruction, whether the primary delivery system is group instruction or individualized instruction.

Those affective objectives relating to developing social interaction skills will require practice in group interaction, but the underlying principles might well be taught by a computer program. Those objectives relating to self-development require *experience of success* in learning, which also may best be insured by computerized instruction.

So while we have no wish to minimize the value of a warm, caring teacher, we do suggest that the teacher seek appropriate instructional materials for both affective and cognitive development. Group instruction for some objectives is best handled when several learners have reached the same point in progress.

You, the reader, may wish at this point to glance back to Chapter 14 to the conditions of learning listed there for categories of outcomes in both domains. Ask yourself, which of these conditions can only be provided, or best provided, by a teacher in charge of 30 learners? Which conditions can be effectively and efficiently provided by some form of individualized instruction? Where is a combination of individual and group learning needed? We will return to these questions later in this chapter.

For a general overview of how domain interactions may be employed in the sequences of lessons chosen for a unit of instruction, and in the design of each lesson, we have reproduced Table 15.1 from Briggs and Wager (1981, p. 95). We suggest that you study this table in preparation for the later sections of this chapter on sequencing of objectives and lesson design.

The teacher's role. Of course, the teacher or instructor has an important role to play in achievement of integration of the affective and cognitive domains. Based on such guidelines as Table 15.1 and the conditions of learning (Chapter 14), the teacher can sequence objectives so as to achieve domain integration, and the teacher can design lessons using appropriate conditions of learning. For example, one condition of learning for many of the affective components is to provide for group discussion opportunities. The teacher, of course, is instrumental in planning and implementing this external condition. Illustrations of how to do this are presented later in this chapter.

The teacher also can be the person to decide when a learner needs more counseling than the teacher can provide. For problems that cannot be foreseen in advance, either by the teacher or the designers of the instructional materials, the teacher is the first and best line of resource for arranging help for special problems. Teachers also sometimes specialize in teaching of exceptional children for whom no packaged instruction is relevant. Instructors for adults after years of absence from school is the province of adult learning specialists. We saw in Chapters 12 and 14 how computers can supplement the role of the instructor for developing self-management skills and learning strategies (Derry, 1984; McCombs, 1981-82).

The computer's role. We have cited (and discussed in earlier chapters) two studies which employed computers for affective objectives and for integrating them with cognitive objectives for young adults who had made a poor showing in basic skills as well as technical training and self-management.

Table 15.1

Inputs

Outputs	Cognitive Strategies	Verbal Information	Motor Skills	Attitudes	Intellectual Skills
Cognitive Strategies	One might develop strategies for developing new strategies. (speculation)	Verbal information may mediate a transfer of learning, allowing learner to adapt old strategies to new situations.		Dogmatism, field dependence, etc., may affect learner's ability to perceive new strategies.	A repertoire of I.S. probably leads to a generalized "strategy" for solving similar problems (Gagne, 1977b).
Verbal Information	Strategies for memorizing work strings, facts, or organizing meaningful knowledge, e.g., megamemory research by Rohwer (1975).	A number of studies show that the learning of one set of information influences the learning of a second set (Ausubel, 1968). Many theories imply organization into propositions "associative" in nature.	Reading may be dependent upon motor coordination (Wilson and Geyer, 1972, p. 160). Clinical application (directional orientation).	Attitudes about source affect perception and probability that information will be learned (Hovland, Janis, and Kelley, 1953).	Appreciation of classification routines may lead to ability to make relational or associative "propositions" enhancing verbal learning (Klausmeier and Davis, 1980).
Motor Skills	Strategies for learning new motor skills may exist, e.g., patterning, faded cues, successive approximation, cognitive routines.	Provides cues for the sequencing of a motor performance.	Developed in a progressive manner so that part skills may be combined to form more complex skills.	Probably affect effort learner will put into learning new skill or improving an existing one.	Executive subroutine which governs the pattern of responding is an intellectual skill that may be previously learned (Gagne, 1977b).
Attitudes	The ability to self-analyze one's attitudes may be facilitated by learning a cognitive strategy, e.g., strategies for resolving dissonance.	May input directly into some attitude objectives; gives learner expectation of reinforcement available for making certain choices.	The attainment of a skill leads to a more positive attitude towards the use and value of that skill.	Attitudes towards persons, places, or things are mutually supportive; changing one may necessitate changing many (cognitive consistency theory).	The attainment of I.S. may lead to a more positive attitude if their practice is reinforcing to the learner.
Intellectual Skills	Affects ways learner can approach task of learning new skills.	Input into I.S. at any level; serves to clarify terminology and mediate learning transfer; also may serve as advance organizers. Defined concepts may first be learned as verbal information.		A positive attitude probably facilitates motivation needed to make work of learning worth doing. A negative attitude probably serves as a perceptual screen.	A hierarchy exists within the intellectual skills domain so that learning a higher level skill is facilitated by recall of previously learned simpler skills.

A domains/function matrix summarizing how learning in various domains may interact (from Briggs and Wager, 1981).

We now cite another example of use of computers for overcoming handicaps. This relates to the use of computers for children without language skills.

Trachtman (1984) has described work by Laura Meyers and Terry Rosegrant on teaching handicapped children to speak, read, and write, using a special system called Programs for Early Acquisition of Language (PEAL). It is a system that "has a flat, touch-sensitive membrane board with large squares for pictures, symbols, and words, connected to an Apple II computer and an Echo II speech synthesizer" (p. 47).

Over one hundred speechless children, age 20 months to 14 years, afflicted by various physical, mental, and emotional handicaps, were taught language skills. When pictures, letters, or words are pressed, the device pronounces the associated sounds, which are soon repeated by the children. One child quipped, "My voice sounds hoarse" (on the device). One child with Down's Syndrome began by pressing the area with her feet because she could not control her hands. Later on, she switched to operation by hand.

The researchers criticize conventional methods in special education because they begin with testing to discover what the child cannot do, thus reemphasizing the child's learned awareness of failure. The researchers begin with what the child wants or *can* do. Children first press the picture of a toy they prefer; the name of the toy is pronounced by the computer, and the child often then pronounces it. In either event, the child is given the toy to play with. Several speechless children acquired a vocabulary of 400 words within eight weeks, and went on to write sentences and then stories on the word processor. One child learned 25 new words in one session; in the prior year, he had learned to speak five words. Remarkable growth was also reported in attention, motivation, interest, and attitude. Children were taught to dwell on their accomplishments, not on their previous failures.

For the youngest or most retarded children, "toys are propped up on the computer, and when a child touched a square and the screen showed its image—or the synthesizer named the toy—the child got to play with it" (p. 47). The children who have learned as early as 20 months that they are failures and people are disappointed in them, soon become able to talk and to emphasize "I can."

A teacher or parent is present at each computer session, because "the computer never asks the child anything and never tells the child what to do next. The computer is the child's tool, not his teacher" (p. 50). The child learns to take initiative; the computer waits for this.

While improvements in physical functioning are noted by the researchers, they caution that they do not cure physical disabilities, and that life will be difficult for the children in spite of their increased language skills. The children are often disappointed when they have improved so much that they are returned to a mainstream classroom.

When one puts together the three projects just cited, a number of suggestions for computer applications for both cognitive and affective development are evident. The advantages include:

1. Adaptive, individualized instruction, which begins where each learner needs to begin.
2. Privacy and non-punitive responses to faulty attempts, and reinforcement for each correct response, thus enhancing self-esteem.
3. Absence of penalty for slow responses, and complete avoidance of errors in front of a group.
4. Boundless patience for slow learners.
5. Opportunity to develop learner strategies for both self-management and cognitive skills.
6. Individual progress unimpeded by the lock-step pacing of group instruction.
7. Avoidance of down time because other learners are behind or ahead of a given individual.
8. Enjoyment of game-like features.
9. Using words, pictures, and actual objects.
10. The potential for learning specific immediate objectives while making progress on affective and cognitive strategy objectives which take considerable time to develop.
11. Reinforcing the link between a personal action and an outcome.
12. Capability for signalling when each learner attains a

particular objective, thus providing the information for forming small groups when interaction with others is needed.

For at least many affective objectives, then, the computer offers much flexibility and an efficiency that a teacher could not provide under normal circumstances. The best plan would appear to be to use computers for conditions of learning it can be programmed to provide, thus freeing teachers to provide conditions which the computer cannot provide.

Although some objectives require social interaction, it would clearly be a mistake to conclude that only teachers and group instruction are able to promote development of all affective aspects of the learner's behavior. So we recommend focusing upon appropriate conditions of learning for each lesson objective, and *then* deciding when to use group methods and when to use individualized study methods, with or without a computer. Often, of course, there will be a combination of individual study and both large- and small-group work.

We do not take space here to provide a similar discussion of media other than the teacher and the computer. Our recommendation for use of other media would be much like the one just made—select the conditions first, then the media.

In summary, we would recommend designing the lessons first, selecting the most appropriate media for each, and *then* putting together a delivery system which can support the total plan.

PLANNING SEQUENCES OF LESSONS

In Part III we dealt with sequencing of instruction at the macro level—from life-long goals through design of curriculum, courses, course units, and lessons. We used audit trails to achieve continuity among these levels of goals and objectives, and to avoid discontinuities which arose by separating the functions of needs assessment, curriculum, and instruction.

In Chapter 8, we showed how to use the macro level audit trail to derive micro level objectives for course units and lessons. In preparation for this closing section of this chapter, lesson design, we now focus on the course unit for designing sequences of lessons.

In Figure 8.1 (Chapter 8) we took the example of a needs analysis which identified six *life-long needs*:

1. Human relations.
2. Occupational and financial sufficiency.
3. Effective citizenship.
4. Leisure time.
5. Adjustment to rapid change.
6. Anticipation and solution of problems.

We suggested that an *audit trail* be drawn up for each of the six needs. (We presented the one for citizenship.) This results in six *curriculum strands* for elementary and secondary education. Then we demonstrated in Chapter 8 how courses, units, and lessons can be developed from the audit trail. Each unit or lesson can consist of these kinds of objectives:

(1) objectives drawn directly from the audit trail;
(2) objectives subordinate to those in the audit trail, developed by use of task analysis, job analysis, or instructional curriculum maps;
(3) objectives drawn from two or more audit trails (linkages across audit trails);
(4) objectives subordinate to those in two or more audit trails; and
(5) combinations of related affective and cognitive objectives.

In Chapter 8 we also gave an example of objectives for a course unit drawn for one objective in the audit trail. So the audit trail provided an objective which later became the "unit objective." For that unit objective, six subordinate objectives were derived. Each of these six could then become lesson objectives, resulting in a unit of six lessons. Then, taking one of those objectives, we derived eight still more subordinate objectives as the objectives for a single lesson.

The above recap of what we presented in Chapter 8 illustrates the continued "top to bottom" direction of analysis when designing curricula, courses, unit, and lessons. In our unit and lesson objectives, we formed linkages between the "citizenship" audit trail and the recommended "occupational" audit trail. Both audit trails were presumed to contain both cognitive and affective objectives.

In Chapter 9 we followed a similar procedure, using a college curriculum to further extend the citizenship objectives for the college graduate. We started that audit trail with the same life-long citizenship need as for the high school graduate, but we built upon the high school curriculum in developing the portion of the audit trail relating to college instruction.

In Chapter 10 we took a single need identified for professional instructional designers (developing instructional materials), and we drew an audit trail having groups of objectives (a) for professional practice, and (b) for a course and other experiences in a doctoral program, for a total of 31 objectives in the audit trail. We then commented that the objectives from the audit trail were expanded to even more specific objectives in the syllabus for a course in developing instructional materials.

In Chapter 11 we presented rules and principles for drawing up a first-draft audit trail. In Chapter 12 we discussed the place of audit trails in industrial training and in military training.

In summary, audit trails furnish the macro outline of courses and units to be developed. Using the objectives in the audit trails, these macro objectives are supplemented by deriving their supporting subordinate objectives, which become the objective for lessons and units in the course.

It is typical for a lesson to cover more than one objective, especially when attempting to integrate instruction for the affective and cognitive domains. A lesson typically consumes one class hour, often plus outside study and preparation by the learners. However a group of objectives which logically belong together may take more or less time. A unit is typically composed of six or eight lessons covering a period of instruction of a few weeks.

We offer these suggestions when grouping objectives for a lesson or for a series of lessons making up a course unit:

1. Pick one cognitive objective and a related affective objective of either a short-term or long-term type (see item No. 3 below.)
2. Pick an affective attitude objective, either one standing alone or related to the cognitive objective in item 1, above.
3. Pick a self-development objective or a learning strategy objective which will take considerable time to develop fully.

4. Pick one socializing or moral development objective which is to be attained over a period of time.

5. Refer back to Chapter 14 for relevant sets of conditions of learning for each category of outcomes.

6. Draw up a lesson or unit plan for complete mastery of the cognitive objective, while achieving or making progress on the other objectives.

7. Decide whether to try to establish the attitude before teaching the cognitive objective, or whether the attitude will be an outcome of mastery of the cognitive objective. (Table 15.1 may be helpful.)

8. If there is to be a group portion of the lesson or unit, design the activity to achieve progress on points No. 3 and No. 4 above.

9. Build upon the hierarchical nature of intellectual skill objectives, and sequence subordinate objectives accordingly.

10. Build upon possible hierarchical relationships between affective and cognitive objectives (Hurst, 1980b), and sequence the two types of objectives accordingly.

11. Work in instruction on learning strategies along with the other objectives.

12. Decide whether some lessons in the unit should relate to cognitive objectives, others to affective ones, or whether all lessons should be a blend of both.

13. Decide when to announce affective objectives to the learners, and when to model or shape the desired behavior.

14. Decide which affective objectives are directly discussed with the learners and which are embedded in the lessons.

15. Separate sessions on drill, practice, and feedback for basic cognitive skills from the more open environment for discussing attitude and value questions.

16. Provide some highly structured lessons for skill learning and some discovery or inquiry sessions for other objectives.

17. Provide both inductive and deductive sessions.

18. Seek out prepared packages of instruction when appropriate for the objectives and when required media equipment is available.

19. Even when considerable use is made of individualized study by

computers and other media, conduct small group work for those at a similar stage of progress, and large group sessions for open value discussions and experience sharing.

20. Ask yourself (a) "how will I divide my time between working with individuals and with large or small groups?"; and (b) "what can the materials, media, and self-study achieve, and what must I do?"

LESSON DESIGN

Examples of lesson design models employing objectives and events of instruction are found in several sources (Briggs, 1970; Briggs, 1972; Briggs, 1977; Briggs & Wager, 1981; Gagné & Briggs, 1970). Most of the examples in those sources pertain to lessons having cognitive objectives. Each source contains worksheets useful for arranging sequences of objectives and events of instruction in the lesson.

Throughout this book we have said that once the objective(s) for a lesson has been decided upon, one can employ the nine "events of instruction" as the building blocks for lesson design. For each of the nine events, one considers how to incorporate the appropriate set of conditions of learning. In this section of this chapter we present a variety of examples of lesson design, covering a range of categories of outcomes, types of learners, and learning situations. We offer comments for each example of lesson design.

Earlier, we have shown how teachers can design lessons (Briggs, 1977, Chapter 8) and how materials development teams can design lessons and lesson materials (Carey & Briggs, 1977). There we pointed out that teachers design lessons, in part, by *selecting* materials and activities, while design teams usually *develop* instructional materials. In both cases the purpose is the same—to supply appropriate instructional events incorporating conditions of learning relevant for the outcome category represented by the lesson objectives. Regardless of the media and delivery system employed, these purposes of lesson design remain the same.

In the following series of examples of lesson design, numbers in parentheses, such as (48), refer to the serially ordered conditions of learning as listed in Chapter 14. These examples, collectively, illustrate flexibility in choosing which instructional events and which conditions of learning to use. Not all events are used in each lesson, nor are all conditions listed for the category of outcome in Chapter 14 used.

A Lesson for a Single Cognitive Objective

Here we present an example of one of the most simple types of lesson—a lesson for a single cognitive objective. Due to the age level of the learners and the nature of the objective, we can illustrate the use of all nine instructional events listed earlier in this book. We also use primarily teacher-conducted, group instruction. We do not always give the teacher's communications verbatim; therefore we refer to a "prescription" rather than to a "script."

Lesson Objective: "Given circles with either the diameter or radius indicated, the learner will demonstrate finding the areas by written computation, with no assistance."

Type of Outcome: Rule using (intellectual skill; cognitive)

Event of Instruction	Medium	Prescription
1. Gaining attention	Teacher Drawings Objects	"Look at all these circles." Drawn on chalkboard; cut out of paper; carpet material (189).
2. Informing learners of the objective	Teacher	"Today you will learn to find the areas of circles, when the radius or diameter is given for each. The answer will be expressed in square inches or square feet" (217).
3. Stimulate recall of prerequisite learning	Teacher	Reviews the formulas for finding areas of other shapes, rectangles, etc. Asks students for meanings of diameter, radius, circumference, and area. Reviews how to square quantities. Reviews value of pi, and what it means in relation to diameter and circumference (196).

4. Present the new stimuli	Teacher Chalkboard	'The formula for finding the area of a circle is: $A = pi\ (\pi)\ r^2$." Write formula on chalkboard. Discuss and demonstrate the rule, stimulating further recall of component concepts and simpler rules: meaning of area, pi, radius, squaring, numbering, diameter (25, 26, 29).
5. Elicit the performance. (Note: Events 5, 6, and 7 may be placed in different orders, and repeated)	Teacher Chalkboard	Draw a circle on the chalkboard, showing a radius of 4 inches. Ask learners to find the area (28).
6. Provide feedback	Teacher	Confirms correct answers and steps in computations; corrects errors (31).
7. Provide guidance to thinking	Teacher	Present another example with diameter given rather than radius. Ask learners how to find area. Give explanations and prompts as necessary. Have learners explain the formula in their own words. Have them provide their own circles and area solutions (32, 34).
8. Provide for transfer and retention (This event will call for problem solving and cognitive strategies for some learners. Our numbered conditions of learning reflect this.)	Teacher	Give students circles cut out of paper, carpet materials, etc. Have them measure diameter and solve for area. Discuss real-life examples. Give an ellipse made of a string. Have them find area (by reshaping into a circle). Provide a shape like this with dimensions: an oblong: ⬭ Have learners solve for area. Have learners design shapes in which area is solvable by forming other shapes. Schedule review sessions (36, 40, 41, 75).
9. Assess attainment	Teacher Written Test	Administer written test and provide feedback (31).

Discussion of the Example

Note that all nine events of instruction were used. They could be placed in different sequences from that shown above. There are often cycles of events 5, 6, and 7, one cycle for each example or each type of example of finding areas of circles. Note also that the prescriptions make use of many of the conditions of learning listed for rule learning in Chapter 14, and also some conditions for other cognitive outcome categories for event 8. This lesson might be the last lesson in a series of lessons about circles. The entries under prerequisite learning suggest what some of the previous lessons covered. Those entries also refer to prior learning in finding areas of shapes other than circles. No affective objective was stated, but the teacher would conduct the lesson so as to stimulate interest, success, and favorable attitude toward the course.

The sequence of events would be different for an inductive method in which learners are led to discover the rule, rather than having it given to them. Perhaps events other than the nine shown would be used for a discovery approach. Also, other events might ultimately be originated for affective objectives. (Students in our instructional design courses have sometimes invented other events, such as "use probing questions.") The criterion for such new events is that they would be generic—applicable for an entire category or domain of objectives, not for a particular lesson only.

Depending upon the known capabilities of the learner, the teacher might not provide some of the events, expecting the learners to be able to supply them for themselves.

The nine events of instruction used for this lesson are the same ones originally listed by Gagné in his first edition of *The Conditions of Learning* (1965). At that time he was concentrating almost exclusively upon the learning of intellectual skills. These nine events fit nicely for teaching intellectual skills. They do not fit so cleanly with lessons in other outcome areas. For example, a fact is not very generalizable; it either can be recalled by the learner or it cannot be recalled. So the event, provide for transfer, is clearly not relevant. On the other hand an intellectual skill, like finding the area of circles, can be applied to thousands of examples (it is generalizable), so the transfer event is applicable.

For attitudes (and other areas of the affective domain), one may not wish to state an objective (to the learners), and an attitude toward one topic may not be transferable to another. So we must examine the relevance of the nine instructional events for categories of outcomes other than intellectual skills. One way to do this, say, for an attitude, is to refer back to the conditions of learning in Chapter 14 for the *specific method* chosen for that attitude, and *then* decide which if any of the nine instructional events are appropriate.

Finally, note that the above lesson could be taught by a computer.

A Lesson for Teacher Training

Rarely do we have access to a research study directly supporting the design of a lesson for a particular objective. But the study by Barbara Martin Hurst (1980b) does provide one of these exceptional opportunities. She conducted a study involving teachers who were learning the process of "implementing a new curriculum called *Individually Guided Education* (IGE)" (p. 296). She drew up an *a priori* learning hierarchy, consisting of objectives in both the affective and the cognitive domains. She employed ordering theory to confirm or disconfirm hypothesized sequential dependencies among objectives in the *a priori* hierarchy.

Using this method, Hurst did not teach lessons aimed at particular objectives. Rather, she validated a sequence of hypothesized objectives. The "lessons" had been previously presented by school administrators and consultants instructing teachers in the use of IGE, or they were currently being presented. The teachers were from five different schools and in different stages of learning about IGE. This enabled Hurst to ascertain how the cognitive and affective objectives interacted at different points in the learning process. This is different from conducting a learning experiment having a similar purpose, as has been done by Gagné, by White (see Hurst, 1980b), and by J. Young (1984).

Hurst took as the terminal objective for her hierarchy the affective objective that teachers would voluntarily choose to implement the method (IGE). Then she listed supporting objectives from both domains, affective and cognitive. She found that "affective skills with substantial cognitive components require as prerequisites at least some of these cognitive skills. The affective skills not heavily dependent on cognitive knowledge formed the bottom layer of the hierarchy and acted as a stimulus for certain cognitive achievements" (p. 301). Teachers first developed a willingness to receive information about IGE; this led to further interest in and satisfying feelings about IGE. Cognitive knowledge related to understanding IGE came next. As those skills were acquired, teachers began to be committed to use IGE. Then higher order cognitive skills related to use and implementation of IGE were acquired, and attitudes were strengthened.

Based on those findings, we now select two adjacent objectives from Hurst's hierarchy to show how instruction could be designed. These, in order, are:

Objective 1: "The learner classifies examples of IGE by determining correct use of components and relationships." Category: defined concepts; intellectual skill: cognitive domain.

Objective 2: "The learner indicates feelings of satisfaction and pleasure with IGE." Category: affective domain; responding (Krathwohl, *et al.*, 1964).

Overall sequence of lessons. The validated hierarchy shows that "lessons" were designated to result in a willingness to receive information about IGE, and lessons to supply that information. So first some affective objectives and some information objectives were dealt with. Based on that, plus some "identify" objectives (recognizing parts of IGE), the learners are ready for the present lesson. Notice that only the cognitive objective is communicated to the learner, under the assumption that the affective objective will be an outcome of mastery of the cognitive objective.

Instructional Events	Medium	Prescription
1. Gaining attention	Instructor Workbook	"Turn to Exercise 10 in your workbook for IGE. Notice that the exercise lists 20 teaching practices drawn from several models of teaching" (189).

2. Informing learners of the (cognitive) objective.	Instructor	"Your task for Exercise 10 is to classify each of the 20 teaching practices as components of IGE or not components of IGE" (217).
3. Stimulating recall of prerequisite learning	Instructor	"First, let's review some of the separate parts of the IGE system." Reviews prior information and concepts relating to how objectives are defined; what criterion-referenced test items are; grouping procedures; record keeping; selection of materials; monitoring pupil progress. Reminds learners of IGE-related concepts used in earlier portions of this unit (modeling) (11, 196).
4. Present the new stimulus and evoke responding	Instructor	"One way to feel comfortable and competent when using IGE is to be able to classify examples and non-examples of practices typical of IGE. Then you can select or design the different components of IGE. In Exercise 10, read each practice described, and classify it as belonging or not belonging in IGE. Study this exercise for 15 minutes, and note your response. We will then discuss each of the 20 practices" (14).
5. Provide feedback and guide thinking	Instructor and trainees	Instructor calls on individual students for a response to one of the 20 practices, and asks for explanation of each response. When necessary, gives prompts for deciding whether a teaching practice belongs to IGE or not. The discussion brings out the reasons why each answer is correct, thus providing review of theory and practices taught in earlier lessons. Also, a discussion of advantages and disadvantages of components is provided here (196, 215).

6. Provide for retention and transfer	Instructor and trainees	Instructor asks each trainee to explain how he or she would plan each of the (correct) teaching practices, selected from the 20 practices in Exercise 10, for a subject area in the teacher's own specialty. Alternatives are discussed, and those most closely following IGE theory are reinforced. Real-life examples are used to illustrate how specific alternatives have been designed and implemented (18, 19, 20, 22, 210).
7. Assessing attainments	Instructor	"Rather than giving you a test now, which could consist of another list of teaching practices for you to classify, we will combine evaluation of your work with the next lesson. In that lesson you will choose either IGE or another approach to teaching, and write a brief description of how your chosen method would address each of the five major components of instruction that we studied in the previous lesson. This paper will present the basis for evaluating success for this series of lessons (215, 216, 219).

Discussion of the Example

Notice first that we combined some of the nine instructional events for this lesson, and that we deferred evaluation of learner performance until the next lesson, the last one in this course unit. As indicated, we could have used a test which would be *another* sample of teaching practices, similar in nature to Exercise 10, but consisting of different examples. We made both of these decisions out of consideration of learner characteristics and in order to save time. Also, we wanted the trainees to have a real-life type of assessment, namely using IGE or another method for planning a unit of instruction. We thought that this decision would be affectively more acceptable to the trainees.

Note that the next lesson permits a *genuine* choice between IGE and another method. This fact itself should result in a favorable attitude toward systematic planning for each major function of instruction, whatever the method. A set of criteria would be drawn up, relating to adequate planning for the components of instruction, whatever the method. (Components refer to grouping procedures, lesson design, material selection, evaluation, etc.— components of all methods of teaching).

During assessment the instructor must be clear about what he/she is assessing. If it is the attitude component, then the choice itself is evaluated; if it is the cognitive component, then correct use of the components is the primary concern. It is possible for a learner to choose IGE, but incorrectly use one or more components; it is also possible to correctly use all components, but not choose to, given a choice situation. In Assessing Attainments in the above example, we are assuming that the learners are cognitively able to use and apply IGE, so we are first assessing their choice to do so, and secondly the cognitive aspects. Of course, if they choose not to use IGE, then another method of assessing the cognitive aspects will be necessary.

It will be up to the instructor to decide whether the next lesson will make a direct attempt to influence trainees to favor IGE over other methods or systems of teaching. If that decision is "yes," then the teacher could select the method desired for influencing attitudes from the methods listed in Chapter 14, along with appropriate sets of conditions of learning (e.g., modeling, persuasive communications, etc.). Modeling was incorporated in the present lesson.

Some instructors might elect to insure that teachers have the cognitive skills necessary to employ several methods of teaching, as recommended by Joyce and Weil (1980), but leave the choice among them up to the trainees. Presumably this could result over time in use of several models of teaching, each selected in consideration of the desired outcome categories and the characteristics of the learners.

Of course, the terminal objective in the hierarchy by Hurst (1980b) was a favorable attitude toward voluntarily adopting IGE, when appropriate. One could instead adopt the terminal cognitive objective of being able to use IGE. But the point of her results was that there is an interaction between the cognitive and affective objectives in her hierarchy, in which attainments in each domain tend to result in attainments in the other domain. Her results indicated that attitudes can be both a cause and an effect of cognitive attainments, and *vice versa*. That's one of the reasons why we wrote this book.

A Lesson for Value Development

In this lesson we present an example of the development of a value structure. By this we mean that the learner will organize two (or more) attitudes into an integrated pattern. The value will be superordinate to either of the attitudes previously developed, and link them in some important way.

We have selected a value related to government fiscal policy. The lesson objective is: "Forms a judgment about U.S. government financial spending and supports a chosen policy with accurate facts and reasons." Category: affective domain; values development. This lesson contributes to the development of three of the curriculum objectives we listed in Chapter 8: numbers 17, 20, and 34. The age group for this lesson could be high school, college, or adult. We have designed it for a high school social studies class.

Overall Sequence of Lessons in the Unit

The learner would have previously demonstrated an understanding of issues related to (a) environmental spending (e.g., use of public funds to maintain and/or upgrade national parks and recreation areas, control industrial pollution, and conserve resources), (b) defense spending (e.g., use of funds to build new weapon systems, develop research programs related to national defense, and upgrade the skills of military personnel), and (c) social policy legislation (e.g., use of funds for social security, child care, and educational programs). In addition, learners have indicated that each separate fiscal policy—environmental, defense, and social—is important to the well-being and health of the nation. That is, they have indicated that the government is responsible for a spending policy in each area and that funds should be allocated (an attitude) in each area.

In this lesson, learners are confronted with the fact that the government has limited funds and must make selective decisions about allocations. This lesson would probably cover several sessions.

Type of Outcome: Affective domain; value development

Instructional Events	Medium	Prescription
1. Gaining attention	Teacher Handouts	"The paper I am giving you has a list of programs and a dollar figure indicating how much it costs the government to fund each program." (The figures could be real or fictitious; learners should be told if they are real figures or not. Learners should also be told that this is a representative list of programs, not all the ones about which the government must make decisions.) "At the top of the page is another dollar figure. That figure indicates how much money the government has to spend on all the programs listed."
		"Your task is to first separate the programs into three groups—those related to environmental, defense, or social policy—and add up the needed funds for each group. Then add your three figures together and see if it is less than or more than the figure at the top of the page." The teacher waits while students do this. "What did you find out?" "Yes, it costs more to finance all the programs than the government has to spend on all the programs" (15, 23, 36).
2. Informing the learner of the objective	Teacher	"In this lesson, we are going to discuss what the government must do in this situation. Your task is to decide how you think the govern-

ment should spend its money. You should be able to defend your position with accurate facts and sound reasoning. There is no right or wrong answer. In Congress, our Representatives and Senators struggle with these decisions each time they meet; each one has his or her own opinion. The President also has an opinion. These are very difficult issues for everyone in the country. Now is the time for you to think about the problem and decide what you think is the best way for the government to spend its money. The decisions you make may influence your voting choices (37, 58, 124).

3. Stimulating recall of prerequisite learning

   Teacher
   Students

   "Before we begin, let's review the different policies and why the government allocates money to each." The teacher reviews the major concepts of environment, defense, and social policy, and describes the purpose of several selected programs. The teacher elicits from students why the government allocates funds for each type of policy (11, 29, 35).

4. Present the new stimuli and provide feedback and guide thinking

   Teacher
   Students
   Media
   Resource-
   People

   The teacher now begins to conduct a discussion about the advantages and disadvantages of cutting or cutting out programs. In doing this, the teacher might bring in newspaper articles and editorials about inadequate defense systems, the "new poor" in America, pollution, etc. Speakers from representative groups, such as social agencies, could be asked to speak; students could contact representatives from government to provide information; parental surveys could be taken.

The consequences to people, the economy, and the world would be discussed. The teacher brings up the idea of necessary vs. luxury items, and relates this to governmental decisions. Tells learners that people differ on what they consider primary and secondary needs (14, 26, 108, 109, 119, 122).

5. Provide transfer	Teacher Chalkboard	The teacher summarizes some of the major points raised and assists learners in comparing issues. Teacher asks students to explain their views and to explain how the issues overlap. If time permits, the teacher shows how students must make similar selective decisions in spending their own money, and how families must also make such decisions (122, 123, 124).
6. Elicit a performance and assess attainment	Teacher	Ask students to write a letter to their Congressional Representative explaining how money should be spent. Tells students that they must support their recommendations with data and/or explain their reasons for the policy decisions they have chosen (125).
7. Provide feedback	Teacher	Reinforces students for tackling a difficult task. Explains that very few of them made the same recommendations, but that each one of them did a fine and thoughtful job (if they did, of course). Have learners brainstorm other important issues where value decisions must be made, e.g., the value of life, relating attitudes about abortion and capital punishment (125, 179, 185, 226).

Discussion of the Example

The purpose of this lesson was to help learners establish a superordinate value structure linking subordinate cognitive and affective elements. Note that we had learners write down a position rather than verbalize one. In a group discussion of even ten students, it is difficult to insure that each student has formulated an opinion. Also, putting a position down on paper often helps students see inconsistencies in their views and assists the teacher in pointing out relationships and/or inconsistencies. Other ways of assessing attainment of the objective might be to use formal or informal debates, role playing, questionnaires, and interviews.

Several of the events of instruction were combined. Since the major vehicle used in this lesson was group discussion, "present the stimuli" and "provide feedback to guide thinking" were accomplished during a discussion. Much of the new stimuli came from the students, as did the feedback. A critical role of the teacher was to point out inconsistencies and relationships among cognitive elements.

"Provide transfer" was separated from the two events above because of the nature of group discussions. The issues can become confusing, students can ramble in making a point, and disruptions can occur (both among students and in form of interruptions such as fire drills, snow days, etc.). Therefore, we think the teacher (or a student) should summarize the preceding discussions, focusing primarily on the relationships among the issues under consideration.

"Elicit a performance" and "Assess attainment" were also combined. In this case, students were asked to formally state their position. Since the teacher is *not assessing their position*, but rather their thinking and reasoning processes and the fact that they now have a position, the two events need not be separated. The teacher, however, may choose to first elicit a performance, provide additional data and discussion, and then assess attainment.

The final event, "Provide feedback," was for the purpose of reinforcing the learners, and for stating again that there is no correct answer. Students should be praised for accomplishing a difficult task, not for a particular position.

This example clearly shows the relationships between the cognitive and affective domains. Students could develop a value without the cognitive prerequisites; however, their opinions would most likely be shallow, based on their own unsupported perceptions and/or based on someone else's ideas that they are merely verbalizing. In designing the lesson as we have, the objective not only helps students develop a value structure, but also increases their cognitive knowledge, strengthens or diminishes existing attitudes, and increases their ability to handle complex subjects and relationships (cognitive strategies). In addition, if learners view the task as a difficult one in which their effort and ability have paid off, they might view themselves more positively and may be willing to address complex issues and tasks in the future.

Referring back to our general suggestions for lesson design (see the heading, *Planning Sequences of Lessons*, earlier in this chapter), one can see that in conducting the lesson plan just presented above, several features could be added. For example, during the discussion phase of the lesson (event 4), the teacher could reinforce students who abide by "discussion rules" previously agreed upon by the class, thus contributing to a long-range social objective. Also, while the students are doing the first assigned individual work (event 1), they may be reminded to use the "self-talk" (self-management) strategy taught earlier. Thus, progress could be made during the lesson toward accomplishment of two long-term objectives in addition to the objective stated at the opening of the lesson plan.

A Lesson for Self-Development

The lesson we present here is for battered women in an abuse clinic. The coordinator of one clinic is presently getting a master's degree in Education with specialization in instructional design. The coordinator is enrolled in one of the author's classes.

One of the key factors in working with abuse victims is to help them feel better about themselves. The coordinator stated that some of the major problems of abused women are that they (a) feel they have caused the abuse and that they deserve it, (b) are unable to leave abusive situations because they have few skills and/or because they have children to take care of (feed, clothe, and provide emotional support), and (c) do not have friends or a support system in whom they can confide and be helped by. The coordinator also stated that making the choice to go to an abuse clinic is an important and very positive step for these women. Fortunately, most women view the clinic not as a temporary reprieve from the abusive partner, but as a first step for permanently altering their lives.

Women who go to clinics stay for varying lengths of time (from days to weeks); some go with clothes, books, and toys for their children while others go with only the clothes they have on; some women have been abused repeatedly, others have not; some have been to a clinic before; for others, it is their first time. The clinic is staffed with volunteers (some of whom were previously abuse victims themselves).

One goal of the clinic is to help abused victims make decisions or choices about getting out of the abusive situation or staying with their partner, assessing the consequences of their decisions, and deciding where to go and what to do if they do decide to get out of the abusive situation. Many though not all of the women are financially supported by their partners.

We have used the information above to design a lesson for self-development. The situation we have described is accurate, the intervention is one we devised and is not used by the abuse clinic to which we are referring. The clinic coordinator is presently working on her own plan.

Lessons in the Unit

Due to the vast differences in the women who go to clinics (e.g., length of stay, skills and abilities, emotional state) and the fact that women go individually rather than in groups, we have designed an individualized program. The program is designed to help women understand their situation and control it. The program consists of several "units." We use the term individualized very loosely; that is, materials are arranged so that any woman can select a "lesson" at any time and complete it without an instructor or group. We do not mean a "lesson" has formal objectives and criterion-referenced evaluation although the lessons could be so designed. The following "units" would be available:

1. Understanding physical abuse (this may include both adult and child abuse).
2. Getting to know the social services agencies that can help you.
3. Assessing your own skills and abilities.
4. Using the newspaper to help you find a job or a new place to live.

The lesson we describe below would be "conducted" by a volunteer. It would occur immediately after the intake session, assuming that the woman is in the physical, mental, and emotional state to do something of this nature. The "lesson" will vary in length of time for completion from woman to woman. The goal is to reinforce the woman's ability to make decisions and to have some control over her life. The objective is: "Each woman will make one comment that shows she understands that going to the clinic was a self-directed, positive step to control her life, and one comment that demonstrates she has the ability/potential to take another step in that direction."

Type of Outcome: Affective domain; self-development

Instructional Events	Medium	Prescription
1. Gaining attention	Volunteer	The volunteer would orient the woman to the activities she could engage in while at the center. The volunteer would show the woman the individualized "packets" and describe how to use them (e.g., showing the woman where supporting materials and resources are located). Inform the woman that some of the information in these packets may be of interest to her and might provide some ideas about what she will do once she leaves the clinic (150, 151, 158, 163).
2. Informing woman of objective	Volunteer	Tell victim that you would like her to leave the clinic feeling better about herself than she did when she arrived. Tell her that after she has used one or more packets, you would like to have a conference with her (155, 161).

3. Present stimulus

Individual-
ized Packets
Volunteers
Other Women
at Clinic

The packet would be designed so
that each "unit" had several lessons. Instructions would include
how to proceed and a list of materials. Each packet would contain the
following:

1. Cognitive information and intellectual skills related to the topic
   of the lesson.
2. Case studies (written or mediated) of women who "took control of their lives."
3. An opportunity to make a decision of some kind; or set a
   personal goal.
4. Directions to interact with another woman (either a volunteer
   or another woman at the clinic).
5. An opportunity to learn something new (a skill, a piece of
   information, a strategy for coping or solving a problem).
6. Interesting and motivational activities.
7. An "evaluation"—space to write
   down a reflection, an idea, or
   new knowledge gained from the
   packet (11, 12, 13, 14, 25, 26,
   38, 53, 60, 61, 75, 116, 119,
   150, 154, 159, 160, 162, 166,
   196, 216).

4. Provide feedback
   and guide think-
   ing and Assess At-
   tainments

Woman
Volunteer

Use probing questions during an
individual interview to assess the
woman's conception of herself and
her situation. Volunteer asks questions designed to elicit positive
self-statements (based on particular
packets used and relying on the
vicarious modeling situation set up
in each) (154, 163, 164, 201).

Volunteer reinforces positive self
statement and helps alter negative

or neutral statements (use internal, stable, controllable attributions where possible). The volunteer also demonstrates how the new learning gained from the packet can help the woman. When the woman makes positive self-statements, the volunteer uses these as the basis for helping the woman decide what to do next. ("Take a look at the packet on social services agencies. The information on day care centers may be very helpful for you.") (165, 183, 218).

Discussion of the Example

We used only a few of the events of instruction in this example because we recommended an individualized approach. Many of the events would have been included in the packets. Although the packets were designed to impart cognitive information, they were also structured to promote self-development. Vicarious modeling was used in each; the opportunity to set a goal and carry it out was included; and interesting materials with worthwhile information was provided so that women would choose to learn things to help themselves, and enjoy doing so.

Notice that the objective was not directly communicated to the woman. She was merely told by the volunteer that they (the clinic personnel) hoped she would leave the clinic feeling better about herself than when she arrived. Our decision to elicit two positive statements was somewhat arbitrary; it could vary depending on the particular woman and her situation. We selected two positive comments because we were assuming that the woman was in the worst possible state. Given that, any positive self-statement would be an achievement.

The crux of implementing this objective is two-fold: (a) the usefulness and worth of the packets, and (b) the session with the volunteer. The stated objective: to elicit two positive self-statements from the woman, is similar to Responding in the taxonomy by Krathwohl, *et al.* (1964), and is directed toward self-development. In order to get a woman to respond positively may take several attempts and may require probing and gentle nudging by the volunteer. Referring often to the vicarious modeling situations in the packets and to other women in the clinic may be necessary. Also, reinforcing the model's behavior, the progress of other women, and the woman's own progress (moving into the clinic) may help move women toward the goal.

Because each woman and her situation is different, competent volunteers who can help an abused woman regard herself more positively is a must. One of the external conditions for self-development is social interaction; we have built it into our lesson. Likewise, women will arrive with varying degrees of academic competence, hence, an individualized program with materials for different degrees of abilities and skills is a desirable component of a program of this type. Another external condition for self-development is to provide the conditions for success.

A lesson such as this could be used in any number of instances in which individualized materials are available or could be developed (presuming the situations warranted it) and in which some personalized attention is possible. Other self-development lessons could be designed for use with groups. Designers should remember to provide conditions for academic success and mastery, opportunities for self-directed behavior, and opportunities for social interaction.

SUMMARY

We opened this chapter by discussing several alternate points at which selection of delivery systems and media could be made, in the overall instructional design process.

We then discussed the role of the teacher and the role of the computer in achieving integration of the affective and cognitive domains in designing lessons and sequences of lessons.

Next we discussed sequencing of lessons that form a unit of instruction, and we listed 20 suggestions for designing sequences so as to achieve both immediate and long-term objectives.

We then presented four examples of lesson plans, and provided a discussion of each. In these lesson plans, we placed in parentheses the serial numbers of the conditions of learning employed, as those conditions are listed in Chapter 14.

This chapter, then, represents the final stage of work in the total course design process which began with needs assessment and audit trails.

Introduction to Part VI:

Looking Backward and Forward

In Chapter 16, we look back at what we have done toward integrating the affective and cognitive domains; we discuss what still needs to be done; and we complete our skeletal outline of a model and theoretical framework for integrating the two domains. We also look ahead to the hopefully positive results of our efforts.

To summarize, we see our book as a mixture of reviewing and interpreting literature, on one hand, and developing an instructional design model and new techniques, on the other. With regard to research, one of our primary goals was to present an eclectic theory base. We have drawn from behavioral, cognitive, developmental, and humanistic theories and positions in determining the components of the affective domain and in deriving the conditions of learning. We have in some cases played our cards close to our vests, that is, we have interpreted the literature quite literally; in other cases, we have been more venturesome. With regard to technique, we presented audit trails in Part III, and we presented four sample lesson plans in Chapter 15, referring by number to the conditions of learning in Chapter 14.

We include the chart on the following page to review the problems we encountered, along with our recommended solutions.

Problems

1. What does the affective domain consist of?

2. What are the major linkages between components of the affective and cognitive domains (domain interactions)?

3. How can affective and cognitive objectives be sequenced to enhance domain interactions?

4. How can lessons be designed to enhance domain interactions?

5. What does a lesson design look like, and how are the conditions of learning selected and used?

Techniques for Solutions

1. Review of the literature (Part II), and design of a new taxonomy of the affective domain (Figure 16.1).

2. Review of the literature (Part II) and design of a taxonomy linking the two domains (Figure 16.2).

3. Use of audit trails (Part III).

4. Use of the conditions of learning given in Part II and in Chapter 14.

5. See examples in Chapter 15.

So, on the applied side, we have basically followed the instructional design model of Gagné and Briggs (1979), greatly expanding their work on attitudes. We have added the technique of audit trails; we have identified conditions of learning for components of the affective domain; and we have faced the need to enhance interaction between the affective and cognitive domains. We have done for the affective domain what Gagné (1979) did for the cognitive domain, and we have linked the domains.

In short, we have presented *a new instructional design model* and we have provided *the beginnings of a theoretical framework for linking the affective and cognitive domains.* At the same time, we have remained as nearly eclectic in theory as we could be.

The major contributions we make in Chapter 16 are:

1. We propose a tentative taxonomy of the affective domain using the components we have identified (Figure 16.1).

2. We make the relationships between the affective and

cognitive domains more explicit by presenting a second taxonomy that shows the major linkages between components of the affective and cognitive domains (Figure 16.2).

3. We provide capability verbs for each component of the affective domain.

In addition, we include (a) a self-assessment of our work, (b) a discussion of the feasibility of our approach, (c) a list of commonly appearing conditions of learning across all categories of the affective domain, (d) a description of needed research, (e) conclusions, and (f) a view of the future. In Chapter 16, then, we try to review our work showing what we did and what we did not do, and we invite further research.

Chapter 16

A Look Backward at Our Work, Recommendations, and Future Directions

OUR PROGRESS AND A SELF-ASSESSMENT

A Look Backward

A Self-Assessment

A PROPOSED TAXONOMY OF THE AFFECTIVE DOMAIN

A Discussion of the Proposed Taxonomy

Linking the Proposed Affective Taxonomy to Cognition

Capability Verbs for the Affective Domain

Capability Verbs for the Cognitive Domain

Summary

COMMONLY APPEARING EXTERNAL CONDITIONS
OF LEARNING FOR THE AFFECTIVE DOMAIN

Eight External Conditions for All
Components of the Affective Domain

Three Additional Conditions of Learning

Chapter 16

A Look Backward at Our Work, Recommendations, and Future Directions

We began this book by explicating our concerns about two aspects of instructional planning: (a) the separation of the affective and cognitive domains in theory, research, and practice; and (b) the gaps and discontinuities among educational needs, life-long goals, curricula, and instruction. In discussing these concerns, we provided possible reasons for present-day practices, and we suggested solutions, in the form of audit trails, conditions of learning, and lesson design, for improving theory and practice. Now, in this closing chapter, we evaluate our progress toward these goals, and we offer some conclusions and recommendations. Specifically, in this chapter we (a) self-assess our work and the progress we have made; (b) propose a new taxonomy of the affective domain, and provide capability verbs for each component; (c) summarize the most commonly appearing conditions of learning for the affective domain; (d) discuss needed research; (e) address the feasibility of our approach for designing instruction linking the two domains, and for closing the gap among needs, life-long goals, curricula, and instruction; (f) list our conclusions; and (g) give our views of the future as they pertain to the issues and concerns we have addressed.

OUR PROGRESS AND A SELF-ASSESSMENT

The two primary problems of interest to us: (a) separation of the affective and cognitive domains, and (b) discontinuities among goals, curricula, and instruction, led us to focus our attention and energy on selected aspects of educational planning, neglecting or merely touching on other aspects. We first discuss our accomplishments; then we discuss what we have left for others to do.

A Look Backward

Any number of authors, researchers, psychologists, and educators have commented on the unnatural separation of the affective and cognitive domains in theory, research, and practice. We, too, noticed it from our research in change theory and instructional design, and from practical experiences, including what students said to us about the heavy emphasis of cognitive knowledge in instructional design models, courses, and literature.

It was readily apparent to us, as it would be to anyone even cursorily searching the literature, that the cognitive domain was considerably more well defined and explained than was the affective domain. Therefore, in order to integrate the two domains, the affective domain demanded attention. Because the affective domain was confusing and ill-defined, there was a consequent lack of integration of knowledge about the two domains.

Believing that taxonomies of outcomes are a valuable tool providing the order needed to design instruction, we first did a review of the major cognitive and affective domain taxonomies. In the cognitive domain, Gagné's work was adopted because it (a) provided a comprehensive typology of outcomes of learning including one aspect of the affective domain, (b) listed conditions of learning and events of instruction for all types of learning (it is a prescriptive taxonomy), and (c) is founded upon psychological learning principles. We were unable to select and use any one of the affective taxonomies we reviewed. The taxonomy by Krathwohl *et al.* (1964) had limitations we could not accept (e.g., omission of a self-development category, and an organizing principle related more closely to learner strategies—responding, valuing—than to affective constructs—attitudes, values); the taxonomy by Gephart and Ingle (1976) was a comprehensive and useful description of the domain, but it was not useful for instructional planning; the Brandhorst taxonomies (1978) were only partially developed; and the others did not offer more, singly or in combination, than the three just mentioned.

The affective domain literature, and definitions of affect *per se*, are diverse; little agreement can be found across schools of thought, disciplines, researchers, or taxonomies. Recognizing that another definition and/or taxonomy could compound the confusion, not diminish it, and always keeping in mind that we wanted to integrate the domains, we provided a working definition of the affective domain to guide our work, and we borrowed the idea of conditions of learning from Gagné (Gagné, 1977; Gagné & Briggs, 1979) to give some order to our search of the affective domain.

We, therefore, began to delineate the affective domain by selecting affective constructs or components which were pervasive and which appear often in the literature (Part II), and we listed conditions of learning for each component or construct (Parts II and V). In a later section of this chapter we propose a taxonomy of the affective domain, further describe it for use in instructional settings, and discuss its potential limitations.

Coupled with our exploration of the affective domain and taxonomies, we began searching for ways to (a) integrate the domains, and (b) close the gap among needs, goals, curricula, and instruction. Our technique of audit trails was developed for this purpose.

Audit trails are a technique for identifying both affective and cognitive outcomes ranging from broad life-long societal goals to instructional objectives (Part III). We assumed that life-long goals (related to leisure time and citizenship, for example) have both affective and cognitive components. Again, we assumed that it is not sufficient for learners to understand and know about, for example, governmental policy; educators want students to form attitudes and values about the government, and to act on their convictions. All too often instructors imply that they are interested in this affective component of learning, but they do not always plan for it explicitly, as they do for cognitive knowledge. One reason is because they do not know how to; another reason is because the affective component, often seen as equally if not more important than the cognitive aspect of instruction, is not as explicitly stated. The reasons are both practical and political.

Audit trails make the affective element of the curriculum more explicit, and they link life-long goals to instructional objectives. Of course, they do not address the political issues.

Procedurally, we suggested that audit trails be developed as the first step of instructional planning after needs assessment to identify long-term goals. Using the goals and objectives identified in the audit trail, further analysis of the audit trail should be done to specify other levels of objectives—curriculum, unit, and instructional. Once objectives have been identified for the lesson design stage, appropriate conditions of learning can also be identified and used. In a later section of this chapter, we will discuss the feasibility of using this approach for both teachers in school settings and for instructional designers.

To summarize, we noted that (a) the affective and cognitive domains were separated in theory and practice; (b) there was little agreement on what constituted the affective domain, and the components that comprised it; (c) there was a lack of integration of knowledge about the two domains; and (d) there were gaps and discontinuities among life-long goals, curricula, and instruction. To address these concerns and problems, we (a) reviewed existing taxonomies, and identified important components of the affective domain; (b) listed conditions of learning for each category of the affective domain that we identified; (c) described and showed examples of the audit trail technique; and (d) provided examples of lessons linking the affective and cognitive domains.

A Self-Assessment

We started many threads of thought in this book; we were explicit about many, and merely touched on others. Here we review what we have not done, or what we have not done completely.

Perhaps the most striking omission we made in writing this book on domain interactions was to exclude the psychomotor domain. We did this because we were particularly interested in the affective and cognitive domains, and because we were more knowledgeable about them than we were about the psychomotor domain. Certainly no theoretical framework for addressing domain interactions can be considered completed unless the psychomotor domain is included, so we acknowledge that further work needs to be done to integrate psychomotor behaviors with affective and cognitive behaviors.

We believe our audit trail technique is viable and consistent with instructional design techniques and procedures. It is a top-down strategy. We have shown that it is possible to develop audit trails (see examples in Chapters 8, 9, and 10), and we have shown how they can be used to identify instructional objectives. We, therefore, provided procedures and examples.

What we have not done is provided any firm procedures for evaluating the adequacy of audit trails once they were developed. We suggested expert review procedures, but we recognize the limitations of that approach. We have taken the stance that a successive approximation to a complete audit trail is better than no audit trail at all. We do not imagine that this stance will satisfy all readers; we hope others, perhaps curriculum or evaluation specialists, will suggest or design other, more objective ways to assess the adequacy of audit trails.

Our review of the literature in the affective domain was reasoned; that is, we searched for literature that both addressed a specific aspect of the affective domain and that linked affect to cognition. However, the literature review is by no means complete. We have made both conscious and unconscious omissions. We have boiled down hugh areas of research literature into only a few pages, and from those we have identified conditions of learning. Other literature may have led us in different directions, so we acknowledge here that we have only made a start toward unraveling the complexities of the affective domain and toward understanding the relationships between the affective and cognitive domains.

The same can be said about our choice of affective constructs to be used in this book—we made conscious and unconscious choices. For example, we omitted creativity. It is an aspect of the affective domain. Should it have been included? What about attributions? Are they underlying factors or truly a component of the domain? What about the aesthetic dimension? The spiritual dimension? Clearly, we have not exhausted all the potential components of the affective domain. There are perhaps even unanticipated objectives or categories that could have been included to take into account unplanned outcomes of an affective nature. We selected what we believed to be important and dominant components. We have, perhaps, made errors of omission and commission (e.g., social competence).

Regarding lesson design, we mentioned or referred to aspects of lesson design that we did not really address extensively or adequately. We made liberal use of the term objectives, but we did not provide techniques for writing affective objectives, nor did we adopt a particular style of objectives. We also made mention of affective evaluation, and we described self-report procedures; however, we did not give a complete account of evaluation in the affective domain. There are all varieties of semantic scales, graphic and numerical rating scales, and observation devices that could be used. In addition, we have discussed only one non-human medium, computers, in any detail. We have left untouched the effects of film, video, slide-tapes, audio, etc., on the affective and cognitive development of learners. Lesson design, at least from an instructional design perspective, is impossible without attention to writing objectives, designing adequate evaluation techniques, and using media effectively. We made the assumption that readers of this book would already have some knowledge of the above, and have, therefore, devoted little space and discussion to these aspects of lesson design. However, in Chapter 2 we did emphasize one of the most neglected aspects of objectives—*why* particular objectives should be adopted. We said that an instructional design effort should address all these questions: who? what? why? when? where? and how?

In summary, our focus has been twofold: first, on identifying components of the affective domain and the related conditions of learning; second, on designing audit trails and lessons that link the two domains and that link life-long goals, curricula, and instruction. We did not address the psychomotor domain, and we have no doubt failed to address all potential aspects of the affective domain. We have only briefly addressed all aspects of lesson design; and we may not have satisfied readers with an objective way to evaluate audit trails. We see these shortcomings as further work to be done.

A PROPOSED TAXONOMY OF THE AFFECTIVE DOMAIN

The taxonomy that we propose below is a tentative and interim one. We are not convinced that the placement of affective components is correct, nor are we convinced that all the components included should be there. We have used only those components discussed in Part II (see Figure 16.1).

Discussion of the Proposed Taxonomy

We have placed self-development as the most inclusive of the affective components. We believe that self-development is "greater than the sum of the parts"; that is, it is more encompassing than values, morals and ethics, continuing motivation, and social competence. However, we also believe that self-development includes each of these dimension of the affective domain. Hence, self-development is at the apex of our taxonomy.

Values are more inclusive than attitudes, and different from morals and ethics. Values refer to an evaluation of worth, what an individual is committed to. Morals and ethics refer to judgment about what is right and wrong, or about right and wrong behavior. We have, therefore, separated values from morals and ethics. While we considered separating morals and ethics into two categories, we did not. Ethics sometimes refers to a more general notion of right and wrong, whereas morals sometimes refers to more specific instances of right and wrong, for example, a moral code of sexual behavior. The terms are, however, also used synomously; we have done so here.

We have directly linked attitudes to both values and morals and ethics, and we have indirectly linked attitudes to continuing motivation and social competence. Attitudes, we believe, form the building blocks for values development and for the development of moral and ethical stances, hence, the direct link. Attitudes, also, of course, influence what individuals choose to be motivated toward, and how they behave in social situations. Attitudes, however, do not appear to be the core of continuing motivation and social competence as they do for values and morals and ethics. We have, therefore, shown direct and indirect links.

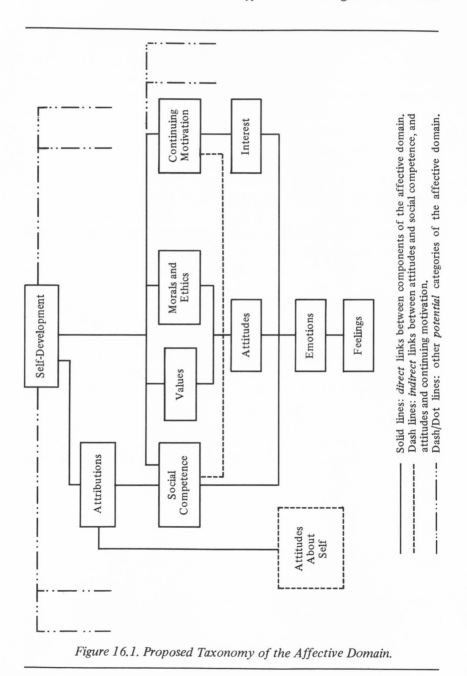

Figure 16.1. Proposed Taxonomy of the Affective Domain.

We placed social competence and continuing motivation on an equal par with values and morals and ethics as prerequisites to self-development. We, therefore, link an individual's social competence and continuing motivation to move towards a goal (e.g., a career, a family, a church, a political organization), to positive self-development.

We suggest that interest is prerequisite to continuing motivation. We also believe that (arousing and sustaining) interest is a category of the affective domain; it is distinct from, but related to, continuing motivation. We did not, however, discuss these categories as separate in Chapter 7.

We believe that the cognitive evaluations that individuals attach to feelings, the category emotions, underlie the individual's development of attitudes, interests, social competence, and the other related affective categories. Feelings, we propose, are generally attached to emotions, at least they are according to the way we have defined them in Chapter 7.

Finally, we include attributions. Of all the placements we make, this is the one about which we are most uneasy and unsure. A first draft of the taxonomy presented in Figure 16.1 placed attributions at the lowest level of the taxonomy with broken lines to indicate that we viewed attributions as an underlying factor to all the affective components. However, on second thought, we realized that many of the components of the domain could be considered underlying factors and therefore we abandoned the idea of depicting attributions as such. We have settled on linking attributions directly to self-development. To make explicit the relationship of attitudes to attributions, we added a subcategory of attitudes, attitudes about self. We also directly linked social competence to attributions. We did this because so many of the evaluations we make about ourselves come from our social interactions, or they come from evaluations of us made by others (see Oden's categories in Chapter 7). As we stated earlier, we feel quite unsure about attributions, both about including it in the domain at all, and its subsequent placement. We offer it to you for your review and critique.

Like Gephart and Ingle (1976), we now include dash/dot lines (see Figure 16.1) to indicate that a more comprehensive taxonomy of the domain is probably desirable, including even unanticipated objectives or an entire unanticipated category.

Perhaps an *alternate* way to think about the affective categories we have presented, or as a useful way to summarize the categories of the affective domain, is to identify *goal or outcome categories* that cut across the categories. Potential affective goals and outcomes for education and training might include:

1. Goals related to positive attitudes toward subject areas or disciplines including aesthetics.
2. Goals related to the development of a rational basis for attitudes and values. These would include analytic thought about and decision making in the realm of morals and ethics.
3. Goals related to affective processes; those indicative of positive directional movement as perceived by the individual.
4. Goals related to developing and sustaining interest and motivation in vocational or avocational pursuits, as well as other areas that are important or are of interest to the learner.

The first three categories were first listed by Hurst (1980a); we added the last. To use the terminology we have used in previous chapters, category one refers to attitudes and feelings about subjects or fields of study, and attitudes about school or education in general; category two refers to attitudes, values, ethics, and morals that require analysis of cognitive information and decision-making; category three refers to self-development and attributions, including the subcategory attitudes about self; category four refers to developing interested and motivated learners, including goals related to developing learner strategies.

Linking the Proposed Affective Taxonomy to Cognition

In reviewing the taxonomies of the affective and cognitive domains for Part II, we found a taxonomic schema that linked the two domains using the taxonomies proposed by Krathwohl *et al.*, (1964) and Bloom (1956). Upon first reading about the integration we were excited; we expected to find precisely what we had been searching for. We were sorely disappointed. The "new" taxonomy did nothing more than list the categories of the domains and it included a few horizontal connecting lines. Krathwohl *et al.* did a similar thing in their *Handbook of the Affective Domain* (Krathwohl *et al.*, 1964). We expected more.

What we are about to present may be viewed in much the same way that we viewed the integrated taxonomy that we discovered in the literature. We have made no substantial theoretical leaps; we only include the taxonomy to re-emphasize our interest in domain interactions, and to make the links between the domains more explicit. The taxonomy, we hope, is self-explanatory; we have not discussed it further. The cognitive components are identified by an asterik (see Figure 16.2).

Capability Verbs for the Affective Domain

We stated in Chapter 3 that the most useful taxonomy was a prescriptive one, a taxonomy that enables teachers and instructional designers to plan lessons and sequences of lessons. The taxonomies presented in Figures 16.1 and 16.2 propose (a) some relationships among the affective components, and (b) relationships between affective and cognitive components. Such taxonomies may help in determining sequences of lessons and the sequencing of instruction within lessons.

We now add one more aspect of instructional design to be used with our taxonomies and the conditions of learning to make them more prescriptive; we add capability verbs for the affective domain. These verbs can be used as aids for writing objectives and designing evaluation instruments, and they can be used to enable clearer communication about aspects of the domain among researchers and practitioners. We use them here to further clarify the components of the affective domain. We will then make a few brief comments about the verbs we have selected. See page 453.

Category of Outcome in the Affective Domain	Capability Verb
Self-development	Progresses toward
Values	Organizes

(Continued on page 453)

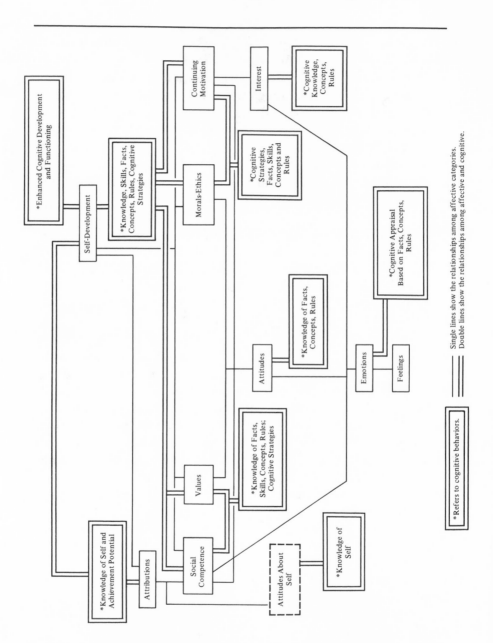

Figure 16.2. Taxonomy Linking the Affective and Cognitive Domains.

(Continued from page 451)

Morals and ethics	Justifies
Attitudes	Chooses
Social competence	Participates
Continuing motivation	Sustains
Interest	Maintains
Emotions and feelings	Expresses
Attributions	Attributes

First, we want to make a general comment related to all the categories. The behaviors educators want to facilitate in the affective domain are generally voluntary. So, we recommend including the word, *voluntarily*, before each capability verb. The reason we did not include it is because there are some instances where an affective behavior may be "forced" in order to set the behavior in motion. Krathwohl *et al.* (1964) named a category in their taxonomy, Acquiscence in responding, to satisfy this need. That term refers to obedience or compliance. We, too, recognize this need, and therefore, have not included voluntarily before each category. We do, however, suggest that *usually affective behaviors are voluntary.* Learners make uncoerced and free choices.

Second, for the categories of values, morals and ethics, and attitudes we would have liked to have stated "acts in accordance with values," or "acts according to self-selected moral precepts." We did not use the behavioral wording because of the weak link between values, attitudes, morals and ethics, and behavior. In each of these categories, what is learned are *capabilities of behaving*, or *tendencies to behave in a particular way*. However, many things can intervene to block an actual behavior, e.g., no opportunity or a superordinate value structure. We, therefore, use the verbs *justify* for morals and ethics and *organize* for values. When writing an objective, teachers and designers may wish to specify some action that would link the value and the behavior. For example, "voluntarily justifies his/her values related to nuclear war by taking some action in accordance with his/her justification." While this is awkward, we hope it makes our point. It implies that the learner has voluntarily expressed a position, and is sufficiently committed to act on the position taken.

We wish to make one final note related to the capability verb for self-development. We selected the verb *progresses toward* to show directional movement. We assume that self-development is a life-long process, not a specific end point. Our verb choice was intended to demonstrate that belief.

Capability Verbs for the Cognitive Domain

Gagné and Briggs (1979) proposed the five-component objective form of writing objectives when precision in expression is required to enable a team of designers to work together on lesson designs and assessments of learner performance.

In that five-component form of writing objectives, two verbs are used: (a) a capability verb and (b) an action verb. The learner's overt and measurable performance of the action verb in a test situation enables one to infer that the intended capability has been attained.

We have mentioned the five-component form of writing objectives frequently in Chapter 14, but not all of our sample objectives completely follow this form. You may recall that in Chapter 11, on how to do an audit trail, we deliberately avoided the five-component form as too restrictive for that design stage. We now wish to present capability verbs for the cognitive domain, and to include illustrative action verbs.

For readers who wish to take a self-instructional package on how to write five-component objectives, see Briggs and Wager (1981, Chapter 4). For readers who wish to know more about the purpose of five-component objectives, see Gagné and Briggs (1979). Examples of five-component objectives are found in both those sources, and in our Chapter 14.

We next list our suggested standard verbs for the cognitive domain. Many of these were first offered by Gagné and Briggs (1979), some were first offered by Briggs and Wager (1981), and a few are first offered here.

So we suggest a rather "free style" of writing objectives when doing an audit trail, but for explicitness in lesson design and evaluation of learner performance, we suggest the five-component form and its capability verbs (especially when a team of designers is working on the same lesson). Readers may wish to try still other specific ways of writing objectives, referred to in Chapters 2 and 14, or they may wish to originate their own ways of defining objectives. Note that in the "free style" in our audit trails (Part III) we often combined cognitive and affective elements in the same objectives. For lesson design, separate cognitive and affective objectives may be used, as in Chapter 15.

Category of Outcome in the Cognitive Domain	Capability Verb	Illustrative Action Verb
Intellectual Skills		
Discriminations	Discriminate	By saying "same" or "different"
Concrete Concepts	Identify	By pointing or sorting
Defined Concepts	Classify	By selecting
Rule Using (principles)	Demonstrate	By computing
Problem Solving (higher order rules)	Generate	By writing
Information Learning		
Verbatim Learning	Recite	Orally
Learning of Facts	State	Orally
Substance Learning	Summarize	In writing
Cognitive Strategies		
As Lesson Objectives	Originate	By giving a novel solution

(Continued on page 456)

(Continued from page 455)

| As Tools for Learning | Revise or Reactivate | By using a new or previously taught or discovered learning strategy |

Summary

In this section, we have proposed two taxonomies. The first (Figure 16.1) proposes a taxonomy of the affective domain; it includes the categories we discussed in Part II of this book, and it gives a cumulative structure for some of the dimensions. We proposed the taxonomy as a tentative one, and we included dash lines to indicate that it is incomplete.

The second taxonomy (Figure 16.2) is one that links the cognitive and affective domains. It is crude but is included to emphasize the interconnectedness of the two domains. The cognitive elements support the affective elements, and the reverse. Our diagram serves the purpose of making this explicit.

Finally, we included capability verbs for each category of the affective domain. The capability verbs could be preceded by the word *voluntarily*, although there are some instances in which learners are coerced into behaving in a particular way. Dissonance theory makes use of this technique as a strategy; however, Krathwohl *et al.* (1964) recommended it as an early outcome. We also remembered the weak link between attitudes, values, morals and ethics, and an action, and discussed several of our verbs in relation to that weak link.

Just after our list of capability verbs for the affective domain, we presented our list of capability verbs for the cognitive domain.

We now turn our attention to the external conditions of learning we proposed in Parts II and IV. We listed a total of 132 for the affective domain. In the next section we make some recommendations for making the most use of these conditions.

COMMONLY APPEARING EXTERNAL CONDITIONS OF LEARNING FOR THE AFFECTIVE DOMAIN

When we made our final count of the external conditions we

had generated for the affective domain we were truly surprised. One hundred and thirty-two are a lot of external conditions! As we reviewed the lists made in Parts II and IV, we began to see some common external conditions across all components of the affective domain. (This is also true in the cognitive domain; for example, "provides examples and non-examples" is an external condition for the categories of discrimination, concrete and defined concepts, and rule using.) We decided that it would be helpful to identify the common external conditions; therefore, in this section, we present eight common external conditions of learning for the affective domain. We also present three conditions that are pervasive, but that were not included for each component.

The eight external conditions of learning listed below are stated in the most general terms possible. For each of these eight conditions, the purpose of providing the condition might change according to the particular category of the affective domain under consideration. An example will clarify what we mean. One external condition across all categories is to provide new cognitive information to learners. When this condition is used in conjunction with developing values, the purpose is help learners establish a cognitive framework. When used for attitude learning, it can serve the purpose of (a) providing a discrepant message, or (b) providing information related to a particular argument. When used for emotional development, new information is provided to change the information base on which the emotion is made. So, while the conditions are general, there are specific uses of each for the various categories of the affective domain. We do not list the specifics again since they have already been given in both Parts II and IV. We give only a very broad description of each of the common external conditions.

Eight External Conditions for All Components of the Affective Domain

1. Provide cognitive information that is new to the learners, or that is presented in a new way.
2. Use successive approximations either to break a task into smaller units so success can be achieved, or to gradually increase the learners' cognitive base or tolerance for an idea.

3. Model attitudes, values, emotions, values, etc., that are consistent with the desired behavior.
4. Use group discussions or social interactions (one-to-one, small groups, role plays, etc.) to assist learners to (a) see another position, (b) take another's perspective, (c) verbalize their own position, and/or (d) solve problems.
5. Use direct reinforcement to (a) establish attitudes, emotions, values, etc., when there is consensus on the desired attitude, emotion, value, etc., and (b) reward cooperation, participation, independence, success, etc.
6. Match the learners' task to their abilities; strive for a moderate level of difficulty.
7. Provide opportunities for learners to take an overt action.
8. Use the principle of contiguity to help learners associate learning in general (school, training sessions), and specific learning (affective or cognitive knowledge and skills) to a pleasant, stimulating environment.

Three Additional Conditions of Learning

We also list three additional external conditions that do not span all categories, but are very pervasive.

9. Relate learner success to his or her ability and effort. Relate failure to lack of effort.
10. Encourage the learners to set goals for themselves, and provide an opportunity for learners to work toward those goals.
11. Use a variety of instructional strategies, and use a variety of external conditions to facilitate affective and cognitive development.

These 11 important conditions of learning can be used singly or in combination to influence a wide range of affective goals. We will have more to say about them in a later section concerning the feasibility of designing instruction using our approach.

NEEDED RESEARCH

We have presented a framework for a theory relating the affective and cognitive domains (e.g., outcome categories of the affective domain; conditions of learning), and we have presented a procedure for integrating affect and cognition in instruction (e.g., audit trails; lesson design). What we have begun is so clearly in its infancy that research is needed on almost all aspects of our proposals. We present here, however, some lines of research we believe should be begun first, and that would be most valuable. We recognize that we have only scratched the surface.

The first need we see is validation of the conditions of learning that we have proposed. Four aspects could be pursued: (a) identification of the most common and pervasive conditions across all categories of the affective domain; (b) identification of unique conditions for specific categories of the affective domain; (c) identification of specific conditions of learning that influence both cognitive and affective development; and (d) identification of conditions that are particularly applicable to particular groups of learners, e.g., college students, adults in non-traditional settings, elementary and/or secondary learners, etc. We assume that the most viable way to approach such research would be to conduct experimental studies employing a control group and an experimental group or groups, but perhaps there are other ways to proceed to test the same hypotheses.

A second line of research we recommend is the study of the relationships among (a) categories of the affective domain and (b) categories of the affective and cognitive domains. For example, we have proposed a tentative taxonomy of the affective domain and a tentative taxonomy of the relationships between the affective and cognitive domains. Research to test the hypothesized relationships is needed. Hurst (1980b) using the taxonomies by Krathwohl *et al.* (1964) and by Gagné (1977) has conducted one such study. Young (in progress) is currently conducting an experimental study testing the relationships between attitudes and information and cognitive skills. The results of research along both of these lines would be valuable for instructional designers, practitioners, and researchers.

A final line of inquiry revolves around the procedures we have developed, specifically related to audit trails. We presented the "how to" in Chapter 11, but ways to determine (a) the adequacy of audit trails are needed, and (b) procedures for developing the most complete and comprehensive audit trails are also desirable.

As to adequacy of audit trails, we have recommended expert review procedures. However, we have not specified how to evaluate completeness or comprehensiveness, nor have we specified how to judge the relative merits of specific objectives or goals within an audit trail. Some types of formative evaluation procedures could be developed and tested for these purposes.

As for the procedures for developing audit trails, again we recommend expert tryouts, reporting the findings in the literature. Perhaps through these tryouts, some more objective means of developing and assessing audit trails will emerge.

We have not mentioned evaluation of lesson designs, *per se*, although procedures are implied in the above recommendations. The relationships among cognitive and affective objectives, necessary conditions of learning, affective evaluative procedures, etc., could all be tested in "classroom" settings. Experimental studies combining the above could be conducted to evaluate the "correctness" of particular lesson designs, and the components within any lesson design (e.g., conditions of learning).

In summary, we recommend needed research on (a) the conditions of learning, (b) the interrelationships among components of the affective domain, and the components of the cognitive and affective domains, and on (c) audit trails. Only with such research will we be able to truly evaluate our hypotheses and proposals.

THE FEASIBILITY OF OUR APPROACH

As we reviewed our own work, we asked ourselves how feasible it was for a teacher or an instructional designer to actually develop instruction based on our recommendations. Two hundred and thirty conditions of learning are overwhelming, audit trails do not exist, and affective goals are often not specified.

First, a few comments about audit trails. We provided three examples of audit trails that we developed for this book. In Chapter 11, we gave the number of clock hours it took one person to develop the audit trails—10 hours for the one presented in Chapter 8, two hours for the one in Chapter 10. While this is certainly not an excessive amount of time to spend on what we believe is so valuable, we do acknowledge that this is a technique we had been thinking about for years. So, while we had never actually done an audit trail until this book, the idea of audit trails was firmly established in our minds. Perhaps we developed our audit trails more rapidly because of this. Granted, good audit trails will take more time to develop initially than when some experience has been gained (remember developing your first hierarchy?); however, with even minimal practice, expertise can come rapidly. We suggest "giving it a shot." We also believe that *any* audit trail that attempts to link life-long needs to lesson objectives, and to link the affective and cognitive domains, is better than no audit trail. We believe, therefore, that *the process is as important as the product*; the process alters the focus of one's thinking from only the concerns of a particular lesson to how a particular lesson is linked to a life-long goal or goals. Additionally, if focuses thinking on both affective and cognitive outcomes.

We have developed a somewhat comprehensive instructional design model including taxonomies, capability verbs, conditions of learning, audit trails, and lesson design procedures. Teachers use instructional design models very differently than do professional instructional designers. For teachers, lesson design is only one of a multitude of activities they engage in each day. This, plus the fact that they generally have little lead time to develop units and lessons, prompts us to recommend our procedures and strategies to them at a broad and general level. We hope teachers will become more aware of the interactions between affective and cognitive outcomes, and how to design lessons that incorporate both types of outcomes. This is one of the reasons we presented the common conditions of learning in this chapter. This list should help teachers select and use several conditions to facilitate development of many affective components.

Thus, on the one hand, we believe what we have developed can be used by teachers and designers who are at an "awareness level" of relationships between the cognitive and affective domains. We hope teachers will more readily think about affective objectives and strategies as they begin to design instruction, and as they work on curriculum committees.

On the other end of the spectrum are professional instructional designers whose job it is to systematically design instruction. These professionals, who often have considerable lead time, and considerable resources for designing instruction, can follow our procedures fairly closely, and employ audit trails, conditions of learning, etc., in their designs. It is from this group that we hope will come many recommendations for improvement of our ideas.

We, of course, believe our approach is feasible (we would not have suggested it otherwise); however, we see an individual's sophistication of use dependent on a number of factors: time, resources, training in instructional design skills and procedures, attitudes, etc. We hope teachers and instructional designers will use what they can, and become increasingly more adept at the procedures, modifying and adapting them to meet specific needs for specific audiences, in specific situations.

CONCLUSIONS

Throughout this book and this chapter we have made or alluded to quite a few conclusions we arrived at during work on the book. In this section, we first make one general conclusion, and then we briefly list the other main ones as a summary of our work.

In general, we believe that instructional designers, teachers, and trainers can positively influence learning and learners by designing and developing instruction that integrates the affective and cognitive domains. In Chapter 2, we listed a rank ordering of influences that affect what and how people learn. We included such determiners of learning as home environment, intelligence, motivation, time on task, etc. These subjective rank orders were based on our perceptions of the present status of both research and practice. We conclude, however, that if our suggestions for integrating the cognitive and affective domains were carried out, four of the influences we listed relatively low on the list might be ranked higher: quality of instruction, learner strategies, attitudes and values, and media selection.

Next, we list the other major conclusions that we believe are important.

1. The affective and cognitive domains have important relation-

ships between them. Instruction can be designed to aid in the development of outcomes in both domains.

2. The affective domain is poorly defined (as a specific entity), and it is difficult to establish boundaries for it.
3. Conditions of learning can be determined for various categories of the affective domain (Part II and IV), and common conditions can be determined that cut across several categories (Chapter 16).
4. Audit trails can be developed to link life-long needs to curricula, course and unit goals, and to lesson objectives.
5. Audit trails can be developed to integrate goals and objectives in both the affective and cognitive domains.
6. Lessons can be designed to integrate cognitive and affective objectives using audit trails, conditions of learning, and individual and group media and strategies.
7. In general, the events of instruction proposed for use with the cognitive domain are also useful for lessons combining the affective and cognitive domains. However, additional conditions of learning might also require identification. On the other hand, informing the learner of the objective should be omitted if the desired behavior is a voluntary one.
8. Research is needed to determine:
   (a) the most important conditions of learning for specific components of the affective domain;
   (b) common conditions of learning across categories of the affective domain;
   (c) conditions of learning for specific audiences;
   (d) conditions that influence both affective and cognitive outcomes;
   (e) the relationship among categories of the affective domain;
   (f) the relationship among categories of the cognitive and affective domains;
   (g) ways to test/evaluate the adequacy of audit trails; and
   (h) procedures for designing the most comprehensive and complete audit trails.
9. Additional work needs to be done on specifying affective objectives, designing affective assessment instruments, and developing affective strategies and media; and on these

components of instructional design as they relate to both cognitive and affective outcomes.

A VIEW OF THE FUTURE

We, the authors, assume that most of our readers are professionals in education or training or students preparing for these professions. That means that all of us are both professionals and citizens. Throughout this book we have often stressed our mutual dual role to improve instruction and to help make this a better world.

As citizens, we are concerned first with survival—with avoiding atomic wars and with assuring our needs for water, food, and energy. We cannot fine-tune our instructional efforts unless these basic needs are met. As instructional professionals, we have a special opportunity for working toward a better informed citizenry as one means of influencing survival decisions made by our political figures. We cannot expect a government better than the total citizenry at making wise choices.

Regular readers of the magazine *The Futurist* realize that we have the means for survival if only we make the right decisions. Most futurists agree on that. What they disagree about is whether those right decisions will be made. Thus, some futurists take an optimistic view of the future, and others take a pessimistic view. The criticality of these survival decisions influenced us to present audit trails in citizenship and to emphasize moral development.

That said, we now turn to the professional role we all have. The purpose of this closing section of the book is to merely sketch out a few of the benefits we believe could result from application of the recommendations we have presented in this book. We will dwell upon these only briefly under two main headings: deciding what to teach, and deciding how to teach it.

What to Teach

It would be a great shame if any of us used the most advanced instructional techniques and media to teach outmoded objectives. Why spend the money and effort to teach well what should not be taught at all? In earlier chapters we have mentioned the tendency for objectives and content to become outdated. Too often curricula reflect traditions from times past. We believe our emphasis upon needs assessment and audit trails could, if put into practice, do much to insure that our objectives are relevant for real life-long needs.

As a corollary of the above, we believe that any instructional design effort should begin with objectives, not with course content. Even some instructional design models begin with analysis of content—usually traditional content. But without an audit trail, how can we know that either course objectives or course content are aimed at a real need? Without a technique like the audit trail, how can we be sure that curriculum and instruction are directed toward long-term goals?

So, our first point of emphasis for future practice is to use audit trails to insure relevance of all lessons, courses, and curricula for clearly established life-long goals. This emphasis will be increasingly important the more quickly the world changes. As needs for new occupations arise due to societal changes, our first attention must be to the issue of what to teach. Thus, we see audit trails as a technique for insuring the current and future relevance of *what* we teach. This *what* we teach, of course, will relate to both affective and cognitive objectives, and in many cases to psychomotor objectives, a domain we do not address in this book.

By such means as discussed here, the future can bring up-to-date relevance to what is taught.

How to Teach

Education and training professionals will be equally concerned with future development in media of instruction, and in techniques for assuring relevance of instruction. However, we should not uncritically adopt new media just because they are new. But one reason why instructional professionals can benefit from reading futuristic literature is to keep abreast of current projections of future trends in the labor market; these have implications for both the selection of objectives and the selection of media.

Our dual responsibility as professionals, then, is to employ means for insuring the relevance of *what* is taught, and to use mature judgment in selecting media and designing lessons and materials, using appropriate conditions of learning.

But it is how media are *programmed* that is more important than the choice of media. Here we refer to the instructional events and conditions of learning we have dwelt upon at length in this book. A carefully selected medium, poorly programmed, is another waste to be avoided. So the conditions of learning we have identified are crucial for effective programming of whatever media are used. As we have also stressed, these conditions of learning are equally useful for the teacher and for the programmer. So we seek the best use of teachers, group instruction, individualized instruction, and media.

Earlier we listed suggestions as to how both teachers or instructors and other media can work, in combination, to enhance achievement of both short-term and long-term objectives, in both the affective and the cognitive domains.

The Future Potential

Viewing this entire chapter and book as a whole, one can visualize effective and enjoyable learning situations in schools, homes, industry, and elsewhere. We can visualize teleconferencing, television, and other group-interactive media as well as sophisticated individual study stations. We have cited work in using computers to enhance self-management and other learner strategies, as well as use for immediate cognitive and affective objectives. We have also cited the literature on the role of the teacher and group discussion for both social and cognitive outcomes. We have even dealt the best we could with feelings and emotions.

In conclusion, we, the authors, just beginning to emerge from our work in writing this book, can visualize happy and effective consequences of our work, provided that we have persuaded enough readers to try some of our recommendations.

We hope also that this book will stimulate research in areas in which we had to break fresh ground. And, as professional instructional designers, we would be most pleased if this book is considered an advance in instructional design models.

References

AAAS Commission on Science Education. (1967). *Science—A process approach.* Hierarchy Chart, New York: Xerox, Inc.

AAAS Commission on Science Education. (1967). *Science—A process approach.* Washington, D.C.: American Association for the Advancement of Science.

Abbett, W.S., Bridgham, R.G., & Elstein, A.S. (1982). Medical education. In H.E. Mitzel (Ed.), *Encyclopedia of educational research* (5th ed.) (pp. 1202-1212). New York: The Free Press.

Abramson, L.Y., Seligman, M.E.P., & Teasdale, J.D. (1978). Learned helplessness in humans: Critique and reformulation. *Journal of Abnormal Psychology, 87,* 1, 49-74.

Adams, G.S. (1983). Attitude measurement. In H.E. Mitzel (Ed.), *Encyclopedia of educational research* (5th ed.) (pp. 180-189). New York: The Free Press.

Adler, A. (1956). *The individual psychology of Alfred Adler.* H.L. Ansbacher & R.R. Ansbacher (Eds.). New York: Basic Books.

Airasian, P.W., & Bart, W.M. (1975). Validating a priori instructional hierarchies. *Journal of Educational Measurement, 12,* 163-173.

Allender, J.S. (1982). Affective education. In H.E. Mitzel (Ed.), *Encyclopedia of educational research* (5th ed.) (pp. 94-103). New York: The Free Press.

Allport, G.W. (1935). Attitudes. In C. Murchinson (Ed.), *Handbook of social psychology* (pp. 798-884). Worcester, MA: Clark University Press.

Allport, G.W. (1935). *Becoming.* New Haven: Yale University Press.

Allport, G.W. (1961). *Pattern and growth in personality.* New York: Holt, Rinehart, and Winston.

American Psychological Association. (1967). *Casebook on ethical standards of psychologists.* Washington, D.C.

American Psychological Association. (1973). *Ethical principles in the conduct of research with human participants.* Washington, D.C.

Arnold, M.B. (1960). *Emotion and personality.* New York: Columbia University Press.

Aronson, D.T., & Briggs, L.J. (1983). Contributions of Gagné and Briggs to a prescriptive model of instruction. In C.R. Reigeluth (Ed.), *Instructional-*

design theories and models: An overview of their current status (pp. 75-100). Hillsdale, NJ: Lawrence Erlbaum Associates.

Ausubel, D.P. (1963). *The psychology of meaningful verbal learning.* New York: Grune & Stratton.

Ausubel, D.P. (1968). *Educational psychology: A cognitive view.* New York: Holt, Rinehart, and Winston.

Ball, S. (1982). Motivation. In H.E. Mitzel (Ed.), *Encyclopedia of educational research* (5th ed.) (pp. 1256-1263). New York: The Free Press.

Bandura, A. (1977a). Self-efficacy: Toward a unifying theory of behavioral change. *Psychological Review, 84*, 191-215.

Bandura, A. (1977b). *Social learning theory.* Englewood Cliffs, NJ: Prentice-Hall.

Bandura, A. (1978). The self system in reciprocal determinism. *American Psychologist, 33*, 344-358.

Baranowski, T. (1981). Toward a definition of concepts of health and disease, wellness and illness. *Health Values, 5*, 246-256.

Bar-Tal, D. (1978). Attributional analysis of achievement-related behavior. *Review of Educational Research, 48*, 259-271.

Bart, W.M., & Airasian, P.W. (1974). Determination of the orderings among seven Piagetian tasks by an ordering-theoretic method. *Journal of Educational Psychology, 66*, 277-284.

Bart, W.M., & Krus, D.J. (1973). An ordering-theoretic method to determine hierarchies among items. *Educational and Psychological Measurement, 33*, 291-300.

Bills, R.E. (1976). Affect and its measurement. *Proceedings of the National Symposium for Professors of Educational Research (NSPER).* Memphis, Tennessee. (ERIC Document Reproduction Service No. ED 157 911.)

Blocher, D.H. (1982). Mental health. In H.E. Mitzel (Ed.), *Encyclopedia of educational research* (5th ed.) (pp. 1212-1218). New York: The Free Press.

Bloom, B.S. (1976). *Human characteristics and school learning.* New York: McGraw-Hill.

Bloom, B.S. (Ed.). (1956). *Taxonomy of educational objectives: The classification of educational goals. Handbook I: Cognitive domain.* New York: Longman.

Bloom, B.S. (1984). The 2 sigma problem: The search for methods of group instruction as effective as one-to-one tutoring. *Educational Researcher, 13*(6), 4-16.

Bloom, B.S., Hastings, J.T., & Madaus, G.F. (1971). *Handbook on formative and summative evaluation of student learning.* New York: McGraw-Hill.

Boutwell, R.C. (1977). Designing a systematized program in instructional design and development. *Journal of Educational Technology Systems, 5*(3), 191-213.

Bower, F.F. (1982). Curriculum development and the Neuman model. In B.M. Neuman (Ed.), *The Neuman Systems Model.* New York: Appleton-Century-Crofts.

Boyer, E. (1983). *High School: A report on secondary education in America.* Carnegie Foundation for the Advancement of Teaching. New York: Harper and Row.

Braden, R.A., & Sachs, S.G. (1983). The most recommended books on instructional development. *Educational Technology, 23*(2), 24-28.

Bradshaw, J. (1972, March 30). The concept of social need. *New Society*, pp. 640-643.

Brandhorst, A.R. (1978). *Reconceptualizing the affective domain.* Williamsburg, Virginia. (ERIC Document Reproduction Service No. ED 153 891.)

Branson, R.K. (1977). Military and industrial training. In L.J. Briggs (Ed.), *Instructional design: Principles and applications* (pp. 353-391). Englewood Cliffs, NJ: Educational Technology Publications.

Branson, R.K. (1978). The interservice procedures for instructional systems development. *Educational Technology, 26*(3), 11-14.

Branson, R.K., Rayner, G.T., Cox, J.L., Furman, J.P., King, F.J., & Hannum, W.H. (1975, August). Interservice procedures for instructional systems development. (5 Vols.), TRA DOC Pam 350-30 and NAVEDTRA 106A). Ft. Monroe, VA: U.S. Army Training and Doctrine Command. NTS No. ADA 019 486 through ADA 019 490.

Bratton, B. (1981). Competencies for the instructional training development professional. *Journal of Instructional Development, 5*(1), 14-15. (Report of the AECT Task Force on Instructional Development Certification.)

Briggs, L.J. (1954). *Development and appraisal of a measure of student motivation.* Lackland Air Force Base, TX: Air Force Personnel and Training Research Center. (AFPTRC-TR-54-31.)

Briggs, L.J. (1959). Teaching machines for training of military personnel in maintenance of electronic equipment. In E. Galanter (Ed.), *Automatic teaching: The state of the art* (pp. 131-145). New York: John Wiley and Sons.

Briggs, L.J. (1960). Teaching machines. In G. Finch (Ed.), *Educational and training media: A symposium* (pp. 150-195). Washington, DC: National Academy of Sciences-National Research Council, Publication 789.

Briggs, L.J. (1970). *Handbook of procedures for the design of instruction* (1st ed.). Pittsburg, PA: American Institutes for Research.

Briggs, L.J. (1972). *Student's guide to handbook of procedures for the design of instruction.* Pittsburg, PA: American Institutes for Research.

Briggs, L.J. (Ed.). (1977). *Instructional design: Principles and applications.* Englewood Cliffs, NJ: Educational Technology Publications.

Briggs, L.J. (1980). Thirty years of instructional design: One man's experience. *Educational Technology, 20*(2), 45-50.

Briggs, L.J. (1982a). Instructional design: Present strengths and weaknesses, and a view of the future. *Educational Technology, 22*(10), 18-23.

Briggs, L.J. (1982b). Systems design in instruction. In H.E. Mitzel (Ed.), *Encyclopedia of educational research* (5th ed.) (pp. 1851-1858). New York: The Free Press.

Briggs, L.J. (1984). Whatever happened to motivation and the affective domain? *Educational Technology, 24*(5), 33-34.

Briggs, L.J., & Reed, H.B. (1943). The curve of retention for substance material. *Journal of Experimental Psychology, 32*, 513-517.

Briggs, L.J., & Roe, R.M. (1953). Morale as a function of opportunity to register complaints. Chanute Air Force Base, Ill.: Technical Training Research Laboratory. (Technical Report 53-4.)

Briggs, L.J., & Wager, W.W. (1981). *Handbook of procedures for the design of instruction* (2nd ed.). Englewood Cliffs, NJ: Educational Technology Publications.

Bruner, J., Goodnow, J.J., & Austin, G.A. (1967). *A study of thinking.* New York: Science Editions, Inc.

Burton, J.K., & Merrill, P.F. (1977). Needs assessment: Goals, needs, and priorities. In L.J. Briggs (Ed.), *Instructional design: Principles and applications* (pp. 21-45). Englewood Cliffs, NJ: Educational Technology Publications.

Carey, J., & Briggs, L.J. (1977). Teams as designers. In L.J. Briggs (Ed.), *Instructional design: Principles and applications*, (pp. 261-307). Englewood Cliffs, NJ: Educational Technology Publications.

Chandler, T.A., & Spies, D.J. (1984). Semantic differential placement of attributions and dimensions in four different groups. *Journal of Educational Psychology, 76*, 1119-1127.

Connelly, R.D. (1972). *A taxonomic approach to the evaluation of prospective elementary teachers in a mathematics course.* (Doctoral dissertation, Kent State University.) *Dissertation Abstracts International, 1973, 34*, 613A-614A. (University Microfilms No. 73-13, 303.)

Conrad, C.F. (1982). Undergraduate instruction. In H.E. Mitzel (Ed.), *Encyclopedia of educational research* (5th ed.) (pp. 1963-1973). New York: The Free Press.

De Landsheere, V. (1977). On defining educational objectives. *Evaluation in Education: International Progress, 1*(2), 73-190. New York: Pergamon Press.

Derr, R.L. (1973). *A taxonomy of social purposes of public schools: A handbook.* New York: Longman.

Derry, S.J. (1984, April). Strategy training: An incidental learning model for CAI. Paper presented at the meeting of the American Educational Research Association, New Orleans, LA.

Dewey, J. (1963). *Experience and education.* New York: Collier. (Originally published in 1938.)

Dick, W. (1977a). Formative evaluation. In L.J. Briggs (Ed.), *Instructional design: Principles and applications* (pp. 311-333). Englewood Cliffs, NJ: Educational Technology Publications.

Dick, W. (1977b). Summative evaluation. In L.J. Briggs (Ed.), *Instructional design: Principles and applications* (pp. 335-348). Englewood Cliffs, NJ: Educational Technology Publications.

Dinero, T.E., & Martin, B.L. (1983, April). *A comparison of Rasch scaling and ordering theory to investigate a hierarchy of cognitive and affective test items.* Paper presented at the meeting of the National Council on Measurement in Education, Montreal, Canada.

Dollard, J., & Miller, N.E. (1950). *Personality and psychotherapy.* New York: McGraw-Hill.

Draguns, J.G. (1982). Personality theory. In H.E. Mitzel (Ed.), *Encyclopedia of educational research* (5th ed.) (pp. 1398-1404). New York: The Free Press.

Dweck, C.S., & Reppucci, N.D. (1973). Learned helplessness and reinforcement responsibility in children. *Journal of Personality and Social Psychology, 25,* 109-116.

Elliott, J.E., & Kearns, J.M. (1978). *Analysis and planning for improved distribution of nursing personnel and services: Final report.* (DHEW Publication No. HRA 79-16.) Hyattsville, MD: U.S. Department of Health, Education, and Welfare. (ERIC Document Reproduction Service No. ED 176 065.)

English, H.B., & English, A.C. (1958). *A comprehensive dictionary of psychological terms.* New York: Longman.

English, H.B., Welborn, E.L., & Killian, C.D. (1934). Studies in substance memorization. *Journal of General Psychology, 2,* 223-259.

Ferguson, M. (Ed.). (1982a). New theory: Feelings code, organize thinking. (Special issue-Part I.) *Brain/Mind Bulletin, 7*(6).

Ferguson, M. (Ed.). (1982b). New theory: Feelings code, organize thinking. (Special issue-Part II.) *Brain/Mind Bulletin, 7*(7).

Festinger, L. (1957). *A theory of cognitive dissonance.* Stanford, CA: Stanford University Press.

Finch, G. (Ed.). (1960). *Educational and training media: A symposium.* Washington, D.C.: National Academy of Sciences–National Research Council, Publication 789.

Fishbein, M. (Ed.). (1967). *Attitude theory and measurement.* New York: Wiley.

Flavell, J.H. (1963). *The developmental psychology of Jean Piaget.* New York: Litton.

Fogel, A. (1982). Emotional development. In H.E. Mitzel (Ed.), *Encyclopedia of educational research* (5th ed.) (pp. 555-559). New York: The Free Press:

Foshay, W.R. (1978). An alternative for task analysis in the affective domain. *Journal of Instructional Development, 1*(2), 22-24.

Freud, S. (1964). New introductory lectures on psychoanalysis. In J. Strachey (Ed.), *The Standard Edition of the Complete Works of S. Freud* (Vol. 22). London: Hogarth Press. (Originally published, 1933.)

Fromm, E. (1947). *Man for himself: An inquiry into the psychology of ethics.* New York: Holt, Rinehart, and Winston.

Furst, E.J. (1981). Bloom's taxonomy of educational objectives for the cognitive domain: Philosophical and educational issues. *Review of Educational Research, 51,* 441-453.

Gagné, R.M. (1962). The acquisition of knowledge. *Psychological Review, 69,* 355-365.

Gagné, R.M. (Ed.). (1962). *Psychological principles in system development.* New York: Holt, Rinehart, and Winston.

Gagné, R.M. (1964). Problem solving. In A.W. Melton (Ed.), *Categories of human learning* (pp. 293-317). New York: Academic Press.

Gagné, R.M. (1965). *The conditions of learning.* New York: Holt, Rinehart, and Winston.

Gagné, R.M. (1970). *The conditions of learning* (2nd ed.). New York: Holt, Rinehart, and Winston.

Gagné, R.M. (1977). *The conditions of learning* (3rd ed.). New York: Holt, Rinehart, and Winston.

Gagné, R.M., & Bassler, O.C. (1963). Study of retention of some topics of elementary nonmetric geometry. *Journal of Educational Psychology, 54,* 123-131.

Gagné, R.M., & Briggs, L.J. (1974). *Principles of instructional design.* New York: Holt, Rinehart, and Winston.

Gagné, R.M., & Briggs, L.J. (1979). *Principles of instructional design* (2nd ed.). New York: Holt, Rinehart, and Winston.

Gagné, R.M., Mayor, J.R., Garstens, H.L., & Paradise, N.E. (1962). Factors in acquiring knowledge of a mathematics task. *Psychological Monographs, 76*(7), 1-19.

Gagné, R.M., & Paradise, N.E. (1961). Abilities and learning sets in knowledge acquisition. *Psychological Monographs, 75*(14), 1-23.

Garbarino, J. (1981). *Successful schools and competent students.* Lexington, MA: Lexington Books.

Gephart, W.J., & Ingle, R.B. (1976). Evaluation and the affective domain. *Proceedings of the National Symposium for Professors of Educational Research (NSPER).* Phoenix, Arizona: (ERIC Document Reproduction Service No. ED 157 911.)

Gerlach, V., & Sullivan, A. (1967). *Constructing statements of outcomes.* Inglewood, CA: Southwest Regional Laboratory for Educational Research and Development.

Gershen, J.A. (1982). Dental professions education. In H.E. Mitzel (Ed.), *Encyclopedia of educational research* (5th ed.) (pp. 439-445). New York: The Free Press.

Gilbert, D. (1969). The young child's awareness of affect. *Child Development, 40,* 629-640.

Gilligan, C. (1982). *In a different voice.* Cambridge, MA: Harvard University Press.

Ginsberg, H., & Opper, S. (1969). *Piaget's theory of intellectual development.* Englewood Cliffs, NJ: Prentice-Hall.

Gordon, I.J. (1970). Affect & cognition: A reciprocal relationship. *Educational Leadership, 27,* 661-664.

Gropper, G.L. (1983). A metatheory of instruction: A framework for analyzing and evaluating instructional theories and models. In C.R. Reigeluth (Ed.), *Instructional-design theories and models: An overview of their current status* (pp. 37-53). Hillsdale: NJ: Lawrence Erlbaum Associates.

Guilford, J.P. (1967). *The nature of human intelligence.* New York: McGraw-Hill.

Guralnik, D.B. (Ed.). (1979). *Webster's new world dictionary, second college edition.* Cleveland, OH: William Collins.

Hannum, W.H., & Briggs, L.J. (1982). How does instructional systems design differ from traditional instruction? *Educational Technology, 22*(1), 9-14.

Harriman, R. (1984). Moving beyond linear logic. *The Futurist, 18*(4), 17-20.

Hawkin, P., Ogilvy, J., & Schwartz, P. (1982). *Seven tomorrows.* New York: Bantam Books.

Henerson, M.E., Morris, L.L., & Fitz-Gibbon, C.T. (1978). *How to measure attitudes.* Beverly Hills, CA: Sage.

Hiatt, H.H. (1976). The responsibilities of the physician as a member of society: The invisible line. *Journal of Medical Education, 51*, 30-38.

Hilgard, E.R., & Bower, G.H. (1966). *Theories of learning* (3rd ed.). New York: Appleton-Century-Crofts.

Hill, P.W., & McGaw, B. (1981). Testing the simplex assumption underlying Bloom's taxonomy. *American Educational Research Journal, 18*, 93-101.

Hoepfner, R., *et al.* (1972). *CSE-RBS test evaluation: Tests of higher order cognitive, affective, and interpersonal skills.* Los Angeles: Center for the Study of Evaluation.

Horney, K. (1937). *The neurotic personality of our time.* New York: Norton.

Hovland, C.I., Janis, I.J., & Kelley, H.H. (1953). *Communications and persuasion.* New Haven: Yale University Press.

Hurst, B.M. (1978). *The validation of a cognitive and affective hierarchy of the adoption process of educational change.* (Doctoral Dissertation, The University of Toledo, 1978.) *Dissertation Abstracts International, 39*, 2032A-2033A. (University Microfilm No. 7818538.)

Hurst, B.M. (1980a, April). Developing hierarchical structures integrating cognition and affect. Paper presented at the meeting of the American Educational Research Association, Boston. (ERIC Document Reproduction Service No. ED 193 316.)

Hurst, B.M. (1980b). An integrated approach to the hierarchical order of the cognitive and affective domains. *Journal of Educational Psychology, 72*, 293-303.

Insko, C.A. (1967). *Theories of attitude change.* New York: Appleton-Century-Crofts.

Irwin, D.M. (1982). Moral development. In H.E. Mitzel (Ed.), *Encyclopedia of educational research* (5th ed.) (pp. 1237-1241). New York: The Free Press.

Jaccard, J. (1975). A theoretical analysis of selected factors important to health education strategies. *Health Education Monograph, 3,* 152-167.

Johnson, H.C., Jr. (1983). Moral education. In H.E. Mitzel (Ed.), *Encyclopedia of educational research* (5th ed.) (pp. 1241-1256). New York: The Free Press.

Joyce, B., & Weil, M. (1980). *Models of teaching* (2nd ed.). Englewood Cliffs, NJ: Prentice-Hall.

Jung, C.G. (1968). *Analytical psychology: Its theory and practice.* New York: Random House, Vintage Books.

Katz, D., & Stotland, E. (1959). A preliminary statement to a theory of attitude structure and change. In S. Koch (Ed.), *Psychology: A study of science* (Vol. 3, pp. 423-475). New York: McGraw-Hill.

Kaufman, R. (1983). Educational excellence: Already at risk. *Educational Technology, 23*(12), 34-35.

Kaufman, R., & English, F.W. (1979). *Needs assessment: Concept and application.* Englewood Cliffs, NJ: Educational Technology Publications.

Keller, J.M. (1983). Motivational design of instruction. In C.M. Reigeluth (Ed.), *Instructional-design theories and models: An overview of their current status* (pp. 386-434). Hillsdale, NJ: Lawrence Erlbaum Associates.

Kiesler, C.A., Collins, B.E., & Miller, N. (1969). *Attitude change: A critical analysis of theoretical approaches.* New York: John Wiley and Sons.

Kohlberg, L. (1969). Stage and sequence: The cognitive-developmental approach to socialization. In D. Golin (Ed.), *Handbook of socialization theory and research.* Chicago: Rand McNally.

Kohlberg, L., & Mayer, R. (1972). Development as the aim of education. *Harvard Educational Review, 42,* 449-496.

Kolb, J.R. (1967-68). Effects of relating mathematics to science instruction on the acquisition of quantitative science behaviors. *Journal of Research in Science Teaching, 5,* 174-182.

Krathwohl, D.R., Bloom, B.S., and Masia, B.B. (1964). *Taxonomy of educational objectives: The classification of educational goals. Handbook II: Affective domain.* New York: Longman.

Krech, D., & Crutchfield, R.S. (1948). *Theory and problems in social psychology.* New York: McGraw-Hill.

Kropp, R.P., & Stoker, H.W. (1966). *The construction and validation of tests of the cognitive processes as described in the taxonomy of educational objectives.* Florida State University, Institute of Human Learning, Tallahassee, FL.

Layton, J.M. (1982). Nursing education. In H.E. Mitzel (Ed.), *Encyclopedia of educational research* (5th ed.) (pp. 1354-1364). New York: The Free Press.

Lazarus, R.S. (1968). Emotions and adaptation: Conceptual and empirical relations. In W.J. Arnold (Ed.), *Nebraska symposium on motivation.* Lincoln: University of Nebraska Press.

Lewy, A. (1968). The empirical validity of major properties of a taxonomy of affective educational objectives. *Journal of Experimental Education, 36,* 70-77.

Lumsdaine, A.A. (1961). *Student responses in programmed instruction.* Washington, D.C.: National Academy of Sciences—National Research Council, Publication 943.

Lumsdaine, A.A., & Glaser, R. (Eds.). (1960). *Teaching machines and programmed learning: A source book.* Washington, D.C.: National Education Association.

Madaus, G.F., Woods, E.M., & Nuttall, R.L. (1973). A causal model analysis of Bloom's taxonomy. *American Educational Research Journal, 10,* 253-262.

Mager, R.F. (1975). *Preparing objectives for instruction* (2nd ed.). Belmont, CA: Fearon.

Markle, D.G. (1977). First aid training. In L.J. Briggs (Ed.), *Instructional design: Principles and applications* (pp. 439-459). Englewood Cliffs, NJ: Educational Technology Publications.

Marlowe, D. (1982). Engineering education. In H.E. Mitzel (Ed.), *Encyclopedia of educational research* (5th ed.) (pp. 559-563). New York: The Free Press.

Martin, B.L. (1984, April). *An empirical validation of the affective domain taxonomy.* Paper presented at the meeting of the American Educational Research Association, New Orleans, LA.

Martin, B.L. (1984). Internalizing instructional design. *Educational Technology, 24*(5), 13-18.

Maslow, A.H. (1962). *Toward a psychology of being.* New York: Harper and Row.

Massey, R.F. (1981). *Personality theories: Comparisons and syntheses.* New York: D. Van Nostrand.

McCombs, B.L. (1981-82). Translating learning strategies into practice: Focus on the student in technical training. *Journal of Instructional Development, 5*(2), 10-17.

Merrill, M.D. (1983). Component display theory. In C.R. Reigeluth (Ed.), *Instructional-design theories and models: An overview of their current status* (pp. 279-333). Hillsdale, NJ: Lawrence Erlbaum Associates.

Merrill, M.D., Barton, K., & Wood, L.E. (1970). Specific review in learning a hierarchical imaginary science. *Journal of Educational Psychology, 61,* 102-107.

Miller, W.G., Snowman, J., & O'Hara, T. (1979). Application of alternative statistical techniques to examine the hierarchical ordering in Bloom's taxonomy. *American Educational Research Journal, 16,* 241-248.

Mitchell, A. (1983). *The nine American lifestyles.* New York: Macmillan.

Mitchell, D.E., & Encornation, D.J. (1984). Alternative state policy mechanisms for influencing school performance. *Educational Researcher, 13*(15), 4-11.

Mitzel, H.E. (Ed.). (1982). *Encyclopedia of educational research* (5th ed.). New York: The Free Press.

Mowrer, O.H. (1950). *Learning theory and personality dynamics.* New York: Ronald Press.

Murphy, G., Murphy, L.B., & Newcomb, T.M. (1937). *Experimental social psychology.* New York: Harper.

National Education Association Commission on Reorganization of Secondary Education. (1918). *Cardinal principles of secondary education.* Washington, D.C.

A Nation at Risk. (1983). The National Commission on Excellence in Education. Washington, D.C.: U.S. Government Printing Office.

Nelson, B. (1983, September 22). Physicians urged to show compassion. Reprinted from the New York Times in the *Tallahassee Democrat.*

Newcomb, T.M., Turner, R.H., & Converse, P.E. (1965). *Social psychology: The study of human interaction.* New York: Holt, Rinehart, and Winston.

Nunally, J.C. (1967). *Psychomometric theory.* New York: McGraw-Hill.

Oden, S. (1982). Social development. In H.E. Mitzel (Ed.), *Encyclopedia of educational research* (5th ed.) (pp. 1715-1723). New York: The Free Press.

Pantelidis, V.S. (1975). *An instructional program on personnel rules and regulations for state employees.* Unpublished doctoral dissertation, Florida State University, Tallahassee, Florida.

Parcel, G.S. (1976). Skills approach to health education: A framework for integrating cognitive and affective learning. *Journal of School Health, 46,* 403-406.

Payne, D.A. (1976). The assessment of affect: nomothetic and idiographic. *Proceedings of the National Symposium for Professors of Educational Research (NSPER).* Baltimore, MD. (ERIC Document Reproduction Service No. ED 157 911)

Pelczar, M.J., Jr. (1982). Graduate education. In H.E. Mitzel (Ed.), *Encyclopedia of educational research* (5th ed.) (pp. 738-743). New York: The Free Press.

Phillips, D.C., & Kelly, M.E. (1975). Hierarchical theories of development in education and psychology. *Harvard Educational Review, 45,* 351-375.

Pressey, S.L. (1926). A simple apparatus which gives tests and scores—and teaches. *School and Society, 23,* 373-376.

Pressey, S.L. (1950). Development and appraisal of devices providing immediate automatic scoring of objective tests and concomitant self-instruction. *Journal of Psychology, 29,* 417-447.

Purcell, J.L. (1968). *Developing an attitude scale using the taxonomy of educational objectives—affective domain.* (Doctoral dissertation, Washington State University, 1968.) *Dissertation Abstracts, 29,* 519A. (University Microfilm No. 68-10, 970.)

Rawls, J. (1971). *A theory of justice.* Cambridge, MA: Belknap Press of Harvard University Press.

Redfield, D.D., & Dick, W. (1984). An alumni-practitioner review of doctoral level competencies in instructional systems. *Journal of Instructional Development, 7*(1), 10-13.

Reigeluth, C.M. (Ed.). (1983a). *Instructional-design theories and models: An overview of their current status.* Hillsdale, NJ: Lawrence Erlbaum Associates.

Reigeluth, C.M. (1983b). Instructional design: What is it and why is it? In C.M. Reigeluth (Ed.), *Instructional-design theories and models: An overview of their current status* (pp. 3-36). Hillsdale, NJ: Lawrence Erlbaum Associates.

Reiser, R.A., & Gagné, R.M. (1983). *Selecting media for instruction.* Englewood Cliffs, NJ: Educational Technology Publications.

Resnick, L.B. (1967). *Design of an early learning curriculum.* Working Paper 16, Learning Research and Development Center, University of Pittsburgh.

Resnick, L.B., & Wang, M.C. (1969). Approaches to the validation of learning hierarchies. *Proceedings of the eighteenth annual regional conference on testing problems.* Princeton, NJ: Educational Testing Service.

Ringness, T.A. (1975). *The affective domain in education.* Boston: Little, Brown, and Company.

Rogers, C.R. (1951). *Client centered therapy.* Boston: Houghton Mifflin.

Rogers, C.R. (1959). A theory of therapy, personality, and interpersonal relationships as developed in the client-centered framework. In S. Koch (Ed.), *Psychology: A study of a science* (Vol. 3). New York: McGraw-Hill.

Rogers, C.R. (1969). *Freedom to learn.* Columbus, OH: Charles E. Merrill.

Rogers, C.R. (1983). *Freedom to learn for the 80's.* Columbus, OH: Charles E. Merrill.

Rokeach, M. (1960). *The open and closed mind.* New York: Basic Books.

Romiszowski, A.J. (1981). *Designing instructional systems.* London: Kogan Page.

Rowher, W.D. (1975). Elaboration and learning in childhood and adolescence. In H.W. Reese (Ed.), *Advances in child development and behavior.* New York: Academic Press.

Ross, C.K. (1981). Factors influencing successful preventive health education. *Health Education Quarterly, 8,* 187-208.

Rotter, J.B. (1975). Some problems and misconceptions related to the construct of internal versus external control of reinforcement. *Journal of Consulting and Clinical Behavior, 43,* 56-67.

Rotter, J.B., Chance, J.E., & Phares, E.J. (1972). *Applications of a social learning theory of personality.* New York: Holt, Rinehart, and Winston.

Runkel, P.J., & Schmuck, R.A. (1982). Group processes. In H.E. Mitzel (Ed.), *Encyclopedia of educational research* (5th ed.) (pp. 743-753). New York: The Free Press.

Schachter, S., & Singer, J. (1962). Cognitive, social, and physiological determinants of emotional state. *Psychological Review, 69,* 379-399.

Schubert, W.H. (1982). Curriculum research. In H.E. Mitzel (Ed.), *Encyclopedia of educational research* (5th ed.) (pp. 420-431). New York: The Free Press.

Scriven, M. (1966). Student values as educational objectives. In *Proceedings of the 1965 Invitational Conference on Testing Problems.* Princeton, NJ: Educational Testing Service, 33-49.

Shama, D.S. (1984). *The development of an academic achievement attribu-*

tion inventory for children using Rasch analysis. Unpublished doctoral dissertation, Kent State University.

Shaver, J.P. (1972). *Values and schooling: Perspectives for school people and parents.* Logan, Utah: Utah State University.

Short, E.C. (1982). Curriculum development and organization. In H.E. Mitzel (Ed.), *Encyclopedia of educational research* (5th ed.) (pp. 405-412). New York: The Free Press.

Silber, K.H. (1982). An analysis of university training programs for instructional developers. *Journal of Instructional Development, 6*(1), 15-28.

Silber, M.B. (1961). A comparative study of three methods of effecting attitude change. (Doctoral dissertation, Ohio State University, Columbus, OH.) *Dissertation Abstracts, 22,* 2488-2489. (University Microfilms No. 61-5126.)

Skinner, B.F. (1958). Teaching machines. *Science, 128,* 969-997.

Smith, B.O. (1966). Teaching and testing values. In *Proceedings of the 1965 Invitational Conference on Testing Problems.* Princeton, NJ: Educational Testing Service, 50-59.

Smith, R.G., Jr. (1951). *The relationship between attitude survey BE 501A (Form B) and the morale scale.* San Antonio, TX: Human Resource Research Center, Lackland Air Force Base. (Research Note TECH 51-5.)

Snelbecker, G.E. (1974). *Learning theory, instructional theory, and psycho-educational design.* New York: McGraw-Hill.

Sprinthall, R.C., & Sprinthall, N.A. (1977). *Educational psychology: A developmental approach* (2nd ed.). Menlo Park, CA: Addison-Wesley.

Sternberg, R.J. (1983). Criteria for intellectual skill training. *Educational Researcher, 12*(2), 6-12.

Sullivan, H.S. (1953). *The interpersonal theory of psychiatry.* New York: Norton.

Swanson, R.A. (1982). Industrial training. In H.E. Mitzel (Ed.), *Encyclopedia of educational research* (5th ed.) (pp. 864-870). New York: The Free Press.

Talmage, H. (Ed.). (1975). *Systems of individualized education.* Berkeley, CA: McCutchan.

Tanner, D. (1982). Curriculum history. In H.E. Mitzel (Ed.), *Encyclopedia of educational research* (5th ed.) (pp. 412-420). New York: The Free Press.

Thurstone, L.L. (1946). Comment. *American Journal of Sociology, 52,* 39-40.

Trachtman, P. (1984, February). Putting computers in the hands of children without language. *Smithsonian,* pp. 42-51.

Transgaard, H. (1973). *The cognitive component of attitudes and beliefs: Structure and empirical methods.* The Danish National Institute of Social Research.

Wadsworth, B.J. (1971). *Piaget's theory of cognitive development.* New York: Longman.

Wadsworth, B.J. (1978). *Piaget for the classroom teacher.* New York: Longman.

Wager, W. (1977). Instructional technology and higher education. In L.J. Briggs (Ed.), *Instructional design: Principles and applications* (pp. 395-419). Englewood Cliffs, NJ: Educational Technology Publications.

Weil, M., Joyce, B., & Kluwin, B. (1978). *Personal models of teaching: Expanding your teaching repertoire.* Englewood Cliffs, NJ: Prentice-Hall.

Weiner, B. (1972). Attribution theory, achievement motivation, and the educational process. *Review of Educational Research, 42,* 203-215.

Weiner, B. (1979). A theory of motivation for some classroom experiences. *Journal of Educational Psychology, 71,* 3-25.

Weiner, B., & Kukla, A. (1970). An attributional analysis of achievement motivation. *Journal of Personality and Social Psychology, 15,* 1-20.

Weiner, B., Nierenberg, R., & Goldstein, M. (1976). Social learning (locus of control) versus attributional (causal stability) interpretations of expectancy of success. *Journal of Personality, 44,* 52-68.

White, R.T. (1973). Research into learning hierarchies. *Review of Educational Research, 43,* 361-375.

White, R.T. (1974a). Indexes used in testing the validity of learning hierarchies. *Journal of Research in Science Teaching, 11*(1), 61-66.

White, R.T. (1974b). A model for validation of learning hierarchies. *Journal of Research in Science Teaching, 11*(1), 1-3.

White, R.T., & Gagné, R.M. (1974). Past and future research on learning hierarchies. *Educational Psychologist, 11,* 19-28.

Wyer, R.S., Jr. (1974). *Cognitive organization and change: An information processing approach.* Potomac, MD: Lawrence Erlbaum Associates.

Young, S.V. (1981). A comparison of two methods of studying college textbook materials: Objectives alone versus objective phrased as adjunct questions in a learning hierarchy with a color-coded underlining system. Unpublished doctoral dissertation, Florida State University, Tallahassee, Florida.

Young, J. (1984). The effects of differential sequencing of learning domain objectives on selected learning outcomes: A domain-interaction study. Unpublished doctoral dissertation prospectus, Florida State University, Tallahassee, Florida.

Zeleny, C.E. (1951). *An investigation of the relation of job satisfaction factors to high and low reenlistment rates.* San Antonio, TX: Human Resource Research Center, Lackland Air Force Base. (Research Note TECH 51-58.)

Zimbardo, P.G. (1979). *Psychology and life* (10th ed.). Glenview, IL: Scott, Foresman and Company.

Zimbardo, P.G., Ebbeson, E.B., & Maslach, C. (1977). *Influencing attitudes and changing behavior* (2nd ed.). Menlo Park, CA: Addison-Wesley.

Zumeta, W., & Solomon, L.C. (1982). Professions education. In H.E. Mitzel (Ed.), *Encyclopedia of educational research* (5th ed.) (pp. 1458-1467). New York: The Free Press.

Author Index

Subject Index

Adaptation-level theory, of attitude change, 116, 118

Adult learners: and locus of control, 181-183; and personal goals, 35; and self-development, 173, 176; and social competence, 209, 214

Affective behaviors, voluntary nature of, 453. *See also* Domain integration; Domain separation

Affective constructs, critique of those selected, 445-446

Affective domain: definition and use, 3, 12-14, 15-16, 49, 50; goals and objectives, xi, 17, 367-370; integrated with cognition, 4, 7, 18; measurement of, 13, 367-370; need for in instruction, 11; taxonomies, 76-89. *See also* Domain taxonomies; Domain integration; Domain separation

Affective needs, of children and adults, 253-254

Affective Taxonomy, proposed, 447-450. *See also* Domain taxonomies

Attitudes: and behavior, 100, 134; components of, 104-105; definitions and conceptions of, 99-101, 107; determiner of learning, 33; dimensions of, 104-107; in Gagné's model, 21, 59, 62; objectives and measurement, 367-370; objectives, issues

for instructional designers, 269-270; philosophical positions on teaching of, 366-367; scales, for measurement of behavior, 369-370; sets and clusters, 103; short-term vs. long-term objectives, 365-366, 368-369; structure, components of, 104-105, 107; types of, 105-106; and values, 102-103

Attitude change: distinct from development, 135; educational implications, 136-140; issues related to, 128, 134-136, 140

Attitude change theories, 107-133: behavioral and cognitive theories of, 107-108; critique of major groups, 111, 117-118; with instructional implications, 118-140; overview of, 109, 110, 112-116. *See also*: Balance, Behavioral, Functional, and Miscellaneous attitude change theories; Yale attitude change program; Dissonance theory; Cognitive balancing; Social judgment theory; Social learning theory

Attributions: and achievement behaviors, 216-220; conditions of learning, 219-220, 377; determiner of learning, 28-29; definition of and dimensions, 28, 216; issues, 217-219; locus of control in, 29; and motivation, 204, 208, 216; types of, 184